SO-AKU-859

When should I travel to get the best airfare?
Where do I go for answers to my travel questions?
What's the best and easiest way to plan and book my trip?

frommers.travelocity.com

Frommer's, the travel guide leader, has teamed up with **Travelocity.com** the leader in online travel, to bring you an in-depth, easy-to-use resource designed to help you plan and book your trip online.

At **frommers.travelocity.com**, you'll find free online updates about your destination from the experts at Frommer's plus the outstanding travel planning and purchasing features of Travelocity.com. Travelocity.com provides reservations capabilities for 95 percent of all airline seats sold, more than 47,000 hotels, and over 50 car rental companies. In addition, Travelocity.com offers more than 2,000 exciting vacation and cruise packages. Travelocity.com puts you in complete control of your travel planning with these and other great features:

Expert travel guidance from Frommer's - over 150 writers reporting from around the world!

Best Fare Finder - an interactive calendar tells you when to travel to get the best airfare

Fare Watcher - we'll track airfare changes to your favorite destinations

Dream Maps - a mapping feature that suggests travel opportunities based on your budget

Shop Safe Guarantee - 24 hours a day / 7 days a week live customer service, and more!

Whether traveling on a tight budget, looking for a quick weekend getaway, or planning the trip of a lifetime, Frommer's guides and Travelocity.com will make your travel dreams a reality. You've bought the book, now book the trip!

Travelocity.com
A Sabre Company

Frommer's®

A New Star-Rating System & Other Exciting News from Frommer's!

In our continuing effort to publish the savviest, most up-to-date, and most appealing travel guides available, we've added some great new features.

Frommer's guides now include a new **star-rating system.** Every hotel, restaurant, and attraction is rated from 0 to 3 stars to help you set priorities and organize your time.

We've also added **seven brand-new features** that point you to the great deals, in-the-know advice, and unique experiences that separate travelers from tourists. Throughout the guide look for:

Finds	Special finds—those places only insiders know about
Fun Fact	Fun facts—details that make travelers more informed and their trips more fun
Kids	Best bets for kids—advice for the whole family
Moments	Special moments—those experiences that memories are made of
Overrated	Places or experiences not worth your time or money
Tips	Insider tips—some great ways to save time and money
Value	Great values—where to get the best deals

We've also added a **"What's New"** section in every guide—a timely crash course in what's hot and what's not in every destination we cover.

Other Great Guides for Your Trip:

Frommer's Caribbean

Frommer's Caribbean Cruises & Ports of Call

Frommer's Caribbean from $70 a Day

Frommer's Caribbean Hideaways

Virgin Islands

6th Edition

by Darwin Porter & Danforth Prince

Here's what the critics say about Frommer's:

"Amazingly easy to use. Very portable, very complete."

—Booklist

"The only mainstream guide to list specific prices. The Walter Cronkite of guidebooks—with all that implies."

—Travel & Leisure

"Complete, concise, and filled with useful information."

—New York Daily News

"Hotel Information is close to encylopedic."

—Des Moines Sunday Register

Hungry Minds™

Best-Selling Books • Digital Downloads • e-Books • Answer Networks •
e-Newsletters • Branded Web Sites • e-Learning
New York, NY • Cleveland, OH • Indianapolis, IN

About the Authors

A native of North Carolina, **Darwin Porter** was a bureau chief for the *Miami Herald* when he was 21 and later worked in television advertising. A veteran travel writer, he is the author of numerous best-selling Frommer's guides, including those to The Bahamas and Bermuda. He is assisted by **Danforth Prince,** formerly of the Paris Bureau of the *New York Times.* They have been frequent travelers to the Caribbean for years, and are intimately familiar with what's good there and what isn't. They have also written *Frommer's Caribbean from $70 a Day,* the most candid and up-to-date guide to budget vacations on the market.

Published by:

Hungry Minds, Inc.
909 Third Avenue
New York, NY 10022

Copyright © 2001 Hungry Minds, Inc. All rights reserved. No part of this book may be reproduced or transmitted in any form or by any means, electronic or mechanical, including photocopying, recording, or by any information storage and retrieval system, without permission in writing from the Publisher.

FROMMER'S is a registered trademark of Arthur Frommer. Used under license.

ISBN 0-7645-6442-0
ISSN 1055-5447

Editor: Myka Carroll
Production Editor: Donna Wright
Photo Editor: Richard Fox
Cartographer: Roberta Stockwell
Production by Hungry Minds Indianapolis Production Services

Front cover photo: A couple snorkeling in Spring Bay, British Virgin Islands
Back cover photo: A view of Trunk Bay, St. John, U.S. Virgin Islands

Special Sales

For general information on Hungry Minds' products and services, please contact our Customer Care department; within the U.S. at 800-762-2974, outside the U.S. at 317-572-3993 or fax 317-572-4002. For sales inquiries and reseller information, including discounts, bulk sales, customized editions, and premium sales, please contact our Customer Care department at 800-434-3422.

Manufactured in the United States of America

5 4 3

Contents

4 St. John   123

5 St. Croix   149

6 The British Virgin Islands   195

Appendix: The Virgin Islands in Depth   239

Index   246

List of Maps

An Invitation to the Reader

In researching this book, we discovered many wonderful places—hotels, restaurants, shops, and more. We're sure you'll find others. Please tell us about them, so we can share the information with your fellow travelers in upcoming editions. If you were disappointed with a recommendation, we'd love to know that, too. Please write to:

Frommer's Virgin Islands, 6th Edition
Hungry Minds, Inc. • 909 Third Avenue • New York, NY 10022

An Additional Note

Please be advised that travel information is subject to change at any time—and this is especially true of prices. We therefore suggest that you write or call ahead for confirmation when making your travel plans. The authors, editors, and publisher cannot be held responsible for the experiences of readers while traveling. Your safety is important to us, however, so we encourage you to stay alert and be aware of your surroundings. Keep a close eye on cameras, purses, and wallets, all favorite targets of thieves and pickpockets.

New! Frommer's Star Ratings & Icons

Every hotel, restaurant and attraction listing in this guide has been ranked for quality, value, service, amenities, and special features using a star-rating scale. In country, state, and regional guides, we also rate towns and regions to help you narrow down your choices and budget your time accordingly. Hotels and restaurants in the Very Expensive and Expensive categories are rated on a scale of one (highly recommended) to three stars (exceptional). Those in the Moderate and Inexpensive categories rate from zero (recommended) to two stars (very highly recommended). Attractions, towns, and regions are rated according to the following scale: zero stars (recommended), one star (highly recommended), two stars (very highly recommended), and three stars (must-see).

In addition to the rating system, we also use seven icons to highlight insider information, useful tips, special bargains, hidden gems, memorable experiences, kid-friendly venues, places to avoid, and other useful information:

(Finds   (Fun Fact   (Kids   (Moments   (Overrated   (Tips   (Value

The following abbreviations are used for credit cards:

AE	American Express	DC	Diners Club	V Visa
DISC	Discover	MC	MasterCard	

Frommers.com

Now that you have the guidebook to a great trip, visit our website at **www.frommers.com** for travel information on nearly 2,000 destinations. With features updated regularly, we give you instant access to the most current trip-planning information available. At Frommers.com, you'll also find the best prices on air fares, accommodations, and car rentals—and you can even book travel online through our travel booking partners. At Frommers.com you'll also find the following:

- Daily Newsletter highlighting the best travel deals
- Hot Spot of the Month/Vacation Sweepstakes & Travel Photo Contest
- More than 200 Travel Message Boards
- Outspoken Newsletters and Feature Articles on travel bargains, vacation ideas, tips & resources, and more!

What's New in the Virgin Islands

This rapidly changing archipelago, controlled by both the United States and Great Britain, explodes with new developments year after year. There's always a new resort opening up or an old one closing down, and the roster of what's hot in dining shifts from year to year. Here are the highlights of the latest developments in the Virgin Islands.

ST. THOMAS Accommodations Good news from **Wyndham Sugar Bay Beach Club,** 6500 Estate Smith Bay (© 800/927-7100): Guests arriving in 2002 will find millions spent on a mammoth restoration, phase two of an overall plan to stay competitive with other East End resorts. Guest rooms have new carpeting, furnishings, electronics, designer wall treatments, and rejuvenated marble bathrooms.

Best Western Emerald Beach Resort, Lindbergh Bay (© 340/776-3426), has bounced back from two hurricanes. It still suffers from its location across from the airport, but this mini-resort also opens onto one of the best white sandy beaches in St. Thomas. It's turning into a family favorite. **Renaissance Grand Beach Resort,** Smith Bay Road (© 340/775-1510), has now fallen under the Marriott umbrella. It joins Frenchman's Reef and Morning Star Beach as another jewel in the crown.

Dining A recent explosion of restaurants in and around Charlotte Amalie keeps enriching the taste buds of islanders and visitors alike. At **Café**

Wahoo, 6300 Estate Smith Bay, Red Hook (© 340/775-6350), diners enjoy an eclectic medley of specialties that are inspired by Europe. Chefs use the finest and freshest of ingredients from the West Indies. In an open-air dining room near the American Yacht Harbor, close to the departure point of the ferry to St. John, the fresh catch of the day—hauled off the little fishing boats just pulling in—is grilled to perfection. Nearby, **The Frigate,** 6501 Red Hook Plaza (© 340/775-6124), is a seaside restaurant that also manages to secure some of the choicest cuts of beef in the U.S. Virgins. As you dine overlooking Red Hook Harbor and the island of St. John, your dinner choice might be the fattest lobster of the take, a steak on the level of the Palm in New York City, or something lighter, perhaps chicken teriyaki.

A funky native bar, **Fungi's on the Beach,** Point Pleasant Resort (© 340/775-4142), has opened on Pineapple Beach, serving regional dishes and brews. Come here for some of the juiciest burgers on island and the most delectable pizza. You can also order Caribbean specialties, such as conch in butter sauce. Visitors to **Blackbeard's Castle,** Blackbeard's Hill (© 340/776-1234), can now enjoy "tower dining" while viewing the port of Charlotte Amalie. The castle's open-air tower has been turned into the setting for a romantic gourmet dinner, featuring a Continental menu.

The most casual place for fun dining on the island has recently become

Molly Molones at the Red Hook American Yacht Harbour (© **340/775-1270**), where you'll be fed an array of everything from baby back ribs to shepherd's pie, all washed down with the island's best selections of beer and ale. The conch fritters are the best in the East End.

Sports & Outdoor Pursuits Tired of escorted tours? **Nauti Nymph Powerboat Rentals,** American Yacht Harbor, Red Hook (© **800/734-7345** or 340/775-5066), reaches out to independent travelers and adventurers. The expert staff here will assist in designing your personal itinerary for a bareboat rental or can hook you up with a captained day trip. A choice of Coast Guard–approved and fully equipped vessels ranging in size from 25 to 29 feet await your decision.

Seeing the Sights The cultures of both America and the Caribbean are explored at the newly opened **American Caribbean Museum,** 32 Raadets Gade (© **340/714-5150**), in Charlotte Amalie. The history of the islands is traced from their volcanic beginnings to their occupation by the Americans.

Shopping The port of Charlotte Amalie, capital of St. Thomas, remains the shopping mecca of the Caribbean. Among the stores that have vastly upgraded their stock is **Amsterdam Sauer,** Main Street (© **340/774-2222**), where the Sauer family remains a leader in jewelry and gems. They've reached out to stock their store with pieces by world-renowned jewelry designers. The Sauers also offer the largest selection of unset gems in the Caribbean. Hot on their trail is the greatly improved stock at **Artistic Jewelers,** 32 Main St. (© **800/653-3113**), which carries exclusive designer jewelry lines, including the "classics" from David Yurman.

Mr. Tablecloth, 6 Main St. (© **340/774-4343**), has received new shipments of top-quality linen from the Republic of China (including Hong Kong). The store now has the best selection of tablecloths and accessories in Charlotte Amalie. **Mussfeldt Design,** International Plaza Mall, (© **340/774-9034**), sells the latest resort wear from around the world—mainly Mexico, Australia, and, of course, the Caribbean itself. Especially delectable are the unique embroideries and prints designed by Peter Mussfeldt.

Finally, it had to happen: **The Virgin Islands Brewing Company,** across from the Havensight Mall (© **340/777-8888**), was originally founded on St. Croix but has invaded St. Thomas with two local beers, Blackbeard Ale and Foxy's Lager. At the company store, you're given free samples and can purchase six-packs of the home-brewed suds along with T-shirts, caps, and polo shirts.

After Dark The major venue for night life in St. Thomas has recently become **The Old Mill,** the largest and newest entertainment complex to open on the island, with three separate venues. The courtyard sports bar offers a variety of games, including four pool tables. The more elegant wine and champagne bar is in a restored 18th-century sugar mill, where guests can relax to the sound of jazz and blues. More than 100 different types of wines and champagnes from all over the world are served here. There's also a dance club, the largest of its kind in the U.S. Virgins.

ST. JOHN Accommodations Seekers of cozy Caribbean B&Bs are heading for the newly opened **Garden by the Sea Bed & Breakfast,** Cruz Bay (© **340/779-4731**), with only a trio of bedrooms overlooking the ocean, just a 10-minute walk from the little port of Cruz Bay. Don't expect telephones or TVs in the bedrooms—this is a getaway, not a communications center. Decoration is in the West

Indian style with elephant-bamboo canopy beds, Japanese fountains, ceiling fans, and wood furnishings.

Dining   The late-breaking culinary news from here is Chef Aaron Willis's eclectic menu served at the **Stone Terrace,** Cruz Bay (📞 **340/693-9370**), overlooking the waterfront at the point where the ferries from St. Thomas dock. In a native stone building—hence its name—the chef serves some of the freshest-tasting dishes of the Caribbean. For inspiration, he roams the world.

Exploring the Island   A new **National Park Visitors Center** (📞 **340/776-6201**) has recently opened in Cruz Bay, offering two floors of information and wall-mounted wildlife displays, plus a video presentation about the culture of the Virgin Islands.

ST. CROIX Accommodations   A place of "barefoot elegance," the newly opened **Diva Carina Bay Resort & Casino** at Carina Bay (📞 **877/FUN-DIVI**) not only has introduced gambling for the first time to the U.S. Virgin Islands, but also has brought a top-of-the-line new resort property to St. Croix. Offering 130 tasteful and well-furnished rooms, plus 20 villas, the property has a sea-toned decor and rooms filled with such amenities as dataports and voicemail. Guest villas come with fully equipped kitchens. A special feature is "The Spa," where experts work you over to create a "new you."

Seeing the Sights   The island has recently launched the **St. Croix Heritage Trail** to help visitors relive its Danish colonial past. Specially designed maps and road signs lead visitors along the trail, which is one of the 50 nationwide Millennium Legacy Trails inaugurated in 2000. The 72-mile route is teeming with historical and cultural sights, and a free brochure and easy-to-follow maps

guide travelers along. The route connects the two major towns of Christiansted and Frederiksted and goes past once-prosperous sugar plantations. A brochure and map are available by calling the St. Croix Heritage Trail office at 📞 **340/713-8563.**

TORTOLA Accommodations   On the major island of Tortola, **The Sugar Mill Hotel,** Apple Bay (📞 **800/462-8834**), has opened a new addition to its property. In keeping with the historic pedigree of this now 24-room Caribbean inn built around the ruins of a 370-year-old sugar mill, the Plantation House suites are designed to reflect the charm of traditional Caribbean architecture, with fine stone work, breezy porches, and lacy gingerbread trim. Plantation House is located just a few steps from the beach.

VIRGIN GORDA Accommodations   On the increasingly posh island of Virgin Gorda, site of some of the finest resorts in the B.V.I., a more democratically priced resort has opened: **Nail Bay Resort** at Nail Bay (📞 **800/871-3551**). The resort reopened after a complete overhaul to give the present resorts some stiff competition. Named for a 19th-century sugar plantation, this remote 147-acre enclave lies below the Gorda Peak National Park. A series of comfortable, tastefully furnished, and spacious rooms, suites, villas, and apartments are linked by illuminated walkways. "Waterfalls," romantic lighting, and panoramic vistas across Sir Francis Drake Channel enhance the allure of the property.

Dining   The only authentic Italian restaurant on island, **Giorgio's Table** in Mahoe Bay (📞 **284/495-5684**), a 15-minute drive north of Spanish Town, brings the tastes of the Mediterranean to this island. The best fresh fish and the most delicious pastas are found here.

1

The Best of the Virgin Islands

Former stamping ground of some of history's most famous seafarers, the Virgin Islands are now invaded by thousands of visitors who arrive daily by cruise ship and plane from Miami and Puerto Rico. These green, hilly islands, some governed by the United States and some by Great Britain, number about 100 in all. Most are tiny and virtually uninhabited, except for a few birds or an adventurous boating party stopping off for a little snorkeling or swimming. For an ultimate tropical getaway, it's even possible to rent an entire island for yourself.

Most Virgin Islands natives are descendants of African slaves who worked the sugar cane plantations. In recent years, the local population has swelled with an influx of "down islanders"—people from other Caribbean islands. Many Puerto Ricans have also come here (it's only 30 minutes by air); they are joined by many mainland Americans. The old ways of the islands are all but gone in bustling St. Thomas and St. Croix, but they may still be found in St. John and some pockets of the British Virgins, especially on laid-back Virgin Gorda. Below you'll find the highlights of this quintessential vacation paradise.

1 The Best Beaches

Many Caribbean islands have only rocky beaches or beaches made of black volcanic sand (which heats up fast in the noonday sun), but those in the Virgin Islands are known for their fine white sand. Best of all, every beach in the Virgin Islands is free (except for Magens Bay in St. Thomas) and open to the public, although in some cases, you'll have to walk across the grounds of a resort (or arrive by private boat) to reach them.

- **Magens Bay Beach** (St. Thomas): This ½-mile loop of pebble-free sand and remarkably calm water is by far the most popular and picturesque beach in the U.S. Virgin Islands. Two peninsulas protect the shore from erosion and strong waves, making Magens an ideal spot for swimming. Expect a lively crowd here in the high season. See chapter 3.

- **Sapphire Beach** (St. Thomas): This beach is one of the finest on St. Thomas and a favorite with windsurfers. Come here for some of St. Thomas's best shore snorkeling and diving (off Pettyklip Point). And, don't worry about equipment—water-sport concessions abound here. Take a moment to enjoy the panoramic view of St. John and other islands. See chapter 3.

- **Caneel Bay** (St. John): Site of a famous resort, Caneel Bay is a string of seven beaches, stretching around Durloe Point to Hawksnest Caneel. Rosewood Hotels, which operates Caneel Bay Resort, admits day guests. See chapter 4.

- **Trunk Bay** (St. John): This beach, which is protected by the U.S. National Park Service, is a favorite with cruise-ship passengers. It's famous for its underwater snorkeling trail. Trunk Bay is consistently ranked among the top 10 Caribbean beaches, most recently by *Condé Nast Traveler*. See chapter 4.

- **Sandy Point** (St. Croix): The biggest beach in the U.S. Virgin Islands, Sandy Point lies in the southwestern part of St. Croix, directly to the west of Alexander Hamilton Airport. Its waters are shallow and calm. Because the beach is a protected reserve and a nesting spot for endangered sea turtles, it's only open to the public on weekends from 9am to 5pm. See chapter 5.

- **Cane Garden Bay** (Tortola): Cane Garden Bay is the most popular beach in the British Virgin Islands and a close rival to Magens Bay (see above) for scenic beauty. Its translucent waters and sugar-white sands are reason enough to visit Tortola; it's also the closest beach to Road Town, the capital. See chapter 6.

2 The Best Snorkeling Spots

A readers' poll by *Scuba Diving* magazine confirmed what Virgin Islanders knew all along: The islands of St. Croix, St. John, and St. Thomas are among the finest places to snorkel in the Caribbean. Here are some of the best spots:

- **Coki Beach** (St. Thomas): On the north shore of St. Thomas, Coki Beach offers superb year-round snorkeling. Especially enticing are the coral ledges near Coral World's underwater tower. See chapter 3.

- **Leinster Bay** (St. John): Easily accessible Leinster Bay, on the northern shore of St. John, offers calm, clear, and uncrowded waters teeming with sea life. See chapter 4.

- **Haulover Bay** (St. John): A favorite with locals, this small bay is rougher than Leinster and is often deserted. The snorkeling, however, is dramatic, with ledges, walls, nooks, and sandy areas set close together. See chapter 4.

- **Trunk Bay** (St. John): The self-guided, 225-yard-long snorkeling trail here has large underwater signs that identify species of coral and other marine life. Above water, the beach's freshwater showers, changing rooms, equipment rentals, and lifeguards make snorkeling more convenient. See chapter 4.

- **Buck Island** (off St. Croix): This tiny island, whose land and offshore waters are classified as a national monument, lies 2 miles off the north coast of St. Croix. More than 250 recorded species of fish swim through its reef system. A variety of sponges, corals, and crustaceans also inhabit Buck Island, which is strictly protected by the National Park Service. See chapter 5.

- **Cane Bay** (St. Croix): One of the island's best diving and snorkeling sites is off this breezy, north-shore beach. On a good day, you can swim out 150 yards to see the Cane Bay Wall, which drops dramatically off to deep waters below. Multicolored fish and elkhorn and brain coral flourish here. See chapter 5.

3 The Best Dive Sites

- **Cow and Calf Rocks** (St. Thomas): This site off the southeast end of St. Thomas (about a 45-minute boat ride from Charlotte Amalie) is the island's best diving spot. It's also a good

The Best of the Virgin Islands

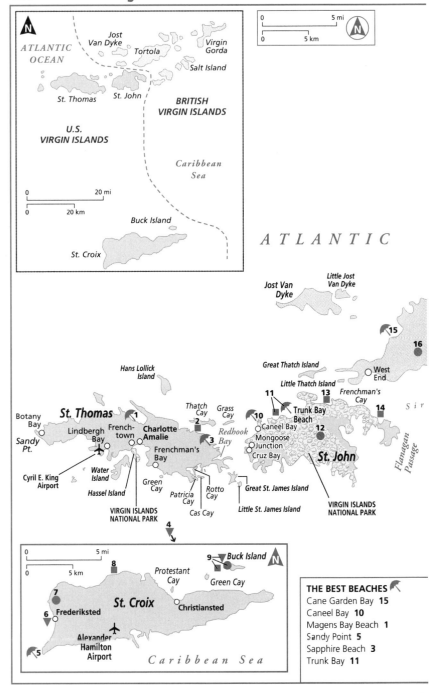

THE BEST BEACHES

Cane Garden Bay **15**
Caneel Bay **10**
Magens Bay Beach **1**
Sandy Point **5**
Sapphire Beach **3**
Trunk Bay **11**

Anegada

The Settlement

Prickly
Pear
Island

Necker Island

Mosquito
Island

Seal Dogs

*North
Sound*

Eustatia

O C E A N

Great Camanoe

George Dog

West Dog

South Sound

Guana
Island

Little
Camanoe

Scrub
Island

Great Dog

Marina Cay

Spanish
Town

Virgin Gorda

Tortola East
End ○ **17** ▼

Beef
Island

C h a n n e l

**Road
Town**

F r a n c i s *D r a k e*

Fallen
Jerusalem

Cooper
Island

19 ▼

○ Round
Rock

*Salt
Island
Passage*

18
▼ **Salt
Island**

Ginger
Island

**Peter
Island**

Norman Island

C a r i b b e a n   S e a

British Virgin Islands

U.S. Virgin Islands

THE BEST SNORKELING ■
SPOTS
Buck Island **9**
Cane Bay **8**
Coki Beach **2**
Haulover Bay **14**
Leinster Bay **13**
Trunk Bay **11**

THE BEST DIVE SITES ▼
Alice in Wonderland **19**
Buck Island **9**
Chikuzen **17**
Cow and Calf Rocks **4**
Frederiksted Pier **6**
The Wreck of the
    HMS Rhone **18**

THE BEST NATURE WALKS ●
The Annaberg Sugar
    Plantation Ruins Walk **12**
Buck Island Walk **9**
The Rain Forest Hike **7**
Sage Mountain
    National Park **16**

bet for snorkeling. You'll discover a network of coral tunnels riddled with caves, reefs, and ancient boulders encrusted with coral. See chapter 3.

- **Buck Island** (off St. Croix): This is one of the major diving meccas in the Caribbean, with an underwater visibility of some 100 feet. There are enough labyrinths and grottoes for more experienced divers, plus massive gardens of fiery coral inhabited by black sea urchins, barracudas, stingrays, and other creatures. See chapter 5.
- **Frederiksted Pier** (St. Croix): Conventional wisdom has designated this pier, located in an old ramshackle town at the west end of St. Croix, the most interesting pier dive in the Caribbean. The original pier was virtually destroyed by Hurricane Hugo in 1989, but a new one opened in 1993. Plunge into a world of exotic creatures, including sponges, banded shrimp, plume worms, and sea horses. See chapter 5.
- **Alice in Wonderland** (Ginger Island): This brilliant coral wall, offshore of a tiny island, slopes from 40 feet to a sandy bottom at 100 feet. Divers often refer to the site as "a fantasy" because of its monstrous overhangs, vibrant colors, gigantic mushroom-shaped corals, and wide variety of sea creatures—everything from conch and garden eels to longnose butterfly fish. See chapter 6.
- **Chikuzen** (Tortola): Although its not the *Rhone* (see below), this 270-foot steel-hulled refrigerator ship, which sank off the island's east end in 1981, is one of the British Virgin Islands' most fascinating dive sites. The hull—still intact under about 80 feet of water—is now home to a vast array of tropical fish, including yellowtail, barracuda, black-tip sharks, octopus, and drum fish. See chapter 6.
- **The Wreck of the HMS *Rhone*** (off Salt Island): The *Rhone* wreck is the premier dive site not only in the Virgin Islands but also in the entire Caribbean. This royal mail steamer, which went down in 1867, was featured in the murky film *The Deep*. See chapter 6.

4 The Best Boating Outfitters

Boating is big in the U.S. Virgin Islands, and it's even bigger in the British Virgins, which are said to have the best cruising in the Caribbean.

- **American Yacht Harbor** (St. Thomas; ✆ 800/736-7294): This is one of the best bareboat or full-crew charter companies on St. Thomas. It's located on Red Hook Marina, which itself is home to numerous boat companies, including both fishing and sailing charters. Whatever craft you're looking for, you're bound to find it here. See chapter 3.
- **Vacation Vistas and Motor Yachts** (St. John; ✆ 340/776-6462): This is your best bet for half- or full-day excursions on St. John. Many boaters head for a day cruise to the famous Baths on Virgin Gorda in the British Virgin Islands. To cut costs, you can go on a regularly scheduled tour; if you have a large group, you can charter your own craft. See chapter 4.
- **The Moorings** (Tortola; ✆ 800/535-7209). This is the finest charter service in the Virgin Islands. It has done more than any other

outfitter to make the British Virgin Islands the destination of choice among the world's yachting class. Its fleet of yachts and boats

is staggering—everything from bareboat rentals to fully crewed vessels with skipper, crew, and cook. See chapter 6.

5 The Best Golf Courses

• **Mahogany Run** (St. Thomas; ✆ **800/253-7103**): This par-70, 6,022-yard course, one of the most scenic in the Caribbean, has breathtaking views of the British Virgin Islands. It's famous for its "Devil's Triangle," a tricky trio of holes (13, 14, and 15). See chapter 3.

• **The Buccaneer** (St. Croix; ✆ **800/255-3881** or 340/773-2100): This 6,117-yard resort course has some spectacular vistas,

especially from its signature third hole, where the seascape stretches from Christiansted to Buck Island. See chapter 5.

• **Carambola** (St. Croix; ✆ **340/778-5638**): This par-72 course at Davis Bay, known for decades as Fountain Valley, is one of the most challenging in the Caribbean. The well-maintained holes are characterized by dangerous water hazards and ravines. See chapter 5.

6 The Best Tennis Facilities

• **Wyndham Sugar Bay Beach Club** (St. Thomas; ✆ **800/WYNDHAM** or 340/777-7100): Some tennis buffs have deserted the Buccaneer on St. Croix (see below) in favor of this resort at Estate Smith Bay. Sugar Bay Plantation offers the U.S. Virgin Islands' first stadium tennis court, as well as six Laykold courts, which are lit at night. See chapter 3.

• **The Buccaneer** (St. Croix; ✆ **800/255-3881** or 340/773-2100): This is where Ted Kennedy

plays when he's on St. Croix. The facilities at this resort have been touted as the best in the Virgin Islands and have played host to several professional tournaments, including the Virgin Islands Tennis Championships in July. There are eight all-weather Laykold courts, two of which are lit at night. Non-guests can play here for a fee. See chapter 5.

7 The Best Nature Walks

• **The Annaberg Sugar Plantation Ruins Walk** (St. John): This paved walk is only ¼ mile long, but it's a highlight of the 10,000-acre U.S. Virgin Islands National Park. The trail traverses the ruins of what was once the most important sugarcane plantation on the island. Slaves' quarters, a windmill tower, and ballast-brick buildings are remnants of a long-vanished era. Stunning views look toward Tortola, Great Thatch Island, and

Jost Van Dyke on the opposite side of Sir Francis Drake Passage. See chapter 4.

• **Buck Island Walk** (off St. Croix): A circumnavigation of this island, which is reached by boat, takes about 2 hours and is rated moderate. Because the island is ringed with white sandy beaches, feel free to take a break for a refreshing swim. There's also a trail that points inland. See chapter 5.

- **The Rain Forest Hike** (St. Croix): At the northwestern end of St. Croix lies the 15-acre "Rain Forest," which is thick with magnificent plant life. The little-traveled four-wheel-drive roads through the area provide great hiking paths. See chapter 5.
- **Sage Mountain National Park** (Tortola): This 3- to 4-hour hike

is one of the most dramatic in the British Virgins. It goes from Brewer's Bay to the top of Mount Sage, the highest peak in the Virgin Islands at 1,780 feet. Along the way, you'll see intriguing ruins of old homes, not to mention the beautiful flora and fauna of the park's primeval forest. See chapter 6.

8 The Best Resorts

- **Marriott Frenchman's Reef Beach Resort** (St. Thomas; ✆ **800/524-2000** or 340/776-8500): This sprawling luxe resort practically put St. Thomas on the tourist map. Today it's linked to its even better sibling next door, Marriott Morning Star Beach Resort. Guests at both properties share the same amenities, facilities, and restaurants. The resort stands on one of the best beaches on the island. See chapter 3.
- **The Ritz-Carlton** (St. Thomas; ✆ **800/241-3333** or 340/775-3333): There is no grander place to stay in the U.S. Virgin Islands. Fronted by white sand beaches, this is the resort for those who want to escape to the Caribbean not like Robinson Crusoe, but as Bill Gates might if he showed up on a yacht. It's got everything that an Italian Renaissance palazzo could offer—and more. See chapter 3.
- **The Buccaneer** (St. Croix; ✆ **800/255-3881** or 340/773-2100): Newer and glitzier competitors have sprouted up, but this large, luxurious, and family-owned resort is still the class act. It not only lies on the island's best beaches but also has the best sports program, the best entertainment, and the best food of any hotel. See chapter 5.

- **Caneel Bay** (St John; ✆ **340/776-6111**): There is no resort in the islands with a greater pedigree than this creation of Laurance S. Rockefeller as the Caribbean's first ecoresort back in the days when no one knew what that was. It is more for Walter Cronkite than Madonna. Even though the resort isn't posh, it's an understated classic, an outpost of refinement without ostentation. See chapter 4.
- **Westin Resort St. John** (St. John; ✆ **800/808-5020** or 340/693-8000): The glitz and glitter missing at Caneel Bay can be found here. Architecturally dramatic and visually appealing, this resort sprawls across 34 landscape acres, opening onto a 1,200-foot white sandy beach. It boasts a huge array of activities with lots of water sports. See chapter 4.
- **Biras Creek Estate** (Virgin Gorda; ✆ **800/608-9661** or 284/494-3555): A private and romantic retreat, this resort resembles a hillside fortress. It's an escapist's hideaway on a 150-acre estate with its own marina. There are no phones and no TVs, but you can have the latest edition of the *Wall Street Journal.* See chapter 6.
- **The Bitter End Yacht Club** (Virgin Gorda; ✆ **800/872-2392** or 284/494-2746): This is the best sailing and diving resort in all of

The Best of the Virgin Islands on the Web

City.net (http://citynet.com/caribbean/caribbean.html) is a great website that will point you toward a wealth of travel information on both the U.S. Virgin Islands and the British Virgin Islands. If you've decided on the U.S.V.I., check out **America's Caribbean Paradise: The U.S. Virgin Islands** (www.usvi.net); for the B.V.I., try **The British Virgin Islands Welcome Tourist Guide On-Line** (www.bviwelcome.com). Another good site is **Caribbean On-Line** (http://caribbean-on-line.com), a series of virtual guidebooks packed with information on hotels, restaurants, shopping, beaches, sports outfitters, and more.

the Virgin Islands. This resort opens onto one of the most unspoiled and secluded deep-water harbors in the Caribbean. You live and dine here in style; you can even stay aboard a 30-foot yacht. See chapter 6.

- **Long Bay Beach Resort** (Tortola; ✆ **800/729-9599** or 284/495-4252): The finest resort at the capital of the B.V.I., this complex borders a mile-long sandy beach. It's the only full-service resort in Tortola, and its deluxe beachfront

rooms and cabanas are quite nice. See chapter 6.

- **Peter Island Resort** (Peter Island; ✆ **800/346-4451** or 284/495-2000): This posh resort lies on its own 1,800-acre tropical island. It opens onto Deadman's Beach, which, in spite of its name, is consistently voted one of the most romantic in the world by various travel magazine reader polls. This is a true retreat, a hedonistic resort and a monument to the good life. See chapter 6.

9 The Best Honeymoon Resorts

Many hotels in the Virgin Islands will help plan your wedding, doing everything from arranging the flowers and the photographer to applying for the marriage license (see chapter 2 for more details). Even you don't actually tie the knot here, the Virgin Islands offer some of the world's most romantic destinations for honeymooning couples.

- **Elysian Beach Resort** (St. Thomas; ✆ **800/524-6599** or 340/775-1000): For a great value, ask about the "Honeymoon Getaway" package, which includes a deluxe room or a one-bedroom suite, champagne on arrival, and free use of the tennis courts, fitness center, freshwater pool, and Jacuzzi. See chapter 3.

- **The Buccaneer** (St. Croix; ✆ **800/ 255-3881** or 340/773-2100): This resort boasts the most extensive facilities on St. Croix, including an 18-hole golf course, eight championship tennis courts, a spa and fitness center, a 2-mile jogging trail, and three beaches. The 1653 sugar mill on the grounds is the most popular wedding spot on the island. We recommend staying in one of the beachside rooms with fieldstone terraces that take you right down to the water. See chapter 5.

- **Biras Creek Estate** (Virgin Gorda; ✆ **800/608-9661** or 284/494-3555): This private and elegant hotel is located on a secluded 150-acre promontory, reached only by launch. Sign-posted nature trails cut through its lush tropical gardens. See chapter 6.

- **Little Dix Bay** (Virgin Gorda; © **888/767-3966** or 284/495-5555): The understated elegance of this luxury resort is popular with older couples and honeymooners alike—in fact, the powerfully amorous atmosphere sometimes makes single guests feel like wallflowers. Spread out over 500 acres on a secluded bay, this resort offers beautiful beaches and sporting activities galore, or plenty of privacy, if that's what you're after. See chapter 6.

10 The Best Family Resorts

- **Bolongo Beach Club** (St. Thomas; © **800/524-4746** or 340/775-1800): The resort staff here offers a huge roster of family activities; there's also a separate program for kids only. When booking, ask about the package that allows children to stay and eat for free with their parents. See chapter 3.
- **Renaissance Grand Beach Resort** (St. Thomas; © **800/421-8181** or 340/775-1510): On 34 acres of the northeast shore, this deluxe resort offers accommodations that are in part like little family townhouses. It's an excellent family resort, with counselors operating a free year-round children's program (ages 3 to 14). See chapter 3.
- **The Buccaneer** (St. Croix; © **800/524-4776** or 340/773-1800): This hotel, located on a 300-acre former sugar estate, is a longtime family favorite. It has on-site facilities for just about every sport you can think of, including tennis, golf, swimming, jogging, sailing, scuba diving, and snorkeling. Children's programs include a half-day sail to Buck Island Reef and nature walks through tropical foliage, where kids can taste local fruit in the wild. See chapter 5.
- **Chenay Bay Beach Resort** (St. Croix; © **800/548-4457** or 340/773-2918): Families staying in these West Indian–style cottages, can keep their 3- to 12-year-olds busy with various organized activities, from swimming and snorkeling to nature walks and story hours. The friendly owners of this barefoot-casual hotel used their own offspring as test cases to design their children's program, which runs during the summer and over holiday periods. See chapter 5.
- **The Bitter End Yacht Club** (Virgin Gorda; © **800/872-2392** or 340/494-2746): Most children's programs at this lively resort are geared toward those age 6 and over and involve all the typical water sports: sailing, windsurfing, snorkeling, swimming, and more. Ask about the packages for families. See chapter 6.

11 The Best B&Bs

- **Villa Blanca** (St. Thomas; © **800/231-0034** or 340/776-0749): Small, intimate, and charming, this B&B stands on 3 acres on a hill overlooking Charlotte Amalie. A homelike atmosphere prevails, and there's also a freshwater pool, though you'll have to drive to the beach. See chapter 3.

- **Villa Santana** (St. Thomas; ✆ **340/776-1311**): At this country villa, originally built for a Mexican general, all rooms are suites. In honor of its previous occupant, the decor is Mexican, and there's a pool, sun deck, and garden. See chapter 3.
- **Garden by the Sea Bed & Breakfast** (St. John; ✆ **340/779-4731**): Overlooking the ocean, this is a small but choice B&B on the least populated of the major U.S. Virgins. With easy access to north shore beaches, it offers beautifully furnished bedrooms with elephant bamboo canopy beds and Japanese fountains. You get style and affordable prices—not bad. See chapter 4.
- **Breakfast Club** (St. Croix; ✆ **340/773-7383**): The best value B&B on St. Croix is a 1950s compound of efficiency apartments with a stone house from the 1930s. Each unit comes with a kitchenette. A sense of home prevails with guests gathering around a hot tub on a raised deck. The breakfast is better than what you might find at most hotels. See chapter 5.
- **Hilty House** (St. Croix; ✆ **340/773-2594**): On a hilltop set against a backdrop of mountains, the island's best B&B is a plantation-style house with a variety of accommodations, ranging from self-catering cottages to master bedrooms with four-poster beds. See chapter 5.
- **The Olde Yard Inn** (Virgin Gorda; ✆ **800/653-9273** or 284/495-5544): The best B&B in the B.V.I. is more like a charming little inn lying outside Spanish Town. Surrounded by tropical gardens, it is an inviting oasis with reasonable prices. Bedrooms are renovated, and French-accented dinners are another reason to check in here. A free shuttle hauls guests to a nearby white sandy beach. See chapter 6.

12 The Best Places to Get Away from It All

Although there are tranquil retreats on St. Croix and even St. Thomas, you'll find even more remote oases on St. John and the British Virgin Islands.

- **St. John:** This is one of the most secluded islands you'll find in the Caribbean. More than two-thirds of its land has been preserved as a national park. That means that unlike St. Thomas and St. Croix, St. John's landscape looks much like it did in the 1950s: white sand beaches and verdant tropical forests. Day-trippers from St. Thomas come over in the morning and usually depart before 5pm. After that, St. John becomes a crowd-free paradise. **Caribbean Villas & Resorts** (✆ **800/338-0987**) offers some of the best values here for those who'd like to rent their own private villa. See chapter 4.
- **Anegada Reef Hotel** (Anegada; ✆ **284/495-8002**): This hotel is located some 20 miles north of Virgin Gorda's North Sound, on a flat mass of coral and limestone; it's one of the most remote spots in the entire Virgin Islands chain. You may never meet any of the 250 local residents, although you'll occasionally see snorkelers, fishers, and scuba divers. We recommend this unpolished hotel for devotees of deserted beaches and laid-back getaways. It's the kind of place where if the bartender isn't around, you make your own cocktails and write down what you had. See chapter 6.

- **Guana Island Club** (Guana Island; ✆ **800/544-8262** or 284/494-2354): This secluded, hilltop hideaway is the only development on a private, 850-acre island off the coast of Tortola. The island is known for its six vacant, virgin beaches; rare species of plant and animal life (look for the roseate flamingo); and excellent nature trails. See chapter 6.
- **Peter Island Resort** (Peter Island; ✆ **800/346-4451** or 284/495-2000): This exquisite resort inn sits on a 1,800-acre private island, which comes complete with five pristine beaches, hiking trails, and gorgeous offshore reefs. Guests also enjoy first-rate water sports facilities, elegant candlelight dining, and secluded beachfront accommodations. See chapter 6.
- **The Sandcastle** (Jost Van Dyke; ✆ **284/495-9888**): The ultimate escapist's dream. This little island, reached by ferry from Tortola, is riddled with good hiking trails, uncrowded sandy beaches, and the ruins of an old military fort. People come to the Sandcastle in search of isolation and relaxation, and that's exactly what they get. See chapter 6.

13 The Best Restaurants

- **Duffy's Love Shack** (St. Thomas; ✆ **340/779-2080**): No one's ever heard of haute cuisine at this laid-back place serving both American standards and zesty Caribbean dishes. If the cowboy steak doesn't interest your kid, maybe the voodoo pineapple chicken will. Wait until your child samples those West Indian egg rolls. See chapter 3.
- **Hervé Restaurant and Wine Bar** (St. Thomas; ✆ **340/ 777-9703**): This newly launched establishment next to the landmark Hotel 1829 has captured much attention, most recently from *Gourmet* magazine. The panoramic view is great, but it's the cuisine that counts, a truly sublime American/Caribbean/Continental repertoire. Nothing beats the black sesame–crusted tuna with a ginger and raspberry sauce. See chapter 3.
- **Virgilio's** (St. Thomas; ✆ **340/ 776-4920**): This cheerful yet elegant spot boasts the best Italian food on the island. Virgilio's lovingly prepares all your favorite Italian classics (try the osso buco or chicken parmigiana), in addition to more than 20 different homemade pasta dishes, and a few surprises too, like cioppino, a kettle of savory seafood stew. Savvy diners always save room for one of the flambé desserts. See chapter 3.
- **Asolare** (St. John; ✆ **809/ 779-4747**): The most beautiful and elegant restaurant on St. John also has some of the best food. Chef Robert Smith produces a fusion of French and Asian cuisine that relies on the island's freshest seafood and produce. Try the prawn and coconut milk soup or the spicy tuna tartare wrapped in somen noodles. The staff is the hippest and most attractive on the island. See chapter 4.
- **Le Château de Bordeaux** (St. John; ✆ **340/776-6611**): Both the view here and the exquisite combination of continental and Caribbean cuisine are winners. Wild game and rack of lamb perfumed with rosemary and a honey-Dijon nut crust appear often on the ever-changing menu. The West Indian seafood chowder is a perfect blend of fish and spices. See chapter 4.

- **Indies** (St. Croix; ☎ **340/692-9440**): San Francisco–born chef Catherine Piav-Driggers applies everything she ever learned in California to the rich bounty of the Caribbean. The result is taste and texture unequaled on the island— spicy Caribbean chicken, spring rolls, and grouper brought to life with coconut milk, shrimp, tomato, ginger, and scallions. The sheltered 19th-century courtyard where meals are served adds to the unforgettable experience. See chapter 5.
- **Kendricks** (St. Croix; ☎ **340/773-9199**): David and Jane Kendrick bring a light continental touch to richly flavored dishes. You might begin with baked brie smothered in perfectly seasoned wild mushrooms, then move on to coconut shrimp in a chive-studded, peppery aïoli. Some of this culinary couple's recipes have been featured in *Bon Appetit* magazine. See chapter 5.
- **Skyworld** (Tortola; ☎ **284/494-3567**): With a 360° view of Tortola and its sister isles, sunsets that turn the whole sky a fiery red, and one or two *Pascha Coladas* (passion fruit juice, rum, and cream of coconut), who cares about dinner? This restaurant does. Its eclectic cuisine is heavy on fresh fish. Don't miss the refreshing Key lime pie, the best on the island. See chapter 6.

14 The Best Shopping Buys

The U.S. Virgin Islands are the shopping mecca of the Caribbean, mostly because there's no sales tax and shoppers can take advantage of the $1,200 duty-free allowance. St. Thomas's capital, Charlotte Amalie, is the nerve center of the shopping activity here. Look for two local publications, *This Week in St. Thomas* or *Best Buys*— either will steer you toward the goods you want.

Before you leave home, try to check out the price of comparable items you hope to buy in St. Thomas; that way, you'll know if you are really getting a bargain or not (see the shopping section in chapter 3 for more details). With that said, your best deals will most likely be found in the following merchandise.

- **Arts and Crafts:** Though arts and crafts here are not the high-priority items they are on such islands as Haiti and Jamaica, you can certainly find them in the Virgin Islands. The **Jim Tillett Gallery** in St. Thomas (☎ **340/775-1929**) is the premier art gallery and craft studio in the U.S. Virgin Islands. The staff's silk screening has been featured in fashion layouts around the world. In St. John, **Mongoose Junction,** in a woodsy roadside area right at Cruz Bay, offers the best assortment of locally produced arts and crafts (all tax-free for U.S. citizens). Handmade pottery, sculpture, and glass are sold here, along with locally made clothing. In Christiansted on St. Croix, seek out **Folk Art Traders** (☎ **340/773-1900**). But if you're looking for handcrafts exclusive to the U.S. Virgin Islands, head for **Many Hands** (☎ **340/773-1990**), also in Christiansted at the Pan Am Pavilion.
- **Fine China and Crystal:** Sometimes (not always) you can find great deals on these wares—many shoppers report savings of 30% to 50%. We noted that Baccarat goblets sold on St. Thomas went for about a third of the price quoted in the U.S. catalog. Again, know

your prices before you land on St. Thomas.

- **Jewelry:** Watches and gold jewelry are often heavily discounted in St. Thomas and St. Croix, especially during the off-season (mid-April to mid-October), when there isn't a traffic jam of cruise ships in their harbors. The sheer volume of jewelry offered in St. Thomas is stunning—diamonds, emeralds, rubies, opals, gold, and platinum, including both world-famous names and one-of-a-kind pieces created by local artists.

- **Liquor:** A recent spot survey showed that prices for liquor in St. Thomas and St. Croix were 50% to 60% less than in New York City. You're allowed to bring 5 liters of liquor back to the United States, or 6 liters if the sixth is locally produced. Local liquor nearly always means rum in the Virgin Islands, but it could also

include Southern Comfort, which is bottled on the island (check the label). Because of the generous U.S. Customs allowances in the Virgin Islands, St. Thomas or St. Croix might be the best places to purchase expensive French brandy, champagne, or liqueurs.

- **Perfumes and Cosmetics:** Be on the lookout for bargains on imported perfumes and beauty products such as bath gels and makeup. How much you save depends on the product. We recently discovered that an ounce of Yves St. Laurent's Opium was $40 cheaper in St. Thomas than in Manhattan. **Tropicana Perfume Shoppes (© 340/774-0010)**, on Main Street in Charlotte Amalie, has the largest selection of fragrances for both women and men in the U.S. Virgin Islands.

15 The Best Nightlife

If you're a serious party animal, you'll want to avoid St. John and most places on the British Virgin Islands and concentrate on St. Thomas and St. Croix. Below are the latest hot spots.

- **The Old Mill** (St. Thomas; © 340/776/3004), is the newest and largest entertainment complex in all of the Virgin Islands. Everything is here, from the island's best sports bar to its most elegant wine and champagne bar for those nighttime revelers who want to go more posh. See chapter 3.

- **Turtle Rock Bar at the Wyndham Sugar Bay Beach Club** (St. Thomas; © 340/777-7100): This place near Red Hook is known for its burgers and bar scene. There's always something going on, whether it's karaoke or live shows by steel-pan bands or other local talent. Happy hour,

from 4 to 6pm, means half-price cocktails. See chapter 3.

- **Blue Moon** (St. Croix; © 340/772-2222): On Thursday and Friday nights, this little dive/bistro is the hottest spot in Christiansted. The crowd here is predominantly local, along with a few savvy visitors. See chapter 5.

- **The Buccaneer** (St. Croix; © 800/255-3881 or 340/773-2100): This deluxe hotel has the best nightlife on the island, often in its bar, the Terrace Lounge. Call to see what's going on during your visit; it could be anything from limbo shows to live reggae. See chapter 5.

- **Divi Casino** (St. Croix; © 340/773-9700): At the Divi Carina Bay Resort, this glittering casino has introduced gambling to the U.S. Virgin Islands for the first time (if you don't count the island's buccaneering days). Built in the midst of a raging controversy over gambling, the 10-million-square-foot casino boasts 12 gaming tables and 275 slot machines. See chapter 5.

- **Bomba's Surfside Shack at Cappoon's Bay** (Tortola; ✆ 284/495-4148): This is one of the most famous bars in the West Indies and the most interesting hangout in the British Virgin Islands. Bomba's decor consists of junk and neon graffiti. The rum punches are always flowing, and the hippest people in town show up here, especially for the notorious all-night Full Moon Parties. See chapter 6.

16 The Most Intriguing Historical Sights

- **Crown House** (St. Thomas): This 18th-century, stone-built mansion served as the home of two former governors. Among the many antiques here are memorabilia of governor Peter von Scholten, who occupied the premises in 1827. A French chandelier in the mansion is said to have come from Versailles. See chapter 3.
- **Fort Christian** (St. Thomas): This fort, which stands in the heart of Charlotte Amalie, was built in 1672 after the arrival of the first Danish colonists. The oldest building on the island, it has been vastly altered over the years and has housed a jail, courthouse, town hall, church, and, most recently, a historical museum. Head to the roof for a stellar view. See chapter 3.
- **Annaberg Ruins** (St. John): The ruins of this sugar plantation are the greatest reminder of St. John's plantation era. The remains of the building have been spruced up rather than restored, and the surrounding land is now lush vegetation. Visitors can explore the former slave quarters. See chapter 4.
- **Fort Christiansvaern** (St. Croix): This fort is one of the best preserved of its type in the West Indies, with a facade that hasn't changed much since the 1820s. It was constructed from ballast bricks imported from Denmark, the island's colonial guardian. The first fort on the spot was built between 1732 and 1749, and part of that structure remains. See chapter 5.
- **Fort Frederick** (St. Croix): This fort, completed in 1760, is said to have been the first to salute the flag of the newly formed United States. It was also here, in 1848, that Gov. Peter von Scholten read a proclamation freeing the island's slaves. A small museum sits on the site today. See chapter 5.

2

Planning Your Trip to the Virgin Islands

A little advance planning can go a long way. In this chapter, we give you all the information you need to know before you go, including how to get the lowest rates on flights, lodging, and car rentals. We also help you decide which island(s) to visit and when to go.

1 Choosing the Perfect Island

Peering at the tiny Virgin Islands chain on a world map, you may find it difficult to distinguish the different islands. They vary widely, however, in looks and personality, and so will your vacation, depending on which island or islands you choose. It's important to plan ahead. For example, if you're an avid golfer, you won't want spend a week on a remote British Virgin Island with only a rinky-dink nine-hole course or no course at all. But that same island might be perfect for a young couple contemplating a romantic honeymoon. By providing detailed information about the character of each island in both the U.S. Virgin Islands and the British Virgin Islands, we hope to guide you to your own idea of paradise.

U.S. VS. BRITISH VIRGIN ISLANDS

American and British cultures have left different imprints on the Virgin Islands. The **U.S. Virgin Islands** (or "U.S.V.I."), except for St. John, offer much of the commercial hustle-and-bustle of the mainland, including supermarkets and fast-food chains. In contrast, the British islands to the east are sleepier. Except for a few deluxe hotels, mostly on Virgin Gorda, they recall the way the Caribbean was

before the advent of high-rise condos, McDonald's, and fleets of cruise ships.

If you want shopping, a wide selection of restaurants and hotels, and night-life, head to the U.S. Virgin Islands, particularly **St. Thomas** and **St. Croix.** With a little research and effort, you can also find peace and quiet on these two islands, most often at outlying resorts. But overall, among the U.S. Virgin Islands, only St. John matches the British Virgins for tranquility. **St. John** is a rugged mixture of bumpy dirt roads, scattered inhabitants, and a handful of stores and services. It's protected by the U.S. Forest Service and remains the least developed of the U.S. islands.

The **British Virgin Islands** (or "B.V.I.") seem to be lingering in the past, but today even year-round residents can't deny that change is in the air. **Tortola** is the most populated British isle, but its shopping, nightlife, and dining are still limited. It's more a spot for boaters of all stripes—it's considered the cruising capital of the Caribbean. To the east, **Virgin Gorda** claims most of the B.V.I.'s deluxe hotels. There are also attractive accommodations and restaurants on the smaller islands, such as Jost Van Dyke, Anegada, and Peter Island.

Fun Fact "Little Timmy Duncan," St. Croix Giant

One of the most popular basketball players in the NBA, San Antonio Spur Tim Duncan is St. Croix born and bred. Growing up on the island, he wanted to be a swimmer, and while still a teenager he became one of the top-ranked swimmers in the United States in his age group. When Hurricane Hugo swept away his team's swimming pool in 1989, Tim gave up swimming and started playing basketball. Starting at 6'2" tall, he shot up to his full height of 7'0" in just two years. At the end of his senior year, he was named both NCAA Player of the Year and the National Defensive Player of the Year and was named ACC Player of the Year for the second straight time. Drafted by the San Antonio Spurs in 1997, he has gone to glory, winning "Rookie of the Year" honors and helping his team to win its first-ever NBA championship title in 1999. In St. Croix he's a local hero, and his portrait stands across from the airport.

Who does every little boy growing up in St. Croix want to be? Tim Duncan, of course, but those are big shoes to fill.

If you'd like to meet and intermingle with locals and get to know the islanders and their lifestyle, it's much easier to do so in the sleepy B.V.I. than in the hustle-bustle of St. Thomas or even St. Croix. The only U.S. Virgin Island that has the laid-back quality of the B.V.I. is St. John, where the atmosphere is far more relaxed than St. Thomas—except that "local native" you are likely to meet on St. John is often an ex-pat from the U.S. mainland, not a Virgin Islander born and bred.

Except for frequent ferry connections between St. Thomas and St. John, traveling among the other islands is a bit difficult, requiring private boats in many cases or airplane flights in others (see the "Getting Around the Islands" section later in this chapter for more details). The day will surely come when transportation from island to island will be made more convenient and frequent, but that day hasn't arrived yet.

THE MAJOR ISLANDS IN BRIEF

The islands previewed below are the most visited and the sites of the most shopping, hotels, restaurants, attractions, and nightlife. For those who want to escape from the masses, the British Virgin Islands have a number of escapist islands such as Peter Island, Mosquito Island, or Guana Island. These are virtual private hideaways, often with expensive resorts (which is the main reason for going there in the first place). Two more remote British Virgin Islands with more democratically priced hotels include Anegada and Jost Van Dyke. Even if you're staying at a resort on Virgin Gorda or Tortola, you still might want to join a boat excursion to visit some of the lesser known islands as part of a sightseeing excursion with some time left for R&R on a nearly deserted beach.

ST. THOMAS

The most developed of the Virgin Islands, St. Thomas resembles a small city at times. There are peaceful retreats here, but you must seek them out. The harbor at **Charlotte Amalie,** the capital, is the cruise-ship haven of the Caribbean. Many locals try to avoid it when the greatest concentration of vessels is in port (usually from December to April). Charlotte Amalie offers the widest selection of duty-free shopping in the Caribbean. However,

The Virgin Islands

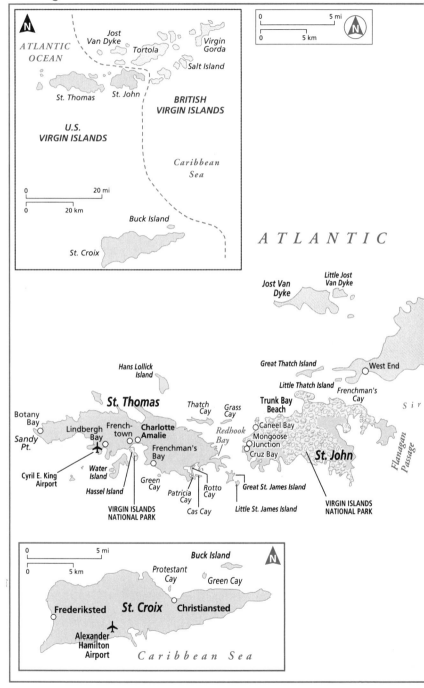

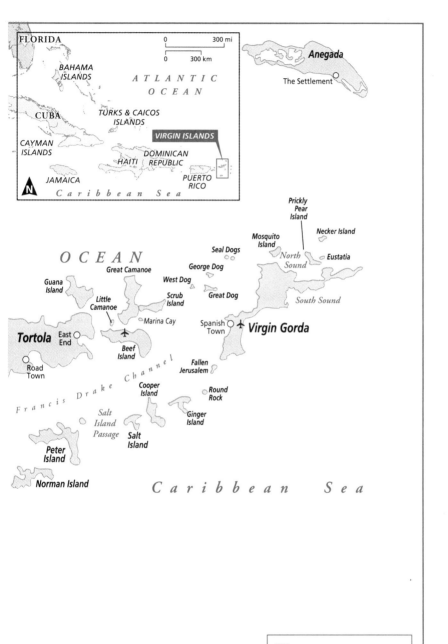

FLORIDA

BAHAMA ISLANDS

A T L A N T I C
O C E A N

0   300 mi
0   300 km

CUBA

TURKS & CAICOS ISLANDS

VIRGIN ISLANDS

CAYMAN ISLANDS

DOMINICAN REPUBLIC

HAITI

JAMAICA

PUERTO RICO

C a r i b b e a n   S e a

N

Anegada

The Settlement

Prickly Pear Island

Mosquito Island

Necker Island

Seal Dogs

North Sound

Eustatia

O C E A N

George Dog

Great Camanoe

West Dog

Guana Island

Scrub Island

Great Dog

South Sound

Little Camanoe

Marina Cay

Spanish Town

Virgin Gorda

Tortola East End

Beef Island

C h a n n e l

Fallen Jerusalem

Road Town

D r a k e

Cooper Island

Round Rock

F r a n c i s

Salt Island Passage

Ginger Island

Salt Island

Peter Island

Norman Island

C a r i b b e a n   S e a

British Virgin Islands

U.S. Virgin Islands

you must browse carefully through the labyrinth of bazaars to find the real bargains.

St. Thomas, like most of the Virgin Islands, gives you plenty of opportunity to get outside and get active, although many visitors come here simply to sit, sun, and maybe go for a swim. **Magens Bay Beach,** with its tranquil surf and sugar-white sand, is one of the most beautiful beaches in the world, but it is likely to be packed, especially on heavy cruise-ship days. More secluded beaches include Secret Harbour and Sapphire Beach in East End.

St. Thomas has only one golf course, **Mahogany Run,** but it's a real gem. The three trickiest holes (13, 14, and 15) are known throughout the golfing world as the "Devil's Triangle."

Yachts and boats anchor at **Ramada Yacht Haven Marina** in Charlotte Amalie and at **Red Hook Marina** on the island's somewhat isolated eastern tip. The serious yachting crowd, however, gathers at Tortola in the British Virgin Islands (see below). Sport fishers angle from the **American Yacht Harbor** at Red Hook. The island also attracts snorkelers and scuba divers—there are many outfitters offering equipment, excursions, and instruction. Kayaking and parasailing are also drawing more beach bums away from the water's edge.

St. Thomas also has the most eclectic and sophisticated restaurant scene in the Virgin Islands, with special emphasis on French and Continental fare. It pays more for its imported (usually European) chefs and secures the freshest of ingredients from mainland or Puerto Rican markets.

The wide selection of restaurants, from Mexican and Italian to Asian and American, adds an international flavor to the island's West Indian fare.

There's also a wide variety of accommodations on St. Thomas, from **Bluebeard's Castle** (a perennial favorite) to more modern beachfront complexes in the East End, including the manicured **Elysian Beach Resort.** Apartment and villa rentals abound, and you can also find handful of old-fashioned B&B–style guest houses.

If St. Thomas has one drawback, it's that it is no longer as safe a destination as it used to be. Crime is on the rise, and muggings are frequent. Wandering the island at night, especially on the back streets of Charlotte Amalie, is not recommended.

ST. JOHN

Our favorite of all the U.S. Virgin Islands, St. John has only two deluxe hotels, but several charming inns and plenty of campgrounds. Its primary attraction is the **U.S. Virgin Islands National Park,** which covers more than half the island. Guided walks and safari bus tours are available to help you navigate the park, which is full of pristine beaches, secret coves, flowering trees, and ghostly remains of sugar cane plantations. A third of the park is underwater. **Trunk Bay,** which also boasts the island's finest beach, has an amazing underwater snorkeling trail. Scuba diving is also a major attraction on St. John, as is hiking, because of the extensive network of trails through the national park.

St. John has a handful of posh restaurants, as well as a number of colorful West Indian eateries. Many

Impressions

Listen you ol' guys from the States. You Bob Doles. You don't need that Viagra. My bush tea will fix you up just fine.

—An old woman vendor yelling at some elderly male cruise ship passengers in Charlotte Amalie, 1999 residents and long-term visitors like to bring cooking supplies over on the ferry from St. Thomas, where prices are lower and the selection broader. Nightlife isn't a major attraction here; it usually consists of sipping rum drinks in a bar in **Cruz Bay** and maybe listening to a local calypso band. After a spending a day outdoors, most visitors on St. John are happy to turn in early.

ST. CROIX

This island is the second major tourist destination in the Virgin Islands. Like St. Thomas, St. Croix is highly developed. Cruise-ship passengers continue to flood **Frederiksted** and the capital, **Christiansted,** looking for duty-free goods and a handful of white sand to take home in a plastic bag. Although parts of the island resemble American suburbia, some of St. Croix's true West Indian–style buildings have been preserved, along with many of its rich cultural traditions.

One of the best reasons for a trip to St. Croix, even if only for a day, is to visit **Buck Island National Park,** just 1½ miles off St. Croix's northeast coast. The park's offshore reef attracts snorkelers and certified divers from around the world. Blue signs posted along the ocean floor guide you through a forest of staghorn coral swarming with flamboyant fish.

St. Croix is the premier golfing destination in the Virgin Islands, mainly because it boasts **Carambola,** the archipelago's most challenging 18-hole course. St. Croix is also a tennis mecca of sorts: The luxurious **Buccaneer Hotel** has some of the best courts in the Virgin Islands and hosts several annual tournaments. Other sports for active vacationers include horseback riding, parasailing, sport fishing, water-skiing, snorkeling, and scuba diving.

The restaurants on St. Croix are not as good as those on St. Thomas, although they claim to be. The highly touted **Top Hat,** for example, prides itself on its Danish dishes, but split-pea soup and *Frikadeller* (meatballs with red cabbage) may not be exactly what you're looking for on a hot Caribbean night. Life after dark is mostly confined to a handful of bars in Christiansted.

As for accommodations, St. Croix has only a few real luxury hotels, but there are a lot of small, attractive inns (we highly recommend **Pink Fancy**). And, as on St. Thomas, it's easy to find villas and condos for rent at reasonable weekly rates.

For the most part, life here is laid-back; however, St. Croix is certainly not problem-free. At night, use discretion and avoid the back streets of Christiansted and, more importantly, Frederiksted, on the western coast.

TORTOLA

Tortola is the hub of the British Virgin Islands, but not always the best place for visitors, especially if you're planning to spend more than a couple of days here—we think Virgin Gorda (see below) has better hotels and restaurants. **Road Town,** the capital, with its minor shopping, routine restaurants, and uninspired architecture, deserves a couple of hours at the most. Once you leave Road Town, however, you'll find Tortola more alluring. The island's best (and most unspoiled) beaches, including Smuggler's Cove with its garden of snorkeling reefs, lie at the island's western tip. Tortola's premier beach is **Cane Garden Bay,** a 1½-mile stretch of white sand. Because of the gentle surf, it's one of the most secure places for families with small children. For hikers on Tortola, a highlight of a visit is the exploration through Sage Mountain National Park with trails leading to

Fun Fact **A Famous Virgin Islander: Kelsey Grammer**

Kelsey Grammer, a native of St. Thomas, is known to TV audiences around the world as Dr. Frasier Crane, the egghead/psychiatrist at the bar in the long-running TV series *Cheers.* In 1993, he launched his own spin-off series, *Frasier,* which has also proved to be a prime-time hit.

the peak at 1,780 feet, offering panoramic views. The park is also rich in flora and fauna, with everything from mamey trees to the mountain dove.

Although many visitors to the Caribbean look forward to fishing, hiking, horseback riding, snorkeling, and surfing, what makes Tortola exceptional is boating. It is *the* boating center of the British Virgin Islands, which are among the most cherished sailing territories on the planet. The island offers some 100 charter yachts and 300 bareboats, and its marina and shore facilities are the most up-to-date and extensive in the Caribbean Basin.

The crystal-clear waters compensate for the island's lackluster bars and restaurants. You can count on the food here being simple and straightforward— we suggest any locally caught fish grilled with perhaps a little lime butter.

VIRGIN GORDA

Our favorite British Virgin Island is Virgin Gorda, the third-largest member of the archipelago, with a permanent population of about 1,000 lucky souls. Many visitors come over just for a day to check out **The Baths,** an astounding collection of gigantic rocks, boulders, and tide pools on the southern tip. Shaped by volcanic pressures millions of years ago, they have eroded into shapes reminiscent of a Henry Moore sculpture. With more than 20 uncrowded beaches, the best known of which are Spring Beach and Trunk Beach, Virgin Gorda is a sun worshiper's dream come true.

Unlike Tortola, Virgin Gorda has some of the finest hotels in the Virgin Islands, including **Little Dix Bay** and **Biras Creek,** but you must be willing to pay the price for the privilege of staying at these regal resorts. There are also more reasonably priced places to stay, such as **Olde Yard Inn,** which feels like an old-fashioned retreat. Outside the upscale hotels, restaurants tend to be simple places serving the local West Indian cuisine. No one takes nightlife too seriously on Virgin Gorda—there isn't very much of it.

2 Visitor Information

IN THE U.S. Before you take off for the U.S. Virgin Islands, you can get information from the **U.S. Virgin Islands Division of Tourism,** 1270 Ave. of the Americas, New York, NY 10020 (© **800/372-USVI** or 212/332-2222; fax 212/332-2223). There are additional offices at the following locations: 245 Peachtree Center Avenue, Suite 760, Atlanta, GA 30303 (© **404/688-0906**); 500 N. Michigan Ave., Suite 2030, Chicago, IL 60611 (© **312/670-8784**); 444 North Capital St. NW, Suite 305, Washington, DC 20001 (© **202/624-3590**); 2655 Le Jeune Rd., Suite 907, Coral Gables, FL 33134 (© **305/442-7200**); and 3460 Wilshire Blvd., Los Angeles, CA 90010 (© **213/739-0138**).

For details on the British Virgin Islands, get in touch with the **British**

Virgin Islands Tourist Board, 370 Lexington Ave., Suite 1605, New York, NY 10017 (© **800/835-8530** or 212/696-0400; fax 212/949-8254). On the West Coast, contact the **B.V.I. Information Office,** 1804 Union St., San Francisco, CA 94123 (© **213/ 736-8931**).

IN CANADA Information about the U.S.V.I. Government Tourist office at 703 Evans Ave., Suite 106, Toronto ON M9C 5E9 (© **416/ 622-7600;** fax 416/622-3431).

IN THE U.K. Information for the British Virgin Islands is available at the **B.V.I. Information Office,** 55 Newman St., London, England W1T 3EB (© **020/7947-8200;** fax 020/ 7947-8279). For the **U.S. Virgin Islands,** information is available at 2 Cinnamon Row, Plantation Wharf, York Place, London, England SW11 3TN (© **020/7978-5262;** fax 020/7924-3171).

3 Entry Requirements & Customs

U.S. and Canadian citizens are required to present some proof of citizenship—a passport, voter registration card, or birth certificate—to enter the Virgin Islands, whether U.S. or British. Though a passport is not necessary, it is by far the best form of identification and will speed you through Customs and Immigration. Also, if you have a passport, you can take an excursion to the nearby Leeward Islands, such as Anguilla or St. Martin, which are foreign destinations.

Visitors from Europe and other parts of the world do need a passport and a U.S. visa to enter the U.S. Virgin Islands. Those who stay less than 6 months in the British Virgin Islands need only a passport and a return or onward ticket. The B.V.I. has a unique system for processing arriving passengers. On entry, there are two lines: one for "belongers" (those born on the B.V.I. or married to a native) and "nonbelongers" (everyone else).

Before you leave home, make two copies (leave one at home) of your most valuable documents, including your passport, driver's license, voter registration card (if you're using that instead of a license), airline tickets, and hotel vouchers. If you're on medication, you should also make copies of prescriptions.

PASSPORT INFORMATION FOR RESIDENTS OF THE U.S.

If you're applying for a first-time passport, you need to do it in person at one of 13 passport offices throughout the United States; a federal, state, or probate court; or a major post office (though not all post offices accept applications; call the number below to find the ones that do). The places that accept the passport application will have the forms you need; you can also download them ahead of time, see the website address below. Some travel agencies also stock the necessary forms. You'll have to present a certified birth certificate as proof of citizenship, and it's wise to bring along your driver's license, state or military ID, and Social Security card as well. You also need two identical passport-sized photos (2 in. by 2 in.), taken at any corner photo shop (not one of the strip photos, however, from a photo-vending machine).

For people over age 15, a passport is valid for 10 years and costs $60 ($45 plus a $15 handling fee); for those ages 15 and under, it's valid for 5 years and costs $40. If you're over age 15, you can renew your passport by mail (within certain limitations) and bypass the $15 handling fee. Allow plenty of time before your trip to apply; processing normally takes 3 weeks, but can take longer during busy periods (especially spring). For more information, call the **National Passport Agency** (© 202/647-0518). To find your regional passport office, call the **National Passport Information Center** (© 900/225-5674; http://travel. state.gov).

FOR RESIDENTS OF CANADA You can pick up a passport application at one of 28 regional passport offices or most travel agencies. The passport is valid for 5 years and costs $60. Children under age 16 may be included on a parent's passport but need their own to travel unaccompanied by the parent. Applications, which must be accompanied by two identical passport-sized photographs and proof of Canadian citizenship, are available at travel agencies throughout Canada or from the central **Passport Office,** Department of Foreign Affairs and International Trade, Ottawa, Ontario K1A 0G3 (© 800/567-6868; www.dfait-maeci. gc.ca/passport). Processing takes 5 to 10 days if you apply in person, or about 3 weeks by mail.

FOR RESIDENTS OF THE U.K. To pick up an application for a regular 10-year passport (the Visitor's Passport has been abolished), visit your nearest passport office, major post office, or travel agency. You can also contact the **London Passport Office** at © 0990/ **210-410** or search its website at www.ukpa.gov.uk. Passports are £28 for adults and £11 for children under age 16.

FOR RESIDENTS OF IRELAND You can apply for a 10-year passport, costing IR£45, at the **Passport Office,** Setanta Centre, Molesworth St., Dublin 2 (© 01/671-1633; www. irlgov.ie). Those under age 18 and over age 65 must apply for a IR£10 3-year passport. You can also apply at 1A South Mall, Cork (© 021/272-525) or over the counter at main post offices.

FOR RESIDENTS OF AUSTRALIA Apply at your local post office or passport office, or search the government website at www.dfat.gov.au. Passports cost A$132 for adults and A$66 for those under age 18.

FOR RESIDENTS OF NEW ZEALAND You can pick up a passport application at any travel agency or Link Centre. For more information, contact the **Passport Office,** P.O. Box 805, Wellington (© 0800/ **225-050;** www.passports.govt.nz). Passports are NZ$80 for adults and NZ$40 for those under age 16.

CUSTOMS

The U.S. Virgin Islands are duty-free ports, which means that many goods imported to the islands are not subject to import taxes and therefore can be sold at a discount. Shoppers can take advantage of the duty-free bargains, but only up to a limit prescribed by their government. On leaving the U.S.V.I., Americans must clear Customs. Customs procedures for Canadian, Australian, British, and other foreign travelers to the U.S.V.I. are the same as on the U.S. mainland.

In the British Virgin Islands (which aren't duty-free ports), there is a customs review upon entry.

Customs restrictions on what you can bring to both the B.V.I. and U.S.V.I. are rather flexible. Usually you are waved through immigration and customs after only a brief question or two, especially if you appear to be a vacationer. You're allowed to bring in a "reasonable" amount of duty-free goods for your personal use; the custom agent has the right to determine what is a reasonable amount. (One or two bottles of perfume—yes. Three dozen? No.) You can also bring in two liters of alcohol and two cartons of cigarettes into both B.V.I. and U.S.V.I., but very few visitors do that, especially in the U.S.V.I.

where discounted liquor is sold. In general, it's a question of what you take out of the Virgin Islands duty-free—not what you can bring in. Of course, the importation of firearms or dangerous materials is forbidden.

BRINGING IT ALL HOME TO THE U.S.

The U.S. government allows U.S. citizens a total of $1,200 worth of duty-free imports from the U.S.V.I. every 30 days—twice the amount allowed for those returning from most foreign-ruled Caribbean islands and three times the amount for those returning from most foreign countries and French islands, such as Guadeloupe or Martinique. The duty-free exemption for purchases made in the British Virgin Islands is $600. Purchases made in the U.S. Virgin Islands over the duty-free exemption are taxed at a flat rate of 5% (10% in the British Virgin Islands).

Family members traveling together can make joint declarations. For a husband and wife with two children, the exemption in the U.S. Virgins is $4,800!

Unsolicited gifts worth up to $100 per day from the U.S. Virgin Islands can be sent to friends and relatives, and they do not have to be declared as part of your $1,200 duty-free allowance. Gifts mailed from the British Virgin Islands cannot exceed $50 per day.

U.S. citizens can bring back 5 liters of liquor duty free, plus an extra liter of rum (including Cruzan rum) if one of the bottles is produced in the Virgin Islands. Goods made on the island are also duty-free, including perfume, jewelry, clothing, and original paintings; however, if the price of an item exceeds $25, you must be able to show a certificate of origin.

Be sure to collect receipts for all purchases in the Virgin Islands, and beware of merchants offering to give you a false receipt—he or she might be an informer to U.S. Customs. Also, keep in mind that any gifts received during your stay must be declared.

If you're concerned about Customs procedures and want more specific guidance, write to the **U.S. Customs Service,** 1301 Constitution Ave., P.O. Box 7407, Washington, DC 20044 (© **202/927-6724;** www.customs.ustreas.gov) to request the free pamphlet *Know Before You Go.* For information on U.S. Virgin Islands requirements, call © **340/774-4554** in St. Thomas.

TO THE U.K. U.K. citizens returning from a non-EU country such as the U.S. Virgin Islands have a customs allowance of: 200 cigarettes, 50 cigars, or 250 grams of smoking tobacco; 2 liters of still table wine; 1 liter of spirits or strong liqueurs (over 22% volume) or 2 liters of fortified wine, sparkling wine, or other liqueurs; 60 cc (ml) perfume; 250 cc (ml) of toilet water; and £145 worth of all other goods, including gifts and souvenirs. People under age 17 cannot have the tobacco or alcohol allowance. For more information, contact **HM Customs & Excise,** Passenger Enquiry Point, 2nd Floor, Wayfarer House, Great South West Rd., Feltham, Middlesex, TW14 8NP (© **020/8910-3744;** from outside the U.K. © 01144/20-8910-3744), or consult their website at www.hmce.gov.uk.

TO CANADA For a clear summary of Canadian rules, write for the booklet *I Declare,* issued by **Revenue Canada,** 2265 St. Laurent Blvd., Ottawa K1G 4KE (© **506/636-5064;** www.ccra-adrc.gc.ca). Canada allows its citizens a $500 exemption. You're allowed to bring back duty-free 200 cigarettes, 200 grams of tobacco, 1.5 liters of liquor, and 50 cigars. In addition, you're allowed to mail gifts to Canada from abroad at the rate of CAN$60 a day, provided they're unsolicited and don't contain alcohol or tobacco (write on the package "Unsolicited gift, under $60 value"). All valuables should be declared on the Y-38 form before departure from Canada, including serial numbers of valuables you already own, such as expensive foreign cameras. *Note:* The $750 exemption can only be used once a year and only after an absence of 7 days.

TO AUSTRALIA The Australian duty-free allowance is A$400 or, for those under age 18, A$200. Personal property mailed back from the Caribbean should be marked "Australian goods returned" to avoid payment of duty. Upon returning to Australia, citizens can bring in 250 cigarettes or 250 grams of loose tobacco, and 1,125 mL of alcohol. A helpful brochure, available from Australian consulates or Customs offices, is *Know Before You Go.* For more information, contact **Australian Customs Services,** GPO Box 8, Sydney NSW 2001 (© **02/9213-2000;** www. customs. gov.au).

TO NEW ZEALAND The duty-free allowance for **New Zealand** is NZ$700. Citizens over age 17 can bring in 200 cigarettes, or 50 cigars, or 250 grams of tobacco (or a mixture of all three if their combined weight doesn't exceed 250 grams); plus 4.5 liters of wine and beer or 1.125 liters of liquor. Most questions are answered in a free pamphlet available at New Zealand consulates and Customs offices: *New Zealand Customs Guide for Travellers,* Notice no. 4. For more information, contact **New Zealand Customs,** 50 Anzac Ave., P.O. Box 29, Auckland (© **09/359-6655;** www.customs.govt.nz).

4 Money

CASH & CURRENCY

Both the U.S. Virgin Islands and the British Virgin Islands use the U.S. dollar as the form of currency.

British and Canadian travelers will have to convert their currency into U.S. dollars. The chart below provides a rough approximation of conversion rates you're likely to find at the time of your trip, but be sure to check them before you leave.

ATMS

Automated teller machines (ATMs) allow travelers to withdraw small amounts of cash as needed—and thus avoid the risk of carrying a fortune around in an unfamiliar environment. Many banks, however, impose a fee every time a card is used at an ATM in a different city or bank. ATMs are linked to a national network that most likely includes your bank at home. **Cirrus** (© **800/424-7787;** www.

mastercard.com) and **Plus** (© **800/ 843-7587;** www.visa.com) are the two most popular networks; check the back of your ATM card to see which network your bank belongs to. Use the network's toll-free number to locate ATMs in your destination.

ATMs are most prevalent in Charlotte Amalie on St. Thomas and in Christiansted on St. Croix. They are also available in Cruz Bay on St. John and in the British Virgin Islands on Tortola and Virgin Gorda. The other islands do not have ATMs.

TRAVELER'S CHECKS

Traveler's checks are something of an anachronism from the days before ATMs made cash accessible at any time. But they still might be a good choice if you want to avoid the small fees charged whenever you use an ATM. Traveler's checks are as reliable as currency but can be replaced if lost

The U.S. Dollar, the British Pound & the Canadian Dollar

At the time of this writing, the British pound trades at an average of 1$US = 67 pence, and the Canadian dollar trades at an average of $1US = $1.50 Canadian. The chart below gives a rough approximation of conversion rates you're likely to find throughout the Caribbean at the time of your trip. Rates fluctuate, so be sure to confirm the exchange rates before you make any major transactions.

U.S. $	U.K. £	Canadian $	U.S. $	U.K. £	Canadian $
0.25	0.17	0.38	30.00	19.98	45.00
0.50	0.33	0.75	35.00	23.31	52.50
0.75	0.50	1.13	40.00	26.64	60.00
1.00	0.67	1.50	45.00	29.97	67.50
2.00	1.33	3.00	50.00	33.30	75.00
3.00	2.00	4.50	60.00	39.96	90.00
4.00	2.66	6.00	70.00	46.62	105.00
5.00	3.33	7.50	80.00	53.28	120.00
6.00	4.00	9.00	90.00	59.94	135.00
7.00	4.66	10.50	100.00	66.60	150.00
8.00	5.33	12.00	125.00	83.25	187.50
9.00	5.99	13.50	150.00	99.90	225.00
10.00	6.66	15.00	175.00	116.55	262.50
15.00	9.99	22.50	200.00	133.20	300.00
20.00	13.32	30.00	250.00	166.50	375.00
25.00	16.65	37.50	500.00	333.00	750.00

or stolen, unlike cash. Be sure to keep a record of the checks' serial numbers, separated from the checks of course, so you're ensured a refund in such an emergency.

You can get traveler's checks at almost any bank. **American Express** offers denominations of $10, $20, $50, $100, $500, and $1,000. You'll pay a service charge ranging from 1% to 4%. You can also get American Express traveler's checks over the phone by calling ✆ **800/221-7282;** by using this number, AmEx gold and platinum cardholders are exempt from the 1% fee. **AAA** members can obtain travelers checks without a fee at most AAA offices. **Visa** offers traveler's checks at Citibank locations nationwide, as well as several other banks, in denominations of $20, $50, $100, $500, and $1,000. The service charge ranges between 1.5% and 2%. **MasterCard** also offers traveler's checks. Call ✆ **800/223-7373** in the United States and Canada, or 813/937-7300, for a location near you.

CREDIT CARDS

Credit cards are invaluable when traveling. They're safer and more convenient than cash and provide a record of all your expenses. You can also withdraw **cash advances** from your credit cards at any bank (though you'll start paying hefty interest on the advance the moment you receive the cash). At most banks, you don't even need to

What Things Cost in St. Thomas	U.S. $
Taxi from airport to an East End hotel	20.00
Local bus from Charlotte Amalie to Red Hook ferry	1.00
Local telephone call	.25
Double at Marriott's Frenchman's Reef (deluxe)	299.00
Double at Villa Blanca (moderate)	125.00
Double at Island View Guesthouse (budget)	77.00
Lunch for one at Banana Tree Grille (moderate)*	18.00
Lunch for one at Eunice's (budget)*	12.00
Dinner for one at Blackeard's Castle (deluxe)*	50.00
Dinner for one at Alexander's (moderate)*	35.00
Dinner for one at Duffy's Love Shack (budget)*	18.00
Pint of beer in a bar	3.50
Coca-Cola in a cafe	1.50
Cup of coffee in a cafe	1.50
Glass of wine in a restaurant	4.00
Roll of ASA 100 color film, 36 exposures	6.50
Admission to Magens Bay Beach	1.00
*Includes tax and tip, but not wine	

go to a teller; you can simply get a cash advance at the ATM if you know your PIN number. If you've forgotten your PIN number or didn't even know you had one, call the phone number on the back of your credit card and ask the bank to send it to you. The process usually takes 5 to 7 business days, though some banks will provide the number over the phone if you tell them your mother's maiden name or pass some other security clearance.

Almost every credit card company has an emergency toll-free number that you can call if your wallet or purse is stolen. The company may be able to wire you a cash advance off your credit card immediately and, in many places, can deliver an emergency credit card in a day or two. **Citicorp Visa's** U.S. emergency number is ✆ **800/336-8472. American Express** cardholders and traveler's check holders should call ✆ **800/221-7282** for all money emergencies. **MasterCard** holders should call ✆ **800/307-7309.**

MONEYGRAMS

If you find yourself out of money, a wire service provided by American Express can help you tap friends and family for emergency funds. Through **MoneyGram** (✆ **800/926-9400;** www.moneygram.com), money can be sent around the world in less than 10 minutes. Senders should call AmEx to learn the address of the closest outlet that handles MoneyGrams. Cash and credit/charge cards are acceptable forms of payment. AmEx's fee for the service is $19 for the first $50, with a sliding scale for larger sums. The service includes a short telex message and a 3-minute phone call from sender to recipient. The beneficiary must present a photo ID at the outlet where the money is received.

5 When to Go

CLIMATE

Sunshine is practically an everyday affair in the Virgin Islands. Temperatures climb into the 80s during the day and drop more comfortably into the 70s at night. Winter is generally the dry season in the islands, but rainfall can occur at any time of year. However, you don't have to worry too much—usually, tropical showers come and go so quickly you don't have time to get off the beach.

HURRICANES The hurricane season, the dark side of the Caribbean's beautiful weather, officially lasts from June through November. The chain of Virgin Islands lies in the main pathway of many a hurricane raging through the Caribbean, and these islands are often hit, frequently having to bounce back. If you're planning a vacation in hurricane season, you'll need to stay abreast of weather conditions. Of course, you can't always know far enough in advance what the weather will be when you actually arrive, but many a placid vacation dream has gone with the wind.

Islanders certainly don't stand around waiting for a hurricane to strike. Satellite forecasts generally give adequate warning to both residents and visitors. And of course, there's always prayer: Islanders have a legal holiday in the third week of July called Supplication Day, when they ask to be spared from devastating storms. In late October, locals celebrate the end of the season on Hurricane Thanksgiving Day.

THE HIGH SEASON & THE OFF-SEASON

High season in the Virgin Islands, when hotel rates are at their peak, runs roughly from mid-December to mid-April. However, package and resort rates are sometimes lower in January, as a tourist slump usually occurs right after the Christmas holidays. February is the busiest month. If you're planning to visit during the winter months, make reservations as far in advance as possible.

Off-season begins when North America starts to warm up, and vacationers, assuming that temperatures in the Virgin Islands are soaring into the 100s, head for less tropical local beaches. However, it's actually quite balmy year-round in the Virgin Islands—thanks to the fabled trade winds—with temperatures varying little more than 5° between winter and summer.

There are many advantages to off-season travel in the Virgin Islands. First, from mid-April to mid-December, hotel rates are slashed a startling 25% to 50%. Second, you're less likely to encounter crowds

Average Temperatures (°F) & Rainfall (Inches) in the U.S. Virgin Islands

	Jan	Feb	Mar	Apr	May	June	July	Aug	Sept	Oct	Nov	Dec
St. Thomas												
Temp	76.8	76.7	77.3	79	78.5	81.6	82.2	82.6	81.7	82.6	80.5	76.9
Precip.	1.86	.95	.97	8.32	9.25	1.62	2.25	3.6	2.04	4.43	7.77	2.46
St. Croix												
Temp.	75.9	75.8	77.5	78.7	79.3	81.9	83	83.3	82.6	82	79.8	78.3
Precip.	2.72	.46	1.44	4.25	7.19	2.35	1.20	4.07	2.11	3.08	7.64	2.77
St. John												
Temp.	75.4	75.1	77.3	78.1	77.8	79.7	80.3	82.6	81.7	80.4	78.3	76.4
Precip.	2.08	1.03	.81	8.02	10.6	1.92	2.55	4.61	1.86	4.02	8.42	3.44

at swimming pools, beaches, resorts, restaurants, or shops. Especially in St. Thomas and St. Croix, a slower pace prevails in the off-season, and you'll have a better chance to appreciate the local culture and cuisine. Of course, there are disadvantages to off-season travel too: Many hotels use the slower months for construction or restoration, fewer facilities are likely to be open, and some hotels and restaurants may close completely when business is really slow.

Additionally, if you're single and planning a trip during the off-season, ask for the hotel's occupancy rate—you may want crowds. The social scene in both the B.V.I. and the U.S.V.I. is intense from mid-December to mid-April. After that, it slumbers a bit. But if you seek escape from the world and its masses, summer is the way to go, especially if you're with someone you want to hang with and aren't depending on meeting others for your social encounters.

HOLIDAYS

In addition to the standard legal holidays observed in the United States, U.S. Virgin Islanders also observe the following holidays: Three Kings' Day (January 6); Transfer Day, commemorating the transfer of the Danish Virgin Islands to the Americans (March 31); Organic Act Day, honoring the legislation that granted voting rights to the islanders (June 20); Emancipation Day, celebrating the freeing of the slaves by the Danish in 1848 (July 3); Hurricane Supplication Day (July 25); Hurricane Thanksgiving Day (October 17); Liberty Day (November 1); and Christmas Second Day (December 26). The islands also celebrate two carnival days on the last Friday and Saturday in April: Children's Carnival Parade and the Grand Carnival Parade.

In the British Virgin Islands, public holidays include the following: New Year's Day; Commonwealth Day (March 12); Good Friday; Easter Monday; Whitmonday (sometime in July); Territory Day Sunday (usually July 1); Festival Monday and Tuesday (during the first week of August); St. Ursula's Day (October 21); Birthday of the Heir to the Throne (November 14); Christmas Day; and Boxing Day (December 26).

THE VIRGIN ISLANDS CALENDAR OF EVENTS

April

International Rolex Cup Regatta. This is one of three regattas in the Caribbean Ocean Racing Triangle (CORT) series. Top-ranked international racers come to St. Thomas to compete in front of the world's yachting press. The St. Thomas Yacht Club hosts the 3-day event. Early April. For more information, call © **340/775-6320.**

BVI Spring Regatta. This is the third leg of the CORT events (see "International Rolex Cup Regatta," above). A range of talents, from the most dedicated racers to bareboat crews out for "rum and reggae," participate in the 4-day race. Mid-April. For more information, contact the BVI Spring Regatta Committee, P.O. Box 200, Road Town, Tortola, B.V.I. (© **284/494-3286;** www.bvispringregatta.org).

St. Thomas Carnival. This annual celebration, with origins in Africa, is the most spectacular carnival in the Virgin Islands. Over the years, the festivities have become Christianized, but the fun remains. "Mocko Jumbies," people dressed as spirits, parade through the streets on stilts nearly 20 feet high. Steel and fungi bands, "jump-ups," and parades bring the event to life. Events take place islandwide, but the most action is on the streets of Charlotte Amalie. After Easter. Contact the visitor center in St. Thomas (© 340/774-8784) for a schedule of events.

July

Carnival of St. John. Parades, calypso bands, and colorful costumes lead up to the selection of Ms. St. John and the King of Carnival. First week of July. Call the St. John Tourist Office (© 340/776-6450) for information.

August

B.V.I. Summer Festival. Many visitors from other Caribbean islands hop over to the Road Town in Tortola for this 3-day party. Join locals as they dance to fungi and reggae bands and take part in the Unity Day Parade and other carnival activities and festivities. Early August. For information, call the B.V.I. Tourist Board Office (© 284/494-3134).

U.S. Virgin Islands Open/ Atlantic Blue Marlin Tournament. This prestigious St. Thomas–centered charity event (proceeds go to the Boy Scouts) is also eco-friendly—trophies are based on the number of blue marlin caught, tagged, and released. The tournament is open to anyone who's interested, and sport fishers come from around the world to participate. Late August (weekend closest to the full moon). For more information, call the VI Council of the Boy Scouts of America (© 888/234-7484).

December

Christmas in St. Croix. This major event launches the beginning of a 12-day celebration that includes Christmas Day, the legal holiday on December 26, New Year's Eve (called "Old Year's Day"), and New Year's Day. It ends January 6, the Feast of the Three Kings, with a parade of flamboyantly attired merrymakers. For information, call the U.S. Virgin Islands Department of Tourism office in Christiansted (© 340/773-0495).

6 The Active Vacation Planner

There's no rule that says you have to confine yourself to a beach chair within arm's length of the bar while visiting the Virgin Islands (though there's no rule against it, either). You will have endless opportunities to sit by the surf sipping rum drinks, but remember that there are many opportunities to explore the islands actively. Coral reefs and stunning beaches provide breathtaking backdrops for a variety of water sports, from snorkeling to sea kayaking, and there's also plenty of golf, tennis, hiking, and even horseback riding. This section presents an overview of all the outdoor activities on the Virgin Islands. See individual chapters for more specific information on locations and outfitters.

CAMPING   The best campsites in the Virgin Islands are on St. John at **Maho Bay** and **Cinnamon Bay,** which is considered one of the finest campgrounds in the Caribbean. Both facilities are open year-round and are so popular that reservations during the winter months need to be made far in advance. In the British Virgin Islands, the best campsite is Tortola's **Brewers Bay Campground,** which rents tents and basic equipment and is open year-round.

FISHING   In the last 25 years or so, more than 20 sport fishing world records have been set from the Virgin Islands, mostly for the mega blue marlin. Other abundant fish in these waters are bonito, tuna, wahoo, sailfish, and skipjack. Sport fishing charters, led by experienced local captains, abound in the islands; both half-day and full-day trips are available. But you needn't go out to sea to fish. On St. Thomas, St. John, and St. Croix, the U.S. government publishes lists of legal shoreline fishing spots (contact local tourist offices for more information). Closer inshore, you'll find kingfish, mackerel, bonefish, tarpon, amberjack, grouper, and snappers.

On St. Thomas, many men line fish from the rocky shore along Mandahl Beach, which is also a popular spot for family picnics. The shore here is not the best place for swimming, because the water drops off dramatically and the surf tends to be rough. On St. John, at the Virgin Islands National Park, the park waters are open to fishermen with hand-held rods. No fishing license is required for shoreline fishing, and government pamphlets available at tourist offices list some 100 good spots. Call ✆ **340/775-6762** for more information.

GOLF   The golfing hub of the Virgin Islands is the challenging **Carambola Golf Course** (✆ **340/778-5638**) in St. Croix. Also on St. Croix is the excellent course at **The Buccaneer** (✆ **340/773-2100**) just outside Christiansted. The highlight on St. Thomas is the **Mahogany Run** (✆ **800/253-7103** or 340/777-6006). There aren't any courses on St. John or the British Virgin Islands.

HIKING   The best islands for hiking are **Tortola** and **St. John.** In Tortola, the best hiking is through Sage Mountain National Park, spread across 92 acres of luxuriant flora and fauna; you can get maps and advice at the tourist office. On St. John the most intriguing hike is the Annaberg Historical Trail, which takes you by some of the most evocative scenes of former plantation life on island. Because most of St. John is itself a

National Park, park rangers can assist in providing maps and general guidance. **St. Croix** also has good hiking in its "Rain Forest" area. **Buck Island,** off the coast of St. Croix, is beloved by snorkelers and scuba divers but also fascinating to hike. You can easily explore the island in a day as it is only half a mile wide and a mile long. You'll encounter many birds and flowers while hiking in the Virgin Islands— but no poisonous snakes. Look for the trumpet-shaped "ginger thomas," the U.S. Virgin Island's official flower.

HORSEBACK RIDING   Equestrians should head for St. Croix. **Paul and Jill's Equestrian Stables** (✆ **340/772-2880**) at Sprat Hall Plantation are the premier stables not only in the Virgin Islands but also in all the Caribbean. The outfit is known for the quality of both its horses and riding trails. Neophytes and experts are welcome.

SAILING & YACHTING   The Virgin Islands are a sailor's paradise, offering crystal-clear turquoise waters, secluded coves and inlets, and protected harbors for anchoring.

For details on chartering your own boat, see the box on p. 36. Most visitors, however, are content with **day sails,** which are easy to organize, especially at the harbors in St. Thomas, Tortola, and Virgin Gorda. Regardless of where you decide to cruise, you really shouldn't leave the islands without spending at least one day on the water, even if you have to load up on Dramamine or snap on your wrist bands before you go.

The most popular cruising area around the Virgin Islands is deep and incredibly scenic **Sir Francis Drake Channel,** which runs from St. John to Virgin Gorda's North Sound. The channel is surrounded by mountainous islands and boasts crisp breezes year-round. In heavy weather, the network of tiny islands shelters yachties from the brute force of the open sea. The waters surrounding St. Croix, to the south, are also appealing, especially near Buck Island.

Outside the channel, the Virgin Islands archipelago contains reefy areas that separate many of the islands from their neighbors. To navigate these areas, you need to use a depth chart (available from charter companies or any marine supply outlet) and have some local knowledge. *Tip:* Locals and temporarily shore-bound sailors willingly offer free advice, often enough to last a couple of drinks, at almost any dockside watering hole.

For more than a quarter of a century, *The Yachtsman's Guide to the Virgin Islands* has been the classic cruising guide to this area (it's updated periodically). The detailed, 240-page text is supplemented by 22 sketch charts, more than 100 photographs and illustrations, and numerous landfall sketches showing harbors, channels, landmarks, and such. Subjects covered include piloting, anchoring, communication, weather, fishing, and more. The guide also covers the eastern end of Puerto Rico, Vieques, and Culebra. Copies are available at major marine outlets, bookstores, and direct from **Tropical Island Publishers,** P.O. Box 610938, North Miami, FL 33261-0938 (© **305/893-4277**), for $15.95 postpaid.

Except for **Anegada,** which is a low-lying atoll of coral limestone and sandstone, all the Virgin Islands are high and easily spotted. The water here is very clear. The shortest distance between St. Thomas and St. Croix is 35 nautical miles; from St. John to St. Croix, 35 nautical miles; from St. Thomas to St. John, 2 nautical miles; from Tortola to St. Thomas, 10 nautical miles; from Virgin Gorda to Anegada, 13 nautical miles; and from St. John to Anegada, 30 nautical miles.

Virgin Gorda to St. Croix is about the longest run, at 45 nautical miles. (Specific distances between the islands can be misleading, though, because often you may need to take roundabout routes from one point to another.)

If you don't know how to sail but would like to learn, contact one of the sailing schools on St. Croix. **Annapolis Sailing School,** 1215 King Cross St., Christiansted, St. Croix, U.S.V.I. 00820 (© **800/638-9192** or 340/773-4709), has three 24-foot daysailers and charges $295 per person for a 2-day course, on Saturdays and Sundays.

Womanship, The Boat House, 137 Conduits St., Annapolis, MD 21401 (© **800/342-9295** in the U.S. or 410/267-6661) offers a sailing program for women of all ages and levels of nautical expertise in the British Virgin Islands. Groups consist of a maximum of six students with two female instructors. Participants sleep aboard the boat, meals included. Courses last a week. The cost is $1,695 from December through April; off-season, $1,595.

The British Virgin Islands are also the headquarters of the **Offshore Sailing School,** Prospect Reef Resort, Road Town (© **284/494-5119**). This school offers sailing instruction year-round. For information before you go, write or call Offshore Sailing School, 16731 McGregor Blvd., Ft. Myers, FL 33908 (© **800/221-4326** or 941/454-1700).

SEA-KAYAKING/ISLAND-CAMPING TOURS   Arawak Expeditions, Cruz Bay, St. John (© **800/238-8687** or 340/693-8312 in the U.S.), is the only outfitter in the Virgin Islands offering multiple-day sea-kayaking/island-camping excursions. Full-day and half-day trips are also available. The vessels are two-person fiberglass kayaks, complete with foot-controlled rudders. The outfit provides all the

Chartering Your Own Boat

There may be no better way to experience the Virgin Islands than on the deck of your own yacht. Impossible? Not really. No one said you had to *own* the yacht.

Experienced sailors and navigators with a sea-wise crew might want to rent a **bareboat charter,** that is, a fully equipped boat with no captain or crew. You'll have to prove you can handle the task before you're allowed to set sail; even then, you may want to take along an experienced local sailor who's familiar with the sometimes tricky waters. If you're not an expert sailor but still yearn to hit the high seas, consider a **fully crewed charter** with captain and cook. The cost of a crewed boat is obviously more than that of a bareboat and varies according to crew size and experience.

Four to six people, maybe more, often charter yachts.measuring from 50 to more than 100 feet. Most are rented on a weekly basis and come with a fully stocked kitchen (or a barbecue) and bar, fishing gear, and water sports equipment. More and more bareboaters are saving money on charters by buying their own provisions, rather than relying on the charter company.

The best outfitter in the Virgin Islands is **The Moorings,** P.O. Box 139, Wickhams Cay, Road Town, Tortola, B.V.I. (© **800/535-7289** or 284/494-2331), which offers both bareboat and fully crewed charters equipped with barbecue, snorkeling gear, dinghy, and linens. It even supplies windsurfers free with crewed boats (for an extra cost with bareboats). The experienced staff of mechanics, electricians, riggers, and cleaners is extremely helpful, especially if you're going out on your own. They'll give you a thorough briefing about Virgin Islands waters and anchorages. Seven-night combined hotel-and-crewed-yacht packages run $1,113 to $2,212 per person, based on a 6-person trip.

To make reservations in the United States or Canada, call © **800/535-7289.** For information, write to The Moorings Ltd., 19345 U.S. 19 North, Suite 402, Clearwater, FL 34624 (© **813/530-5424**).

kayaking gear, healthy meals, camping equipment, and experienced guides. The cost of a full-day trip is $75, half-day, $40; multiple-day excursions range in price from $995 to $1,195.

SNORKELING & SCUBA DIVING These sports are popular on all the islands. On St. Croix, the best site for both is **Buck Island,** easily accessible by day sails from the harbor in Christiansted. St. Croix is also known for its dramatic "drop-offs," including the famous Puerto Rico Trench.

On St. Thomas, all major hotels rent fins and masks for snorkelers, and most day-sail charters have this equipment onboard. Many outfitters, like the St. Thomas Diving Club, also feature scuba programs.

As for the British Virgin Islands, the best snorkeling is around **The Baths,** Virgin Gorda's major attraction. **Anegada Reef,** which lies off Anegada Island, has been a "burial ground" for ships for centuries; an estimated 300 wrecks, including many pirate ships, have perished here. The wreckage of the **RMS *Rhone,*** near the westerly tip of Salt Island, is the most celebrated dive spot in the B.V.I. This ship went under in 1867 in one of the most disastrous hurricanes ever to hit the Virgin Islands.

TENNIS

Tennis is a becoming a major sport in the Virgin Islands. Most courts are all-weather or Laykold. Because of intense midday heat, many courts are lit for night games. Pro shops, complete with teaching pros, are available at the major tennis resorts, especially on St. Croix and St. Thomas.

St. Thomas has six public (and free) tennis courts that operate on a first-come, first-served basis. If the courts at the major hotels aren't booked by resident guests, you can usually play there for a minimal fee as long as you call a day in advance. Both **Bolongo Bay** and **Marriott's Frenchman's Reef Beach Resort** have four courts.

The best tennis facilities in the Virgin Islands are on St. Croix at **The Buccaneer,** which has eight meticulously maintained courts and a state-of-the-art pro shop. The island also has seven public courts, but they're rather rough around the edges.

On Tortola, there are six courts at **Prospect Reef;** they're often open to non-guests for a fee. If you're a serious tennis buff and are planning to stay on Virgin Gorda, consider **Little Dix Bay,** which has seven beautiful courts reserved for guests only.

7 Getting Married in the Virgin Islands

THE U.S. VIRGIN ISLANDS   No blood tests or physical examinations are necessary, but there is a $25 license fee, a $25 notarized application, and an 8-day waiting period, which is sometimes waived, depending on circumstances. Civil ceremonies before a judge of the territorial court cost $200 each; religious ceremonies performed by clergy are equally valid. Fees and schedules for church weddings must be negotiated directly with the officiant. More information is available from the **U.S. Virgin Islands Division of Tourism,** 1270 Ave. of the Americas, New York, NY 10020 (© **212/332-2222**). The guide *Getting Married in the U.S. Virgin Islands* is distributed by U.S.V.I. tourism offices; it gives information on all three islands, including wedding planners, places of worship, florists, and limousine services. It also provides a listing of island accommodations that offer in-house wedding services.

Couples can apply for a marriage license for St. Thomas or St. John by contacting the **Territorial Court of the Virgin Islands,** P.O. Box 70, St. Thomas, U.S.V.I. 00804 (© **340/774-6680**). For weddings on St. Croix, contact the **Territorial Court of the Virgin Islands,** Family Division, P.O. Box 929, Christiansted, St. Croix, U.S.V.I. 00821 (© **340/778-9750**).

THE BRITISH VIRGIN ISLANDS
There's no requirement of island residency, but a couple must apply for a license at the attorney general's office, and stay on the B.V.I. for at least 3 days while the paperwork is processed. You'll need to present a passport or original birth certificate and photo identification, plus certified proof of your single marital status, including any divorce or death certificates pertaining to former spouses. Two witnesses must accompany the couple. The license fee is $110. Local registrars will perform marriages, or you can choose your own officiant. For information and an application for a license, contact the **Registrar's Office,** P.O. Box 418, Road Town, Tortola, B.V.I.   (© **284/494-3701** or 284/494-3134).

8 Health & Insurance

STAYING HEALTHY

Finding a good doctor in the Virgin Islands is not a problem. See "Fast Facts" later in this chapter and also in individual island chapters for specific names and addresses.

If you experience **diarrhea,** moderate your eating habits, and drink only bottled water until you recover. If symptoms persist, you should consult a doctor.

The Virgin Islands sun can be brutal. To protect yourself, consider wearing sunglasses and a hat, and use **sunscreen** (SPF 15 and higher) liberally. Limit your time on the beach the first few days. If you do overexpose yourself, stay out of the sun until you recover. If your sunburn is followed by fever, chills, a headache, or a feeling of nausea or dizziness, see a doctor.

Mosquitoes do exist in the Virgin Islands, but they aren't the malaria-carrying mosquitoes that you might find elsewhere in the Caribbean. They're still a nuisance, though. **No-see-ums,** which appear mainly in the evening, are the bigger menace. Screens can't keep these critters out, so carry your bug repellent.

Pack **prescription medications** in your carry-on luggage. Carry written prescriptions in generic, not brand-name form, and dispense all prescription medications from their original labeled vials. Also bring along copies of your prescriptions in case you lose your pills or run out. If you wear **contact lenses,** pack an extra pair in case you lose one.

If you do get sick, you may want to ask the concierge at your hotel to recommend a local doctor—even his or her own physician. This will probably yield a better recommendation than any toll-free number would.

INSURANCE

Rule number one: Check your existing policies before you buy any additional coverage. That said, there are three kinds of travel insurance: trip cancellation (in case you can't travel due to illness or emergency and in case a tour operator/outfitter cancels the trip), lost luggage, and medical. **Trip cancellation insurance** might be a good idea if you have paid a large portion of your vacation expenses up front. This kind of insurance costs approximately 6% to 8% of the total value of your vacation.

Your homeowner's insurance should cover stolen **luggage.** The airlines are responsible for $1,250 on domestic flights if they lose your luggage; if you plan to carry anything more valuable than that, keep it in your carry-on bag.

Your existing **health insurance** should cover you if you get sick while on vacation (though if you belong to an HMO, you should check to see whether you are fully covered when away from home). Members of **Blue Cross/Blue Shield** can now use their cards at select hospitals in most major cities worldwide (© **800/810-BLUE** or www.bluecares.com for a list of hospitals). Some **credit card companies** (American Express and certain gold and platinum Visa and MasterCard, for example) may insure you against travel accidents if you buy plane, train, or bus tickets with their cards.

Before purchasing additional insurance, read your policies and agreements carefully, and call your insurers or credit card companies if you have any questions.

If you do decide you need more protection, try one of the following independent providers: **Access**

America (© 800/284-8300, www. accessamerica.com); **Travel Guard International** (© 800/826-1300, www.travel-guard.com); **Travel Insured International, Inc.** (© 800/ 243-3174, www.travelinsured.com); **Travelex Insurance Services** (© 800/ 228-9792, www.travelex-insurance. com); or **The Divers Alert Network (DAN)** (© 800/446-2671 or 919/ 684- 8111; www.diversalertnetwork. org), which insures scuba divers. Don't pay for more insurance than you need. For example, if you need only trip cancellation insurance, don't purchase coverage for lost or stolen property.

INSURANCE FOR BRITISH TRAVELERS

Most big travel agents offer their own insurance and will probably try to sell you their package. Think before you sign. Britain's Consumers' Association recommends that you insist on reading the policy before buying it. You should also shop around for deals. You might contact **Columbus Travel Insurance Ltd.** (© 020/7375-0011) in London, or, for students, **Campus Travel** (© 0870/240-1010), also in London. Columbus Travel will only sell insurance to travelers who have been official British residents for at least 1 year.

9 Tips for Travelers with Special Needs

TIPS FOR TRAVELERS WITH DISABILITIES

A disability shouldn't stop anyone from traveling. There are more resources out there than ever before. *A World of Options,* a 658-page book of resources for disabled travelers, covers everything from biking trips to scuba outfitters. It costs $35 ($30 for members) and is available from **Mobility International USA,** P.O. Box 10767, Eugene, OR 97440 (© **541/ 343-1284** voice and TDD; www.miusa.org). Annual membership for Mobility International is $35, which includes their quarterly newsletter, *Over the Rainbow.* In addition, **Twin Peaks Press,** P.O. Box 129, Vancouver, WA 98666 (© **360/ 694-2462**), publishes travel-related books for people with disabilities.

The **Moss Rehab Hospital** (© 215/ 456-9600, www.mossresourcenet. org) has been providing friendly and helpful phone advice and referrals to disabled travelers for years through its **Travel Information Service.**

You can join **The Society for the Advancement of Travel for the Handicapped (SATH),** 347 Fifth Ave. Suite 610, New York, NY 10016 (© **212/447-7284;** fax 212/725-8253; www.sath.org) for $45 annually, $30 for seniors and students, to gain access to a vast network of connections in the travel industry. The society provides information sheets on travel destinations and referrals to tour operators that specialize in traveling with disabilities. Its quarterly magazine, *Open World for Disability and Mature Travel,* is full of good information and resources. A year's subscription is $18 ($35 outside the United States).

Some resorts on St. Thomas and St. Croix have made some inroads in catering to persons with disabilities. St. John and all of the British Islands lag far behind in this regard. If planning a vacation to the U.S. Virgin Islands, a person with disabilities should carefully check with a travel agent or else call the hotel of his or her choice (which is much better) and discuss one's requirements realistically and see if a particular resort is prepared to cater to one's needs. It's only the price of a phone call and a lot of

---

(Tips For British Travelers with Disabilities

RADAR (Royal Association for Disability and Rehabilitation), Unit 12, City Forum, 250 City Rd., London EC1V 8AF (© **020/7250-3222;** fax 020/7250-0212), publishes vacation "fact packs," which provide information on trip planning, travel insurance, specialized accommodations, and transportation abroad.

---

questions can be cleared up, and specific information obtained. As of this writing, about a third of the major resorts (and none of the cheaper guest houses or villas) in St. Thomas or St. Croix are prepared to cope with vacationers who have disabilities.

Travelers with disabilities may also want to consider joining a tour that caters specifically to them. One of the best operators is **Flying Wheels Travel,** 143 West Bridge (P.O. Box 382), Owatonna, MN 55060 (© **800/ 535- 6790**). It offers various escorted tours and cruises, with an emphasis on sports, as well as private tours in minivans with lifts. Other reputable specialized tour operators include **Access Adventures** (© 716/889-9096), which offers sports-related vacations; **Accessible Journeys** (© 800/TINGLES or 610/521-0339), for slow walkers and wheelchair travelers; **The Guided Tour, Inc.** (© 215/782-1370); **Wilderness Inquiry** (© 800/728-0719 or 612/ 379-3858); and **Directions Unlimited** (© 800/533-5343).

You can obtain a copy of *Air Transportation of Handicapped Persons* by writing to Free Advisory Circular No. AC12032, Distribution Unit, **U.S. Department of Transportation,** Publications Division, M-4332, Washington, DC 20590.

Visually impaired travelers should contact the **American Foundation for the Blind,** 11 Penn Plaza, Suite 300, New York, NY 10001 (© **800/ 232-5463**), for information on traveling with Seeing Eye dogs.

TIPS FOR GAY & LESBIAN TRAVELERS

The Virgin Islands, along with Puerto Rico, are some of the most gay-friendly destinations in the Caribbean. This is partly because of the multicultural influences, from both the U.S. mainland and Britain, that barrage the archipelago. Although many gay and lesbian travelers still flock to St. Thomas, St. Croix now has more specific hotels and places catering primarily to the gay market, none better than the Cormorant Beach Club (see p. 158). Here are some organizations that specialize in travel for gay people and can help you plan your trip.

The **International Gay & Lesbian Travel Association (IGLTA),** (© **800/ 448-8550** or 954/776-2626; fax 954/776-3303; www.iglta.org), with around 1,200 members, links travelers up with appropriate gay-friendly service organizations or tour specialists. It offers quarterly newsletters, marketing mailings, and a membership directory. Most members are gay or lesbian businesses, but individuals can join for $150 yearly, plus a $100 administration fee for new members. Members are kept informed of gay and gay-friendly hoteliers, tour operators, and airline and cruise-line representatives. Contact the IGLTA for a list of its member agencies, who will be tied into IGLTA's information resources.

Gay and lesbian travel agencies include **Above and Beyond Tours** (© **800/397-2681;** they cater primarily to gay men), and **Kennedy**

Travel (© 800/988-1181 or 516/352-4888).

TIPS FOR SENIORS

Don't be shy about asking for discounts, and always carry some kind of identification, such as a driver's license, that shows your date of birth. Many hotels offer special rates for seniors; ask when you make your reservations. In many cities, seniors qualify for reduced admission to theaters, museums, and other attractions, and discounted fares on public transportation.

Members of the **American Association of Retired Persons (AARP),** 601 E St. NW, Washington, DC 20049 (© **800/424-3410** or 202/434-AARP; www.aarp.org), get discounts not only on hotels but also on airfares and car rentals. AARP offers a wide range of special benefits, including *Modern Maturity* magazine and a monthly newsletter.

The National Council of Senior Citizens, 8403 Colesville Rd., Suite 1200, Silver Spring, MD 20910 (© **301/578-8800;** www.ncscinc.org), a nonprofit organization, offers a newsletter six times a year (partly devoted to travel tips) and discounts on hotel and auto rentals; annual dues are $13 per person or couple.

Sears Mature Outlook, P.O. Box 9390, Des Moines, IA 50306 (© **800/336-6330**), began as a travel organization for people over age 50, though it now caters to people of all ages. Members receive a bimonthly magazine and discounts on hotels (as well as free coupons for discounts from Sears). Annual membership is $39.95.

The Mature Traveler, a monthly 12-page newsletter on senior citizen travel is a valuable resource. It's available by subscription ($32 a year) from GEM Publishing Group, Box 50400, Reno, NV 89513-0400. GEM also publishes *The Book of Deals,* a collection of more than 1,000 senior discounts on airlines, lodging, tours, and attractions around the country; it's available for $9.95 by calling © 800/460-6676. Another helpful publication is *101 Tips for the Mature Traveler,* available from **Grand Circle Travel,** 347 Congress St., Suite 3A, Boston, MA 02210 (© **800/221-2610** or 617/350-7500; fax 617/346-6700).

Grand Circle Travel is also one of the hundreds of travel agencies specializing in vacations for seniors. Many of these packages are of the tour-bus variety, with free trips thrown in for those who organize groups of 10 or more. Seniors seeking more independent travel should probably consult a regular travel agent. **SAGA International Holidays,** 222 Berkeley St., Boston, MA 02116 (© **800/343-0273**), offers inclusive tours and cruises for those age 50 and older. SAGA also sponsors the more substantial "Road Scholar Tours" (© **800/621-2151**), which are fun-loving but with an educational bent.

TIPS FOR FAMILIES

All of the Virgin Islands, both U.S. and British, are viewed as family friendly, although St. Thomas and St. Croix have the most facilities and attractions for families. Some of the smaller and less developed islands don't cater much to children, unless a family's idea of a good time is to hang out on the beach all day. But St. Thomas, for example, offers plenty of diversions for families with such attractions as Coral World and the Paradise Point Tramway. When compared with some of the other major destinations of the Caribbean (such as Jamaica where crime is high), the U.S. Virgins are generally safe destinations. The British Virgin Islands are even safer but with significantly fewer family-oriented activities.

Several books on the market offer tips for those traveling with kids.

Family Travel (Lanier Publishing International), *How to Take Great Trips with Your Kids* (Harvard Common Press), and *Adventuring with Children* (Foghorn Press) are full of good general advice.

Family Travel Times newsletter costs $40 (online only, www. familytraveltimes.com), and it's updated every 2 weeks. Subscribers also can call in with travel questions but only on Wednesday from 10am to 1pm Eastern Standard Time. Contact *Family Travel Times,* 40 5th Ave., New York, NY 10011 (© **888/822-4322** or 212/477-5524).

TIPS FOR WOMEN TRAVELERS

St. John and the British Virgin Islands have a low crime rate. St. Thomas and St. Croix have the highest crime rate against women in the archipelago. However, you are far safer in the Virgin Islands than you would be walking the streets of any major U.S. city. A woman is far more likely to get raped in a city such as New Orleans than she is in Charlotte Amalie. Still, the usual precautions are always advised. Some of the local men (those who have not had sensitivity training) still regard a single woman as an object to hassle with unwanted attention, but such encounters happen in the Virgin Islands no more often than in most urban areas. The usual precautions that you'd follow if you live in any major U.S. city should also be your guidelines for travel to the Virgin Islands.

Several books on the market cater to the concerns of the female traveler. *Safety and Security for Women Who Travel,* by Sheila Swan Laufer and Peter Laufer, is well worth $12.95, and *Adventures in Good Company: The Complete Guide to Women's Tours and Outdoor Trips* ($16.95) is also a very

good resource. On the Web, check out **The Executive Woman's Travel Network** (www.delta.com/prog_serv/ exec_womans_travel/), the official woman's travel site of Delta Airlines, which offers tips on staying fit, eating well, finding special airfares, and dealing with many other travel issues.

TIPS FOR SINGLE TRAVELERS

St. Thomas has the most youth-oriented scene of any of the Virgin Islands, British or American. Some areas of St. Thomas are more popular than others with young people, especially the bars and restaurants around Red Hook. The major resorts at Flamboyant Point and the East End of St. Thomas cater mainly to a middle-aged or elderly crowd. Many young people who visit St. Thomas stay in the guest houses in and around Charlotte Amalie. Beyond St. Thomas, the island of St. Croix attracts a large array of young single travelers, mainly to the inns in and around Christiansted and Frederiksted.

Travel Companion Exchange (© **800/392-1256**) is one of the nation's oldest companion finders for single travelers. Register with this organization to find a travel mate who will split the cost of the room with you and be around as little or as often as you like during the day. Several tour organizers cater to solo travelers as well. **Experience Plus** (© **800/ 685-4565;** fax 970/493-0377) offers an interesting selection of single-only trips.

Travel Buddies (© **800/998-9099**) runs single-friendly tours with no singles supplement. **The Single Gourmet Club,** 133 E. 58th St., New York, NY 10022 (© **212/980-8788;** fax 212/980-3138), is an international social, dining and travel club for singles, with offices in 21 cities in the United States and Canada.

10 Flying to the Virgin Islands

The bigger islands, like St. Thomas, have regularly scheduled air service from North American carriers, and the smaller islands are tied into this vast network through their own carriers.

If you're coming from the United Kingdom, you'll likely fly first to Miami then take American Airlines or some other carrier on to your final destination. Although there are special deals, round-trip fares from New York to St. Thomas range from $391 to $1,140 per person, from Miami to St. Thomas $374 to $1,155 round-trip.

For more information on how to reach each island by plane, refer to the "Getting There" sections in the individual island chapters.

FLYING FOR LESS: TIPS FOR GETTING THE BEST AIRFARES

Passengers within the same airplane cabin rarely pay the same fare for their seats. Business travelers who need to purchase tickets at the last minute, change their itinerary at a moment's notice, or get home before the weekend pay the full fare. Passengers who can book their tickets well in advance, who don't mind staying over Saturday night, or who are willing to travel on a Tuesday, Wednesday, or Thursday after 7pm, will pay a fraction of the full fare. Here are a few other easy ways to save.

- **Ask about special discounted fares.** Airlines periodically lower prices on popular routes. Check your newspaper for advertised discounts or call the airlines directly and ask if any promotional rates or special fares are available. If you already hold a ticket when a sale breaks, it may even pay to exchange your ticket, which usually incurs a charge of $50 to $75. Note, however, that the lowest-priced fares are often nonrefundable, require advance purchase of 1 to 3 weeks, require a certain length of stay, and carry penalties for changing dates of travel.

- **Contact a consolidator.** Consolidators, also known as bucket shops, buy seats in bulk from the airlines and then sell them to the public at prices below even the airlines' discounted rates. Their small boxed ads usually run in the Sunday travel section of local newspapers. Before you buy from a consolidator, however, ask for a record locator number and confirm your seat with the airline itself. Be prepared to book your ticket with a different consolidator—there are many to choose from—if the airline can't confirm your reservation. Also be aware that bucket shop tickets are usually nonrefundable or rigged with stiff cancellation penalties, often as high as 50%–75% of the ticket price.

  Council Travel (© 888/COUNCIL; www.counciltravel. com) and STA Travel (© 800/781-4040; www.sta-travel.com) cater especially to young travelers, but their bargain basement prices are available to people of all ages. Other reliable consolidators include **1-800-FLY-CHEAP** (www.1800flycheap.com), **TFI Tours International** (© 800/745-8000 or 212/736-1140), and **Travel Avenue** (© 800/333-3335 or 312/876-1116).

- **Look into courier flights.** If you fly as a courier, you'll give up your luggage allowance; in return, you'll get a deeply discounted ticket. These flights are often offered at the last minute. **Now**

Voyager, open Monday to Friday from 10am to 5:30pm and Saturday from noon to 4:30pm (☎ 212/431-1616), flies from New York. Voyager also offers noncourier discounted fares now.

• **Join a travel club** such as **Moment's Notice** (☎ 718/234-6295) or **Sears Discount Travel Club** (☎ 800/433-9383), which supply unsold tickets at discounted prices. You pay an annual membership fee to get the club's hotline number. Of course, you're limited to what's available, so you have to be flexible.

TIPS FOR FLYING IN COMFORT

• You'll find the most legroom in a bulkhead seat, in the front row of each airplane cabin. Consider, however, that you will have to store your luggage in the overhead bin, and you won't have the best seat in the house for the in-flight movie.

• When you check in, ask for one of the emergency-exit-row seats, which also have extra legroom. They are assigned at the airport, usually on a first-come, first-served basis. In the unlikely event of an emergency, however, you'll be expected to open the emergency-exit door and help direct traffic.

• Ask for a seat toward the front of the plane. You'll be one of the first to disembark after the gangway is in place.

• When you make your reservation, order a special meal if you have dietary restrictions. Most airlines offer a variety of special meals, including vegetarian, macrobiotic, kosher, and meals for the lactose intolerant.

• Wear comfortable clothes and dress in layers. The climate in airplane cabins is unpredictable. You'll be glad to have a sweater or jacket to put on or take off as the temperature onboard dictates.

• Pack some toiletries for long flights. Airplane cabins are notoriously dry places. Take a travel-size bottle of moisturizer or lotion to refresh your face and hands at the end of the flight. If you wear contact lenses, bring eye drops.

• If you're flying with a cold or chronic sinus problems, use a decongestant 10 minutes before ascent and descent, to minimize pressure buildup in the inner ear.

• Drink plenty of water before your departure and during your flight to avoid dehydration.

• If you're flying with kids, don't forget a deck of cards, toys, extra bottles, pacifiers, diapers, and chewing gum to help them relieve ear pressure buildup during ascent and descent.

11 Cruising to the Virgin Islands

A high percentage of Caribbean cruises make at least one stop in the Virgin Islands. Charlotte Amalie in St. Thomas is the most popular port, followed by historic Frederiksted in St. Croix, and Road Town in Tortola.

Miami is the cruise capital of the world, but ships also leave from San Juan, New York, Port Everglades, Los Angeles, and other points. Most cruise ships travel at night, arriving the following morning at ports of call, where passengers can go ashore for sightseeing and shopping.

WHICH CRUISE LINE IS FOR YOU?

Once you've decided that a cruise to the Virgin Islands is right for you, you'll need to choose your cruise line. Two great resources for choosing a cruise line are *Frommer's Caribbean Cruises and Ports of Call* and *Cruise Vacations For Dummies* (Hungry

Minds, Inc.). Below you'll find a rundown of various ships cruising the Virgin Islands.

Carnival Cruise Lines (© **800/ 327-95021** or 305/599-2200; www. carnival.com) offers affordable vacations on some of the biggest and most brightly decorated ships afloat. It's the richest, boldest, brashest, and most successful mass-market cruise line in the world. Its boats leave from Miami, Tampa, New Orleans, Port Canaveral, and San Juan and stop over at selected ports throughout the eastern and western Caribbean, including St. Thomas, St. Lucia, San Juan, Guadeloupe, Grenada, Grand Cayman, and Jamaica. Most of its cruises offer good value, last between 4 and 16 days (in most cases, 7 days), and feature nonstop activities, lots of glitter, and the hustle and bustle of armies of passengers and crew members embarking and disembarking at every port.

Celebrity Cruises (© **800/ 437-3111** or 305/539-6000; www. celebrity-cruises.com) maintains five newly built, medium-to-large size ships offering cruises of between 7 and 15 nights to such ports as Key West, San Juan, Grand Cayman, St. Thomas, Ocho Rios, Antigua, and Cozumel, Mexico, among others. The line is unpretentious but classy, several notches above mass-market, but with pricing that's nonetheless relatively competitive. Accommodations are roomy and well equipped, and the cuisine is among the most refined of any of its competitors afloat.

Norwegian Cruise Line (© **800/ 327-7030**) or 305/436-4000; www. ncl.com), controller of the cruise world's most diverse collection of ships, appeals to all ages and income levels. The line features Scandinavian officers, an international staff, and a pervasive modern Viking theme. One of its ships, *Norwegian Dream,* is based year-round in San Juan, Puerto Rico, and leaves on 7-day excursions

stopping at such ports as Aruba, Curaçao, Tortola, Virgin Gorda, St. Thomas, St. Lucia, Antigua, St. Kitts, and St. Croix.

Princess Cruises (© **800/ 421-0522** or 310/553-1770; www. princesscruises.com) places more emphasis on luxury living on a mass scale than any other line afloat. The company's ships usually carry fewer passengers than similarly sized vessels on other lines. Its cruises last between 7 and 11 days, and include stops at such islands as Aruba, Caracas, Dominica, Grenada, St. Lucia, St. Martin, St. Kitts, and St. Thomas. In 1998, the line launched the largest ship in the history of the cruise industry, the 109,000-ton *Grand Princess.*

Royal Caribbean International (RCI) (© **800/327-6700** or 305/539-6000; www.royalcaribbean. com) leads the industry in the development of megaships. This mainstream, mass-market cruise line encourages a restrained house-party atmosphere that's somehow a bit less frenetic than that of other "party-style" cruise lines. Though accommodations and accouterments are more than adequate, they are not upscale, and cabins aboard some of the line's older vessels tend to be a bit more cramped than the industry norm. Using either Miami or San Juan as their home port, Royal Caribbean ships call regularly at such ports as St. Thomas, San Juan, Ocho Rios, St. Martin, Grand Cayman, St. Croix, and Curaçao. Most of the company's cruises last for 7 days, although some weekend jaunts from San Juan to St. Thomas are available for 3 nights.

Seabourn Cruise Line © (**800/ 929-9595** or 415/391-7444; www. seabourn.com) is an upscale, expensive outfit known for luxurious, small-scale ships. Two of its three ships spend significant time within the Caribbean. Their ports of call include Jamaica, St. Barts, St. Martin,

St. Lucia, Bequia, Tobago, Barbados, St. Croix, and Virgin Gorda. There are more activities than you'd expect aboard such relatively small ships (10,000 tons), and an absolutely amazing amount of onboard space per passenger. Cuisine is superb, served within a dining room that's unapologetically formal.

HOW TO GET THE BEST DEAL ON YOUR CRUISE

Cruise lines operate like airlines, setting rates for their cruises and then selling them in a rapid-fire series of discounts, offering almost whatever it takes to fill their ships. Because of this, great deals come and go in the blink of an eye, and most are available only through travel agents.

If you have a travel agent you trust, leave the details to him or her. If not, try contacting a travel agent who specializes in booking cruises. Some of the most likely contenders include the following: **Cruises, Inc.,** 5000 Campuswood Dr. E., Syracuse, NY 13057 (© **800/854-0500** or 315/463-9695); **Cruise Fairs of America,** Century Plaza Towers, 2029 Century Park E., Suite 950, Los Angeles, CA 90067 (© **800/456-4FUN** or 310/556-2925); **The Cruise Company,** 10760 Q St., Omaha, NE 68127 (© **800/289-5505** or 402/339-6800); **Kelly Cruises,** 1315 W. 22nd St., Suite 105, Oak Brook, IL 60523 (© **800/837-7447** or 630/990-1111); **Hartford Holidays Travel,** 129 Hillside Ave., Williston Park, NY 11596 (© **800/828-4813**

or 516/746-6670); and **Mann Travel and Cruises American Express,** 6010 Fairview Rd., Suite 104, Charlotte, NC 28210 (© **800/849-2301** or 704/556-8311).

A FEW MONEY-SAVING TIPS

- **Book early:** You can often get considerable savings on a 7-day cruise by booking early. Ask a travel agent or call the cruise line directly.
- **Book an inside cabin:** If you're trying to keep costs down, ask for an inside cabin (one without a window). They're often the same size and offer the same amenities as the more expensive outside cabins. If you're planning on using the space only to sleep, who needs natural light during the day?
- **Take advantage of senior discounts:** The cruise industry offers some discounts to seniors (usually defined as anyone age 55 or older), so don't keep your age a secret. Membership in AARP, for example, can net you substantial discounts; always ask your travel agent about these types of discounts when you're booking.
- **Don't sail alone:** Cruise lines base their rates on double occupancy, so solo passengers usually pay between 150% and 200% of the per-person rate. If you're traveling alone, most lines have a program that allows two solo passengers to share a cabin.

12 Package Deals

Travelers to the Virgin Islands can often save money by purchasing a package tour. With these deals (which are not the same as escorted tours), the cost of airfare, accommodation, meals, and sometimes sightseeing and car rentals are combined in one package,

neatly tied up with a single price tag. Is it too good to be true?

Well, maybe. There are some drawbacks to packages. First, you usually have to pay the entire cost up front. Second, you have to take what the package gives you. Even if you find yourself in a hotel that you dislike intensely, you probably won't be able to change it. Finally, you'll pay a lot more if you want to travel alone—most of these deals are based on double occupancy.

Nevertheless, the remarkable savings that package tours provide—especially for popular destinations like the Virgin Islands—are often worth the drawbacks. In some cases, a package that includes airfare, hotel, and transportation to and from the airport will cost you less than just the hotel alone would have had you booked it yourself. That's because packages are sold in bulk to tour operators, who then resell them to the public at a considerable discount.

Just be sure to do your homework, because package deals vary widely. Some offer a better class of hotels than others. Some offer the same hotels for lower prices. Some offer flights on scheduled airlines, whereas others book charters. Some packages let your choose between escorted vacations and independent vacations; others will allow you to add a few excursions or escorted day trips (also at lower prices than you could locate on your own) without booking an entirely escorted tour. If you take the time to shop around, you will save in the long run.

FINDING A PACKAGE DEAL

The best place to start your search for a package deal is the travel section of your local Sunday newspaper. Also check the ads in the back of national travel magazines like *Arthur Frommer's Budget Travel, Travel & Leisure, National Geographic Traveler,* and *Condé Nast Traveler.* **Liberty Travel** (℗ **888/271-1584;** www.libertytravel. com) is one of the biggest packagers in the Northeast. **Certified Vacations** (℗ **800/241-1700**) is another option.

Another good resource is the airlines themselves, which often package their flights together with accommodations. Among the airline packagers, your options include **American Airlines Vacations** (℗ **800/321-2121;** www.aavacations.com), **Delta Dream Vacations** (℗ **800/872-7786;** www. deltavacations.com), and **US Airways Vacations** (℗ **800/455-0123;** www. usairwaysvacation.com). Pick the airline that has the best service to your hometown.

The biggest hotel chains and resorts also offer package deals. If you already know where you want to stay, call the place itself and ask if they can offer land/air packages.

Other tour operators include the following:

Caribbean Concepts Corp., 99 Jericho Turnpike, Jericho, NY 11793 (℗ **800/423-4433** or 516/417-9917), offers low-cost air-and-land packages to the islands, including apartments, hotels, villas, and condo rentals, plus local sightseeing (which can be arranged separately).

The best diving cruises are packaged by **Oceanic Society Expeditions,** Fort Mason Center, Building E, San Francisco, CA 94123 (℗ **800/ 326-7491** or 415/441-1106; www. oceanic-society.org). It also offers whale-watching and some research-oriented trips. Another specialist in this field is **Tropical Adventures,** P.O. Box 4337, Seattle, WA 98104 (℗ **800/247-3483** or 206/441-3483; www.divetropical.com).

Globus & Cosmos, 5301 S. Federal Circle, Littleton, CO 80123 (℗ **800/ 851-0728,** ext. 7518), gives escorted island-hopping expeditions to three or four islands, focusing on the history and culture of the Caribbean.

Club Med, Club Med Sales, P.O. Box 4460, Scottsdale, AZ 85261-4460 (℗ **800/258-2633;** www. clubmed.com), has various all-inclusive options throughout the Caribbean and the Bahamas.

PACKAGES FOR BRITISH TRAVELERS

Package tours can be booked through **BVI Holidays,** a division of Wingjet Travel Ltd., 11-13 Hockerill St., Bishop's Stortford, Herts, England CM23 2DH (✆ **01279/ 656111;** www.bviholidays.co.uk). This company is the major booking agent for all the important hotels in the B.V.I. You can even arrange to stay in several hotels around the islands in one trip. The company also offers staffed yacht charters and bareboat charters.

Caribbean Connections, Concorde House, Canal Street, Chester CH1 4ES (✆ **01244/355-300;** www.caribbean-connections.co.uk), offers all-inclusive packages (airfare and hotel) to the Caribbean and customized tours for independent travel. Other Caribbean specialists operating out of Great Britain include **Kuoni Travel,** Kuoni House, Dorking, Surrey RH5 4AZ (✆ **01306/742-222**), and **Caribtours,** 161 Fulham Rd., London SW3 6SN (✆ **020/7751-0660;** www.caribtours.co.uk), a small, very knowledgeable outfit.

13 Planning Your Trip Online

With a mouse, a modem, and a certain do-it-yourself determination, Internet users can tap into the same travel-planning databases that were once accessible only to travel agents. Sites such as **Travelocity, Expedia,** and **Orbitz** allow consumers to comparison shop for airfares, book flights, learn of last-minute bargains, and reserve hotel rooms and rental cars.

But don't fire your travel agent just yet. Although online booking sites offer tips and hard data to help you bargain shop, they cannot endow you with the hard-earned experience that makes a seasoned, reliable travel agent an invaluable resource, even in the Internet age. And for consumers with a complex itinerary, a trusty travel agent is still the best way to arrange the most direct flights to and from the best airports.

Still, there's no denying the Internet's emergence as a powerful tool in researching and plotting travel time. The benefits of researching your trip online can be well worth the effort:

- **Last-minute specials,** known as "E-savers," such as weekend deals or Internet-only fares, are offered by airlines to fill empty seats. Most of these are announced on

Tuesday or Wednesday and must be purchased online. They are only valid for travel that weekend, but some can be booked weeks or months in advance. Sign up for weekly e-mail alerts at airline websites or check mega-sites that compile comprehensive lists of E-savers, such as Smarter Living (smarterliving.com) or WebFlyer (www.webflyer.com).

- Some sites will send you **e-mail notification** when a cheap fare becomes available to your favorite destination. Some will also tell you when fares to a particular destination are lowest.

- The best of the travel planning sites are now **highly personalized;** they track your frequent-flier miles, and store your seating and meal preferences, tentative itineraries, and credit-card information, letting you plan trips or check agendas quickly.

- All major airlines offer **incentives**—bonus frequent-flier miles, Internet-only discounts, sometimes even free cellphone rentals—when you purchase online or buy an e-ticket.

- Advances in mobile technology provide business travelers and

Frommers.com: The Complete Travel Resource

For an excellent travel planning resource, we highly recommend **Arthur Frommer's Budget Travel Online** (www.frommers.com). We're a little biased, of course, but we guarantee you'll find the travel tips, reviews, monthly vacation giveaways, and online-booking capabilities thoroughly indispensable. Among the special features are: **"Ask the Expert"** bulletin boards, where Frommer's authors answer your questions via online postings; **Arthur Frommer's Daily Newsletter,** for the latest travel bargains and inside travel secrets; and Frommer's **Destinations archive,** where you'll get expert travel tips, hotel and dining recommendations, and advice on the sights to see for more than 200 destinations around the globe. Once your research is done, the **Online Reservation System** (www.frommers.com/booktravelnow) takes you to Frommer's favorite sites for booking your vacation at affordable prices.

other frequent travelers with **the ability to check flight status, change plans, or get specific directions** from handheld computing devices, mobile phones, and pagers. Some sites will e-mail or page a passenger if a flight is delayed.

TRAVEL PLANNING & BOOKING SITES

The best travel planning and booking sites cast a wide net, offering domestic and international flights, hotel and car-rental bookings, plus news, destination information, and deals on cruises and vacation packages. Keep in mind that free (one-time) registration is often required for booking. Because several airlines are no longer willing to pay commissions on tickets sold by online travel agencies, be aware that these online agencies will either charge a $10 surcharge if you book a ticket on that carrier—or neglect to offer those air carriers' offerings.

The sites in this section are not intended to be a comprehensive list, but rather a discriminating selection to get you started. Recognition is given to sites based on their content

value and ease of use and is not paid for—unlike some website rankings, which are based on payment. Remember: This is a press-time snapshot of leading websites—some undoubtedly will have evolved or moved by the time you read this.

- **Travelocity** (www.travelocity.com or www.frommers.travelocity.com) and **Expedia** (www.expedia.com) are the most longstanding and reputable sites, each offering excellent selections and searches for complete vacation packages. Travelers search by destination and dates coupled with how much they are willing to spend.
- The latest buzz in the online travel world is about **Orbitz** (www.orbitz.com), a site launched by United, Delta, Northwest, American, and Continental airlines. It shows all possible fares for your desired trip, offering fares lower than those available through travel agents. (Stay tuned: At press time, travel-agency associations were waging an antitrust battle against this site.)
- **Qixo** (www.qixo.com) is another powerful search engine that allows

you to search for flights and hotel rooms on 20 other travel-planning sites (such as Travelocity) at once. Qixo sorts results by price, after which you can book your travel directly through the site.

SMART E-SHOPPING

The savvy traveler is one armed with good information. Here are a few tips to help you navigate the Internet successfully and safely.

- **Know when sales start.** Last-minute deals may vanish in minutes. If you have a favorite booking site or airline, find out when last-minute deals are released to the public. (For example, Southwest's specials are posted every Tuesday at 12:01am central time.)
- **Shop around.** Compare results from different sites and airlines—and against a travel agent's best fare, if you can. If possible, try a range of times and alternate airports before you make a purchase.
- **Follow the rules of the trade.** Book in advance, and choose an off-peak time and date if possible. Some sites will tell you when fares to a particular destination tend to be cheapest.
- **Stay secure.** Book only through secure sites (some airline sites are not secure). Look for a key icon (Netscape) or a padlock (Internet Explorer) at the bottom of your web browser before you enter credit card information or other personal data.
- **Avoid online auctions.** Sites that auction airline tickets and frequent-flier miles are the number-one perpetrators of Internet fraud, according to the National Consumers League.

- **Maintain a paper trail.** If you book an e-ticket, print out a confirmation, or write down your confirmation number, and keep it safe and accessible—or your trip could be a virtual one!

ONLINE TRAVELER'S TOOLBOX

Veteran travelers usually carry some essential items to make their trips easier. Following is a selection of online tools to bookmark and use.

- **Visa ATM Locator** (www.visa.com/pd/atm) or **MasterCard ATM Locator** (www.mastercard.com/atm). Find ATMs in hundreds of cities in the United States and around the world.
- **Mapquest** (www.mapquest.com). This best of the mapping sites lets you choose a specific address or destination, and in seconds, it will return a map and detailed directions.
- **Cybercafes.com** (www.cybercafes.com) or **Net Café Guide** (www.netcafeguide.com/mapindex.htm). Locate Internet cafes at hundreds of locations around the globe. Catch up on your e-mail and log on to the Web for a few dollars per hour.
- **Universal Currency Converter** (www.xe.net/currency). See what your dollar or pound is worth in more than 100 other countries.
- **U.S. State Department Travel Warnings** (www.travel.state.gov/travel_warnings.html). Reports on places where health concerns or unrest might threaten U.S. travelers. It also lists the locations of U.S. embassies around the world.

14 Getting Around the Islands

Be sure to check out the "Getting Around" sections in the individual island chapters.

BY PLANE

Travelers can fly between St. Thomas and St. Croix and between St. Thomas and Tortola (at Beef Island) or Virgin Gorda. St. John doesn't have an airport; passengers usually land first at St. Thomas, then travel to St. John by boat. **American Eagle** (© 800/433-7300) offers eight daily flights from St. Thomas to St. Croix; a one-way fare is $95. **Seabourne** (© 340/773-6442) also makes this 30-minute trip 16 times daily. To travel between St. Thomas and Tortola or Virgin Gorda by plane, contact **American Eagle** (© 800/ 433-7300), **St. Thomas Air** (© 800/ 522-3084), or **LIAT** (© 800/ 468-0482). The one-way cost for one of the 12 flights between St. Thomas and Tortola is $53 per person from Monday through Friday, $132 Saturday and Sunday.

BY CAR

A rented car is often the best way to get around the Virgin Islands. Just remember the most important rule: In both the U.S. and the British Virgin Islands, **you must drive on the left.**

All the major car-rental companies are represented in the U.S. Virgin Islands, including **Avis** (© 800/ 331-2112), **Budget** (© 800/ 472-3325), and **Hertz** (© 800/ 654-3001); many local agencies also compete in these markets (for detailed information, refer to the "Getting Around" sections in individual island chapters). On St. Thomas and St. Croix, you can pick up most rental cars at the airport. On St. John there are car-rental stands at the ferry dock. During the high season, cars might be in short supply, so reserve as far in advance as possible.

Parking lots in the U.S. Virgin Islands can be found in Charlotte Amalie, in St. Thomas, and in Christiansted on St. Croix (in Frederiksted,

you can generally park on the street). Most hotels, except those in the congested center of Charlotte Amalie, have free parking lots.

In the British Virgin Islands, many visitors don't even bother renting a car. Be aware that some of the roads are like roller-coaster rides. Vehicles come in a wide range of styles and prices, including Jeeps, Land Rovers, minimokes, and even six- to eight-passenger Suzukis. Weekly rates are usually slightly cheaper. To rent a car on the B.V.I., you must purchase a local driver's license for $10 from police headquarters or at the car-rental desk, and you must be at least 25 years old. Major U.S. companies are represented in these islands, and there are many local companies as well.

GASOLINE There are plenty of service stations on St. Thomas, especially on the outskirts of Charlotte Amalie and at strategic points in the north and the more congested East End. On St. Croix, most gas stations are in Christiansted, but there are also some along the major roads and at Frederiksted. On St. John, make sure your tank is filled up at Cruz Bay before heading out on a tour of the island.

On the British Virgin Islands, gas stations are not as plentiful. Road Town, the capital of Tortola, has the most gas stations; fill up here before touring the island. Virgin Gorda has a limited but sufficient number of gas stations. Chances are you won't be using a car on the other, smaller British Virgin Islands. At press time, gas prices range from $2.30 to $2.50 a gallon.

ROAD MAPS Adequate maps are available for free on the islands at their tourist offices. If you arrive by plane, go to the tourist information office at the airport for a map. If you plan to drive your rental car to your hotel, ask a staff member at the tourist office or car-rental desk to trace the best route for you.

BREAKDOWNS   All the major islands, including St. Thomas, St. John, St. Croix, Tortola, and Virgin Gorda, have garages that will tow vehicles, but always call the rental company first if you have a breakdown. If your car requires extensive repairs because of a mechanical failure, a new one will be sent to replace it.

DEMYSTIFYING RENTER'S INSURANCE   Before you drive off in a rental car, be sure you're insured. Hasty assumptions about your personal auto insurance or a rental agency's additional coverage could end up costing you lots of money.

If you already hold a private auto insurance policy, you are most likely covered in the United States for loss of or damage to a rental car and for liability in case of injury to any other party involved in an accident. (Coverage probably doesn't extend outside the United States, however, so be sure to find out whether you are covered in the area you are visiting.) Check to see whether your policy extends to all persons who will be driving the rental car, how much liability is covered in case of an accident, and whether the type of vehicle you are renting is included under your contract. (Rental trucks, sport utility vehicles, and luxury vehicles may not be covered.)

Most major credit cards provide some rental car insurance as well—provided they were used to pay for the rental. They usually cover damage or theft of a rental car for the full cost of the vehicle. If you are uninsured, your credit card provides the only coverage, assuming you decline the rental agency's insurance. If you already have insurance, your credit card will provide secondary coverage—which basically covers your deductible. Credit cards will not cover liability or the cost of injury to an outside party and/or damage to an outside party's vehicle.

Bear in mind that each credit card company has its own peculiarities. Most American Express Optima cards, for instance, do not provide any insurance. American Express does not cover vehicles valued at over $50,000; new, luxury vehicles; or vehicles built on a

---

Tips **Saving Money on a Rental Car**

Car-rental rates vary even more than airfares. The price you pay will depend on the size of the car, the length of the rental period, how far you drive it, whether you purchased insurance, and a host of other factors. You could save hundred of dollars by asking a few key questions, including: Are special promotional rates available? Are weekend rates lower than weekday rates? Is a weekly rate cheaper than the daily rate? Is it cheaper to pick up the car at the airport compared to another island location? How much does the rental company charge to refill your gas tank if you return with the tank less than full?

Don't forget that if you're a member of AARP, AAA, a frequent-flier programs, or a trade union, you may well be entitled to car-rental discounts of up to 30%. Also, many package deals include airfare, accommodations, and a rental car with unlimited mileage. Compare these prices with cost of booking airline tickets and renting a car separately to see if a package might offer a good deal.

truck chassis. MasterCard does not provide coverage for loss, theft, or fire damage and only covers collision if the rental period does not exceed 15 days. Call your own credit card company for details.

If you do not hold an insurance policy or if you are driving outside the United States, you may want to consider purchasing additional liability insurance from your rental company. Be sure to check the terms, however. Some rental agencies only cover liability if the renter is not at fault; even then, the rental company's obligation varies.

The basic insurance coverage offered by most care rental companies, known as the Loss/Damage Waiver (LDW) or Collision Damage Waiver (CDW), can cost much as $20 per day. It varies according to the company policy, but usually covers the full value of the vehicle, with no deductible if an outside party causes an accident or other damage to the rental car. If you are at fault in an accident, however, you will be covered for the full replacement value of the car, but not for liability. Most rental companies will require a police report to process any claims you file, but your private insurer will not be notified of the accident.

BY TAXI

Taxis are the main mode of transport on all the Virgin Islands. On **St. Thomas,** taxi vans carry up to a dozen passengers to multiple destinations, and smaller private taxis are also available. Rates are posted at the airport, where you'll find plenty of taxis on arrival. On **St. John,** both private taxis and vans for three or more passengers are available. On **St. Croix,** taxis congregate at the airport, in Christiansted, and in Frederiksted, where the cruise ships arrive. Many hotels often have a "fleet" of taxis available for guests. Taxis here are unmetered,

and you should always negotiate the rate before taking off.

On the **British Virgin Islands,** taxis are sometimes the only way to get around. Service is available on Tortola, Virgin Gorda, and Anegada, and rates are fixed by the local government.

BY BOAT

Ferry service forms the vital link between St. Thomas and St. John; private water taxis also operate on this route. Launch services link Red Hook, on the East End of St. Thomas, with both Charlotte Amalie in St. Thomas and Cruz Bay in St. John.

In the B.V.I., ferries and private boats link Road Town, Tortola, with the island's West End; there's also service to and from Virgin Gorda and some of the smaller islands, such as Anegada and Jost Van Dyke. However, on some of the really remote islands, boat service may only be once a week. Many of the private islands, such as Peter Island, provide launches from Tortola.

You can travel from Charlotte Amalie (St. Thomas by public ferry to West End and Road Town on Tortola, a 45-minute voyage. Boats making this run include **Native Son** (© 284/ 495-4617), **Smith's Ferry Service** (© 284/495-4495), and **Inter-Island Boat Services** (© 284/495-4166). The latter specializes in a somewhat obscure routing—that is, from St. John to the West End on Tortola.

For details on specific ferry connections, including sample fares, see the "Getting Around" sections of the individual island chapters.

BY BUS

The only islands with a really recommendable bus service are St. Thomas and St. Croix. On St. Thomas, buses leave from Charlotte Amalie and circle the island; on St. Croix, air-conditioned buses run from Christiansted to Frederiksted. Bus service elsewhere is highly erratic; it's mostly used by locals going to and from work.

BY BICYCLE
Much of the hilly terrain of the Virgin Islands does not lend itself to cycling.

St. John, however, is a decent place for bike rides, and St. Croix is ideal. For specific information on bicycle rentals, see the "Getting Around" sections of the individual island chapters.

15 Tips on Accommodations & Dining

ACCOMMODATIONS
Resorts and hotels in the Virgin Islands offer package deals galore, and though they have many disadvantages, the deals are always cheaper than rack rates. Therefore it's always best to consult a reliable travel agent to find out what's available in the way of land-and-air packages before booking accommodations.

There is no rigid classification of hotel properties on the islands. The word "deluxe" is often used, or misused, when "first class" might be more appropriate. First class itself often isn't always what it's touted to be. For that and other reasons, we've presented fairly detailed descriptions of the properties, so that you'll get an idea of what to expect. However, even in the deluxe and first-class properties, don't expect top-rate service and efficiency. Life here moves pretty slowly, and that can have its disadvantages.

The facilities available at hotels in the Virgin Islands vary widely. All the big, first-class hotels have swimming pools and are usually located on or near a beach. If you book at a less expensive accommodation, you can often pay a small fee to use the facilities of the larger, more expensive resorts.

The good news: During the **off-season** (from mid-April to mid-December) hotels slash prices 25% to 50%. Many resorts in the Virgin Islands will allow you to book in on an all-inclusive plan where you pay one price for your room and all your meals, with drinks costing extra. In theory at least, this is less expensive than dining (la carte all the time. The

major disadvantage is that you're locked into one place for most of your meals and you can't get out and dine around the island for more flavor, diversity, and local color. If you want to save money but also sample some of the local restaurants, request "MAP"—that is, the Modified American Plan with breakfast and dinner included. At least that way you'll be free to dine away from the hotel for at least one meal a day.

TIPS FOR SAVING ON YOUR HOTEL ROOM
The rack rate is the maximum rate that a hotel charges for a room. It's the rate you'd get if you walked in off the street and asked for a room for the night. Hardly anybody pays these prices, however, and there are many ways around them.

- **Don't be afraid to bargain.** Get in the habit of asking for a lower price than the first one quoted. Most rack rates include commissions of 10% to 25% or more for travel agents, which many hotels will cut if you make your own reservations and haggle a bit. Always ask politely whether a less expensive room is available, or whether any special rates apply to you. Remember that you may qualify for corporate, student, military, senior citizens, or other discounts. Be sure to mention membership in AAA, AARP, frequent-flier programs, or trade unions, which may entitle you to special deals as well.
- **Rely on a qualified professional.** Certain hotels give travel agents

discounts in exchange for steering business their way, so if you're shy about bargaining, an agent may be better equipped to negotiate discounts for you.

- **Dial direct.** When booking a room in a chain hotel, call the hotel's local line, as well as the toll-free number, and see where you get the best deal. A hotel makes nothing on a room that stays empty. The clerk who runs the place is more likely to know about vacancies and will often give deep discounts to fill up.

- **Remember the law of supply and demand.** Resort hotels are most crowded and therefore most expensive on weekends; so discounts are usually available for midweek stays. Avoid high-season stays whenever you can: Planning your vacation just a week before or after official peak season can mean big savings.

- **Look into group or long-stay discounts.** If you come as part of a large group, you should be able to negotiate a bargain, since the hotel can then guarantee occupancy in a number of rooms. Likewise, if you're planning a long stay on the island (usually from 5 days to a week) you may qualify for a discount. As a general rule, you will receive 1 night free after a 7-night stay.

- **Look for deals on the Web.** If you book your hotel through **Arthur Frommer's Budget Travel** (**www.frommers.com**), you can often save up to 50%. **Microsoft Expedia** (**www.expedia.com**) features a "Travel Agent" that will also direct you to affordable lodgings.

RENTING YOUR OWN VILLA OR VACATION HOME

You might decide to rent a villa, condo, apartment, or even your own cottage on the beach while in the Virgin Islands.

Private apartments are more of a no-frills option than villas and condos. They can be rented with or without maid service. Cottages usually contain a simple bedroom with a small kitchen and bathroom. Many open onto a beach, whereas others are clustered around a communal swimming pool. In the high season, reservations should be made at least 5 to 6 months in advance.

Sometimes local tourist offices will advise you on vacation home rentals if you write or call them directly. In addition, dozens of agencies throughout the United States and Canada offer rentals in the Virgin Islands. Here are some of the best:

Home Abroad, 405 E. 56th St., Suite 6-H, New York, NY 10022 (© **212/421-9165;** fax 212/752-1591), has a roster of private homes, villas, and condos for rent in St. Thomas, St. John, Tortola, and Virgin Gorda; maid service is included in the price.

Caribbean Connection Plus Ltd., P.O. Box 261, Trumbull, CT 06611 (© **800/893-1100** or 203/261-8295; www.islandhoppingexpert.com), offers island-hopping itineraries and a variety of accommodations, including condos and villas. It specializes in the less developed Caribbean islands. The best part about Caribbean Connection is that it caters to four different budgets: shoestring, comfortable, deluxe, and fantasy.

Hideaways International, 767 Islington St., Portsmouth, NH 03801 (© **800/843-4433** or 603/430-4433 in the U.S.; www.hideaways.com), publishes *Hideaways Guide,* a 148-page pictorial directory describing home rentals throughout the Caribbean. Rentals range from cottages to staffed villas to entire islands! In most cases, you deal directly with the owners. Other services include

The West Indian Guest House

Most Caribbean natives stay in guest houses when they travel to the Virgin Islands. Some are surprisingly comfortable, with private bathrooms in each room, air-conditioning or ceiling fans, and swimming pools. Don't expect the luxuries of a first-class resort, but for the money the guest house can't be beat. The guest houses we've recommended in this book are clean and comfortable.

specialty cruises, yacht charters, airline ticketing, car rentals, and hotel reservations. Annual membership is $99; a 4-month trial membership is $39.

If you're interested in a condo rental, contact **Paradise Properties of St. Thomas,** P.O. Box 9395, St. Thomas, U.S.V.I. 00801 (© **340/ 775-3115**), which currently represents six condo complexes. Rental units range from studio apartments to four-bedroom villas. A minimum stay of 3 days is required in any season, 7 nights during Christmas.

Island Villas, Property Management Rentals, 3025 Estate Friedenstual Christiansted, St. Croix, U.S.V.I. 00820 (© **800/626-4512** or 340/ 773-8821; fax 340/773-8823), offers some of the best properties on St. Croix. This outfit specializes in villas, condos, and private homes; many are on the beach. One- to six-bedroom units are available, with prices from $1,200 to $10,000 per week.

Villas of Distinction, P.O. Box 55, Armonk, NY 10504 (© **800/ 289-0900** or 914/273-3331 in the U.S.), offers "complete vacations," including car rental and domestic help. Its private villas have one to six bedrooms, and almost every villa has a swimming pool.

RENTING YOUR OWN ISLAND

Extremely well-heeled escapists can look into renting a private island in the British Virgin Islands. Here's what's up for grabs (and see chapter 6 for more details):

- **Guana Island:** For a negotiable fee, up to 30 guests can take over this privately owned, 850-acre island, the sixth largest of the British Virgin Islands. Guana Island is a nature sanctuary, with seven pristine beaches and a network of hiking trails.

- **Mosquito Island:** Guests can sail their yachts to this sandy 125-acre island, about a 5-minute jaunt north of Virgin Gorda. On arrival, they take over Drake's Anchorage Resort Inn, which has 12 units. Mosquito Island is the perfect hideaway—we're talking four deserted beaches and no TVs, phones, or any other modern amenities.

- **Necker Island** (© **800/557-4255**): This 74-acre hideaway is enveloped by its own unpolluted coral reef. It's owned by Richard Branson (of Virgin Atlantic Airways), who is well acquainted with its trio of sugar-white beaches. When he's not around, he leases the entire island to friends like Eddie Murphy. At the core of the island is a 10-bedroom villa, surrounded by two 1-bedroom guest houses. Sun pours into the lush tropical garden, which has a private freshwater pool and Jacuzzi. The daily rate is $14,000 to $29,000, depending on the number of guests, and includes food, drinks, and activities (tennis, snorkeling, windsurfing, boating, and sea kayaking to name a few) for up to 24 people.

DINING

Dining in the Virgin Islands is generally more expensive than it is in North America because, except for locally caught seafood, many of the ingredients have to be imported. This also means that sometimes they aren't as fresh as they could be. Whenever possible, stick to regional food, which is fresher.

Overall, the food on the islands is better than ever. Many fine talents, including some top-notch chefs from California, now cook here. These chefs often combine mainland recipes with local ingredients to come up with a Caribbean/American cuisine. Nevertheless, whatever you do, try to eat at some of the local places as well. The prices there are more reasonable, and the fare is more adventurous. For details on island food see "The

Cuisine: A Taste of the Virgin Islands" in the appendix.

TIPPING   A 10% to 15% service charge is automatically added to most restaurant tabs. If the service has been good, you should tip a bit extra.

WHAT TO WEAR   In some of the posh resorts, such as Caneel Bay on St. John, it is customary for men to wear a jacket, but in summer, virtually no establishment requires it. If in doubt, always ask the restaurant. At the better places, women's evening attire is casual-chic. During the day it is proper to wear something over your bathing suit if you're in a restaurant.

RESERVATIONS   Check to see if reservations are required before going to a restaurant. In summer, you can almost always get in, but in winter, all the tables may be taken at some of the famous but small places.

16 Tips on Shopping

St. Thomas and St. Croix, with their fabled duty-free deals, are the top shopping destinations in the entire Caribbean. We've recommended numerous shops in the individual island chapters ahead, but we thought you might appreciate a few insider tips on shopping in the Virgin Islands.

The **U.S. Virgin Islands** are duty-free ports, which means that many goods imported to the islands are not subject to import taxes and therefore can be sold at a discount. Shoppers can take advantage of these duty-free bargains, but only up to a limit prescribed by their government. U.S. residents are entitled to $1,200 worth of duty-free exports from the U.S. Virgin Islands every 30 days—that's three times the exemption allowed from most foreign destinations. (For more details, see "Entry Requirements & Customs," earlier in this chapter.) One way to get the most out of your **duty-free allowance** is to send gifts home. You can ship up to $100 worth

of unsolicited gifts per day without paying duty, and you don't have to declare such gifts on your Customs form when leaving the islands.

Goods in the **British Virgin Islands** are taxed at the same rate as any other foreign destination—there are no duty-free bargains. In general, the shopping scene in the B.V.I. pales in comparison to that of St. Croix and especially St. Thomas. The smart shopper will still, however, find some good buys in Road Town, Tortola, usually on British fabrics, china, and other goods.

If you're in the market for a particular item, it's wise to check the price at home before you go. Sometimes even the duty-free items on the islands can be bought just as cheaply at home.

Theoretically, bargaining is not the rule on the islands, but over the years we have found merchant after merchant willing to do so, particularly on expensive items, such as jewelry and perfume. The slow summer, late spring, and fall seasons are the best times to try to make deals with local vendors.

BEST BUYS IN THE U.S. VIRGIN ISLANDS

The best buys are **liquor** (because of the generous U.S. allowance), **jewelry,** and **china.** You may find bargains on crystal, certain clothing, beauty items, porcelain, leather goods, watches, and even furs. Cigarettes are also cheaper. (See also "The Best Shopping Buys" in chapter 1.)

In **clothing,** the best buys are woolen items, such as sweaters. Cashmere sweaters are also sometimes good values. Also look for fashions from the Far East, especially China, and European and U.S. designer labels. But remember, you may find the same (or better) discounts back on the mainland.

Jewelry is the most common item for sale in St. Thomas. Look carefully over the selections of gold and gemstones (emeralds are traditionally considered the finest savings). Gold that is marked 24K in the United States and Canada is marked 999 (99.9% pure gold) on European items. Gold marked 18K in the United States and Canada has a European marking of 750 (or 75% pure), and 14K gold is marked 585 (or 58.5% pure). You can also often get deals on name-brand **watches,** which are sold throughout Charlotte Amalie and, to a lesser degree, St. Croix.

When shopping for **porcelain and crystal,** you'll find that the best European brands are *usually* priced lower than in the States; it pays to know what the going rate is at home before you leave. Most stores will arrange for items to be shipped.

The most popular **island-made items** include leather sandals, paintings, island dolls, locally made clothing, pottery, boutique canvas bags, locally recorded music, straw products, batiks, and unusual handmade jewelry.

 FAST FACTS: **The U.S. Virgin Islands**

American Express Visitors to St. Thomas and St. John should contact **Caribbean Travel Agency/Tropic Tours,** 14ab The Guardian Building (© **340/774-1855**). On St. Croix, the AmEx rep is **Southerland,** Chandler's Wharf, Gallows Bay (© **340/773-9500**).

Banks Several major banks, including Citibank and Chase Manhattan are represented on the islands; most are open Monday through Thursday from 9am to 2:30pm, Friday from 9am to 2pm and 3:30 to 5pm.

Business Hours Typically, Monday through Friday from 9am to 5pm, Saturday from 9am to 1pm. On Sundays, businesses will open or close depending on how many cruise ships are in port.

Cameras & Film Most name-brand film, like Kodak, is sold here, but it's not cheap and neither is developing it. Protect your camera, not only from theft but also from sun, salt water, and sand. For the best commercial camera stores in the U.S.V.I., see the individual island chapters.

Currency U.S. currency is used on the U.S. Virgin Islands.

Driving Rules Drive on the left, and obey speed limits (20 m.p.h. in town, 35 m.p.h. outside).

Drugstores There are many drugstore outlets in St. Thomas and St. Croix, fewer on St. John. See specific island chapters for local recommendations.

Electricity The electrical current in the Virgin Islands is the same as on the U.S. mainland: 110 volts AC, 60 cycles.

Embassies & Consulates There are no embassies or consulates here. If you have a passport issue, go to the local police station, which in all islands is located at the center of government agencies. Tell your problem to whomever is at reception, and you'll be given advice about what agency might come to your assistance.

Emergencies To reach the police in an emergency, call ✆ **911**; fire, **921**; ambulance, **922**; coast guard, **340/776-3497**.

Hitchhiking It isn't illegal, but it isn't widely practiced. We don't recommend it anywhere.

Holidays See "When to Go," earlier in this chapter.

Hospitals See "Fast Facts" in each individual island chapter.

Laundry See "Fast Facts" under the individual island listings for the names of laundromats.

Liquor Laws You must be 21 years of age or older to purchase liquor at a store or in a restaurant.

Mail Postage rates are the same as on the U.S. mainland: 20¢ for a postcard and 34¢ for a letter to U.S. addresses. For international mail, a first-class letter of up to ½ ounce costs 80¢ (60¢ to Canada or Mexico); a first-class postcard costs 70¢ (50¢ to Canada or Mexico); and a preprinted postal aerogramme costs 70¢.

Maps Tourist offices provide free maps of all three islands. If you plan on extensive touring, purchase a copy of the *Official Road Map of the United States Virgin Islands,* available in most local bookstores.

Newspapers & Magazines Daily U.S. newspapers are flown into St. Thomas and St. Croix. Local papers, such as the *Virgin Island Daily News,* also carry the latest news. St. Croix has its own daily newspaper, the *St. Croix Avis;* St. John's paper is *Tradewinds.*

Pets To bring your pet, you must have a health certificate from a mainland veterinarian and show proof of vaccination against rabies. Very few hotels allow animals, so check in advance. If you're strolling with your dog through the national park on St. John, you must keep it on a leash. Pets are not allowed at campgrounds, picnic areas, or on public beaches. Both St. Croix and St. Thomas have veterinarians listed in the Yellow Pages.

Police For local stations see "Police" under "Fast Facts" for the individual islands. In an emergency, call ✆ **911**.

Radio & TV All three islands receive both cable and commercial TV stations. Radio weather reports can be heard at 7:30pm and 8:30am on 99.5 FM.

Safety U.S. Virgins—St. John is relatively safe, even at night, but St. Thomas, especially around its capital, Charlotte Amalie, has the highest crime rate in the Virgin Islands. You may want to avoid it at night. St. Croix has less crime than St. Thomas but caution is advised, especially if you plan night visits to the dives of Frederiksted or Christiansted where muggings might occur.

Taxes There is no departure tax for the U.S. Virgin Islands. Hotels add an 8% tax—this tax is not always included in the rate quoted to you. Always ask.

Telephone, Telex, & Fax Local calls at a telephone booth cost 25¢. From all points on the mainland you can dial direct to the U.S. Virgin Islands using the area code **340**. Most hotels have telex and fax machines, as do local post offices.

Time The U.S. Virgins are on Atlantic Time, which is one hour ahead of Eastern Time. However, the islands do not observe Daylight Saving Time, so in the summer, the Virgin Islands and the East Coast of the U.S. are on the same time. In winter, when it's 6am in Charlotte Amalie, it's 5am in Miami; during daylight saving time it's 6am in both places.

Tipping Tip as you would on the U.S. mainland.

Tourist Offices See "Visitor Information," earlier in this chapter. In St. Thomas, the visitor center is at Emancipation Square (© **340/774-8784**); in St. Croix at 41 A Queen Cross St. (© **340/773-0495**), Christiansted, and also in the Customs House Building, Strand Street, Frederiksted (© **340/772-0357**); and in St. John at Cruz Bay (© **340/776-6450**).

Visas U.S. and Canadian citizens do not need a visa to enter the U.S. Virgin Islands. Visitors from other nations should have a passport and a U.S. visa. Those visitors may also be asked to produce an onward ticket. See "Entry Requirements & Customs," earlier in this chapter.

Water Most visitors drink the local tap water with no harmful aftereffects. Those with more delicate stomachs might want to stick to bottled water.

 ## FAST FACTS: The British Virgin Islands

American Express The local representative is Travel Plan, Ltd., located at Waterfront Drive (© **284/494-2347**), in Tortola, and across from Virgin Gorda Yacht Harbour (© **284/495-5586**) in Virgin Gorda.

Banks Banks are generally open Monday through Thursday from 9am to 3pm, Friday from 9am to 5pm. To cash traveler's checks, try Bank of Nova Scotia, Wickhams Cay (© **284/494-2526**) or Barclays Bank, Wickhams Cay (© **284/494-2171**), both near Road Town.

Bookstores The best bookstore on the island is the National Educational Services Bookstore, Wickhams Cay, in Road Town (© **284/494-3921**).

Business Hours Most offices are open Monday through Friday from 9am to 5pm. Government offices are open Monday through Friday from 8:30am to 4:30pm. Shops are generally open Monday through Friday from 9am to 5pm and Saturday from 9am to 1pm.

Cameras & Film The best place for supplies and film developing on Tortola is Bolo's Brothers, Wickhams Cay (© **284/494-3641**).

Currency The U.S. dollar is the legal currency, much to the surprise of some British travelers.

Customs See "Entry Requirements & Customs," earlier in this chapter.

Dentist For dental emergencies, contact **Dental Surgery** (© **284/494-3274**), which is in Road Town, Tortola, behind the Police Station.

Driving Rules You need a valid driver's license and must pay $10 for a 3-month British Virgin Islands driving permit. Remember to drive on the left.

Drugstores The best place to go is J. R. O'Neal, Ltd., Main Street, Road Town (© **284/494-2292**), in Tortola; closed Sunday.

Electricity The electrical current is 110 volts AC, 60 cycles, as in the United States.

Embassies & Consulates There are none in the B.V.I.

Emergencies Peebles Hospital, Porter Road, Road Town (© **284/494-3497**), has X-ray and laboratory facilities; call if you have an emergency. Your hotel can put you in touch with the local medical staff. For police and fire emergencies call © **911**.

Hitchhiking Travel by thumb is illegal.

Hospitals In Road Town, you can go to Peebles Hospital, Porter Road (© **284/494-3497**).

Laundry & Dry Cleaning In Tortola, one of the best places is Freeman's Laundry and Dry Cleaning, Purcell Estate (© **284/494-2285**).

Liquor Laws The legal minimum age for purchasing liquor or drinking alcohol in bars or restaurants is 21. Alcoholic beverages can be sold any day of the week, including Sunday. You can have an open container on the beach but be careful not to litter, or you might be fined.

Lost Property Go to the police station (see "Police" listing below). Sometimes they'll broadcast notice of your lost property on the local radio station.

Mail Most hotels will mail letters for you, or you can go directly to the post office. Allow 4 days to 1 week for letters to reach the North American mainland. Postal rates in the B.V.I. have been raised to 35¢ for a postcard (airmail) to the United States or Canada, and 50¢ for a first-class airmail letter (½ ounce) to the United States or Canada, or 40¢ for a second-class letter (½ ounce) to the United States or Canada.

Maps The best map of the British Virgin Islands is published by Vigilate and is sold at most bookstores in Road Town.

Newspapers & Magazines Papers from the mainland, such as the *Miami Herald,* are flown into Tortola and Virgin Gorda daily, and copies of the latest issues of *Time* and *Newsweek* are sold at hotel newsstands and at various outlets in Road Town. The B.V.I. have no daily newspaper, but the *Island Sun,* published Wednesday and Friday, is a good source of information on local entertainment.

Nudity Unlike in some parts of the Caribbean, nudity is an offense punishable by law in the B.V.I.

Police The main police headquarters is on Waterfront Drive near the ferry docks on Sir Olva Georges Plaza (© **284/494-3822**) in Tortola. There is also a police station on Virgin Gorda (© **284/495-9828**) and on Jost Van Dyke (© **284/495-9345**).

Radio & TV The B.V.I. has two local FM stations with nonstop music, including Z-HIT (94.3) and Z-WAVE (97.3). There's one local TV station and one cable station.

Safety Crime is rare here; in fact, the British Virgin Islands are among the safest places in the Caribbean. Still, you should take all the usual precautions you would anywhere, and don't leave items unattended on the beach.

British Virgins—Crime virtually does not exist on many of the remote islands of the B.V.I. chain. The most crime, usually minor robberies, occurs in Tortola, with less theft reported on Virgin Gorda. The usual precautions a discerning person would follow anywhere are advised, of course.

Taxes There is no sales tax. A government tax of 7% is imposed on all hotel rooms. A $10 departure tax is collected from everyone leaving by air, $5 for those leaving by sea.

Telephone, Telex, & Fax You can call the British Virgin Islands from the continental United States or from the U.S. Virgin Islands by dialing area code **284,** followed by **49,** and then five digits. Once here, omit both the 284 and the 49 to make local calls. From all public phones and from some hotels, you can access **AT&T Direct** by dialing © **800/872-2881.** Most hotels (not the small guest houses) will send a fax or telex for you.

Time The islands operate on Atlantic standard time year-round. In the peak winter season, when it's 10am in the British Virgins, it's 9am in Florida. However, when Florida and the rest of the East Coast go on daylight saving time, the clocks do not change here.

Tipping & Service Charges Most hotels add on a 5% to 15% service charge; ask if it's already included when you're initially quoted a price. A 10% service charge is often (but not always) added on to restaurant bills; you can leave another 5% if you thought the service was unusually good. You usually don't need to tip taxi drivers, because most own their own cabs, but you can tip 10% if they've been unusually helpful.

Tourist Offices The headquarters of the B.V.I. Tourist Board is in the center of Road Town (Tortola), close to the ferry dock, south of Wickhams Cay (© **284/494-3134**).

Visas Visitors who stay for fewer than 6 months don't need a visa if they possess a return or onward ticket.

Water The tap water in the British Virgin Islands is safe to drink.

3

St. Thomas

St. Thomas, the busiest cruise-ship harbor in the West Indies, is not the largest of the U.S. Virgins—St. Croix, 40 miles south, holds that distinction. But bustling Charlotte Amalie at the heart of the island is the capital of the U.S. Virgin Islands, and it remains the shopping hub of the Caribbean. The beaches on this island are renowned for their white sand and calm, turquoise waters, including the very best of them all, Magens Bay. *National Geographic* rated the island as one of the top destinations in the world for sailing, scuba diving, and fishing.

Charlotte Amalie, with its white houses and bright red roofs glistening in the sun, is one of the most beautiful towns in the Caribbean. It's most famous for shopping, but the town is also filled with historic sights, like Fort Christian, an intriguing 17th-century building constructed by the Danes. The town's architecture reflects the island's culturally diverse past. You'll pass Dutch doors, Danish red-tile roofs, French iron grillwork, and Spanish-style patios.

Because of St. Thomas's thriving commercial activity—as well as its lingering drug and crime problems—the island is often referred to as the most "unvirgin" of the Virgin Islands. Charlotte Amalie's Main Street is virtually a 3- to 4-block-long shopping center. Although this area tends to be overcrowded, the island's beaches, major hotels, most restaurants, and entertainment facilities are, for the most part, removed from the cruise-ship chaos. And you can always find seclusion at a hotel in more remote sections of the island. Hotels on the north side of St. Thomas look out at the Atlantic; those on the south side front the calmer Caribbean Sea.

St. Thomas has much to recommend it—not only perfect sandy beaches but the best dining in the islands and a string of the most upmarket resorts. But no one ever said St. Thomas was the friendliest of the Virgin Islands. It is, in fact, the unfriendliest—a rather impersonal place overrun with cruise-ship passengers and locals who cast a rather cynical eye toward tourists. It can even be dangerous at night, especially on the back streets of Charlotte Amalie. As for its service personnel, they almost parallel what you'd find in New York City—with all that that implies.

If you want to escape the hordes, don't come here, as the rush-hour traffic in and out of Charlotte Amalie will reveal. If you're seeking something laid-back, with friendlier people, all you have to do is take the ferry over to St. John (see chapter 4), and you'll enter a world that's more evocative of the sleepier 1950s. St. Thomas is for those who want action.

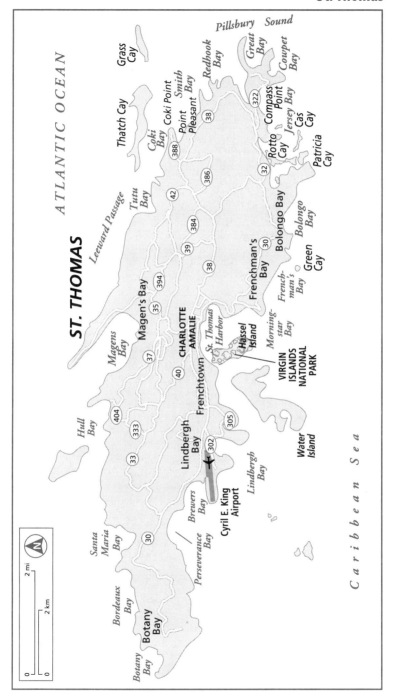

1 Orientation

ARRIVING

BY PLANE

If you're flying to St. Thomas, you will land at the **Cyril E. King Airport** (© **340/774-5100**), to the west of Charlotte Amalie on Route 30. From here, you can easily grab a taxi to your hotel or villa. Chances are you will be staying east of Charlotte Amalie, so keep in mind that getting through town often involves long delays and traffic jams.

Nonstop flights to the U.S. Virgin Islands from New York City and Atlanta take 3¾ and 3½ hours, respectively. Flight time from Miami is about 2½ hours. Flight time between St. Thomas and St. Croix is only 20 minutes. Flying to San Juan from mainland cities and connecting to St. Thomas may cost less than regular nonstop fares.

American Airlines (© **800/433-7300**; www.aa.com) offers frequent nonstop service to St. Thomas from the U.S. mainland, with five daily flights from New York City (summer flights vary; call for schedules). Passengers coming from other parts of the world are usually routed through American hubs in Miami or San Juan, both of which offer daily nonstop service. Connections from Los Angeles or San Francisco to St. Thomas are usually through New York, San Juan, or Miami. American Airlines also arranges discount land-and-air packages to St. Thomas and other Virgin Islands destinations.

The most reliable and frequent flights from Puerto Rico to the U.S. Virgin Islands are on **American Eagle** (© **800/433-7300**), with 13 nonstop flights daily, going to St. Thomas (from which boat connections can be made to St. John) and to St. Croix. It's now easier than ever to travel between St. Thomas and St. Croix: American Eagle has three flights a day, costing $61 per person one-way.

Delta (© **800/221-1212**; www.delta.com) offers two daily nonstop flights between Atlanta and St. Thomas, one in the morning and one in the afternoon. The later flight continues on to St. Croix. **Continental Airlines** (© **800/ 525-0280**; www.continental.com) flies daily from Newark International Airport to St. Thomas. **TWA** (© **800/221-2000**; www.twa.com) does not fly nonstop to any of the Virgin Islands, but offers connections on other carriers through San Juan. TWA flies into San Juan three to five times daily from New York's JFK Airport and twice on Saturday and Sunday from St. Louis with a touchdown in Miami. **USAirways** (© **800/428-4322**; www.usairways.com) now has one daily nonstop flight from Philadelphia to St. Thomas.

Cape Air (© **800/352-0714**; www.flycapeair.com) has service between St. Thomas and Puerto Rico. This Massachusetts-based airline offers seven flights daily. Cape Air has expanded its service to include flights from San Juan to St. Croix and flights between St. Croix and St. Thomas. Canadian travelers can fly Air Canada to Miami and then take another flight into St. Thomas or St. Croix. British passengers can fly from London to Miami, perhaps on British Airways, then on to St. Thomas or St. Croix on another carrier.

A final hint: Bargain-seekers should ask their airline representative to connect them with the tour desk, which can arrange discounted hotel rates if a hotel reservation is booked simultaneously with airline tickets.

BY BOAT

Charlotte Amalie is the busiest cruise-ship port in the Caribbean. For details on cruise-ship travel, see the "Cruising to the Virgin Islands" section in chapter 2.

If you're in the British Virgin Islands, you can take a boat to Charlotte Amalie from Tortola. Trip time is only 45 minutes between these two capitals, and a one-way ticket is $23 ($41 round-trip). The major carriers to and from Tortola are **Smith's Ferry** (© 340/775-7292) and **Native Son** (© 340/774-8685), which are both based in Charlotte Amalie. Boats arrive and depart from Tortola's West End.

St. Thomas is also linked by boat to St. John, about 3 to 5 miles away. Ferries depart from Red Hook Marina on the East End of St. Thomas and arrive at Cruz Bay on St. John. Trip time is about 20 minutes; the cost is $3 one-way. For complete ferry schedules, call © **340/776-6282.**

It's also possible to take a ferry service from Puerto Rico to St. Thomas with a stop in St. John. The service, however, is only available once every 2 weeks—maybe more often if demand increases. Trip time between San Juan and Charlotte Amalie (St. Thomas) is about 2 hours and 15 minutes. The cost is $80 one-way, but only $100 round-trip. For more information, call Transportation Services at © **340/776-6282.**

VISITOR INFORMATION

In St. Thomas, the **visitor center** at Emancipation Square (© **340/774-8784**) dispenses a helpful booklet, *St. Thomas This Week,* which has maps of St. Thomas and St. John plus up-to-date touring information and current event listings. The two-page St. Thomas map has a clear, easy-to-follow street plan of Charlotte Amalie, plus the locations of important landmarks and all of the city's leading shops. The visitor center is open Monday through Friday from 8am to 5pm, Saturday from 9am to noon.

CHARLOTTE AMALIE LAYOUT

For a map of the landmarks and attractions discussed below, see "Walking Tour: Charlotte Amalie" on p.107.

MAIN STREETS & ARTERIES

Charlotte Amalie, the capital of St. Thomas, is the only town on the island. Its seaside promenade is called **Waterfront Highway,** or simply, the Waterfront. From here, you can take any of the streets or alleyways into town to **Main Street** or Dronningens Gade. Principal links between Main Street and the Waterfront include **Raadets Gade, Tolbod Gade, Store Tvaer Gade,** and **Strand Gade.**

Main Street is home to all the major shops. The western end (near the inter-section with Strand Gade) is known as **Market Square,** once the site of the biggest slave market auctions in the Caribbean Basin. Today, it's an open-air cluster of stalls where native farmers and gardeners gather daily (except Sunday) to peddle their produce. Go early in the morning to see the market at its best.

Running parallel to and north of Main Street is **Back Street** or Vimmelskaft Gade, which is also lined with many stores, including some of the less expensive ones.

Note: It can be dangerous to walk along Back Street at night, but it's reasonably safe for daytime shopping.

In the eastern part of town, between Tolbod Gade and Fort Pladsen (northwest of Fort Christian), lies **Emancipation Park,** commemorating the liberation of the slaves in 1848. Most of the major historical buildings, including the Legislature, Fort Christian, and Government House, lie within a short walk of this park.

Southeast of the park looms **Fort Christian.** Crowned by a clock tower and painted rusty red, it was constructed by the Danes in 1671. The **Legislative**

FAST FACTS: **St. Thomas**

American Express The service is provided by Caribbean Travel Agency/Tropic Tours, 9716 Estate Thomas, Havensight (© **340/ 774-1855**).

Area Code The area code is **340**. You can dial direct from North America.

Banks Several major U.S. banks are represented on St. Thomas. including **Chase Manhattan Bank,** 11A Curaçao Gade (© **340/776-2222**), and **Citibank,** 42–46 Norre Gade, Grand Galleria (© **340/776-3350**). Hours vary, but most are open Monday through Thursday from 9am to 2:30pm, Friday from 9am to 2pm, and 3:30 to 5pm.

Bookstores Dockside Bookshop, Havensight Mall (© **340/774-4937**), where the cruise ships dock, also sells cards and maps.

Business Hours Typical business and store hours are Monday through Friday 9am to 5pm, Saturday 9am to 1pm. Some shops open Sunday for cruise-ship arrivals. Bars are usually open daily from 11am to midnight or 1am, although some hot spots stay open later.

Cameras & Film Try Blazing Photos, Veterans Drive (© **340/774-5547**), in Charlotte Amalie, with a branch office at Havensight Mall (© **340/776-5547**), where cruise-ship passengers arrive. Other locations are at American Yacht Harbor at Red Hook (© **340/776-4587**) and Nisky Shopping Center (© **340/774-1005**).

Dentist The Virgin Island Dental Association (© **340/775-9110**) is a member of the American Dental Association and is also linked with various specialists. Call for information or an appointment.

Doctor Doctors-on-Duty, Vitraco Park (© **340/776-7966**) in Charlotte Amalie, is a reliable medical facility.

Driving Rules See "Getting Around," above.

Drugstores For over-the-counter and prescription medications, go to Drug Farm, 2 4 Ninth St. (© **340/776-7098**), or Havensight Pharmacy, Havensight Mall, Building #4 (© **340/776-1235**).

Embassies & Consulates St. Thomas has no embassies or consulates.

Emergencies For the police, call © **911**; ambulance, **922**; fire, **921**.

Hospitals The St. Thomas Hospital is at 48 Sugar Estate (© **340/776-8311**), Charlotte Amalie.

Hotlines Call the police at © **911** in case of emergency. If you have or witness a boating mishap, call the U.S. Coast Guard Rescue (© **787/729-6800**, ext. 140), which operates out of San Juan, Puerto Rico. Scuba divers should note the number of a decompression chamber (© **340/776-8311**) at the Roy Schneider Community Hospital on St. Thomas.

Laundry & Dry Cleaning The major hotels provide laundry service, but it's more expensive than a Laundromat. For dry cleaning go to One Hour Martinizing, Barbel Plaza (© **340/774-5452**), in Charlotte Amalie. A good full-service Laundromat is 4-Star Laundromat, 68 Kronprindsens Gade (© **340/774-8689**), in Charlotte Amalie.

Liquor Laws Persons must be at least 21 years of age to patronize bars or purchase liquor in St. Thomas.

Maps See "Visitor Information," earlier in this chapter.

Newspapers & Magazines Copies of U.S. mainland newspapers, such as *The New York Times, USA Today,* and the *Miami Herald,* arrive daily in St. Thomas and are sold at hotels and newsstands. The latest copies of *Time* and *Newsweek* are also for sale. *St. Thomas Daily News* covers local, national, and international events. *Virgin Islands Playground* and *St. Thomas This Week,* both of which are packed with visitor information, are distributed free all over the island.

Post Office The main post office is at 9846 Estate Thomas (© **340/774-1950**), Charlotte Amalie, open Monday through Friday from 7:30am to 5:30pm and Saturday from 7:30am to 2:30pm.

Rest Rooms You'll find public toilets at beaches and at the airport, but they are limited in town. Most visitors use the facilities of a bar or restaurant.

Safety St. Thomas has an unusually high crime rate, particularly in Charlotte Amalie. Don't wander around town at night, particularly on Back Street. Single women should avoid frequenting Charlotte Amalie's bars alone at night. Guard your valuables. Store them in hotel safes if possible, and make sure you keep your doors and windows shut at night.

Taxes The only local taxes are an 8% surcharge added to all hotel tariffs.

Taxis See "Getting Around," earlier in this chapter.

Telephone, Telex, & Fax All island phone numbers have seven digits. It is not necessary to use the 340 area code when dialing within St. Thomas. Numbers for all three islands, including St. John and St. Croix, are found in the U.S. Virgin Islands phone book. Hotels will send faxes and telexes for you, usually for a small service charge. Make long distance, international, and collect calls as you would on the U.S. mainland.

Transit Information Call © **340/774-7457** to order a taxi 24 hours a day. Call © **340/774-5100** for airport information and © **340/776-6282** for information about ferry departures for St. John.

Weather For weather reports, call Vietema at © **340/774-2244**.

Building, seat of the elected government of the U.S. Virgin Islands, lies on the harbor side of the fort.

Kongens Gade (or King's Street) leads to **Government Hill,** which overlooks the town and St. Thomas Harbor. **Government House,** a white brick building dating from 1867, stands atop the hill.

Between **Hotel 1829** (a mansion built that year by a French sea captain) and Government House is a staircase known as the **Street of 99 Steps.** Actually, someone miscounted: It should be called the Street of 103 Steps. Regardless, the steps lead to the summit of Government Hill.

Close by are the remains of the 17th-century **Fort Skytsborg,** also known as Blackbeard's Tower. The notorious 18th-century pirate is said to have spied from here on galleons approaching the harbor.

Blackbeard's Tower should not be confused with **Bluebeard's Tower,** which crowns a 300-foot hill at the eastern edge of town. This is the site of the best-known (but not the best) hotel in the Virgin Islands, Bluebeard's Castle.

OUTLYING NEIGHBORHOODS
The most important of the outlying neighborhoods is **Frenchtown.** Some of the older islanders still speak a distinctive Norman-French dialect here. Because the heart of Charlotte Amalie is dangerous at night, Frenchtown, with its finer restaurants and interesting bars, has become the place to go after dark.

To reach Frenchtown, take Veterans Drive west of town along the Waterfront, turning left (shortly after passing the Windward Passage Hotel on your right) at the sign pointing to the Villa Olga.

The only other neighborhood worth mentioning is **Frenchman's Hill.** The Huguenots built many old stone villas here, and they open onto panoramic views of the town and its harbor.

2 Getting Around

BY BUS
St. Thomas has the best public transportation of any island in the U.S. chain. Buses, called **Vitrans,** leave from street-side stops in the center of Charlotte Amalie, fanning out east and west along all the most important highways. They run between 5:30am and 10:30pm daily, and you rarely have to wait more than 30 minutes during the day. A ride within Charlotte Amalie is 75¢; anywhere else, $1. The service is safe, efficient, and comfortable. For schedule and bus stop information, call ⓒ **340/774-5678.**

BY TAXI
Taxis are the major means of transportation on St. Thomas. They're not metered, but fares are controlled and widely posted; however, we still recommend that you negotiate a fare with the driver before you get into the car. A typical fare from Charlotte Amalie to Sapphire Beach is $10 per person. Surcharges from $1.50 to $2 are added after midnight. If you want to hire a taxi and a driver (who just might be a great tour guide) for a day, expect to pay about $30 for two passengers for 2 hours of sightseeing; each additional passenger pays $12. You'll pay $1 per bag for luggage. For 24-hour radio dispatch taxi service, call ⓒ **340/774-7457.**

Taxi vans transport 8 to 12 passengers to multiple destinations on the island. It's cheaper to take a van instead of a taxi if you're going between your hotel and the airport. The cost for luggage ranges from 50¢ to $1 per bag.

BY CAR
DRIVING RULES Always **drive on the left.** The speed limit is 20 m.p.h. in town, 35 m.p.h. outside town. Take extra caution when driving in St. Thomas, especially at night. Many roads are narrow, curvy, and poorly lit.

RENTING A CAR There is no tax on car rentals in the Virgin Islands. **Avis** (ⓒ **800/331-2112**), **Budget** (ⓒ **888/227-3359**), and **Hertz** (ⓒ **800/ 654-3001**) have offices at the airport in St. Thomas, but you can often save money by renting from a local agency, although vehicles sometimes aren't as well maintained. Try **Dependable Car Rental,** 3901 B Altona, behind the Bank of

Nova Scotia and the Medical Arts Complex (© **800/522-3076** or 340/774-2253), which will pick up prospective renters at the airport or their hotel. A final choice is the aptly named **Discount Car Rental,** 14 Content, outside the airport on the main highway (© **340/776-4858**), which grants drivers a 12% discount on rivals' rates. Their rates are usually among the most reasonable on the island, beginning at $46.95 per day in winter.

Warning: St. Thomas has a high accident rate. Visitors are not used to driving on the left, the hilly terrain shelters blind curves and entrance ramps, roads are narrow and poorly lit, and drivers often get behind the wheel after too many drinks. To be on the safe side, consider getting **collision-damage insurance,** which usually costs an extra $14 to $16 per day. Be aware that even with this insurance, you could still get hit with a whopping deductible: The Hertz deductible is the full value of the car; at Avis and Budget it's $250.

PARKING Because Charlotte Amalie is a labyrinth of congested one-way streets, don't try to drive within town looking for a parking spot. If you can't find a place to park along the waterfront (free), go to the sprawling lot to the east of Fort Christian, across from the Legislature Building. Parking fees are nominal here, and you can park your car and walk northwest toward Emancipation Park, or along the waterfront until you reach the shops and attractions.

ON FOOT

Trust us: This is the *only* way to explore the heart of Charlotte Amalie. All the major attractions and the main stores are within easy walking distance. However, other island attractions, like Coral World or Magens Bay, require a bus or taxi.

3 Accommodations

Nearly every beach on St. Thomas has its own hotel, and the island also has more quaint inns than anyplace else in the Caribbean. If you want to stay in St. Thomas on the cheap, consider staying at one of the guest houses in the Charlotte Amalie area. All the glittering, expensive properties lie in the East End. The choice of hotels in St. Thomas divides almost evenly between places to stay in Charlotte Amalie or the grand resorts along the East End that front the fabulous beaches. There are advantages and disadvantages to both, and your choice of where to stay becomes a matter of personal taste. If you're in St. Thomas for shopping (it is the shopping mecca of the Caribbean), and you want to be near the best stores, the widest choice of restaurants and bars, and nearly all the historic attractions, chances are you'll elect to stay in Charlotte Amalie. The downside is that you'll have to take a shuttle over to a good beach, a ride of no more than 10 to 15 minutes from most Charlotte Amalie properties. If you want the isolation of a resort but the convenience of easily reaching Charlotte Amalie, with its attractions and its shops, you can book into one of the Marriott properties directly to the east of Charlotte Amalie at Flamboyant Point and within relatively easy access.

If your dream is to arrive in St. Thomas and anchor yourself directly on a beach, then the East End is your best choice. All the properties here are grand resorts and have many attractions, including water sports, nightlife, and greater luxury. The downside is that if you don't want to take expensive transportation, or else drive along narrow, dark, and unfamiliar roads at night, you'll be resort-bound for the evening, as commutes to some of the island's best restaurants are difficult at night. You'll also have to spend time and money getting into Charlotte Amalie for shopping.

St. Thomas Hotels at a Glance

	Access for disabled	A/C in bedrooms	Child-care facilities	Children are welcome	Convention facilities	Credit cards accepted	Directly beside beach	Fitness facility	Golf course nearby	Live entertainment	Marina facilities	Restaurant & bar	Spa facilities	Swimming pool	Tennis courts	TV in bedroom	Water sports
Admiral's Inn		✓		✓					✓			✓			✓	✓	
Best Western Carib Beach Resort	✓	✓	✓	✓	✓	✓	✓	✓		✓		✓		✓	✓	✓	✓
Best Western Emerald Beach		✓	✓	✓		✓	✓	✓		✓		✓		✓	✓	✓	✓
Blackbeard's Castle		✓		✓		✓				✓		✓		✓		✓	
Bluebeard's Castle	✓	✓		✓	✓	✓		✓		✓		✓		✓	✓	✓	✓
Bolongo Beach Club	✓	✓	✓		✓	✓	✓				✓	✓	✓		✓	✓	✓
Bunkers Hill Hotel		✓		✓		✓										✓	
Danish Chalet Inn				✓		✓											
Elysian Beach Resort		✓		✓	✓	✓	✓	✓		✓		✓	✓	✓	✓	✓	✓
Galleon House		✓		✓								✓		✓			
Holiday Inn Windward Passage	✓	✓	✓	✓	✓	✓						✓		✓		✓	
Hotel 1829		✓		✓								✓		✓		✓	
Hotel Mafolie		✓			✓							✓		✓		✓	
Island Beachcomber		✓			✓							✓		✓		✓	
Island View Guesthouse		✓		✓		✓			✓			✓		✓			
Mariott Frenchman's	✓	✓	✓	✓	✓	✓	✓	✓		✓		✓		✓	✓	✓	✓
Mariott Morning Star	✓	✓	✓	✓	✓	✓	✓	✓		✓		✓		✓	✓	✓	✓
Pavilions and Pools	✓	✓		✓		✓	✓					✓		✓		✓	✓
Point Pleasant Resort	✓	✓		✓		✓	✓	✓	✓			✓		✓	✓	✓	✓
Renaissance Grand	✓	✓	✓	✓	✓	✓	✓	✓			✓	✓	✓	✓	✓	✓	✓
Ritz-Carlton	✓	✓	✓	✓	✓	✓	✓	✓	✓			✓		✓	✓	✓	✓
Secret Harbour	✓	✓	✓	✓		✓	✓	✓				✓		✓	✓	✓	✓
Villa Blanca		✓		✓								✓		✓			
Villa Santana		✓		✓								✓		✓			
Wyndham Sugar Bay	✓	✓	✓	✓	✓	✓	✓	✓				✓		✓	✓	✓	✓

The really bad news is that almost without exception the East End beachfront resorts are invariably expensive. If you want budget accommodations, or even some moderately priced inns, you'll have to stay close to Charlotte Amalie.

However, by their sheer patronage, most visitors to St. Thomas make the East End their choice. In spite of the high costs, these hotels attract by far the most customers who want the decadent resort life that is impossible at the smaller inns of Charlotte Amalie.

It's your choice. As one hotelier said to us, "That's why we print menus."

Remember that hotels in the Virgin Islands slash their prices in summer by 20% to 60%. Unless otherwise noted, the rates listed below do *not* include the 8% government tax.

CHARLOTTE AMALIE
EXPENSIVE

Best Western Emerald Beach ⚡ Its big draw? It's on a white sandy beach. Its major drawback? It lies just across from the busy airport, 4 miles to the west of Charlotte Amalie, to which it is linked by free shuttle service. As such it appeals to business people who find the East End properties such as the Marriott Resort too far away. Emerald Beach also attracts family vacationers as well, because it sits on one of the best beaches in St. Thomas. It's more of a resort hotel than its neighbors, Island Beachcomber and Carib Beach. All of the tastefully furnished bedrooms face the sands. Accommodations contain two double beds or one king bed, lovely bathrooms with marble tops, mirrored closets, and tropical plants. Each room opens onto its own patio or oceanfront balcony. All of the rooms here are of equal quality.

8070 Lindbergh Bay, St. Thomas, U.S.V.I. 00802. ☎ 800/233-4936 in the U.S., or 340/777-8800. Fax 340/776-3426. http://emeraldbeach.com. 90 units. Winter $189–$259 double; off-season $149–$199 double. Children under age 12 stay free in parents' room. AE, DC, MC, V. **Amenities:** Restaurant, bar; shuttle to town; fitness; pool; tennis court. *In room:* A/C, TV, coffeemaker, hair dryer; iron/ironing board.

Blackbeard's Castle ⚡ Once a private residence, this is now one of the most charming and atmospheric inns in the Virgin Islands, exceeding in romantic appeal its closest rival, Bluebeard's Castle (see below). Perched high on a hillside above the town, it lies at the site of a 1679 tower that the Danish governor ordered erected of chiseled stone. The tower served as a lookout for unfriendly ships, and legend says that Blackbeard himself lived in the tower half a century later. It's not located on the sands, and the nearest beach is a 10-minute taxi ride

---

Tips Renting a Condo, Apartment, or Villa

Sometimes you can make a deal on a moderately priced condo, apartment, or villa. We've found that **Calypso Realty** (☎ **800/747-4858** or 340/774-1620; www.CalypsoRealty.com), has the best offers, especially on rentals from April to mid-December. A condo overlooking St. John often goes for $350 and more per week.

Another source to check is **McLaughlin Anderson Vacations Ltd.** (☎ **800/666-6246** or 340/776-0635; www.mclaughlinanderson.com), which has rentals not only on St. Thomas but also on St. John and St. Croix. A one-bedroom villa begins at $1,285 per week in winter, with off-season rates at $985.

You can also contact **Paradise Properties** of St. Thomas (☎ **800/524-2038** or 340/779-1540; fax 340/779-6109; www.st-thomas.com/paradiseproperties), which currently represents six condo complexes. Rental units range from studio apartments to four-bedroom villas suitable for up to eight people; each has a fully equipped kitchen. A minimum stay of 3 days is required in any season, and 7 nights around Christmas. The prices range from $220 to $395 per day in winter and from $175 to $325 per day in the off-season.

Antilles Resorts (☎ **340/775-2600**; fax 340/775-5901; www.antillesresorts.com) enjoys a repeat business of some 60%. Among other offerings, it rents condo suites featuring private balconies with ocean views, a short walk from the beach.

away (you can rely on cabs if you don't want to rent a car). Most of the well-furnished bedrooms and all of the suites are spacious. The garden rooms are much smaller and have no balconies, though they're located near a private pool area; travelers on a budget might choose these. Accommodations are decorated with tile floors or dark wood, with much use made of Caribbean mahogany furnishings. Each unit is equipped with a well-maintained shower bathroom.

Blackbeard's Hill (P.O. Box 6227), Charlotte Amalie, St. Thomas, U.S.V.I. 00801. ✆ 800/344-5771 in the U.S., or 340/776-1234. Fax 340/776-4321. www.blackbeardscastle.com. 16 units. Winter $125 garden room; $205–$235 balcony or junior suite. Off-season $95 garden room; $135–$160 balcony or junior suite. AE, MC, V. **Amenities:** Restaurant (see "Dining" below), bar; pool. *In room:* A/C, TV, minibar.

Bluebeard's Castle ⚑ This is a popular resort set on the side of the bay overlooking Charlotte Amalie (it's not on a beach, but it offers free shuttle service to Magens Bay). It was once the island's number-one hotel, but it's long been surpassed by newer, more deluxe East End resorts, such as the Ritz-Carlton. The hill surrounding the hotel is now heavily built up with everything from offices to time shares. The guest rooms come in a wide variety of shapes and sizes, all pleasantly but blandly decorated. Many units have a sitting room. Rooms are priced according to view. Standard rooms have no views, whereas deluxe units have a vista of both harbor and town. Some in-between units open onto the cruise-ship docks.

Bluebeard's Hill (P.O. Box 7480), Charlotte Amalie, St. Thomas, U.S.V.I. 00801. ✆ 800/524-6599 in the U.S., or 340/774-1600. Fax 340/774-5134. www.st-thomas.com. 170 units. Winter $195–$250 double. Off-season $140–$195 double. Extra person $35. AE, DC, DISC, MC, V. **Amenities:** 3 restaurants, bar; pool; 2 tennis courts; fitness center. *In room:* A/C, TV.

Holiday Inn St. Thomas ⚑ Even though its charm is not immediately visible, this modern, many-balconied hotel enjoys one of the highest rates of return bookings of any hotel on St. Thomas. It's especially favored by business travelers and sports teams, who are willing to forsake the atmosphere and charms found at "the Beards" (Bluebeard's and Blackbeard's Castles—see reviews above). Renovated in 1998, it's designed around a massive atrium, which is loaded with tropical plants and has a pleasant cafe and brasserie. The 54 harborfront rooms have views of some of the world's largest cruise ships, but are subject to noise from the busy waterfront boulevard. Many frequent visitors request a room overlooking the adjacent Emile Griffith Park, where baseball games, floodlit at night, provide entertainment. Even so, we still opt for the oceanview rooms in spite of the greater noise from traffic. Rooms are comfortably modern, with new mattresses, and each comes with a shower-only bathroom.

Veterans Drive, P.O. Box 640, St. Thomas, U.S.V.I. 00804. ✆ 800/524-7389 or 340/774-5200. Fax 340/774-1231. www.holidayinn.st-thomas.com. 151 units. Winter $175–$195 double, $215–$295 junior suite. Off-season $130–$160 double, $195–$220 junior suite. Rates include continental breakfast. AE, DC, DISC, MC, V. Free parking. **Amenities:** Brasserie, cafe, bar; pool; exercise room; dive shop; massage; salon; car rentals; shuttle to Magens Bay Beach; room service; laundry/dry cleaning; baby-sitting. *In room:* A/C, TV, coffeemaker, fridge, hair dryer, safe, iron/ironing board.

MODERATE

Best Western Carib Beach Resort This Best Western hotel is recommendable for its location (only about a 3-minute walk from the good beach at Lindbergh Bay) and its affordable, air-conditioned, oceanview rooms with private terraces. It's not the fanciest place on the island, and it's not as good as Emerald Beach, another Best Western. The bedrooms are comfortable, but not large. Each has a refrigerator and one queen bed or two double beds (the mattresses

Charlotte Amalie Accommodations

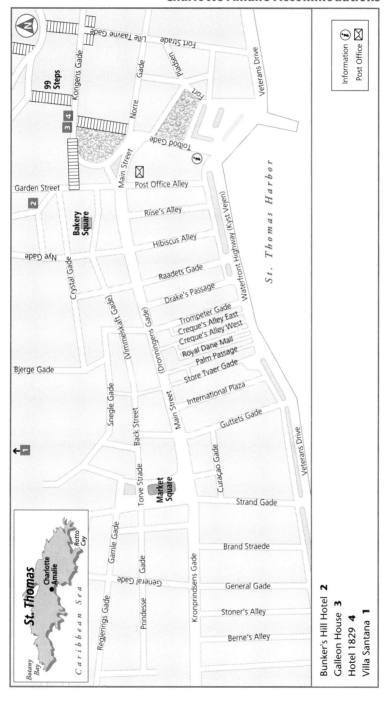

Information ⓘ
Post Office ⊠

99 Steps

Lille Taavne Gade
Fort Strade
Kongens Gade
Gade
Norre Gade
Toldbod Gade
Fort
Pladsen
Veterans Drive

Garden Street

St. Thomas Harbor

Main Street
Post Office Alley

Nye Gade

Bakery Square

Riise's Alley

Hibiscus Alley

Crystal Gade

Raadets Gade

Waterfront Highway (Kyst Vejen)

Drake's Passage

(Vimmelskaft Gade)

Trompeter Gade
Creque's Alley East
Creque's Alley West
Royal Dane Mall
Palm Passage
Store Tvaer Gade

(Dronningens Gade)

Bjerge Gade

International Plaza

Snegle Gade

Guttets Gade

Back Street

Main Street

Veterans Drive

Curaçao Gade

Torve Strade

Market Square

Strand Gade

Gamle Gade

Brand Straede

General Gade

Kronprindsens Gade

General Gade

Prindesse Gade

Regierings Gade

Stoner's Alley

Berne's Alley

St. Thomas

Botany Bay
Caribbean Sea
Charlotte Amalie
Hotto Cay

Bunker's Hill Hotel **2**
Galleon House **3**
Hotel 1829 **4**
Villa Santana **1**

are comfortable). This hotel is a favorite with business travelers, but is equally suitable for vacationers as well. The accommodations are housed in pink-and-blue concrete structures—one with two stories, the other with three—with five cottages closer to the sea. Ask for one of the "Sea Wing" bedrooms opening onto the ocean. We prefer rooms 207 to 216 (they're the best). Dinner is served only in winter; otherwise, guests are shuttled free to the Emerald Beach Resort.

70-C Lindbergh Bay, St. Thomas, U.S.V.I. 00801. © **800/792-2742** in the U.S., or 340/774-2525. Fax 340/777-4131. www.caribbeachresort.com. 66 units. Winter $135–$152 double. Off-season $95–$115 double. Children ages 11 and under stay free in parents' room. AE, MC, V. **Amenities:** Restaurant, bar; pool. *In room:* A/C, TV, coffeemaker, refrigerator.

Island Beachcomber Hotel *(Value)*   This rather standard hostelry near the airport is known for its affordable rates and its beautiful location near one of the island's best sandy beaches. Many guests are one-nighters staying over between yacht charters. A beach-party atmosphere prevails here, and there's also a Tahiti aura to the place, with its tropical foliage, birdcages, bridges, and thatched umbrellas. The bedrooms are clean and well maintained, although their furnishings are a bit worn. Rooms are medium in size, with louvered doors and jalousies, small refrigerators, excellent lighting, and ceiling fans, plus a patio or porch. The standard rooms contain two double beds, whereas superiors are fitted with single king-size beds; each has a fine and comfortable mattress and a bathroom with a good shower. Accommodations face either the garden or the beach, and naturally those opening onto the water are grabbed up first.

P.O. Box 302579, Lindbergh Bay, St. Thomas, U.S.V.I. 00803. © **800/982-9898** in the U.S., or 340/774-5250. Fax 340/774-5615. www.st-thomas.com/islandbeachcomber. 47 units. Winter $130–$145 double. Off-season $100–$115 double. Children $20 extra. AE, DC, DISC, MC, V. **Amenities:** Restaurant, bar; shuttle to town. *In room:* A/C, TV, refrigerator.

Hotel 1829 *✱*   This is one of the leading small hotels in the Caribbean. In charm and authenticity, it far exceeds the more commercialized Bluebeard's. Now a national historic site, the inn has serious island charm. It was designed by an Italian architect in a Spanish motif, with French grillwork, Danish bricks, and sturdy Dutch doors. Danish and African labor completed the structure in 1829 (hence the name), and since then it has entertained the likes of Edna St. Vincent Millay and Mikhail Baryshnikov. The place stands right in the heart of town, on a hillside 3 minutes from Government House. Magens Bay Beach is about a 15-minute drive or taxi ride away. It's a bit of a climb to the top of this multitiered structure—note that there are many steps but no elevator. Amid a cascade of flowering bougainvillea are the upper rooms, which overlook a central courtyard with a miniature pool. The rooms in the main house are well designed and attractive, and most face the water. All have old island decor, such as wood beams and stone walls, and each has small, tiled bathroom with shower stall. The smallest units, in the former slave quarters, are the least comfortable. Some guest rooms are four flights up, so be duly warned if you have a problem with stairs. When we stay here we always opt for one of the front bedrooms as they're the most scenic and spacious.

Kongens Gade (P.O. Box 1567), Charlotte Amalie, St. Thomas, U.S.V.I. 00804. © **800/524-2002** in the U.S., or 340/776-1829. Fax 340/776-4313. www.hotel1829.com. 15 units. Winter $110–$250 double; from $250 suite. Off-season $75–$145 double; from $170 suite. Rates include continental breakfast. AE, DISC, MC, V. **Amenities:** Restaurant; pool. *In room:* A/C, TV, minibar.

Villa Blanca *✱ (Value)*   Small, intimate, and charming, this hotel lies 1½ miles east of Charlotte Amalie on 3 secluded acres of hilltop land, among the most panoramic on the island, with views over the harbor and the green rolling hills. The hotel's main building served as the private home of its present owner, Blanca Terrasa Smith, between 1973 and 1985. After the death of her husband, Mrs. Smith added a 12-room annex in the garden and opened her grounds to paying guests. Today, a homey and caring ambience prevails. Each room contains tile floors, a ceiling fan and/or air-conditioning, a shower-only tiled bathroom, a well-equipped kitchenette, a good bed with a firm mattress, and a private balcony or terrace with sweeping views either eastward to St. John or westward to Puerto Rico and the harbor of Charlotte Amalie. No meals are served. On the premises are a freshwater pool and a large covered patio where you can enjoy the sunset. The closest beach is Morningstar Bay, about a 4-mile drive away.

4 Raphune Hill, Rte. 38, Charlotte Amalie, St. Thomas, U.S.V.I. 00801. ✆ **800/231-0034** in the U.S., or 340/776-0749. Fax 340/779-2661. www.st-thomas.com/villablanca. 14 units. Winter $125–$145 double. Off-season $75–$120 double. AE, DC, MC, V. **Amenities:** Pool. *In room:* Ceiling fan, TV. No phone.

Villa Santana ⋆   This unique country villa is an all-suite property and is more luxurious than its closest competitor, Villa Blanca (which is also good). It was originally built by General Antonio Lopez de Santa Anna of Mexico in the 1850s. It offers a panoramic view of Charlotte Amalie and the St. Thomas harbor. The shopping district in Charlotte Amalie is just a 5-minute walk away; Magens Beach is a 15-minute drive north. Guest rooms are located at La Mansion, the former library of the general; La Terraza, originally the wine cellar; La Cocina de Santa Anna, once the central kitchen for the entire estate; La Casa de Piedra, once the bedroom of the general's most trusted attaché; and La Torre, the old pump house, which has been converted into a modern lookout tower. All rooms have fully equipped kitchens, firm mattresses, ceiling fans, and tiled shower-only bathrooms. The Mexican decor features clay tiles, rattan furniture, and stonework. The property has a pool, sundeck, and small garden with hibiscus and bougainvillea.

Denmark Hill, St. Thomas, U.S.V.I. 00802. ✆ and fax **340/776-1311.** www.st-thomas.com/villasantana. E-mail: santana@islands.vi. 7 units. Winter $125–$195 suite for two. Off-season $85–$135 suite for two. AE, MC, V. **Amenities:** Pool. *In room:* Ceiling fan, TV.

INEXPENSIVE
The Admiral's Inn   This little inn is set on a peninsula in Frenchtown, near the western entrance to Charlotte Amalie's harbor, just a short walk from town. In former days it was both a bordello and the Russian embassy (not at the same time). It often attracts divers and other travelers who aren't too particular about where they spend the night. Although the Admiral's Inn has had its share of admirers, it still disappoints many readers, who complain about lack of security and a sometimes unhelpful staff. Motel-like accommodations contain one or two queen-size beds, plus dressing areas flanking well-maintained shower-only bathrooms. Some of the units also have a small refrigerator. The cheaper accommodations face the harbor and open onto balconies shared with other guests; the more expensive units have ocean views and more upmarket furnishings as well as private balconies. A saltwater beach and sea pool lie a few paces from the lanai-style oceanview units.

Villa Olga (P.O. Box 306162), Frenchtown, Charlotte Amalie, St. Thomas U.S.V.I. 00803. ✆ **800/423-0320** in the U.S., or 340/774-1376. Fax 340/774-8010. www.admirals-inn.com. 12 units. Winter $129–$159 double. Off-season $95–$115 double. Children ages 11 and under stay free in parents' room. Rates include continental breakfast. AE, DISC, MC, V. **Amenities:** Bar; pool. *In room:* A/C, TV.

Bunker Hill Hotel   We really only recommend this guest house if the others recommended below are fully booked (as is often the case). In this price range we'd stay at the Danish Chalet Inn (see below) if it has rooms available. Bunker Hill Hotel is not the safest district in St. Thomas, so caution is advised, especially at night. But this clean and centrally located guest lodge is suitable for anyone who will sacrifice some comfort (you'll have to put up with some street noise) for economy's sake. At this laid-back place, guests share a communal kitchen. Four rooms have balconies, and some offer a view of the lights of Charlotte Amalie and the sea. The furnishings are simple and often threadbare. Rooms are small, and mattresses are well worn; they seem like they came from a dormitory.

7 Commandant Gade, Charlotte Amalie, St. Thomas, U.S.V.I. 00802. ✆ **340/774-8056.** Fax 340/774-3172. www.st-thomas.com/bunkerhill. 18 units. Winter $90 double; $115 suite. Off-season $70 double; $95 suite. Rates include continental breakfast. AE, MC, V. **Amenities:** On-site deli. *In room:* A/C, TV, refrigerator.

Danish Chalet Inn   Set high above Charlotte Amalie on the western edge of the cruise-ship harbor, a 5-minute walk from the harborfront, this trio of buildings sits on a steeply inclined acre of land dotted with tropical shrubs and bougainvillea. The heart and soul of the place is the panoramic terrace, which has a 180° view over the cruise ships. The bedrooms are small but neat, clean, and colorful. All but two of the units contain air-conditioning. Much of this hotel's business stems from its willingness to accept one-night guests (many other small island hotels insist on bookings of several nights).

9E–9J Nordsidevej (Solberg Road) (P.O. Box 4319), Charlotte Amalie, St. Thomas, U.S.V.I. 00803. ✆ **800/635-1531** in the U.S., or 340/774-5764. Fax 340/777-4886. www.danishchalet-inn.com. 11 units, 6 with bathroom. Winter $79 single or double without bathroom, $89–$99 single or double with bathroom. Off-season $68 single or double without bathroom, $74–$88 single or double with bathroom. Extra person $15. Rates include a continental breakfast. MC, V. **Amenities:** Jacuzzi. *In room:* A/C (in some rooms), ceiling fan, refrigerator.

Galleon House   At the east end of Main Street, about a block from the main shopping area, Galleon House is reached after a difficult climb, especially in sweltering heat. Nevertheless, its rates are among the most competitive in town, if you don't mind a place operated without state-of-art maintenance and a staff attitude many readers have complained about. You walk up a long flight of stairs to reach a concrete terrace doubling as the reception area. The small rooms are scattered hillside buildings, each with a ceiling fan, a firm mattress, and so-so air-conditioning, plus a cramped shower-only bath. If you want character, check into the older rooms in the main building. More spacious units with better views lie up the hill in a pair of dull apartment buildings. If you check in, say hi to the iguanas for us. Breakfast is served on a veranda overlooking the harbor, and Magens Beach is 15 minutes by car or taxi from the hotel.

Government Hill (Pl. (P.O. Box 6577), Charlotte Amalie, St. Thomas, U.S.V.I. ✆ **800/524-2052** in the U.S., or 340/774-6952. Fax 340/774-6952. www.st-thomas.com/galleonhouse. 14 units, 12 with bathroom. Winter $79 double without bathroom; $99 double with bathroom. Off-season $59 double without bathroom, $89 double with bathroom. Rates include continental breakfast. AE, DISC, MC, V. **Amenities:** Pool. *In room:* A/C, TV, coffeemaker, hair dryer, refrigerator.

Hotel Mafolie   An old favorite, with plenty of fans and only a few detractors, the Mafolie enjoys a tranquil location with a panoramic view of the harbor (often filled with cruise ships). This sprawling guest house–type hotel—often called a family-style bunkhouse—is perched about 850 feet over Charlotte Amalie. The ambience is not the stuff of dreamy postcards, but the rooms are

St. Thomas Accommodations

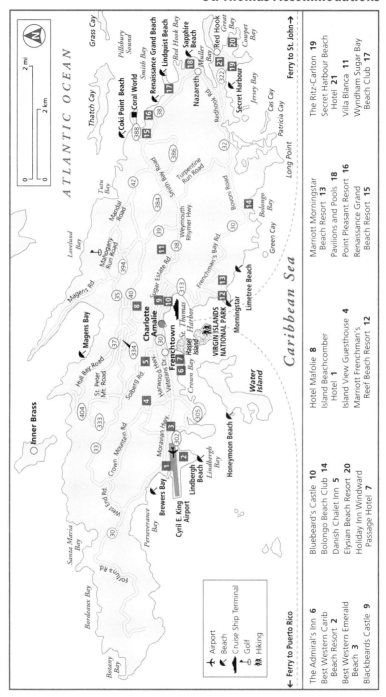

Ferry to St. John →

The Ritz-Carlton **19**
Secret Harbour Beach
  Hotel **21**
Villa Blanca **11**
Wyndham Sugar Bay
  Beach Club **17**

Marriott Morningstar
  Beach Resort **13**
Pavilions and Pools **18**
Point Pleasant Resort **16**
Renaissance Grand
  Beach Resort **15**

Hotel Mafolie **8**
Island Beachcomber
  Hotel **1**
Island View Guesthouse **4**
Marriott Frenchman's
  Reef Beach Resort **12**

Ferry to Puerto Rico ←

Bluebeard's Castle **10**
Bolongo Beach Club **14**
Danish Chalet Inn **5**
Elysian Beach Resort **20**
Holiday Inn Windward
  Passage Hotel **7**

The Admiral's Inn **6**
Best Western Carib
  Beach Resort **2**
Best Western Emerald
  Beach **3**
Blackbeards Castle **9**

79

comfortably furnished, though with a rather uninspired decor. Bathrooms are like those of a cheap mainland motel, with a set of thin towels and a shower stall. Some of the rooms are better than others—a trio offers private patios and a few open directly onto the pool. No. 7 is preferred.

7091 Estate Mafolie, Mafolie Hill, Charlotte Amalie, St. Thomas, U.S.V.I. 00802. © **800/225-7035** or 340/774-2790. Fax 340/774-4091. www.mafolie.com. 22 units. Winter $105–$115 double; $145 minisuite for up to four. Off-season $75–$80 double; $105 minisuite. Children ages 11 and under stay free in parents' room; children ages 12 and over $15 each. AE, MC, V. **Amenities:** Restaurant, bar; pool; shuttle to Magens Bay Beach. *In room:* A/C, TV, refrigerator.

Island View Guesthouse ⚑ (Value)   The casual Island View is located in a hilly neighborhood of private homes and villas about a 7-minute drive west of Charlotte Amalie and a 20-minute drive from the nearest beach at Magens Bay. Set 545 feet up Crown Mountain, it has sweeping views over Charlotte Amalie and the harbor. In its category, it makes previously recommended places such as the Galleon and Danish Chalet look like gone-to-seed properties. It contains main-floor rooms (two without private bathroom) and some poolside rooms. The most desirable rooms are the six luxe chambers recently added with panoramic balcony views and an interior that looks like a good motel room in Florida. All of these upmarket six rooms contain air-conditioning. Among the standard rooms opt for numbers 1 and 2 for the best vistas. If possible, avoid rooms 6 to 9 on the second level because they open onto the dining area. The bedrooms are cooled by breezes and fans, and the newer ones have air-conditioning. Each comes with a shower-only bathroom. Furnishings are very basic, but the price is right. A self-service, open-air bar on the gallery operates on the honor system. A terrace, with gorgeous views, is the site for breakfast each morning, and cocktails in the evening.

11-C Contant (P.O. Box 1903), Charlotte Amalie, St. Thomas, U.S.V.I. 00803. © **800/524-2023** for reservations only, or 340/774-4270. Fax 340/774-6167. www.st-thomas.com/islandviewguesthouse. 16 units (14 with private bathroom). Winter $77 double without bathroom; $110 double with bathroom; $115 suite. Off-season $55 double without bathroom; $80 double with bathroom; $90 suite. Rates include continental breakfast. AE, MC, V. From the airport, turn right onto Rte. 30; then cut left and continue to the unmarked Scott Free Rd., where you turn left; look for the sign. No children under age 15. **Amenities:** Pool. *In room:* Ceiling fan, TV.

FLAMBOYANT POINT
VERY EXPENSIVE

Marriott Frenchman's Reef Beach Resort ⚑⚑⚑   Lying 3 miles east of Charlotte Amalie on the south shore, this is the largest hotel in the U.S. Virgin Islands, but with the opening of the Ritz-Carlton it is no longer the plushest or most glamorous. The resort has an excellent location: on a bluff overlooking both the harbor and the Caribbean. This is a full-service, American-style megaresort; it's not suited to those seeking cozy island ambience. (Go to Hotel 1829 for that.) Everywhere you look are facilities devoted to the good life. To reach the private beach, for example, you take a glass-enclosed elevator. The bedrooms vary greatly, but in general are traditionally furnished and quite comfortable, though we find the rooms more luxurious at the hotel's neighbor, the Morning Star (see review below). Nonetheless, the accommodations here have all you'll need for comfort, and the bathrooms with combo tub and shower are generally spacious. All units have private balconies with sea views.

There is enough variety in dining to make a stay here intriguing even if you don't leave the premises at night. The cuisine has been much improved. In general, we prefer the seafood to the frozen meat imported from the U.S. mainland.

Estate Bakkeroe, Flamboyant Point (P.O. Box 7100), St. Thomas, U.S.V.I. 00801. © **800/524-2000** in the U.S., or 340/776-8500. Fax 340/776-3054. www.marriott.vi. 408 units. Winter $299–$395 double; $495–$575 suite. Off-season $250–$290 double; from $350 suite. MAP (breakfast and dinner) $45 per person extra. Ask about packages. AE, DC, DISC, MC, V. **Amenities:** 6 restaurants, 6 bars; spa; 4 tennis courts; fitness center; 2 pools; water-sports center; dive shop; Sunfish sailboats windsurfers; sauna; steam room; children's program; 24-hour room service; laundry; baby-sitting. *In room:* A/C, TV, dataport, minibar, coffeemaker, hair dryer, iron/ironing board.

Renaissance Grand Beach Resort ⭐⭐⭐   This resort, which occupies 34 acres on the northeast shore of St. Thomas, is perched on a steep hillside above a beautiful though small white-sand beach. In luxury it tops its two siblings (see above and below), but is outpaced by the Ritz-Carlton. Grand Beach has a friendlier layout and design than does one of its major competitors, Wyndham Sugar Bay Beach Club. The accommodations, all stylishly outfitted, are in seven two-story buildings designed like beach houses and staggered so that each unit has its own view. The Bougainvillea section is adjacent to the beach, and the units in the Hibiscus section are literally carved into the hillside. All rooms have quality mattresses, marble foyers, wall-to-wall carpeting, marble bathrooms with tubs and showers, robes, and private patios or balconies with views of the Caribbean. The two-story town-house suites and one- or two-bedroom suites have whirlpool spas. For better views, try to book in the 02 to 23 series of accommodations. This is a good family resort; trained counselors operate a free year-round children's program for ages 3 to 14.

Rte. 38, Smith Bay Rd. (P.O. Box 8267), St. Thomas, U.S.V.I. 00801. © **800/421-8181** in the U.S., or 340/775-1510. Fax 340/775-2185. www.renaissancehotels.com. 290 units. Winter $295–$345 double; $445 one-bedroom suite; $550 two-bedroom suite. Off-season $145–$210 double; $270 one-bedroom suite; $350 two-bedroom suite. MAP (breakfast and dinner) $50 per person extra. Ask about packages. AE, DC, DISC, MC, V. **Amenities:** 2 restaurants, 2 bars; 2 pools; 6 tennis courts; children's programs; water sports center; Sunfish sailboat; kayaks; windsurfers; deep-sea fishing; fitness center; sauna; steam room; spa services; 24-hour room service; laundry; baby-sitting. *In room:* A/C, TV, minibar, coffeemaker, hair dryer, iron/ironing board, safe.

Marriott Morning Star Beach Resort ⭐⭐⭐   Built right on white sands, this is the even better neighbor of the Frenchman's Reef Beach Resort. If you're a guest you can wander between the two properties, which gives you a broader range of restaurant choices and facilities than any other hotel on island can offer. Recently upgraded to the tune of $6 million, this beachside enclave has been enhanced with a striking new Caribbean decor. Both its public areas and its plushly outfitted accommodations are among the best on the island. Its five cottage-style buildings each contain between 16 and 24 units. Guests have the amenities and attractions of the large hotel nearby yet maintain the privacy of this more intimate property. Each unit has rattan furniture and views of the garden, beach, or the lights of Charlotte Amalie from your own veranda. Bedrooms are roomy and spacious, with fine furnishings and tasteful fabrics; the tiled bathrooms come with tub and shower combos.

#5 Estate Bakkeroe, Flamboyant Point (P.O. Box 7100), St. Thomas, U.S.V.I. 00801. © **800/524-2000** or 340/776-8500. Fax 340/776-3054. www.marriott.vi. 96 units. Winter $299–$395 double. Off-season $250–$290 double. MAP (breakfast and dinner) $45 per person extra. AE, DC, DISC, MC, V. **Amenities:** Shared with Frenchman's Reef (see above). *In room:* A/C, TV, dataport, minibar, coffeemaker, hair dryer.

The Ritz-Carlton ⭐⭐⭐   Fronted by white sand beaches, this is the toniest resort in all the U.S. Virgin Islands. To the other luxury hotels on the island, it can say, "Eat my dust." The chic Ritz-Carlton chain took over the Grand Palazzo, a 15-acre oceanfront estate at the island's eastern tip, 4½ miles southeast of Charlotte Amalie. The Ritz is set amid landscaped gardens, blending European elegance with Caribbean style. Bubbling fountains and hidden courtyards create the feel of a Mediterranean villa.

Accommodations are in half a dozen three-story villas designed with Italian Renaissance motifs and Mediterranean colors. Guests register in a reception palazzo, whose arches and accents were inspired by a Venetian palace. From the monogrammed bathrobes to the digital in-room safes, the accommodations here have more amenities than those at any other hotel on the island. They all have full marble bathrooms with fine toiletries, excellent-quality linens, and balconies. The least desirable units are those on the ground floor with only partial views. Service is up to usual high Ritz-Carlton standards.

The elegant dining room captures the best scenic views of Great Bay and St. John, and serves a refined and deluxe cuisine that's complemented by an excellent wine list.

Great Bay, St. Thomas, U.S.V.I. 00802. Ⓒ **800/241-3333** or 340/775-3333. Fax 340/775-4444. www.ritz carlton.com. 152 units. Winter $450–$520 double; $2,000 suite. Off-season $210–$370 double; $910 suite. Ask about packages. AE, DC, DISC, MC, V. **Amenities:** 3 restaurants, 3 bars; 3 tennis courts; fitness center; deep-sea fishing; 24-hour room service; massages; children's programs; baby-sitting. *In room:* A/C, TV, minibar, hair dryer, safe.

Wyndham Sugar Bay Beach Club ⚐   In the East End, a 5-minute ride from Red Hook, this hotel is much improved but still lags behind the Marriott sisters. It has panoramic views, although its secluded beach is really too small for a resort of this size. Many of the attractive rooms are decorated with rattan pieces and pastels, and they have roomy marble bathrooms with tub and shower combos.

After a recent $5 million renovation, guest rooms have new carpeting, furnishings, electronics, wall treatments, and rejuvenated plumbing. Although all the accommodations open onto balconies, some units are sans ocean view.

6500 Estate Smith Bay, St. Thomas, U.S.V.I. 00802. Ⓒ **800/WYNDHAM** in the U.S., or 340/777-7100. Fax 340/777-7200. www.wyndham.com. 230 units. All-inclusive rates: winter $535–$620 double; from $725 suite. Off-season $370–$445 double; from $565 suite. Rates include all meals, snacks, drinks, activities, tax, and service. AE, DC, MC, V. **Amenities:** Restaurant, bar; 3 pools; 2 tennis courts; fitness center; water sports; dive shop; children's club; baby-sitting. *In room:* A/C, TV, fax, dataport, fridge, coffeemaker, hair dryer, safe.

EXPENSIVE

Bolongo Beach Club ⚐ *Value*   This is an unpretentious, barefoot kind of place. You'll find a half-moon-shaped white-sand beach and a cluster of pink, two- and three-story buildings, plus some motel-like units closer to the sands. There's also a social center consisting of a smallish pool and a beachfront bar replete with palm fronds. Bolongo is a hangout sort of place, attracting those who shun the more formal Marriott properties and who would never check into a Ritz-Carlton. It's a relatively small property, but it offers all the facilities of a big resort. Many guests check in on the continental plan, which includes breakfast; others opt for all-inclusive plans that include all meals, drinks, a sailboat excursion to St. John, and use of scuba equipment. Rooms are simple, summery, and filled with unremarkable but comfortable furniture. Each unit has its own balcony or patio, a refrigerator, and one king or two double beds, plus tiled, shower-only bathrooms. Villas (that is, apartment-style condos with full kitchens) are in a three-story building, and all of those units have full kitchens. The best rooms to ask for are the oceanfront villas with full kitchens. Want to travel more frugally? Seek one of the accommodations in "Bayside Inn," the resort's budget annex.

7150 Bolongo, St. Thomas, U.S.V.I. 00802. ⓒ 800/524-4746 or 340/775-1800. Fax 340/775-3208. www.bolongo.com. 75 units, 20 villas. Winter $215 double with no meals; $480 all-inclusive double; $265 studio villa; $325 one-bedroom villa; $425 two-bedroom villa. Off-season $155 double with no meals; $425 all-inclusive double; $165–$190 studio villa, $175–$225 one-bedroom villa; $255–$265 two-bedroom villa. Ask about packages and various meal plans. AE, MC, V. **Amenities:** 2 restaurants, 2 bars; 3 pools; 2 tennis courts; fitness center; dive shop; boating; windsurfing; dock deep-sea fishing; baby-sitting. *In room:* A/C, TV, coffeemaker, hair dryer, refrigerator.

Elysian Beach Resort ⓐ   This time-share resort on Cowpet Bay in the East End, a 20-minute drive from Charlotte Amalie, is imbued a certain European Resort chic, although now outclassed by its next-door neighbor, the Ritz-Carlton. The beautiful white sand beach is the most compelling reason to stay here. Stay here if you seek tranquillity and seclusion without all the razzle-dazzle of other East End competitors, such as the Marriott trio. The thoughtfully planned bed-rooms contain balconies, and 14 offer sleeping lofts reached by a spiral staircase. The decor is tropical, with rattan and bamboo furnishings, ceiling fans, and natural-wood ceilings. The rooms are in a bevy of four-story buildings connected to landscaped gardens. Of the various units, 43 can be converted into one-bedroom suites, 43 into two-bedroom suites, and 11 into three-bedroom suites. Designer fabrics and white ceramic-tile floors make the tropical living quite grand. Try to avoid rooms in buildings V, W, X, Y, and Z as they are some distance from the beach. Each unit comes with a full tiled bathroom.

6800 Estate Nazareth, Cowpet Bay, St. Thomas, U.S.V.I. 00802. ⓒ 800/524-6599 or 340/775-1000. Fax 340/776-0910. www.where2stay.com. 180 units. Winter $275 double; $295 suite. Off-season $200 double; $225 suite. AE, DC, DISC, MC, V. **Amenities:** 2 restaurants, 2 bars; pool; tennis court; fitness center; snorkel gear; canoes; Sunfish sailboats; open-air shuttle to town; massage therapist; baby-sitting. *In room:* A/C, TV, some with kitchen.

Pavilions and Pools ⓐ   Ideal for a honeymoon, this resort lets you have your own villa with floor-to-ceiling glass doors opening onto your own private swimming pool. It's ideal for those who want to run around nude as Adam and Eve, Eve and Eve, or Adam and Adam. The resort, 7 miles east of Charlotte Amalie, is a string of condominium units, tastefully rebuilt and furnished. After checking in and following a wooden pathway to your attached villa, you don't have to see another soul until you leave, if you so wish—the fence and gate around your space are that high. Your swimming pool is encircled by a deck and plenty of tropical greenery. Inside, a room divider screens a full, well-equipped kitchen. The place is not posh, and an average good motel in the States will have better-quality furniture. The bathroom has an outdoor garden shower where you can rinse off after a swim or trip to the beach. The resort adjoins Sapphire Bay, which boasts one of the island's best beaches and many water sports concessions. Honeymooning couples should inquire about packages.

6400 Estate Smith Bay, St. Thomas, U.S.V.I. 00802. ⓒ 800/524-2001 or 340/775-6110. Fax 340/775-6110. www.pavilionsandpools.com. 25 units. Winter $270–$295 double. Off-season $197–$217 double. Rates include continental breakfast. AE, DISC, MC, V. **Amenities:** Restaurant; laundry; free snorkeling gear; pool; day sails. *In room:* A/C, TV, coffeemaker, kitchen, fridge, hair dryer, safe.

Point Pleasant Resort ⓐ   This is a very private, resort on Water Bay, on the northeastern tip of St. Thomas, a 5-minute walk from lovely Stouffer's Beach. It's a worthy competitor to Secret Harbour (see below), except the latter resort opens directly onto a beach. These condo units, which are rented when their owners are not in residence, are set on a 15-acre bluff with flowering shrubbery, century plants, frangipani trees, secluded nature trails, old rock formations, and lookout points. The villa-style accommodations have light and airy furnishings, mostly rattan and floral fabrics. Beds are very comfortable with fine linen and firm mattresses. Every unit has a full kitchen with a microwave. From your living room, you'll have a gorgeous view over Tortola, St. John, and Jost Van Dyke.

The restaurant, Agavé Terrace, is one of the finest on the island. The cuisine, featuring seafood, is a blend of nouvelle American dishes and Caribbean specialties. Local entertainment is provided several nights a week.

6600 Estate Smith Bay, St. Thomas, U.S.V.I. 00802. ℂ 800/777-1700 or 340/775-7200. Fax 340/776-5694. www.pointpleasantresort.com. 95 units. Winter $255–$285 junior or superior suite; $355 deluxe suite; $529 two-bedroom suite. Off-season $175–$195 junior or superior suite; $235 deluxe suite; $345 two-bedroom suite. Ask about package deals. Children under age 12 stay free in parents' room. AE, DC, DISC, MC, V. **Amenities:** 2 restaurants, bar; 3 pools; tennis courts; fitness center. *In room:* A/C, TV, kitchen, coffeemaker, hair dryer, iron/ironing board, safe.

Secret Harbour Beach Resort *Kids*   A favorite with honeymooners, this all-suite combo resort is on the stunning white-sand beach at Nazareth Bay, just outside Red Hook Marina. If you demand full resort activities, this secluded and tranquil haven is not for you—check into one of the Marriotts or Wyndham Sugar Bay. All four contemporary buildings have southwestern exposure (great for sunsets), and each unit has a private deck or patio and a full kitchen. You'll be just steps from the sand, and great snorkeling is right offshore. There are three types of accommodations: studio apartments with a bed/sitting-room area, patio, and dressing-room area; one-bedroom suites with a living/dining area, a separate bedroom, and a sundeck; and the most luxurious, a two-bedroom suite with two bathrooms and a private living room. The aforementioned honeymooners are most likely to show up in the winter months. In summer this is a family-friendly place, as children under the age of 12 stay free.

Kids Family-Friendly Hotels

Secret Harbour *(see p. 84)*   Children under age 12 stay free at this Nazareth Bay hotel. Many units have kitchenettes where families can prepare light meals. Beach facilities are right at your doorstep.

Renaissance Grand Beach Resort *(see p. 81)*   Special family rates and children's menus in the restaurants make this a good choice. Plus, baby-sitting can be arranged around the clock. The Kid's Club, offering a daily program of activities supervised by experienced counselors, operates year-round for kids ages 4 to 12.

Emerald Beach Resort *(see p. 73)*   In spite of its major drawback (it's located across from the airport), this family resort opens onto one of the best beaches on the island. It's a safe, friendly place for those with kids, and children under age 12 stay free in their parents' room. The price is right, too.

Island Beachcomber Hotel *(see p. 76)*   For the family on a budget, this hotel near the airport is appealing. It's not grand in any way, but it's clean and decent. Many of its rooms have two double beds, so families can double up. A beach party atmosphere prevails, and kids and their families find the place festive, if a little worn.

6280 Estate Nazareth, Nazareth Bay, St. Thomas, U.S.V.I. 00802. ⓒ **800/524-2250** or 340/775-6550. Fax 340/775-1501. http://secretharbourvi.com. 60 units. Winter $255–$295 studio double; $275–$355 one-bedroom suite; $465–$565 two-bedroom suite. Off-season $135–$195 studio double; $179–$225 one-bedroom suite; $279–$345 two-bedroom suite. Rates include continental breakfast. AE, MC, V. **Amenities:** Restaurant, bar; 4 tennis courts; fitness center; massage; dive shop; boat rentals; snorkeling; windsurfing; pool; Jacuzzi; baby-sitting; laundry/dry-cleaning, car-rental desk. *In room:* A/C, TV, kitchen, coffeemaker, hair dryer, safe, iron/ironing board.

4 Dining

The dining scene in St. Thomas these days is among the best in the West Indies, but it has its drawbacks. Fine dining (and even not-so-fine dining) tends to be expensive, and the best spots (with a few exceptions) are not right in Charlotte Amalie and can only be reached by taxi or car.

You'll find an eclectic mix of cuisines on St. Thomas, including American, Italian, Mexican, and Asian. We recommend digging into some of the local Caribbean dishes at least once or twice, especially the seafood specialties like "ole wife" and yellowtail, which are usually prepared with a spicy Creole mixture of peppers, onions, and tomatoes. The winner among native side dishes is *fungi* (pronounced *foon*-gee), made with okra and cornmeal. Most local restaurants serve johnnycake, a popular fried, unleavened bread.

CHARLOTTE AMALIE
EXPENSIVE
Beni Iguana's Sushi Bar ⓕ JAPANESE   It's the only Japanese restaurant on St. Thomas, a change of pace from the Caribbean, steak, and seafood choices nearby. Along with a handful of shops, it occupies the sheltered courtyard and an old cistern across from Emancipation Square Park. You can eat outside, or pass through wide Danish colonial doors into a red- and-black-lacquered interior devoted to a sushi bar and a handful of simple tables. A perennial favorite is the "13" roll, stuffed with spicy crabmeat, salmon, lettuce, cucumbers, and scallions.

In the Grand Hotel Court, Veteran's Dr. ⓒ **340/777-8744.** Reservations recommended. Sushi $5.50–$15 per portion (two pieces); main courses $8–$17; combo plates for four to five diners $25.50–$35.50 each. AE, MC, V. Daily 11:30am–10pm.

♦ Blackbeard Castle's Restaurant ⓕⓕ CONTINENTAL/ASIAN   "Tower dining" is enjoyed while taking in the most stunning view of the port of Charlotte Amalie. The castle's open-air tower has been turned into the setting for a romantic gourmet dinner. It is said that the pirate Blackbeard once kept watch for invaders from this tower. Chefs roam the world for inspiration and try to pack a lot of flavor into every dish without destroying an item's natural goodness. Try the pan-seared crab cake with an Asian vegetable slaw flavored with sesame dressing, or dig into the calamari and sweet potato chowder, which is flavored with basil and chili (how often do you see that on a menu?). Those old American favorites, such as filet mignon or stuffed Caribbean lobster, appear on the menu, but we gravitate more to the red snapper baked with nut crust.

You can also dine in the inn's regular restaurant, where a piano bar makes the evening special.

Blackbeard's Hill. ⓒ **340/776-1234.** Reservations needed 1 week in advance. Main courses $19–$45. AE, MC, V. Sun–Fri 11am–2pm; daily 5:30–10pm.

Hervé Restaurant & Wine Bar ⭐⭐ AMERICAN/CARIBBEAN/FRENCH
This is the hottest restaurant on St. Thomas, surpassing all the competition in town, including its next-door neighbor, Hotel 1829. A panoramic view of Charlotte Amalie and a historic setting are minor benefits—it's the cuisine that matters here. Hervé P. Chassin, whose experience has embraced such stellar properties as the Hotel du Cap d'Antibes, is a restaurateur with a vast classical background. Here in his own unpretentious setting, he offers high-quality food at reasonable prices.

There are two dining areas: a large open-air terrace and a more intimate wine room. Contemporary American dishes are served with the best of classic France, along with Caribbean touches. Start with the pistachio-encrusted Brie, shrimp in a stuffed crab shell, or conch fritters with mango chutney. From here, you can let your taste buds march boldly forward with red snapper poached with white wine, or a delectable black sesame–crusted tuna with a ginger-raspberry sauce. Well-prepared nightly specials of game, fish, and pasta are features. Desserts here are equally divine—you'll rarely taste a creamier crème caramel or a lighter, fluffier mango or raspberry cheesecake.

Government Hill (next to the Hotel 1829). ☎ **340/777-9703.** Reservations requested. Main courses $7.50–$16.50 at lunch, $15.50–$26 at dinner. AE, MC, V. Daily 11am–3pm and 6–10pm.

Hotel 1829 ⭐ CONTINENTAL   Hotel 1829 is graceful and historic, and its restaurant serves some of the finest food on St. Thomas. Guests head for the attractive bar for cocktails before being seated on a 19th-century terrace or in the main room, with walls made from ships' ballast and a floor crafted from 200-year-old Moroccan tiles. The cuisine has a distinctively European twist, with many dishes prepared and served from trolleys beside your table. This is one of the few places in town that serves the finest caviar; other appetizers include goat cheese bruschetta with roasted red pepper hummus. A ragoût of swordfish is made more inviting with pine nut–basil pesto, and the sautéed snapper in brown butter is always a reliable choice. Mint-flavored roast rack of lamb and Châteaubriand for two are other possibilities.

Kongens Gade (at the east end of Main St.). ☎ **340/776-1829.** Reservations recommended, but not accepted more than 1 day in advance. Main courses $17–$22. AE, DISC, MC, V. Daily 6–10pm.

Virgilio's ⭐ NORTHERN ITALIAN   This is the best northern Italian restaurant in the Virgin Islands. Virgilio's neobaroque interior is sheltered under heavy ceiling beams and brick vaulting. A well-trained staff attends to the tables. Owner Virgilio del Mare serves meals against a backdrop of stained-glass windows, crystal chandeliers, and soft Italian music. The *cinco peche* (clams, mussels, scallops, oysters, and crayfish simmered in a saffron broth) is a delectable house special, and the lobster ravioli here is the best there is. Classic dishes are served with a distinctive flair—the rack of lamb, for example, is filled with a porcini mushroom stuffing and glazed with a roasted garlic aïoli. The marinated grilled duck is served chilled. You can even order an individual pesto pizza.

18 Dronningens Gade (entrance on a narrow alley running between Main St. and Back St.). ☎ **340/776-4920.** Reservations recommended. Main courses $9–$25 at lunch, $12–$35 at dinner. AE, MC, V. Mon–Sat 11am–10:30pm.

MODERATE
Banana Tree Grille INTERNATIONAL   This place offers candlelit dinners, sweeping views over the busy harbor, and a decor that includes genuine banana

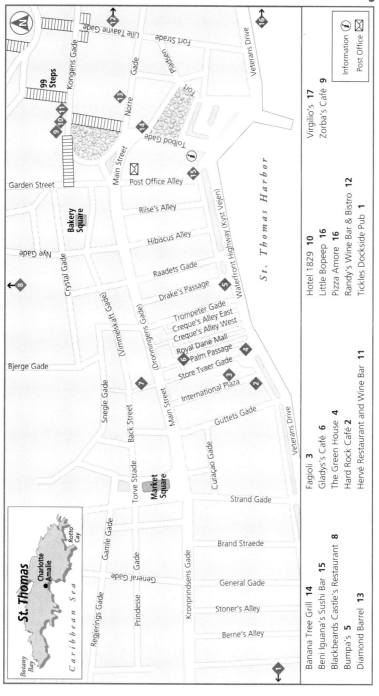

Information ⓘ

Post Office ⊠

Virgilio's **17**
Zorba's Café **9**

Hotel 1829 **10**
Little Bopeep **16**
Pizza Amore **16**
Randy's Wine Bar & Bistro **12**
Tickles Dockside Pub **1**

Hervé Restaurant and Wine Bar **11**

Fagioli **3**
Gladys's Café **6**
The Green House **4**
Hard Rock Café **2**

Banana Tree Grill **14**
Beni Iguana's Sushi Bar **15**
Blackbeards Castle's Restaurant **8**
Bumpa's **5**
Diamond Barrel **13**

St. Thomas Harbor

Waterfront Highway (Kyst Vejen)

Veterans Drive

99 Steps

Bakery Square

Market Square

St. Thomas

Charlotte Amalie

Caribbean Sea

Botany Bay

Rotto Cay

Post Office Alley
Riise's Alley
Hibiscus Alley
Raadets Gade
Drake's Passage
Trompeter Gade
Creque's Alley East
Creque's Alley West
Royal Dane Mall
Palm Passage
Store Tvaer Gade
International Plaza
Guttets Gade

Garden Street
Bjerge Gade

Main Street
Back Street

Snegle Gade
(Vimmelskaft Gade)
(Dronningens Gade)
Nye Gade
Crystal Gade

Kongens Gade
Lille Taavne Gade
Fort Strade
Norre Gade
Tolbod Gade

Veterans Drive

Curaçao Gade
Strand Gade
Brand Straede
General Gade
Stoner's Alley
Berne's Alley

Torve Strade
Gamle Gade
General Gade
Prindesse Gade
Regjerings Gade
Kronprindsens Gade

plants artfully scattered through the two dining rooms. The cuisine is creative, the patrons often hip and laid-back. Start off with one of the accurately named "fabulous firsts," such as tuna wontons with a zippy orange sambal sauce or bacon-wrapped horseradish shrimp grilled and dancing over a mango glaze. Main dishes are filled with flavor, especially the house specialties of sugarcane coco-lacquered tuna, lobster tail tempura with an orange sambal sauce, and the divine mango mustard-glazed salmon. Try the aïoli shank, a house specialty, if it's offered: The shank of lamb is slowly braised in Chianti and served with an aïoli sauce over white beans and garlic mashed potatoes. The desserts are truly decadent.

In Bluebeard's Castle Hotel, Bluebeard's Hill. ⓒ **340/776-4050.** Reservations recommended. Main courses $12.50–$24.75. AE, MC, V. Tues–Sun 6–9:30pm.

Fagioli ITALIAN   Set directly on the waterfront, in the heart of Charlotte Amalie, this is one of the most handsome and appealing new restaurants in town. You can take a seat in the open-air courtyard, one end of which has a view of the harbor; or within an air-conditioned dining room with dark wood and rows of exposed wine racks, creating a welcome feeling of Mediterranean intimacy. Menu items are firmly entrenched in the Italian tradition and include prosciutto with melon, carpaccio of beef, fettuccine with spinach and mozzarella, eggplant alla parmigiana, osso buco, and roasted lamb shank with either Marsala or white wine sauce. The house specialty dessert, tiramisu, is made fresh every day.

21 Dronningens Gade. ⓒ **340/777-8116.** Reservations recommended. Lunch main courses $9.95–$16.95; dinner main courses $14–$24. AE, MC, V. Mon–Sat 11:30am–3pm and 5:30–10pm.

The Green House AMERICAN/CARIBBEAN   Fronted with big sunny windows, this waterfront restaurant attracts cruise-ship passengers who have shopped and need a place to drop. The food here is not the island's best, but it's satisfying if you're not too demanding. Many diners drop in during the afternoon to sample one of the cook's tasty omelets, especially the Caribbean Creole three-egg concoction. The house specializes in chicken, often with exotic fruit flavors, such as mango banana chicken or coconut chicken. The excellent appetizers range from conch fritters to stuffed jalapeño peppers. A kettle of soup is always on the stove. You can also make a meal of the freshly made salads. The most popular item on the menu is the big, juicy burger made with certified Angus beef. There's also a wide selection of seafood, as well as such chef's specialties as baby back ribs. On Wednesday and Friday nights you can hear live reggae music here; on other nights the sounds are selected by a DJ.

Veterans Drive. ⓒ **340/774-7998.** Main courses $12–$25. AE, DISC, MC, V. Sun–Thurs 11am–10pm; Fri–Sat 11–1am.

• **Randy's Wine Bar & Bistro** *(Finds* CONTINENTAL   This is a local oddity, catering to deli devotees (usually from New York), cigar aficionados, and bistro fans. The on-site store sells a good selection of wines, along with the standard liquors and cigars. The deli serves the usual sandwiches and salads (some quite good), whereas the bistro dishes up a quite delectable cuisine. Look for one of the daily specials, such as pork tenderloin in a Dijon mustard sauce. At lunch you might want to try the portobello mushroom sandwich marinated in balsamic vinegar with a basil mayonnaise, or the Carnegie Reuben with half a pound of sliced meat enclosed within. For dinner, shrimp scampi is always a local favorite and understandably so. Tuesday night brings out the locals eager to sample the chef's prime rib.

In Al Cohen's Plaza, 4002 Raphune Hill. (C) **340/775-5001**. Main courses $14–$35; lunch $6.95–$12.95. AE, MC, V. Bistro daily 10–1am; deli daily 9am–5pm.

Zorba's Café GREEK   This is the place for Greek food. Jimmy Boukas is the owner of this casual, friendly establishment located in a 19th-century building in the heart of Charlotte Amalie. Guests can sit out on the courtyard surrounded by banana and palm trees. We highly recommend the Greek lemon chicken and the perfectly seasoned and tender Greek-style lamb shanks. Be sure to save room for the homemade baklava.

1854 Hus, Government Hill. (C) **340/776-0444**. Main courses $15–$25; lunch $8–$15. AE, MC, V. Mon–Sat 11am–3:30pm and 6–10pm; Sun 6–10pm.

INEXPENSIVE

● **Bumpa's** AMERICAN   This deli-style, open-air joint isn't that special, but it's an ideal choice for a good, filling, inexpensive breakfast or lunch. It's on the second level of a little old West Indian house with a canvas-roof porch offering a panoramic view of the harbor. The hordes of shoppers find this a favorite refueling stop. The cook prepares a fresh soup for lunch, and you can also get sandwiches and freshly made salads. Many patrons stop in just to order some ice cream, one of the homemade pies, or a refreshing lemonade on a hot day.

38-A Waterfront. (C) **340/776-5674**. Reservations not accepted. Main courses $4.50–$8. No credit cards. Daily 7am–5pm. Closed Sept.

Diamond Barrel AMERICAN/WEST INDIAN   This popular local eatery and hangout is active throughout the day. The decor (what there is of it) is appropriately nautical, with rattan pieces and murals of sea life. Breakfast is fairly standard fare, but at lunch you can sample some good regional dishes, including the catch of the day and various chicken dishes. You might begin with the oxtail soup or whatever's in the kettle that day. If you want to go really local, opt for the stewed mutton or the pickled pigs' feet, although you might settle more happily for the salmon patties. On-site is a bakery providing fresh pastries and other baked goods. Expect cafeteria-style service.

18 Norre Gade. (C) **340/774-5071**. Main courses $7–$13. Breakfast $3.50–$6.50. No credit cards. Daily 6am–5pm.

Gladys's Café ✦ (Finds) WEST INDIAN/AMERICAN   Antigua-born Gladys Isles is a warm, gracious woman who makes a visit here all the more special. Gladys's Café is housed in a 1700 pump house with a stonework courtyard that has a well (one of only three on the island) in the middle. The breakfast here is the best value in town. The lunch offerings are various sandwiches, salads, and fresh seafood, including an excellent swordfish and dumplings. The house specialty is the hot chicken salad made with pieces of sautéed breasts with red-wine vinegar, pine nuts, and dill, all nestled on a bed of lettuce. Dinner is served only on Friday, when a popular jazz band plays from 8pm to midnight. Try a local lobster, or else shrimp, fresh pasta, fresh fish, or steak.

Royal Dane Mall. (C) **340/774-6604**. Reservations required for parties of four or more. Main courses $7–$15; breakfast $3.50–$7.50. AE, MC, V. Mon–Thurs and Sat 7am–5pm, Fri 7am–11pm, Sun 8am–2pm.

Hard Rock Cafe AMERICAN   Go here if you must. Occupying the second floor of a pink-sided mall whose big windows overlook the ships moored in the harbor, this restaurant is a member of the international chain that defines itself as the Smithsonian of rock 'n' roll. Entire walls are devoted to the memorabilia of John Lennon, Eric Clapton, Bob Marley, and others. Throughout most of the day the place functions as a restaurant, serving barbecued meats, salads, sand-wiches, burgers (including a well-flavored veggie burger), fresh fish, steaks, and the best fajitas in the Virgin Islands. The hamburgers are good; as for the other stuff, you've had better versions. But the food is incidental to the good times people have here. On Friday and Saturday, a live band performs, at which time a small dance floor gets busy, and the bar trade picks up considerably.

In International Plaza, the Waterfront. (✆ **340/777-5555.** Main courses $9–$20. AE, MC, V. Mon–Sat 11am–11pm, Sun 10am–3pm.

Little Bopeep ⟨Value⟩ CARIBBEAN This plain little brick tavern serves up some of the best West Indian food on the island. No one puts on any airs here. Breakfast is strictly take-out, but it's the least expensive morning meal in town. You can order (to go) meat patties and sandwiches, such as egg, bacon, and cheese. Lunch gets more interesting and a lot spicier, with jerk chicken (a secret recipe), curried chicken, and curried conch. Fried plantains accompany most dishes.

Barber Plaza. (✆ **40/774-1959.** Reservations not accepted. Main courses $5.50–$13. Breakfast $3–$7. No credit cards. Mon–Sat 7:30–11am (take-out only) and 11:30am–4pm.

Pizza Amore PIZZA/SANDWICHES/SALADS This small pizzeria serves New York–style pizza with a wide range of toppings. You can also get salads and sandwiches—salami, ham, and heroes on French loaves. Round out your meal with an espresso and cappuccino.

18 Estate Thomas. (✆ **340/774-2822.** Meals $5–$23. No credit cards. Mon–Sat 9am–8pm, Sun 11am–5pm.

Tickles Dockside Pub AMERICAN This joint is dedicated to the concept of fun, comfort, and reasonably priced food in a friendly atmosphere. Diners at this open-air restaurant can sit back and relax while watching the sailboats and cruise ships on the water. The menu features a simple American fare of burgers (not as good as Hard Rock's), including a vegetarian burger, and sandwiches. The renowned Reuben is made with your choice of ham, turkey, or corned beef, grilled with Tickles's own special Russian dressing, Swiss cheese, and sauerkraut. Start off with a plate of "gator eggs" (lightly breaded jalapeño peppers stuffed with cheese) or "sweet lips" (strips of sweet, fried chicken served with a honey-mustard sauce). If you're in the mood for seafood, try the beer-battered white fish fried and served with Swiss-fried potatoes. The cooks also turn out an array of classic dishes found throughout America: chicken Alfredo, prime rib, baby back ribs, fried catfish, and a fisherman's platter served over pasta.

Crown Bay Marina. (✆ **340/776-1595.** Main courses $9–$23; lunch $7–$12. AE, DC, MC, V. Daily 7am–10:30pm.

AT FRENCHTOWN
MODERATE

Alexander's ⟨★⟩ AUSTRIAN/ITALIAN/SEAFOOD West of town, this restaurant offers 12 tables in air-conditioned comfort, with picture windows overlooking the harbor. There's a heavy emphasis on seafood, plus an increasing Italian slant to the menu. The bacon-wrapped chicken breast stuffed with spinach and Swiss cheese is prepared to perfection, as is the pan-seared herb-crusted lamb tenderloin with a mint port sauce. At lunch, you can enjoy mari-nated tuna steak or penne in a basil pesto cream sauce, or go for one of the sandwiches, such as a veggie burger. The top dish, however, is the seafood pasta

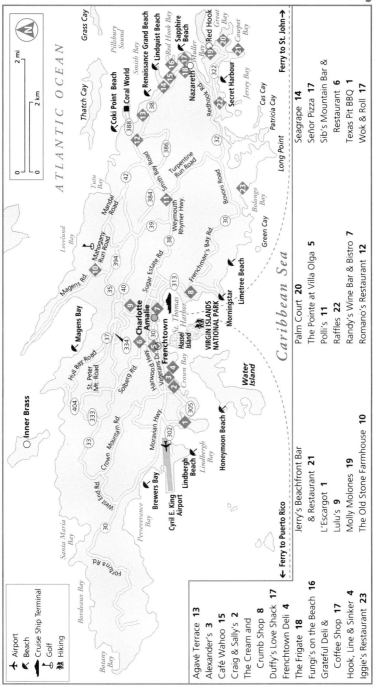

St. Thomas Dining

Map Legend:
- Airport
- Beach
- Cruise Ship Terminal
- Golf
- Hiking

Dining Listings:

Agavé Terrace **13**
Alexander's **3**
Café Wahoo **15**
Craig & Sally's **2**
The Cream and
  Crumb Shop **8**
Duffy's Love Shack **17**
Frenchtown Deli **4**
The Frigate **18**
Fungi's on the Beach **16**
Grateful Deli &
  Coffee Shop **17**
Hook, Line & Sinker **4**
Iggie's Restaurant **23**

Jerry's Beachfront Bar
  & Restaurant **21**
L'Escargot **1**
Lulu's **9**
Molly Molones **19**
The Old Stone Farmhouse **10**

Palm Court **20**
The Pointe at Villa Olga **5**
Polli's **11**
Raffles **22**
Randy's Wine Bar & Bistro **7**
Romano's Restaurant **12**

Seagrape **14**
Señor Pizza **17**
Sib's Mountain Bar &
  Restaurant **6**
Texas Pit BBQ **1**
Wok & Roll **17**

← Ferry to Puerto Rico

← Ferry to St. John →

Map labels:

ATLANTIC OCEAN

Caribbean Sea

Grass Cay
Bordeaux Bay
Botany Bay
Santa Maria Bay
Inner Brass
Brewers Bay
Magens Bay
Lindbergh Beach
Cyril E. King Airport
Honeymoon Beach
Water Island
Hassel Island
Charlotte Amalie
Frenchtown
Crown Bay
VIRGIN ISLANDS NATIONAL PARK
Morningstar
Limetree Beach
Coki Point Beach
Coral World
Renaissance Grand Beach
Lindquist Beach
Sapphire Beach
Red Hook
Great Bay
Coupet Bay
Secret Harbour
Jersey Bay
Cas Cay
Patricia Cay
Green Cay
Bolongo Bay
Long Point
Nazareth
Muller Bay
Redhook Bay
Smith Bay
Pillsbury Sound
Thatch Cay
Loveland Bay
Tutu Bay
Magens Bay

91

with an array of mussels, shrimp, clams, crab, and fresh fish. The vegetarian spring rolls are mouthwatering.

Rue de St. Barthélemy. ✆ **340/776-4211**. Reservations recommended. Main courses $10–$20 at lunch, $16–$24 at dinner. AE, MC, V. Mon–Sat 11:30am–3pm and 5:30–10pm.

Craig & Sally's ⊛ INTERNATIONAL This Caribbean cafe is set in an airy, open-sided pavilion in Frenchtown. Its eclectic cuisine is, according to the owner, "not for the faint of heart, but for the adventurous soul." Views of the sky and sea are complemented by a cuisine that ranges from pasta to seafood, with influences from Europe and Asia. Roast pork with clams, filet mignon with macadamia-nut sauce, and grilled swordfish with a sauce of fresh herbs and tomatoes are examples from a menu that changes every day. The lobster-stuffed, twice-baked potatoes are inspired. The wine list is the most extensive and sophisticated on St. Thomas.

22 Honduras. ✆ **340/777-9949**. Reservations recommended. Main courses $14.50–$35. AE, MC, V. Wed–Fri 11:30am–3pm; Wed–Sun 5:30–10pm.

The Pointe at Villa Olga STEAKS/SEAFOOD This upscale restaurant is known for serving the finest cut of prime rib on island. But it also features grilled seafood, which on occasion is even better. The stripped-down 19th-century villa that contains the Chart House was the Russian consulate during the island's Danish administration. It lies a short distance beyond the most densely populated area of Frenchtown village. The dining gallery is a spacious open terrace fronting the sea. Cocktails start daily at 5pm, when the bartender breaks out the ingredients for his special Bailey's banana colada. Calamari, pasta dishes, coconut shrimp, and Hawaiian chicken are part of the expanded menu. For dessert, order the famous mud pie.

Villa Olga. ✆ **340/774-4262**. Reservations recommended. Main courses $14–$35. AE, DC, DISC, MC, V. Daily 6–10pm.

Hook, Line & Sinker AMERICAN Both locals and visitors flock to this rendezvous, where they get friendly service, good food at reasonable prices, and a panoramic view of the harbor. The setting evokes a New England seaport village; the building has a pitched roof and skylights, along with wraparound French doors and windows. A *Cheers*-like crowd frequents the bar. Breakfast, except for Sunday brunch, is the standard old menu. Lunch choices range from a Caesar salad to various grilled chicken dishes. The dinner menu is usually a delight. The mango rum tuna is especially good. You can also order jerk swordfish and yellowtail stuffed with mushrooms and red peppers and covered in a garlic sauce. Locals call the hearty soups "outrageous."

2 Honduras, Frenchtown. ✆ **340/776-9708**. Main courses $9–$25; lunch $7–$12; Sun brunch $8–$14. AE, MC, V. Mon–Sat 8–10am, 11:30am–4pm, and 6–10pm; Sun 10am–2:30pm.

INEXPENSIVE

Frenchtown Deli DELI Some of the island's best and thickest sandwiches are served here, along with Frenchtown's best coffee. Most dinners are $14.95 for two people, making this the bargain of St. Thomas. House-baked breads, fresh salads, and beer, soda, and wine are also sold. You can eat your dinner on the premises or else take it out.

24A Honduras, Frenchtown Mall, between the harbor and the airport on the outskirts of Charlotte Amalie. ✆ **340/776-7211**. Meals $3.50–$14.95. AE, MC, V. Mon–Fri 6am–8pm, Sat 7am–6pm, Sun 8am–5pm.

SUB BASE

L'Escargot ✒ FRENCH/CARIBBEAN   This place has been in and out of fashion for so long it's a virtual island legend for its sheer endurance alone. One of the oldest restaurants on St. Thomas, it has been going strong for more than three decades. It also serves a first-rate cuisine. Its focal point is a low-slung semi-outdoor terrace with close-up views of Crown Bay Marina. Menu items include the standard repertoire of French dishes, including rack of lamb with rosemary sauce, scampi in pesto sauce with linguine, grilled swordfish with spicy mango sauce, onion soup, fresh mushroom salad, and chocolate mousse. Many dishes—changed daily—have Caribbean zest and flavor. The sautéed or steamed yellowtail is always perfectly prepared, and many local habitués opt for one of the grilled steaks along with plenty of tropical drinks, of course.

12 Sub Base. ✆ **340/774-6565.** Reservations recommended. Main courses $15–$24. AE, MC, V. Daily 11:30am–3pm and 6–10pm.

NEAR MAFOLIE HILL

Lulu's MEDITERRANEAN   This newly established restaurant doesn't necessarily have the best food on St. Thomas, but it's sure got the best view. Originally built in the 1950s on some of the island's highest terrain, it stands in an isolated but panoramic spot whose views sweep out over Magens Bay. Over the years various chefs and owners have experimented with different cuisines, before the present occupants decided to go trendy with "Mediterranean." Many guests prefer to arrive when the bar opens at 4pm to enjoy the greatest place in St. Thomas for sunset cocktails. By the time dinner is served, it's "Who cares?" Others more demanding come here for the cuisine, which is more familiar than imaginative but quite satisfying, especially the appetizer of crab cakes we had with an endive salad. Portobello mushrooms please the palate with fresh mozzarella. For a main course, most of the ingredients are imported but taste just fine in such dishes as sea bass with fresh herbs or an aromatically seasoned rack of lamb. Locals also demand filet mignon, and it remains forever on the menu.

Route 33, Crown Mountain Rd. ✆ **340/774-6800.** Reservations recommended. Main courses $13–$30. AE, MC, V. Tues–Sat 6–9:30pm. Bar Tues–Sat 4–11:30pm.

Sibs Mountain Bar & Restaurant AMERICAN   Sibs combines food with pool tables, electronic bar games, and an ongoing presentation of sports events. You can drink at the front bar or head out to the rear dining room, which offers an outdoor terrace and sweeping views of Charlotte Amalie. Menu items are generously proportioned and well seasoned and include burgers, some of the best ribs in St. Thomas, pastas, pizzas, and fresh fish.

Mafolie Hill. ✆ **340/774-8967.** Reservations not necessary. Main courses $8–$25. AE, MC, V. Daily 5–10pm; bar daily 4pm–4am.

COMPASS POINT

Raffles ✒ CONTINENTAL/SEAFOOD   Named after the legendary hotel in Singapore, this place is filled with South Seas accents. Peacock chairs and ceiling fans set the mood. We always look for the nightly specials, such as fresh West Indian–style fish (with tomato, garlic, and herbs)—although the regular menu is also enticing. Starters include sautéed conch and the lobster bisque. Everything is accompanied by homemade bread. The chef's excellent seafood pasta is loaded with shrimp, scallops, and mahi-mahi. The peanut chicken is a delight. One specialty rarely encountered in the Caribbean is beef Wellington in a delectable mushroom duxelle in puff pastry. The pièce de resistance is marinated duck, which is steamed, baked, and served with an orange ginger sauce.

6300 Frydenhoj, Compass Point, off Rte. 32 (1 mile west of Red Hook). (℗ **340/775-6004.** Reservations recommended. Main courses $16–$25. AE, MC, V. Mon–Fri 11:30am–2:30pm. Tues–Sun 5:30–10:30pm.

AT BOLONGO & COWPET BAYS

Iggie's Restaurant AMERICAN/CONTINENTAL   Sports fans and others patronize this action-packed seaside place. It's the island's best sports bar and grill, with giant TVs broadcasting the latest games. To make things even livelier, karaoke singalongs are staged. The place has "indestructible" furniture, lots of electronic action, and an aggressively informal crowd. Bring the kids along; no one will mind if they make a ruckus, and they can order such favorites as burgers, oversized sandwiches, and pastas. The menu changes nightly; there's often a theme, such as lobster night or Italian night. Most popular is carnival night, when a West Indian all-you-can-eat buffet is presented along with a limbo show. Call to find out what the theme is. Adults can order such tropical drinks as Iggie's Queen (coconut cream, crème de Noyaux, and rum) or the "Ultimate Kamikazi," the ingredients of which are a secret.

At the Bolongo Bay Beach Club, Bolongo Bay, 50 Estate Bolongo (Route 30). (℗ **340/775-1800.** Burgers and sandwiches $7.95–$9.95; main courses $11–$25. AE, MC, V. Daily 11:30am–11pm.

Jerry's Beachfront Bar & Restaurant ITALIAN/SEAFOOD   This is a refreshing and relaxing waterside and panoramic spot for a meal near the East End. The decor includes lots of exposed, very weathered wood, checked gingham tablecloths, and a large bar where nobody seems to mind dallying a bit before a table becomes available. The owners—veterans and survivors of several other popular waterfront eateries around the island—are proud of such specialties as seafood bisque, shrimp Sambuca, pasta bayou (in a creamy pink sauce, with andouille sausage, shrimp, and smoked Gouda), barbecued baby back ribs, and both red and white versions of conch and scampi.

In the Anchorage Condos (next to the St. Thomas Yacht Club), Cowpet Bay. (℗ **340/779-2462.** Reservations recommended in winter. Main courses $10–$18. Set-price menu $22.95. AE, MC, V. Daily 6–9:30pm.

(Finds On the Trail of a Good Barbecue

Locals will direct you to one of three locations for **Texas Pit BBQ:** at the Waterfront, at Red Hook, and Seabay. The owners brought their secret barbecue recipe from Texas, where they learned how to make a fiery sauce to wake up your palate—"and everything else," a habitué confided. These are mere take-out stands but are favored by yachties, St. Thomas cowboys, and frugal families. Chicken, tender ribs, or Texas-style beef are dished up in hearty portions, along with rice, coleslaw, and potato salad, each tasting homemade. One local pronounced these ribs the island's best, and so they are. The Waterfront joint is open Monday to Saturday 4 to 10pm, Red Hook Monday to Saturday 3 to 10pm, and Seabay Monday to Saturday noon to 6pm. For information, call (℗ **340/776-9579.**

EN ROUTE TO THE EAST END

Polli's TEX-MEX   This likable restaurant is set near a splashing fountain within a garden-style pavilion, without walls, that lies adjacent to a collection of arts and crafts boutiques. Its roster of frozen margaritas (try the golden margarita) is tailor-made as a preface to a savory Tex-Mex meal. Menu items include fajitas (made with your choice of beef, chicken, seafood, or tofu), burritos supreme, seafood enchilada platters, quesadillas, and some of the best-priced and juiciest steaks on the island. Children's plates, including tacos and cheese quesadillas or enchiladas, are also dished up, along with some juicy, smoked ribs with a fiery Texas barbecue sauce.

Tillet Gardens, 4125 Anna's Retreat, Route 38, midway between Red Hook and Charlotte Amalie. © **340/775-4550.** Reservations not necessary. Lunch main courses $6–$13.95; dinner main courses $8–$17. AE, DC, MC, V. Mon–Thurs 11:30am–9:30pm; Fri–Sat 11:30am–10:30pm.

IN & AROUND RED HOOK BAY (EAST END)
EXPENSIVE

Café Wahoo ⚓ ASIAN/CARIBBEAN   Diners enjoy an eclectic medley of specialties inspired by Asia, although the chefs concoct dishes using some of the freshest and finest ingredients of the West Indies. In an open-air dining near the American Yacht Harbor, close to the departure point for the ferry to St. John, the fresh catch of the day—hauled off the little fishing boats just pulling in—is delivered to the kitchen, where it's grilled to perfection. The yellowfin tuna keeps us coming back. The chef is also adept at preparing a tuna and salmon sushi platter. The blackened lobster is always a pure delight. The decor is rustic, with outdoor dining and wooden tables.

6300 Estate Smith Bay. © **340/775-6350.** Reservations required. Main courses $20–$25. AE, MC, V. Daily 5:30–10pm. Closed Sept 15–Oct 15.

The Frigate ⚓ AMERICAN/CARIBBEAN   In the center of Red Hook, within the Game Fishing Building, this seaside restaurant manages to secure some of the best beef in the U.S. islands as well as some of the freshest fish. As you dine overlooking the harbor at Red Hook and the island of St. John, your choice might be the fattest lobster caught that day or a steak on the level of The Palm in New York. Want something lighter? Make it chicken teriyaki. Hemingway clones opt for the grilled wahoo, and the surf-and-turf on the menu takes us back to the 1950s. The chefs amuse with a seafood kebab nightly. This is a spacious dining area with a nautical decor. Art on the walls—mainly seascapes—is for sale.

6501 Red Hook Plaza. © **340/775-6124.** Reservations not needed. Main courses $18–$30. AE, DC, MC, V. Daily 5:30–10:30pm.

Palm Court ⚓ INTERNATIONAL   When the shopping bazaars and the cruise-ship passengers flooding Charlotte Amalie have got you down, head here for a sylvan retreat. Palm Court offers cuisine, decor, and service that achieve a subtler European flare than anywhere else on St. Thomas. The breakfast plates are a great value. The place is also a lovely choice for a winter lunch, beginning with conch fritters and going on to one of the sandwiches such as the Caribbean club or else the Caribbean Reuben. There's always a pasta of the day prepared with imaginative flair or a fresh fish grilled to perfection. But at night the chefs really shine. From the mainland they ship in the finest New York strips or filet mignons, and you can always count on the rack of lamb. Even the routine baked half chicken is given added flair with the addition of the fresh pineapple sauce. Grilled red snapper and the delectable swordfish in a lemon and caper sauce are also good choices. The champagne Sunday brunch is one of the island's finest. But perhaps the best time to come here is for the Friday night Caribbean buffet, when a steel band entertains.

In Elysian Beach Resort, 6800 Estate Nazareth, Cowpet Bay. © **340/775-1000.** Reservations recommended. Main courses $16.95–$27.50; lunch $7.95–$13.95; Sun brunch $21.95 adults, $12.95 children. AE, DC, DISC, MC, V. Year-round Thurs–Sun 7:30–10:30am and 6:30–10pm; Dec–Apr also 11:30am–2:30pm.

MODERATE

Fungi's on the Beach CARIBBEAN   Opening onto Pineapple Beach, this is a funky native bar. It's a lot of fun, and the food is good, too. Come here for some of the juiciest burgers on island and the most delectable pizza. You can also order Caribbean specialties, such as conch in butter sauce and roast suckling, along with such island favorites as johnnycakes, plantains, rice and beans, and callaloo soup. Stewed chicken is a local favorite. The place has an outdoorsy atmosphere with a reggae theme. Nightly entertainment—reggae and more reggae—is also a feature.

Point Pleasant. © **340/775-4145.** Reservations not needed. Main courses $7–$20. AE, MC, V. Daily 11:30am–10pm.

Molly Molones IRISH/CARIBBEAN   At the Red Hook American Yacht Harbour, you can join the good ol' boys and dig into the best baby back ribs on island. If you're nostalgic for the Emerald Isle, go for the shepherd's pie. The conch fritters are also the best in the East End, and no one can drink more brew than the boisterous crowd who assembles here every night to let the good times roll. Launch yourself with a bowl of savory conch chowder, and the night is yours. In one of the wildest culinary offerings we've seen lately, an "Irish/Caribbean stew" is a nightly feature. If the catch netted a big wahoo, those game fish steaks will be on the menu that night at Molly's. You can dine outdoors under a canopy right on the dock at the eastern end of Red Hook, where the ferry from St. John pulls in.

6100 Red Hook Quarter. © **340/775-1270.** Reservations not needed. Main courses $15–$25. AE, MC, V. Daily 7am–2am.

INEXPENSIVE

Duffy's Love Shack ★ *(Finds)* AMERICAN/CARIBBEAN   This is a fun and happening place where you can mingle with the locals. As the evening wears on, the customers become the entertainment, often dancing on tables or forming conga lines. Yes, Duffy's also serves food, a standard American cuisine with Caribbean flair and flavor. The restaurant is open-air, with lots of bamboo and a thatched roof over the bar. Even the menu appears on a bamboo stick, like an old-fashioned fan. Start with a Caribbean egg roll or black-bean cakes, then move on to cowboy steak or voodoo pineapple chicken (in a hot garlic-and-pineapple sauce). Surf-and-turf here means jerk tenderloin and mahi-mahi. After 10pm, a late-night menu appears, mostly sandwiches. The bar business is huge, and the bartender is known for his lethal rum drinks.

650 Red Hook Plaza, Rte. 38. © **340/779-2080.** Main courses $9–$16. No credit cards. Daily 11:30am–2am.

Grateful Deli & Coffee Shop AMERICAN DELI   The breakfast menu at this affordable place isn't just of the usual dull ham 'n' eggs order, but includes such delectable offerings as "designer omelets" and glazed waffles served with

---

(Kids) Family-Friendly Restaurants

The Cream and Crumb Shop *(see p. 99)* This is an eternal favorite with kids, and not just because it serves the best pizza on St. Thomas. It also makes the best deli sandwiches, and its ice cream, cakes, and pastries are unsurpassed on the island.

Seagrape *(see p. 97)* Kids love dining at Sapphire Beach, where they can quickly choose from a special menu and then head out to the wide, sandy beach.

Texas Pit BBQ *(see p. 94)* Kids love barbecue, and all three different outlets of this restaurant make it better than anyone else. The owners brought their secret barbecue recipe from Texas. George W. tried it and went on to become president, so who knows?

Wok & Roll *(see p. 97)* For your family's "Chinese fix," head to this small and reasonably priced restaurant at Red Hook across from the ferry dock. Kiddie favorites include the spring rolls and the chow mein.

---

strawberries and whipped cream. Sometimes you can get low-cost regional fare here at lunch, including stewed chicken with rice or vegetable lasagna, or even pumpkin or black-bean soup. But most guests show up for one of the sandwiches, which are Red Hook's, or even the island's, finest—everything from Black Forest ham with Saga blue cheese to a triple-decker club with pastrami, corned beef, and Swiss cheese. Each day 12 different salads are made. You might also opt for the Greek pasta made with feta cheese, olives, and sweet peppers.

6500 Red Hook Plaza (across from the St. John ferry dock), Suite 125. (℃ 340/775-5160. Sandwiches and burgers $5.95–$9. AE, MC, V. Mon–Fri 7am–6pm, Sat 7am–5pm, Sun 8am–3pm.

Señor Pizza PIZZA Red Hook's best pizza is served here; each generous slice is practically a lunch all by itself. If you're staying nearby, the staff will deliver, or else you can settle into one of the on-site picnic tables. If you're not in the mood for pizza, try one of the tasty calzones.

Red Hook (across from the ferry dock). (℃ 340/775-3030. Pizza $2.50 (slice) to $18 (supreme). No credit cards. Mon–Sat 11am–9pm, Sun noon–8pm.

Wok & Roll CHINESE This small Chinese restaurant, below the Warehouse Bar, is housed in a cinder-block building with a blue roof, attracting a lot of families on a budget. A patio seats about 25 people, but the majority of the business is take-out. The restaurant serves typical Asian dishes, such as chow mein and sweet-and-sour pork, along with such specials as Shanghai spring rolls, shrimp in a lobster sauce, and Hong Kong lo mein. The famous dish at this place is the crab Rangoon, and it's worth a try.

6200 Smith Bay, Red Hook (across from the ferry dock). (℃ 340/775-6246. Main courses $5.50–$12. No credit cards. Mon–Thurs 11am–10pm, Fri–Sat 11am–10:30pm, Sun 5–10pm.

SAPPHIRE BEACH

Seagrape CONTINENTAL/AMERICAN This family favorite dining room along the eastern shore opens onto Sapphire Beach. But the sound of the waves and the light sea breezes that permeate the restaurant are only part of Seagrape's allure—the staff is well trained and the food first class. The day begins early here, with such delights as Belgian waffles. For lunch, you can savor the gazpacho or a teriyaki chicken breast sandwich. Kids enjoy it more during the day. It's more romantic in the evening, when you might begin with a smoked salmon pâté on a bed of field greens or else tenderloin carpaccio with a mustard and herb sauce. Ask your server about the day's ocean offering, which can be broiled, pan-fried, grilled, or blackened. A good choice is red snapper fra diablo, simmered in a spicy sauce. You can also dig into the crab cakes served with a tropical salsa and a Chinese pepper rémoulade. Meat eaters will find tender New York strip steaks or filet mignon. On Friday through Sunday, prime ribs are served in huge portions.

In the Sapphire Beach Resort and Marina, Route 6, Smith Bay Road ✆ **340/775-6100**. Reservations recommended. Main courses $12.95–$24.95; breakfast from $5.25, lunch from $9. AE, MC, V. Mon–Sat 7:30–10:30am, 11am–3pm, and 6–10pm; Sun 11am–3pm and 6–10pm.

NORTH COAST
EXPENSIVE

Agavé Terrace ⚑ CARIBBEAN   Perched high above a steep, heavily forested hillside on the eastern tip of St. Thomas, this restaurant, one of the island's best, offers a sweeping panorama and unparalleled romance. The house drink is Desmond Delight, a combination of Midori, rum, pineapple juice, and a secret ingredient. After a few Delights, you may opt for the house appetizer: an Agavé sampler prepared for two, which includes portions of crab meat, conch fritters, and shrimp cocktail. Six different fish usually turn up as catches of the day; they can be prepared in seven different ways, including grilled with a choice of nine different sauces. Some of the island's best steaks are served here, ranging from tenderloin to Kansas City strip. One dish after another delights, including red snapper with lobster medallions and jumbo prawns sautéed in a garlic cream sauce with linguine. All dinners are served with freshly baked breads and the house pasta or rice. There are also vegetarian selections. The wine list is extensive. A live steel drum band draws listeners Tuesday and Thursday nights.

Point Pleasant Resort, 6600 Estate Smith Bay. ✆ **340/775-4142**. Reservations recommended. Main courses $18–$40. AE, MC, V. Daily 6–10pm.

Romano's Restaurant ITALIAN   Located near Coral World, this hideaway is owned by New Jersey chef Tony Romano, who specializes in a flavor-filled and herb-laden cuisine that some diners yearn for after too much Caribbean cooking. House favorites include linguine con pesto, four-cheese lasagna, a tender and well-flavored osso buco, scaloppini Marsala, and broiled salmon. All desserts are made on the premises. The restaurant, marked by exposed brick and well-stocked wine racks, always seems full of happy, lively diners.

97 Smith Bay Rd. ✆ **340/775-0045**. Reservations recommended. Main courses $19–$30; pastas $14.95–$21. AE, MC, V. Mon–Sat 6–10:30pm. Closed Aug and 1 week in Apr for Carnival. Take the Vitran bus.

ON THE NORTH COAST

The Old Stone Farmhouse AMERICAN/INTERNATIONAL   Set in a wooden valley, close to the 11th hole of the Mahogany Run Golf Course, this restaurant dates from the 1750s. Once it was a stable for a nearby Danish sugar plantation, with walls more than 2 feet thick. Ceiling fans and breezes blowing through the valley keep the place cool. For more than a quarter of a century, it has been feeding golfers and those who love them from an eclectic menu that is rotated to take advantage of the best of a season's produce. Various fresh fish

Tips Picnic Fare & Where to Eat It

Because there are dozens of small restaurants and beachside cabanas sell-ing burgers and beer, many would-be picnickers tend to forgo the picnic basket in favor of a quick bite on the sand. But if you crave a real American-style picnic, consult the culinary experts at **The Cream and Crumb Shop,** Building 6, Havensight Mall (© **340/774-2499;** open 6:30am to 5pm), where most cruise ships dock. This cheerful, modern shop is easy to miss amid the cluster of tax-free jewelers and perfume stores. Its thickly layered deli sandwiches ($4.50–$7.50), fresh salads (shrimp, chicken, potato, or crab meat), and homemade pastries are all excellent options for take-out. The shop also specializes in pizza and serves frozen yogurt and ice cream. After stocking up, you can head for your favorite beach. We recommend Magens Bay Beach, not just for its beauty but for its picnic tables, too. Other ideal spots are Drake's Seat and any of the secluded high-altitude panoramas along the island's western end.

dishes still remain your best option. More innovative items, such as sushi, have been added to the menu. Begin, perhaps, with snails in garlic butter or some-thing trendier, such as grilled portobello mushrooms with roasted couscous. Many of the regulars come here for a well-prepared steak.

Mahogany Run. © **340/777-6277.** Reservations recommended. Main courses $16–$29. AE, DISC, MC, V. Tues–Sun 5:30–10pm.

5 Beaches

Chances are, your hotel will be right on the beach, or very close to one. All the beaches in the Virgin Islands are public, and most lie anywhere from 2 to 5 miles from Charlotte Amalie.

THE NORTH SIDE   The gorgeous white sands of **Magens Bay**—the family favorite of St. Thomas—lie between two mountains 3 miles north of the capi-tal. The turquoise waters here are calm and ideal for swimming, though the snorkeling isn't as good. The beach is no secret, and it's usually terribly over-crowded, though it gets better in the mid-afternoon. Changing facilities, snor-keling gear, lounge chairs, paddleboats, and kayaks are available. There is no public transportation to get here (though some hotels provide shuttle buses); from Charlotte Amalie, take Route 35 north all the way. The gates to the beach are open daily from 6am to 6pm (after 4pm, you'll need insect repellent). Admission is $1 per person and $1 per car. Don't bring valuables and certainly don't leave anything of value in your parked car. Break-ins of cars and a few iso-lated muggings are reported monthly.

A marked trail leads to **Little Magens Bay,** a separate, clothing-optional beach (especially popular with gay and lesbian visitors). This is also former pres-ident Clinton's preferred beach on St. Thomas (no, he doesn't go nude).

Coki Point Beach, in the northeast near Coral World, is good but often very crowded with both singles and families. It's noted for its warm, crystal-clear water, ideal for swimming and snorkeling (you'll see thousands of rainbow-hued fish swimming among the beautiful corals). Locals even sell small bags of fish food, so you can feed the sea creatures while you're snorkeling. From the beach,

Two Great Escapes

Water Island, a quarter mile off the coast from the harbor of Charlotte Amalie, is the fourth largest of the U.S. Virgins, with 500 acres of land. At palm-shaded **Honeymoon Beach,** you can swim, snorkel, sail, water-ski, or sunbathe, then order lunch or a drink from the beach bar. With a name like Honeymoon Beach, you know what to expect—loving couples. A ferry runs between Crown Bay Marina and Water Island several times a day. (Crown Bay Marina is part of the St. Thomas submarine base.) Water Island Ferry Service (© **340/690-8071**) leaves from Crown Bay Marina in St. Thomas, costing $3 one-way.

In the same bay, and even closer to shore, is **Hassel Island,** which is also favored by couples. It's almost completely deserted, and is protected as part of a national park. There are no hotels or services of any kind here, and swimming is limited to narrow, rocky beaches. Even so, many visitors hire a boat to drop them off for an hour or two. A hike along part of the shoreline is a welcome relief from the cruise-ship congestion of Charlotte Amalie. Bring water and food if you plan to spend more than 3 hours here. A ferry service at Crown Bay Marina makes the trip here as well.

there's a panoramic view of offshore Thatch Cay. Concessions can arrange everything from water-skiing to parasailing. An East End bus runs to Smith Bay and lets you off at the gate to Coral World and Coki. Watch out for pickpockets.

Also on the north side is luscious **Renaissance Grand Beach,** one of the island's most beautiful, attracting mainly families and couples. It opens onto Smith Bay and is near Coral World. Many water sports are available here. The beach is right off Route 38.

THE EAST END   Small and special, **Secret Harbour** is near a collection of condos and has long been favored by singles of either sex and by those of all sexual persuasions. With its white sand and coconut palms, it's the epitome of Caribbean charm. The snorkeling near the rocks is some of the best on the island. No public transportation stops here, but it's an easy taxi ride east of Charlotte Amalie heading toward Red Hook.

Sapphire Beach is set against the backdrop of the Doubletree Sapphire Beach Resort and Marina, where you can have lunch or order drinks. Like Magens Beach, this good, wide, safe beach is one of the most frequented by families. There are good views of offshore cays and St. John, a large reef is close to the shore, and windsurfers like this beach a lot. Snorkeling gear and lounge chairs can be rented. Take the East End bus from Charlotte Amalie, going via Red Hook. Ask to be let off at the entrance to Sapphire Bay; it's not too far to walk from here to the water.

White-sand **Lindquist Beach** isn't a long strip, but it's one of the island's prettiest. It's between Wyndham Sugar Bay Beach Club and the Sapphire Beach Resort. Many films and TV commercials have used this photogenic beach as a backdrop. It's not likely to be crowded, as it's not very well known, although many couples who know of this place retreat here for sun and romance.

THE SOUTH SIDE   Morning Star (also known as Frenchman's Bay Beach) is near the Marriott Frenchman's Reef Beach Resort, about 2 miles east of Charlotte Amalie. Here, among the often young crowds (many of whom are gay), you can don your skimpiest bikini. Sailboats, snorkeling equipment, and lounge chairs are available for rent. The beach is easily reached by a cliff-front elevator at Frenchman's Reef. The beach attracts mainly hip singles and savvy couples, as does **Limetree Beach,** set against a backdrop of seagrape trees and shady palms, lures those who want a serene spread of sand where they can bask in the sun and even feed hibiscus blossoms to iguanas. Snorkeling gear, lounge and beach chairs, towels, and drinks are available. There's no public transportation, but the beach can easily be reached by taxi from Charlotte Amalie.

WEST OF CHARLOTTE AMALIE   Near the University of the Virgin Islands in the southwest, **Brewer's Bay** is one of the island's most popular beaches for families. The strip of white coral sand is almost as long as the beach at Magens Bay. Unfortunately, this isn't the place for snorkeling. Vendors sell light meals and drinks. From Charlotte Amalie, take the Fortuna bus heading west; get off at the edge of Brewers Bay, across from the Reichhold Center.

Lindbergh Beach, with a lifeguard, rest rooms, and a bathhouse, lies at the Island Beachcomber Hotel and is used extensively by locals, who sometimes stage political rallies here as well as Carnival parties. Many beach-loving couples are also attracted to this beach. It's not good for snorkeling. Drinks are served on the beach. Take the Fortuna bus route west from Charlotte Amalie.

6 Sports & Outdoor Pursuits

DEEP-SEA FISHING   The U.S. Virgins have excellent deep-sea fishing—some 19 world records (8 for blue marlin) have been set in these waters in recent years. Outfitters abound at the major marinas like Red Hook. We recommend angling off the *Fish Hawk* (© **340/775-9058**), which Captain Al Petrosky sails out of Fish Hawk Marina Lagoon on the East End. His 43-foot diesel-powered craft is fully equipped with rods and reels. All equipment (but not meals) is included in the price: $500 per half day for up to six passengers. Full-day excursions start at $950.

Finds Hidden Beach Discoveries

At this point you'd think all the beaches of overrun St. Thomas had been destroyed. But there are two less trampled strands of sand we recently came upon. A sparkling beach of white sand, **Vessup Bay,** is found at the end of Bluebeard's Road (Route 322) as it branches off Route 30 near the hamlet of Red Hook. Against a rocky backdrop, the beach curves around a pristine bay studded with vegetation, including cacti, agave plants, and seagrape. One end of the beach is less populated than the other. A water sports concessionaire operates here. The beach is popular with singles and couples. Another find is **Hull Bay,** on the north shore, just west of Magens Bay, which is overpopulated these days with cruise-ship passengers. Surfers are attracted to the waves along the western tip of Hull Bay, and local St. Thomas fishermen anchor in the more tranquil strands. Part of the beach is in shade. Don't expect much in the way of water sports, but there is a combined restaurant and open-air bar.

Taking to the Seas

On St. Thomas most of the boat business centers around the Red Hook and Yacht Haven marinas.

The 50-foot *Yacht Nightwind,* Sapphire Marina (② **340/775-4110,** 24 hours a day), offers full-day sails to St. John and the outer islands. The $100 price includes continental breakfast, champagne buffet lunch, and an open bar aboard. You're also given free snorkeling equipment and instruction.

New Horizons, 6501 Red Hook Plaza, Suite 16, Red Hook (② **340/ 775-1171**), offers wind-borne excursions amid the cays and reefs of the Virgin Islands. The two-masted, 63-foot ketch has circumnavigated the globe and has been used as a design prototype for other boats. Owned and operated by Canadian Tim Krygsveld, it contains a hot-water shower, serves a specialty drink called a New Horizons Nooner (with a melon-liqueur base), and carries a complete line of snorkeling equipment for adults and children. A full-day excursion, with an Italian buffet lunch and an open bar, costs $100 per person ($55 for children ages 2 to 12). Excursions depart daily, weather permitting, from the Sapphire Beach Resort and Marina. Call ahead for reservations and information.

New Horizons has another vessel, *New Horizons II,* a 44-foot custom-made speedboat that takes you on a full-day trip to some of the most scenic highlights of the British Virgin Islands, costing $115 for adults or $95 for children ages 2 to 12.

You can avoid the crowds by sailing aboard the *Fantasy,* 6700 Sapphire Village, no. 253 (② **340/775-5652;** fax 340/775-6256), which departs from

FITNESS CENTERS   The most reasonably priced club on the island is the **Bayside Fitness Center,** 7140 Bolongo (② **340/693-2600**), part of the Bolongo Beach complex. The club offers weights, cardio, treadmills, and a sauna. The cost of a day pass is $12 for nonresidents; it's free to guests of the Bolongo complex. Hours are Monday to Friday from 6am to 9pm and Saturday and Sunday 8am to 5pm.

GOLF   **Mahogany Run,** on the North Shore at Mahogany Run Road (② **800/253-7103**) is an 18-hole, par-70 course. This beautiful course rises and drops like a roller coaster on its journey to the sea; cliffs and crashing sea waves are the ultimate hazards at the 13th and 14th holes. Greens fees are $100 for 18 holes, reduced to $90 in the late afternoon. Carts are included.

HORSE & PONY TOURS   **Half Moon Stables** (② **340/777-6088**) offers horse and pony tours of the East End. Riders go along a secluded trail that winds through lush, green hills to a pebble-covered beach. These hour-long guided tours are a great way to explore areas of the island rarely seen from tour buses or rental cars. The cost is $55 per person per hour. Western or English saddles are available.

KAYAK TOURS   **Virgin Island Ecotours** (② **340/779-2155** for information) offers 2½-hour kayak trips through a mangrove lagoon on the southern coastline. The cost is $50 per person. The tour is led by professional naturalists who allow enough time for 30 minutes of snorkeling.

the American Yacht Harbor at Red Hook at 9:30am daily. It takes a maximum of six passengers to St. John and nearby islands for swimming, snorkeling, beachcombing, and trolling. Snorkel gear with expert instruction is provided, as is a champagne lunch; an underwater camera is available. The full-day trip costs $100 per person. A half-day sail, morning or afternoon, lasts 3 hours and costs $65. Sunset tours are also popular, with an open bar and hors d'oeuvres, costing $50 per person.

American Yacht Harbor, Red Hook (© **800/736-7294** or 340/775-6454), offers both bareboat and fully crewed charters. It leaves from a colorful yacht-filled harbor set against a backdrop of Heritage Gade, a reproduction of a Caribbean village. The harbor is home to numerous boat companies, including day-trippers, fishing boats, and sailing charters. There are also four restaurants on the property, serving everything from continental to Caribbean cuisine.

Another reliable outfitter is **Charteryacht League,** at Flagship (© **800/ 524-2061** or 340/774-3944).

Sailors may want to check out the *Yachtsman's Guide to the Virgin Islands,* available at major marine outlets, at bookstores, through catalog merchandisers, or direct from **Tropic Isle Publishers,** P.O. Box 610938, North Miami, FL 33261-0938 (© **305/893-4277**). This annual guide, which costs $15.95, is supplemented by sketch charts, photographs, and landfall sketches and charts showing harbors and harbor entrances, anchorages, channels, and landmarks, plus information on preparations necessary for cruising the islands.

SCUBA DIVING & SNORKELING   With 30 spectacular reefs just off St. Thomas, the U.S. Virgin Islands have been rated one of the most beautiful areas in the world for scuba diving and snorkeling by *Skin Diver* magazine. For snorkeling, we like the waters off **Coki Point,** on the northeast shore of St. Thomas; especially enticing are the coral ledges near Coral World's underwater tower. **Magens Bay** also has great snorkeling year-round. For information on snorkeling cruises, see the box "Taking to the Seas," above.

The best dive site off St. Thomas, especially for novices, is **Cow and Calf Rocks,** off the southeast end (45 minutes from Charlotte Amalie by boat); here you'll discover a network of coral tunnels riddled with caves, reefs, and ancient boulders encrusted with coral. The *Cartanser Sr.,* a sunken World War II cargo ship that lies in about 35 feet of water, is beautifully encrusted with coral and now home to myriad colorful resident fish. Another popular wreck dive is the *Maj. General Rogers,* the stripped-down hull of a former Coast Guard cutter.

Experienced divers may want to dive at exposed sheer rock pinnacles like **Sail Rock** and **French Cap Pinnacle,** which are encrusted with hard and soft corals and frequented by lobsters and green and hawksbill turtles. They are also exposed to open-ocean currents that can make these very challenging dives.

St. Thomas Diving Club, 7147 Bolongo Bay (© **877/LETSDIVE** or 340/776-2381), is a full-service, PADI five-star IDC center, the best on the island. An open-water certification course, including four scuba dives, costs

---

⌒ *Moments* Under the Sea

If you really want to get to the bottom of it all, board the air-conditioned *Atlantis* submarine, which takes you on a 1-hour voyage (the whole experience is really 2 hours when you include transportation to and from the sub) to depths of 90 feet, where an amazing world of exotic marine life unfolds. You'll have up-close views of coral reefs and sponge gardens through the sub's 2-foot windows. *Atlantis* divers swim with the fish and bring them close to the windows for photos.

Passengers take a surface boat from the West Indies Dock, right outside Charlotte Amalie, to the submarine, which is near Buck Island (the St. Thomas version, not the more famous Buck Island near St. Croix). The fare is $72 for adults, $36 for ages 4 to 17; children ages 3 and under are not allowed. The *Atlantis* operates daily November through April, Tuesday through Saturday May through October. Reservations are a must (the sub carries only 30 passengers). For tickets, go to the Havensight shopping mall, building 6, or call ✆ **340/776-5650.**

$385. An advanced open-water certification course, including five dives that can be accomplished in 2 days, goes for $275. Every Thursday, participants are taken on an all-day scuba excursion that includes a two-tank dive to the wreck of the **HMS *Rhone*** in the British Virgin Islands; the trip costs $125. A scuba tour of the 350-foot wreck of the ***Witshoal*** is offered every Saturday for experienced divers only; the cost is $95. You can also enjoy local snorkeling for $35.

DIVE IN!, in the Sapphire Beach Resort and Marina, Smith Bay Road, Route 36 (✆ **800/524-2090** or 340/775-6100), is a well-recommended, complete diving center that offers some of the finest services in the U.S. Virgin Islands, including professional instruction (beginner to advanced), daily beach and boat dives, custom dive packages, underwater photography and videotapes, snorkeling trips, and a full-service PADI dive center. An introductory course costs $65, with a one-tank dive going for $62, two-tank dives for $75. A six-dive pass costs $203.

TENNIS The best tennis on the island is at the **Wyndham Sugar Bay Beach Club** ⚐, 6500 Estate Smith Bay (✆ **340/777-7100**), which has the Virgin Islands' first stadium tennis court, seating 220, plus six additional Laykold courts lit at night. The cost is $8 an hour. There's also a pro shop.

Another good resort for tennis is the **Bolongo Bay Beach Resort,** Bolongo Bay (✆ **340/775-1800**), which has two courts lit until 10pm. They're free to members and hotel guests, but cost $10 for nonguests.

Marriott Frenchman's Reef Tennis Courts, Flamboyant Point (✆ **340/776-8500,** ext. 444), has four courts. Again, nonguests are charged $8 per hour per court. Lights stay on until 10pm.

WINDSURFING This sport is available through the major resorts and at some public beaches, including Brewer's Bay, Morning Star Beach, and Limetree Beach. The **Renaissance Grand Beach Resort,** Smith Bay Road, Route 38 (✆ **340/775-1510**), is the major hotel offering windsurfing. It's available only to guests with no charge. You might want to stay here if you plan to do a lot of windsurfing.

Finds **Bringing Out the Sir Francis Drake in You**

Tired of escorted tours? **Nauti Nymph Powerboat Rentals,** American Yacht Harbor, Red Hook (© **800/734-7345** in the U.S., or 340/775-5066), reaches out to the independent traveler and adventurer. The knowing staff here will assist in designing your personal itinerary for a bareboat rental or can hook you up with a captained day trip. A choice of Coast Guard–approved and fully equipped vessels ranging in size from 25 to 29 feet await you as you become your own mariner. Boats are kept in top-of-the-line condition. On your own you can explore the British Virgin Islands, including such little-known islands as Jost van Dyke and Norman Island, the sea trail already having been blazed before you by Sir Francis Drake. Norman Island, incidentally, was the inspiration for Robert Louis Stevenson's *Treasure Island.*

7 Seeing the Sights

ATTRACTIONS IN CHARLOTTE AMALIE

The color and charm of the Caribbean come to life in the waterfront town of **Charlotte Amalie,** capital of St. Thomas, where most visitors begin their visit to the island. Seafarers from all over the globe used to flock to this old-world Danish town, as did pirates and sailors of the Confederacy, who used the port during the American Civil War. At one time, St. Thomas was the biggest slave market in the world.

Old warehouses, once used for storing stolen pirate goods, have been converted to shops. In fact, the main streets, called "Gade" (a reflection of their Danish heritage), now coalesce into a virtual shopping mall. The streets are often packed. Sandwiched among these shops are a few historic buildings, most of which can be seen on foot in about 2 hours. Try the walking tour below to visit the city's attractions.

Additionally, the **Paradise Point Tramway** (© **340/774-9809**) affords visitors a dramatic view of Charlotte Amalie harbor, with a ride to a 697-foot peak, although you'll pay dearly for the privilege. The tramway, similar to those used at ski resorts, operates four cars, each with a 10-person capacity, for the 15-minute round-trip ride. It transports customers from the Havensight area to Paradise Point, where they can disembark to visit shops and the popular restaurant and bar. The tramway runs daily from 9am to 5pm, costing $12 per adult round-trip, $6 for children.

American Caribbean Museum   The cultures of both America and the Caribbean are united in this museum, whose exhibits trace the history of the Virgin Islands from their volcanic beginnings through the Indian settlements and the "discovery" of the archipelago by Christopher Columbus. The museum traces Danish colonization of the islands; the transfer of the islands from Denmark to the United States under President Woodrow Wilson in 1917; and the impact of the American Revolution and the Civil War on the islands. Photographs show the landing of Charles Lindbergh in his plane *The Spirit of St. Louis* in 1928; the great aviator touched down at Mosquito Bay, whose name

---

Finds **A Thrilling Dive for Non-Divers**

Virgin Islands Snuba Excursions ((📞 **340/693-8063**) are ideal for beginning swimmers. These special excursions are offered both at Coral World on St. Thomas and Trunk Bay on St. John. With Snuba's equipment, even novices can breathe easily underwater without the use of heavy restrictive dive gear. The Snuba operations begin in waist-deep shallow water and make a gradual descent to a depth of 20 feet. It's fun for the entire family from ages 8 and up, and no snorkeling or scuba experience is needed. Most orientation and guided underwater tours take 1½ hours, costing $57 per person on St. John. On St. Thomas, a pass to Coral World is included, and the rate is $60 for adults and $57 for children under 12.

---

was later changed to Lindbergh Bay. Life-like historical figures are used to explain the history.

32 Raadets Gade (between Waterfront and Main Streets). 📞 **340/714-5150**. Admission $8 for adults, $4 for children. Daily 9am–3pm.

WALKING TOUR CHARLOTTE AMALIE

Start: King's Wharf.

Finish: Waterfront.

Time: 2½ hours.

Best Time: Before 10am to avoid cruise ship passengers.

Worst Time: Around midday to 4pm when traffic and pedestrians are at their most plentiful.

Begin your tour along the eastern harborfront at:

❶ King's Wharf

This is the site of the Virgin Islands Legislature, which is housed in the apple-green military barracks dating from 1874. From here walk away from the harbor up Fort Pladsen to:

❷ Fort Christian

The fort dates from 1672. Named after the Danish king Christian V, this structure was a governor's residence, police station, court, and jail until it became a national historic landmark in 1977. A museum here illuminates the island's history and culture. Cultural workshops and turn-of-the-century furnishings are just some of the exhibits you can expect to see. A museum shop features local crafts, maps, and prints. Fort Christian

(📞 **340/776-4566**) is open Monday through Friday from 8:30am to 4:30pm. Continue walking up Fort Pladsen to:

❸ Emancipation Park

This is where a proclamation freeing African slaves and indentured European servants was read on July 3, 1848. The park is now mostly a picnic area for local workers and visitors. Near the park is the:

● Grand Hotel

From here, a visitor center dispenses valuable travel information about the island. When this hotel was launched in 1837, it was indeed a grand address, but it later fell into decay, and finally closed in 1975. The former guest rooms upstairs have been turned into offices and a restaurant.

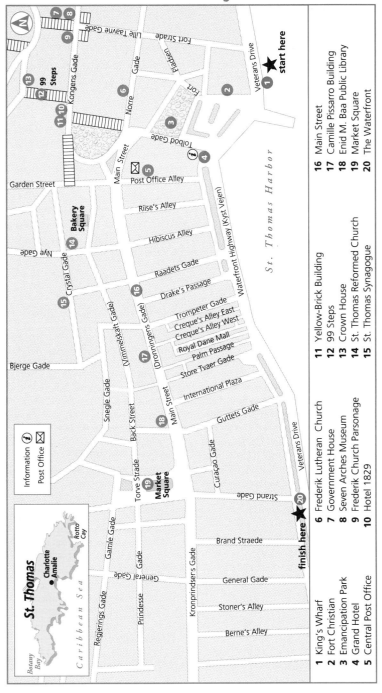

start here

99 Steps

Kongens Gade

Lille Taarne Gade

Fort Strade

Fort Strade

Pladsen

Fort

Veterans Drive

Norre Gade

Tolbod Gade

Main Street

Post Office Alley

Garden Street

Riise's Alley

Bakery Square

Hibiscus Alley

Nye Gade

Crystal Gade

Raadets Gade

Drake's Passage

Trompeter Gade

Creque's Alley East

Creque's Alley West

Royal Dane Mall

Palm Passage

Store Tvaer Gade

International Plaza

Guttets Gade

Bjerge Gade

Snegle Gade

(Vimmelskaft Gade)

(Dronningens Gade)

Back Street

Main Street

Curaçao Gade

Veterans Drive

Waterfront Highway (Kyst Vejen)

St. Thomas Harbor

Torve Strade

Market Square

Strand Gade

Gamle Gade

General Gade

Kronprindser's Gade

Prindesse Gade

Regierings Gade

finish here

Brand Straede

General Gade

Stoner's Alley

Berne's Alley

Information (i)

Post Office ⊠

St. Thomas

Charlotte Amalie

Botany Bay

Rotto Cay

Caribbean Sea

1 King's Wharf
2 Fort Christian
3 Emancipation Park
4 Grand Hotel
5 Central Post Office

6 Frederik Lutheran Church
7 Government House
8 Seven Arches Museum
9 Frederik Church Parsonage
10 Hotel 1829

11 Yellow-Brick Building
12 99 Steps
13 Crown House
14 St. Thomas Reformed Church
15 St. Thomas Synagogue

16 Main Street
17 Camille Pissarro Building
18 Enid M. Baa Public Library
19 Market Square
20 The Waterfront

Northwest of the park, at Main Street and Tolbod Gade, stands the:

⑤ Central Post Office

On display here are murals by Stephen Dohanos, who became famous as a *Saturday Evening Post* cover artist. From the post office, walk east along Norre Gade to the:

● Frederik Lutheran Church

This church was built between 1780 and 1793. The original Georgian-style building, financed by a free black parishioner, Jean Reeneaus, was reconstructed in 1825 and again in 1870 after it was damaged in a hurricane. Exiting the church, walk east along Norre Gade to Lille Taarne Gade. Turn left (north) and climb to Kongens Gade (King Street), passing through a neighborhood of law firms, to:

⑦ Government House

This is the administrative headquarters for the U.S. Virgin Islands. It's been the center of political life in the islands since it was built around the time of the American Civil War. Visitors are allowed on the first two floors, Monday through Saturday from 8am to noon and 1 to 5pm. Some paintings by former resident Camille Pissarro are on display, as are works by other St. Thomas artists. Turn left on Kongens Gade. After leaving Government House, turn immediately to your left and look for the sign for:

● Seven Arches Museum

Browsers and gapers love checking out this museum at Government Hill (© **340/774-9295**), the private home of longtime residents Philibert Fluck and Barbara Demaras. This 2-century-old Danish house has been completely restored and furnished with antiques. Walk through the yellow ballast arches into the Great Room, which has a great view of the Caribbean's busiest harbor. The $5 admission fee includes a cold tropical drink served in a beautiful walled flower garden. Open Tuesday through Sunday from 10am to 3pm, or by appointment.

After visiting the museum, return to Government House. Next to the building, is:

● Frederik Church Parsonage

This building dates from 1725; it's one of the oldest houses on the island. It's the only structure in the Government Hill district to retain its simple 18th-century lines.

Continue west along Kongens Gade until you reach:

① Hotel 1829

Formerly known as the Lavalette House, it was designed by one of the leading merchants of Charlotte Amalie. This is a landmark building and a charming hotel that has attracted many of the island's most famous visitors over the years.

TAKE A BREAK
Hotel 1829, Kongens Gade, provides the perfect veranda, with a spectacular view, for a midday drink or a sundowner. You may just fall in love with the place, abandon this tour, and stick around for dinner. The bar is open daily from 10am to midnight. (See "Dining," above.)

Next door (still on the same side of the street), observe the:

⑪ Yellow-Brick Building

This structure was built in 1854 in what local architects called "the style of Copenhagen." You can go inside and browse the many shops within.

At this point, you might want to double back slightly on Kongens Gade and climb the famous:

⑫ 99 Steps

These steps, which were erected in the early 1700s, take you to the summit of Government Hill, from where you'll see the 18th-century:

⑬ Crown House

The house is immediately to your right on the south side of the street. This stately private house was the home of von Scholten, the Danish ruler who issued the famous proclamation of emancipation in 1848 (see Emancipation Park, above).

Walk back down the steps and continue right (west) along Kongens Gade, then down a pair of old brick steps until you reach Garden Street. Go right (north) on Garden Street and take a left onto Crystal Gade. On your left, at the corner of Nye Gade and Crystal Gade, you'll see:

⑭ St. Thomas Reformed Church

This building dates from 1844. Much of its original structure, which was designed like a Greek temple, has been preserved intact.

Continue up Crystal Gade. On your right (north side), you'll come to:

⑮ St. Thomas Synagogue

This is the oldest synagogue in continuous use under the American flag and the second oldest in the Western Hemisphere. It was erected in 1833 by Sephardic Jews, and it still maintains the tradition of having sand on the floor, commemorating the exodus from Egypt. The structure was built of local stone along with ballast brick from Denmark and mortar made of molasses and sand. It's open to visitors from 9am to 4pm, Monday through Friday. Next door, the **Weibel Museum** showcases 300 years of Jewish history. It keeps the same hours.

Retrace your steps (east) to Raadets Gade and turn south toward the water, crossing the famous Vimmelskaft Gade or "Back Street" (it can get a bit seedy at night). Continue along Raadets Gade until you reach:

⑯ Main Street

This is Charlotte Amalie's major artery and most famous shopping street. Turn right (west) and walk along Main Street until you come to the mid–19th-century:

⑰ Camille Pissarro Building

The structure will be on your right, at the Amsterdam Sauer Jewelry Store. Pissarro, a Spanish Jew who became one of the founders of French Impressionism, was born in this building as Jacob Pizarro in 1830. Before moving to Paris, he worked for his father in a store along Main Street.

Continuing west along Main Street, you will pass on your right the:

⑱ Enid M. Baa Public Library

This building, formerly the von Bretton House, dates from 1818. Keep heading west until you reach:

⑲ Market Square

This was the center of a large slave-trading market before the 1848 emancipation. Today it's an open-air fruit and vegetable market, selling, among other items, *genips* (to eat one, break open the skin and suck the pulp off a pit). The wrought-iron roof covered a railway station at the turn of the century. The market is open Monday through Saturday, its busiest day.

If the genip doesn't satisfy you, take Strand Gade down (south) to:

⑳ The Waterfront

Also known as Kyst Vejen, this is where you can purchase a fresh coconut. One of the vendors here will whack off the top with a machete, so you can drink the sweet milk from its hull. Here you'll have an up-close preview of one of the most scenic harbors in the West Indies, though it's usually filled with cruise ships.

ATTRACTIONS IN THE WEST

Route 30 (Veterans Drive) will take you west of Charlotte Amalie to **Frenchtown.** (Turn left at the sign to The Admiral's Inn.) Early French-speaking settlers arrived on St. Thomas from St. Bart's after they were uprooted by the Swedes. Many island residents today are the direct descendants of those long-ago immigrants, who were known for speaking a distinctive French patois.

This colorful village contains a bevy of restaurants and taverns. Because Charlotte Amalie has become somewhat dangerous at night, Frenchtown has picked up its after-dark business and is the best spot for dancing, drinking, and other local entertainment.

Further west, Harwood Highway (Route 308) will lead you to **Crown Mountain Road,** a scenic drive opening onto the best views of the hills, beaches, and crystal-clear waters around St. Thomas. Eventually, you'll arrive at a popular pit stop called **Mountain Top,** Crown Mountain (© **340/774-2400**). This modern building has a restaurant and bar, plus eight shops. Most people come here to enjoy the view and sip the famous banana daiquiris—the bar here supposedly invented them in 1949! This is perhaps the most scenic perch in St. Thomas, featuring a view of Sir Francis Drake Channel, which separates the U.S. Virgin Islands from the British Virgin Islands. It's open daily 9am to 5pm.

CORAL WORLD & NEARBY ATTRACTIONS

Coral World Marine Park & Underwater Observatory ⟨ᴋ⟩   This marine complex, which is St. Thomas' number-one tourist attraction, features a three-story underwater observation tower 100 feet offshore. Inside, you'll see sponges, fish, coral, and other aquatic creatures in their natural state. An 80,000-gallon reef tank features exotic marine life of the Caribbean; another tank is devoted to sea predators, with circling sharks and giant moray eels. Activities include daily fish and shark feedings and exotic bird shows. The latest addition to the park is a semi-submarine that lets you enjoy the panoramic view and the "down under" feeling of a submarine without truly submerging.

Coral World's guests can take advantage of adjacent **Coki Beach** for snorkel rentals, scuba lessons, or simply swimming and relaxing. Lockers and showers are available. Also included in the marine park are the Tropical Terrace Restaurant, duty-free shops, and a nature trail.

6450 Coki Point, a 20-minute drive from Charlotte Amalie off Route 38. © **340/775-1555**. Admission $18 adults, $9 children ages 3–12. Daily 9am–5pm.

Estate St. Peter Greathouse Botanical Gardens   This estate consists of 11 acres set at the foot of volcanic peaks on the northern rim of the island. The grounds are laced with self-guided nature walks that will acquaint you with some 200 varieties of West Indian plants and trees, including an umbrella plant from Madagascar. From a panoramic deck in the gardens, you can see some 20 of the Virgin Islands, including Hans Lollick, an uninhabited island between Thatched Cay and Madahl Point. The house itself, filled with local art, is worth a visit.

At the corner of Rte. 40 (6A St. Peter Mountain Rd.) and Barrett Hill Rd. © **340/774-4999**. Admission $10 adults, $5 children ages 4–12 years. Daily 9am–4pm.

⟨*Moments* **Into the Deep for Nondivers**

For the first time nondivers can get some of the thrill long known to scuba aficionados by participating in **Sea Trek at the Coral World Marine Park & Underwater Observatory.** For $68 you can get a full immersion undersea with no experience needed. Participants are given a helmet and a tube to breathe through. The tube is attached to an air source at the observatory tower. You then enjoy a 200-yard, 20-minute stroll in water that's 18 feet deep. You're on the sea floor taking in the rainbow-hued tropical fish and the coral reefs as you go along. It's a marvelous way to get to experience the world as seen from the eyes of a fish.

⌒Kids Especially for Kids

Coral World *(see p. 110)*   This is *the* place on St. Thomas to take your children. It's a hands-on experience—kids can even shake hands with a starfish at the Touch Pond. Later they can discover exotic Marine Gardens, where 20 aquariums showcase the Caribbean's incredible natural marine treasures.

Magens Bay Beach *(see p. 112)*   This beach is one of the finest in the world, with calm waters, white sand, and lots of facilities, including picnic tables.

Atlantis Submarine *(see p. 104)*   Children are thrilled by this unique underwater adventure. Onboard, they'll dive to depths of up to 150 feet and see exotic fish, colorful sea gardens, coral formations, and unusual marine creatures. Children must be at least 4 years old.

EXCURSIONS

A driving tour is the best way to see the island; see the itinerary below for our suggestions. **Tropic Tours,** 14AB Estate Thomas (© **340/774-1855**), a representative of American Express, offers a rather dull tour of St. Thomas, including Mountain Top, Drake's Seat, and Charlotte Amalie shopping. The cost is $25 per person.

An even better option is a **day trip to St. John,** home of the world-famous Trunk Bay Beach. To get there, you can take one of the many ferry services. Boats depart from Charlotte Amalie or, more frequently, from Red Hook and arrive in St. John's Cruz Bay. The one-way fare is $3 for adults, $1 for children under age 11. Near the access ramp of the pier in Cruz Bay, you'll find rows of independently operated taxis and their drivers, who will take you on a tour of the island. A 2-hour guided tour costs about $30 per person for two passengers, or $12 per person for six passengers. If you want to skip the tour of St. John and head right to the beach at Trunk Bay for the day, simply negotiate a fare with one of the taxi drivers at the pier. Be sure to arrange a time to be picked up at the end of the day, too. The cost of a one-way trip is usually around $3 to $5 per person.

▊ DRIVING TOUR ▊ ST. THOMAS

Start: Fort Christian.
Finish: Magens Bay Beach.
Time: 2½ hours.
Best Time: Sunday, when traffic is lightest.
Worst Times: Wednesday and Saturday, when traffic is heaviest.

Begin at Fort Christian in the eastern part of Charlotte Amalie and head west along the waterfront. To your left you'll see cruise ships anchored offshore and to your right all the stores. Continue west on Route 30 and pass the Cyril E. King Airport on your left. As the road forks toward the airport, keep right along Route 30, which runs parallel to the airport.

At about 2.4 miles from Fort Christian on your right will be:

❶ The University of the Virgin Islands

This is the major university in the Virgin Islands. It's a modern complex with landscaped campus grounds. Continue west on Route 30 until you reach:

❷ Brewers Bay

The bay will be on your left. You may want to park and go for a swim, as this is one of the better beaches on the island.

Continue 3.8 miles west, climbing uphill through scrub country along a hilly drive past the junction with Route 301. This far west stretch of Route 30 is called:

❸ Fortuna Road

It's one of the most scenic areas of St. Thomas, with sweeping views of the water and offshore islands on your left. Along the way you'll come across parking areas where you can pull off and enjoy the view (the **Bethesda Hill vista** is particularly panoramic). The districts you pass through—Bonne Esperance and Perseverance—are named after the old plantations that once stood here. The area is now primarily residential. At Bordeaux Hill you descend sharply, and the road narrows until you come to a dead end.

At this point, turn around and head back east along Route 30. Be careful: The road is poorly marked at this point. At the junction with Route 301, turn left and head northeast. You will come to another junction at:

● Crown Mountain Road

This is the most scenic road in the Virgin Islands. Turn left here onto Route 33. The road will sweep northward before it makes an abrupt switch to the east. You will be traversing the mountainous heartland of St. Thomas. Expect hairpin turns during your descent. You'll often have to reduce your speed to 10 m.p.h., especially in the Mafolie district. The road will eventually lead to the junction with Route 37, where you should go left, but only for a short distance, until you reach the junction with Route 40. At one point Routes 37 and 40 become the same highway. When they separate, turn right and stay on Route 40 to:

❺ Drake's Seat

This is where Sir Francis Drake is said to have looked out over the sea and charted the best routes through the Virgin Islands. Continue left onto Route 35. The road will veer northwest. Follow it all the way to:

● Magens Bay Beach

Magens Bay is hailed as one of the most beautiful beaches in the world. Here you can rent Sunfish sailboats, glass-bottom paddleboats, and sailboards. Lounge chairs, changing facilities, showers, lockers, and picnic tables are also available.

WINDING DOWN
Magens Bay Bar and Grill, Magens Bay Beach (© 340/ 777-6270), is an ideal place for light meals on this heart-shaped beach. You can order sandwiches, salads, pizza by the slice, and soft drinks. Daily 9:30am to 5pm.

8 Shopping

The discounted, duty-free shopping in the Virgin Islands (see "Entry Requirements & Customs," in chapter 2) makes St. Thomas a shopping mecca. It's possible to find well-known brand names here at savings of up to 60% off mainland prices. But be warned—savings are not always so good. Make sure you know the price of the item back home to determine if you are truly getting a good deal. Having sounded that warning, we'll mention some St. Thomas shops where we have indeed found really good buys.

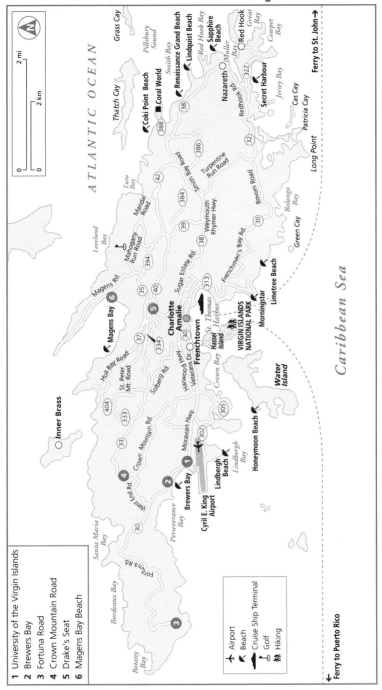

1 University of the Virgin Islands
2 Brewers Bay
3 Fortuna Road
4 Crown Mountain Road
5 Drake's Seat
6 Magens Bay Beach

Most shops, some of which occupy former pirate warehouses, are open Monday through Saturday from 9am to 5pm. Some stores are open Sunday and holidays if a cruise ship is in port.

SHOPPING DISTRICTS

Nearly all the major shopping in St. Thomas is along the harbor of Charlotte Amalie. Cruise-ship passengers mainly shop at the **Havensight Mall** at the eastern edge of Charlotte Amalie, where they disembark. The principal shopping street is **Main Street** or Dronningens Gade (its old Danish name). To the north is another merchandise-loaded street called **Back Street** or Vimmelskaft. Many shops are also spread along the **Waterfront Highway** (also called Kyst Vejen). Between these major streets is a series of side streets, walkways, and alleys—all filled with shops. Other shopping streets are Tolbod Gade, Raadets Gade, Royal Dane Mall, Palm Passage, Storetvaer Gade, and Strand Gade.

THE BEST BUYS & WHERE TO FIND THEM

The best buys on St. Thomas include china, crystal, perfumes, jewelry (especially emeralds), Haitian art, fashions, watches, and items made of wood. Cameras and electronic items, based on our experience, are not the good buys they're reputed to be. St. Thomas is also the best place in the Caribbean for discounts in porcelain, but remember that U.S. brands may often be purchased for 25% off the retail price on the mainland. Look for the imported patterns for the biggest savings.

It is illegal for most street vendors (food vendors are about the only exception) to ply their trades outside of the designated area called **Vendors Plaza,** at the corner of Veterans Drive and Tolbod Gade. Hundreds of vendors converge here at 7:30am; they usually pack up around 5:30pm, Monday through Saturday. (Very few hawk their wares on Sunday, unless a cruise ship is scheduled to arrive.)

When you tire of French perfumes and Swiss watches, head for **Market Square,** as it's called locally, or more formally, Rothschild Francis Square. Here under a Victorian tin roof, locals with machetes slice open fresh coconuts so you can drink the milk, and women wearing bandannas sell akee, cassava, or breadfruit.

Other noteworthy shopping districts include **Tillett Gardens,** a virtual oasis of arts and crafts—pottery, silk screen fabrics, candles, watercolors, jewelry, and more—located on the highway across from Four Winds Shopping Center. The Jim Tillett Gallery here is a major island attraction in itself (see listing below).

At **Mountain Top,** near the center of the island, there's also a modern shopping mall—a bit too tourist-tacky for us—that contains about eight shops; the views are much better than the merchandise.

All the major stores in St. Thomas are located by number on an excellent map in the center of the publication *St. Thomas This Week,* distributed free to all arriving plane and boat passengers and available at the visitor center. A lot of the stores on the island don't have street numbers or don't display them, so look for their signs instead.

Tips Shopping Tip

Friday is the biggest cruise-ship visiting day at Charlotte Amalie (one time we counted eight ships at once), so try to avoid shopping then.

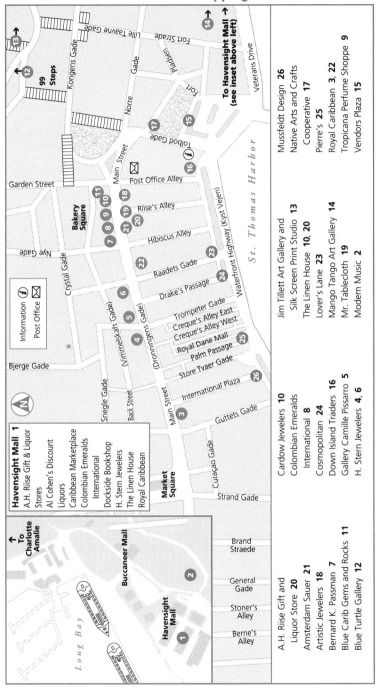

Havensight Mall **1**
A.H. Riise Gift & Liquor
Stores
Al Cohen's Discount
Liquors
Caribbean Marketplace
Colombian Emeralds
International
Dockside Bookshop
H. Stern Jewelers
The Linen House
Royal Caribbean

To
Charlotte
Amalie

Buccaneer Mall

Havensight
Mall

Long Bay

Market
Square

Bjerge Gade

Snegle Gade

Back Street

Main Street

International Plaza

Guttets Gade

Curaçao Gade

Strand Gade

Brand
Straede

General
Gade

Stoner's
Alley

Berne's
Alley

A.H. Riise Gift and
Liquor Store **20**
Amsterdam Sauer **21**
Artistic Jewelers **18**
Bernard K. Passman **7**
Blue Carib Gems and Rocks **11**
Blue Turtle Gallery **12**

Cardow Jewelers **10**
Colombian Emeralds
International **8**
Cosmopolitan **24**
Down Island Traders **16**
Gallery Camille Pissarro **5**
H. Stern Jewelers **4, 6**

Jim Tillett Art Gallery and
Silk Screen Print Studio **13**
The Linen House **10, 20**
Lover's Lane **23**
Mango Tango Art Gallery **14**
Mr. Tablecloth **19**
Modern Music **2**

Mussfeldt Design **26**
Native Arts and Crafts
Cooperative **17**
Pierre's **25**
Royal Caribbean **3, 22**
Tropicana Perfume Shoppe **9**
Vendors Plaza **15**

St. Thomas Harbor

Waterfront Highway (Kyst Vejen)

Veterans Drive

To Havensight Mall
(see inset above left)

Fort Strade

Little Taavne Gade

Kongens Gade

Norre Gade

Fort Gade

99
Steps

Garden Street

Post Office Alley

Bakery
Square

Riise's Alley

Hibiscus Alley

Raadets Gade

Drake's Passage

Trompeter Gade
Creque's Alley East
Creque's Alley West
Royal Dane Mall
Palm Passage
Store Tvaer Gade

Nye Gade

Crystal Gade

(Vimmelskaft Gade)

(Dronningens Gade)

Main Street

Tolbod Gade

Pladsen

Information ⓘ
Post Office ⊠

115

SHOPPING A TO Z

ART

Bernard K. Passman   Bernard K. Passman is the world's leading sculptor of black coral art and jewelry. He's famous for his *Can Can Girl* and his four statues of Charlie Chaplin. On Grand Cayman he learned to fashion exquisite treasures from black coral found 200 feet under the sea. After being polished and embellished with gold and diamonds, some of Passman's work has been treasured by royalty. There are also simpler and more affordable pieces for sale. 38A Main St. ✆ 340/777-4580.

Gallery Camille Pissarro   This art gallery, reached by climbing stairs, is located in the house where Pissarro, a paragon of Impressionism, was born in 1830. In three high-ceilinged and airy rooms, you can see Pissarro paintings relating to the islands. Many prints of local artists are available, and the gallery also sells original batiks, alive in vibrant colors. Caribbean Cultural Centre, 14 Dronningens Gade. ✆ 340/774-4621.

Jim Tillett Art Gallery and Silk Screen Print Studio   Since 1959, Tillett Gardens, once an old Danish farm, has been the island's arts-and-crafts center. This tropical compound is a series of buildings housing studios, galleries, and an outdoor garden restaurant and bar. Prints in the galleries start as low as $10. The best work of local artists is displayed here—originals in oils, watercolors, and acrylics. The Tillett prints on fine canvas are all one of a kind. The famous Tillett maps on fine canvas are priced from $30. Tillett Gardens, 4126 Anna's Retreat, Tutu. ✆ 340/775-1929. Take Route 38 east from Charlotte Amalie.

Blue Turtle Gallery   This is a showcase of the works of Virgin Islands painters, notably Lucina Schutt, best known for her Caribbean land- and seascapes. At this gallery, to the west of Marisol Restaurant, Schutt not only sells artwork beginning at $25 but teaches watercoloring to students. Government Hill. ✆ 340/774-9440.

Mango Tango Art Gallery   This is one of the largest art galleries in St. Thomas, closely connected with half a dozen internationally recognized artists. Original artwork begins at $200; prints and posters are cheaper. Represented are internationally reputed artists who spend at least part of their year in the Virgin Islands, many of them sailing during breaks from their studio time. Examples include Don Dahlke, Max Johnson, Anne Miller, David Millard, Dana Wylder, and Shari Erickson. Al Cohen's Plaza, Raphune Hill, Route 38. ✆ 340/777-3060.

Native Arts and Crafts Cooperative   This is the largest arts and crafts emporium in the U.S. Virgin Islands, combining the output of 90 different artisans into one sprawling shop. Contained within the former headquarters of the U.S. District Court, a 19th-century brick building adjacent to Charlotte Amalie's tourist information office, it specializes in items small enough to be packed into a suitcase or trunk. Examples include spice racks, paper towel racks, lamps crafted from conch shells, salad utensils and bowls, crocheted goods, and straw goods. Tarbor 1. ✆ 340/777-1153.

BOOKS

Dockside Bookshop   If you need a beach read, head for this well-stocked store near the cruise-ship dock. It has the best selection of books on island lore as well as a variety of general reading selections. Havensight Mall. ✆ 340/774-4937.

BRIC-A-BRAC

Carson Company Antiques   Its clutter and eclectic nature might appeal to you. This shop's small spaces are loaded with merchandise, tasteless and otherwise, from virtually everywhere. Much of it is intended to appeal to the tastes of cruise-ship patrons. Bakelite jewelry is cheap and cheerful, and the African artifacts are often interesting. Royal Dane Mall, off Main Street. (C) **340/774-6175.**

CAMERAS & ELECTRONICS

Royal Caribbean   This is the largest camera and electronics store in the Caribbean. It carries Nikon, Minolta, Pentax, Canon, and Panasonic products. It's a good source for watches, too, including such brand names as Seiko, Movado, Corum, Fendi, and Zodiac. And there's a complete collection of Philippe Charriol watches, jewelry, and leather bags, and a wide selection of Mikimoto pearls, 14- and 18-karat jewelry, and Lladró figurines. Another branch is located at Havensight Mall ((C) **340/776-8890**). 33 Main St. (C) **340/776-4110.**

EROTIC WARES

Lover's Lane   This store's inventory is as earthy and, in some cases, raunchy as anything you'll find on St. Thomas. That doesn't prevent a visit here from being amusing, if you're in the mood for it. Amid an ever-so-tasteful decor of muted grays and mirrors, the shop sells provocative lingerie; edible panties; inflatable men, women, and sheep; massage aids of every conceivable type; vibrators; and all the lace, leather, or latex you'll need to make your dreams come true. Raadets Gade 33 (besides Veteran's Drive, on the second floor). (C) **340/777-9616.**

FRAGRANCES

Tropicana Perfume Shoppe   This outlet is billed as the largest perfumery in the world. It offers all the famous names in perfumes, skin care, and cosmetics, including Lancôme and La Prairie. Men will also find Europe's best colognes and aftershave lotions here. 2 Main St. (C) **800/233-7948** or 340/774-0010.

FASHION

Cosmopolitan   This store draws a lot of repeat business. Its shoe salon features Bally of Switzerland, including Bally handbags. In swimwear, it offers one of the best selections of Gottex of Israel for women and Gottex, Hom, Lahco of Switzerland and Fila for men. The menswear section features Paul and Shark from Italy and Burma Bibas sports shirts. The shop also has ties by Gianni Versace and Pancaldi of Italy (at least 30% less than U.S. mainland prices), and Nautica sportswear for men (discounted at 10%). Drakes Passage and the Waterfront. (C) **340/776-2040.**

Mussfeldt Design stocks its shelves with the latest resort wear from around the world—mainly Mexico, Australia, and, of course, the Caribbean itself. Especially delectable are the unique embroideries and prints designed by Peter Mussfeldt himself. International Plaza Mall, near the Hard Rock Café. (C) **340/774-9034.**

GIFTS & LIQUORS

Al Cohen's Discount Liquors   One of St. Thomas's most famous outlets occupies a big warehouse at Havensight, across from the West Indian Company docks where cruise-ship passengers disembark. Inside is a huge storehouse of liquor and wine. The wine department is especially impressive. The quarters have been recently expanded and remodeled, and there are now more brands

---

Tips **A Taste of the Local Brew**

It had to happen. **The Virgin Islands Brewing Company** (© **340/ 777-8888**), across from the Havensight Mall, was originally founded on St. Croix but has invaded St. Thomas with two local beers, Blackbeard Ale and Foxy's Lager. At the company store, you're given free samples and can purchase six-packs of the home-brewed suds along with T-shirts, caps, and polo shirts.

---

and items on sale than ever before. You can also purchase fragrances, T-shirts, and souvenirs. Long Bay Road. © **340/774-3690.**

A. H. Riise Gift & Liquor Stores   This is St. Thomas's oldest outlet for luxury items, such as jewelry, crystal, china, and perfumes. It also offers the widest sampling of liquors on the island. Everything is displayed in a 19th-century Danish warehouse, extending from Main Street to the waterfront. The store boasts a collection of fine jewelry and watches from Europe's leading craftspeople, including Vacheron Constantin, Bulgari, Omega, and Gucci, as well as a wide selection of Greek gold, platinum, and precious gemstone jewelry. Imported cigars are stored in a climate-controlled walk-in humidor. There's also a vast selection of fragrances for both men and women, along with the world's best-known names in cosmetics and treatment products. Waterford, Lalique, Baccarat, and Rosenthal, among others, are featured in the china and crystal department. Specialty shops in the complex sell Caribbean gifts, books, clothing, food, art prints, note cards, and designer sunglasses. Delivery to cruise ships and the airport is free. 37 Main St. at A. H. Riise Gift & Liquor Mall (perfume and liquor branch stores at the Havensight Mall). © **800/524-2037** or 304/776-2303.

Caribbean Marketplace   The best selections of Caribbean handcrafts are found here, including Sunny Caribbee products, a vast array of condiments (ranging from spicy peppercorns to nutmeg mustard), and botanical products. Other items range from steel-pan drums from Trinidad to wooden Jamaican jigsaw puzzles, Indonesian batiks, and bikinis from the Cayman Islands. Do not expect very attentive service. Havensight Mall (Building III). © **340/776-5400.**

Down Island Traders   The aroma of spices will lead you to these markets, which have Charlotte Amalie's most attractive array of spices, teas, seasoning, candies, jellies, jams, and condiments, most of which are packaged from natural Caribbean products. The owner also carries a line of local cookbooks, as well as silk-screened T-shirts and bags, Haitian metal sculpture, handmade jewelry, Caribbean folk art, and children's gifts. Veterans Drive. © **340/776-4641.**

JEWELRY

Amsterdam Sauer   The Sauer family remains a leading purveyor of jewelry and gems. They've stocked their store with some of the best of world designers, and they also offer the largest selection of unset gems in the Caribbean. Main St. © **340/774-2222.**

Artistic Jewelers   This outlet is hot on the trail of Amsterdam Sauer as a leading merchant of jewelry and gems. Before making any serious purchase, perhaps you'll check out the offerings of both. 32 Main St. © **800/653-3113.**

Blue Carib Gems and Rocks   For a decade, the owners of this store have scoured the Caribbean for gemstones. The raw stones are cut, polished, and then fashioned into jewelry by the lost-wax process. On one side of the premises you can see the craftspeople at work; on the other, you can view their finished products. A lifetime guarantee is given on all handcrafted jewelry. Because the items are locally made, they are duty-free and not included in the $1,200 Customs exemption. 2 Back St. (behind Little Switzerland). ✆ **340/774-8525.**

Cardow Jewelers Often called the Tiffany's of the Caribbean, Cardow Jewelers boasts the largest selection of fine jewelry in the world. This fabulous shop, where more than 20,000 rings are displayed, offers savings because of its worldwide direct buying, large turnover, and duty-free prices. Unusual and traditional designs are offered in diamonds, emeralds, rubies, sapphires, and Brazilian stones, as well as pearls. Cardow also has a whole wall of Italian gold chains, and features antique-coin jewelry as well. The Treasure Cove has cases of fine gold jewelry priced under $200. 39 Main St. ✆ **340/776-1140.**

Colombian Emeralds International This store is renowned throughout the Caribbean for offering the finest collection of Colombian emeralds, set and unset. You buy direct from the source, which can mean significant savings. In addition to jewelry, the shop also stocks fine watches. There's another outlet on Main Street. Havensight Mall. ✆ **340/774-2442.**

H. Stern Jewellers This international jeweler is one of the most respected in the world, with some 175 outlets. It's Cardow's leading competitor (see above). Besides this branch, there are two more on Main Street and one at Marriott's Frenchman's Reef. Stern gives worldwide guaranteed service, including a 1-year exchange privilege. Havensight Mall. ✆ **800/524-2024** or 340/776-1223.

Pierre's Connoisseurs of colored gemstones consider this store one of the most impressive repositories of collector's items in the Caribbean. It's a branch of a store based in Naples, Florida. In its inventory are glittering and mystical-looking gemstones you might never have heard of before. Look for alexandrites (garnets in three shades of green); spinels (pink and red); sphenes, yellow-green sparklers from Madagascar (as reflective as high-quality diamonds); and tsavorites, a green stone from Tanzania. 24 Palm Passage. ✆ **800/300-0634** or 340/776-5130.

LINENS
The Linen House The Linen House is the best store for linens in the West Indies. You'll find a wide selection of place mats, decorative tablecloths, and many hand-embroidered goods, much of them crafted in China. A. H. Riise Mall. ✆ **340/774-1668.**

Mr. Tablecloth This shop receives a constant supply of new shipments of top-quality linen from China, including Hong Kong. Now it has the best selection of tablecloths and accessories, plus doilies, in Charlotte Amalie. Also check out their display of placemats, aprons, and runners. 6 Main St. ✆ **340/774-4343.**

MUSIC
Modern Music This store features nearly every genre of music, from rock to jazz to classical, and especially Caribbean. You'll find new releases from Caribbean stars, such as Jamaica's Byron Lee and the Virgin Islands' The Violators, as well as U.S. artists. There are two other branches as well, at the Nisky Center (✆ **340/777-7877**) and at Four Winds Mall (✆ **340/775-3310**). Across from Havensight Mall and cruise-ship docks. ✆ **340/774-3100.**

9 St. Thomas After Dark

St. Thomas has more nightlife than any other island in the U.S. or British Virgin Islands, but it's not as extensive as you might think. Charlotte Amalie is no longer the swinging town it used to be. Many of the streets are dangerous after dark, so visitors have relatively abandoned it, except for a few places, such as the Greenhouse. Much of the action has shifted to **Frenchtown,** which has some great restaurants and bars. However, just as in Charlotte Amalie, some of these little hot spots are along dark, badly lit roads. The primary problem here is mugging. Some of the criminal activity appears drug-related. Sexual assault is known to occur but rather infrequently.

The big hotels, such as Marriott's Frenchman's Reef Beach Resort and Bluebeard's, have the most lively after-dark scene. After a day of sightseeing and shopping in the hot West Indies sun, sometimes your best bet is just to stay at your hotel in the evening, perhaps listening to a local fungi band playing traditional music on homemade instruments.

THE PERFORMING ARTS

Reichhold Center for the Arts   This artistic center, the premier venue in the Caribbean, lies west of Charlotte Amalie. Call the theater or check with the tourist office to see what's on at the time of your visit. The lobby displays a frequently changing free exhibit of paintings and sculptures by Caribbean artists. A Japanese-inspired amphitheater is set into a natural valley, with seating space for 1,196. The smell of gardenias adds to the beauty of the performances. Several different repertory companies of music, dance, and drama perform here. Performances usually begin at 8pm. University of the Virgin Islands, 2 John Brewer's Bay. © 340/693-1559. Tickets $12–$40.

BARS & CLUBS

The Bar at Paradise Point   Any savvy insider will tell you to head to this bar for watching the sunset. It's located 740 feet above sea level, across from the cruise-ship dock, and provides excellent photo ops and panoramic sunset views. Cruise-ship passengers, usually a middle-aged crowd, flock to this bar. A tram takes you up the hill. Get the bartender to serve you a "Bushwacker" (his specialty). Sometimes a one-man steel band is on hand to serenade the sunset watchers. You can also order inexpensive food here, such as barbecued ribs, hot dogs, and hamburgers, beginning at $4. Happy hour, with discounted drinks, begins at 5pm. Paradise Point. © 340/777-4540.

Baywinds   This posh poolside club, cooled by the tradewinds, is a romantic place to be in the evening. Couples in their 20s and 30s dance at the side of the luxurious pool as moonlight glitters off the ocean in the background. Music ranges from jazz to pop. Open nightly, with live music and dinner from 6pm to midnight. At the Renaissance Grand Beach Resort, Smith Bay Road. © 340/775-1510.

Dungeon Bar   There's piano-bar entertainment nightly at this scenic spot overlooking the yacht harbor. It's a popular gathering spot for both residents and visitors, who are mainly in their 30s and 40s. You can dance from 8pm to midnight on Thursday and from 8pm to 1am on Saturday. Entertainment varies from month to month, but a steel band usually comes in on some nights, and other nights are often devoted to karaoke or jazz. There's no cover. Open Tuesday to Friday from 4pm to midnight and Saturday to Monday 4pm to 1am. Bluebeard's Hill. © 340/774-1600.

Jugglers, dancers and an assortment of acrobats fill the street.

She shoots you a wide-eyed look as a seven-foot cartoon character approaches.

What brought you here was wanting the kids

to see something magical while they still believed in magic.

Travelocity® and Travelocity.com are trademarks of Travelocity.com LP and Sabre®
is a trademark of an affiliate of Sabre Inc. © 2001 Travelocity.com LP. All rights reserved.

America Online Keyword: Travel

With 700 airlines, 50,000 hotels and over 5,000 cruise and vaca-

tion getaways, you can now go places you've always dreamed of.

Travelocity.com
A Sabre Company
Go Virtually Anywhere.

"WORLD'S LEADING TRAVEL WEB SITE, 5 YEARS IN A ROW." WORLD TRAVEL AWARDS

I HAVE TO CALL THE TRAVEL AGENCY AGAIN. DARN, OUT TO LUNCH. NOW I HAVE TO CALL THE AIRLINE. I HATE CALLING THE AIRLINES. I GOT PUT ON HOLD AGAIN. "INSTRUMENTAL TOP-40" ... LOVELY. I HATE GETTING PUT ON HOLD. TICKET PRICES ARE ALL OVER THE MAP. HOW DO I DIAL INTERNATIONALLY? OH SHOOT, FORGOT THE RENTAL CAR. I'M STILL ON HOLD. THIS MUSIC IS GIVING ME A HEADACHE. I WONDER IF SOMEONE ELSE HAS CHEAPER FLIGHTS. FORGET IT, CAN'T TAKE IT ANYMORE ... I'M HANGING UP.

YAHOO! TRAVEL
100% MUZAK-FREE

Booking your trip online at Yahoo! Travel is simple. You compare the best prices. You click. You go have fun. Tickets, hotels, rental cars, cruises & more. Sorry, no muzak.

YAHOO!®
Travel
travel.yahoo.com

Tips Safety Note

Sexual harassment can be a problem in certain bars in Charlotte Amalie, where few single women would want to be alone at night anyway. Any of the major resort hotels are generally safer, and any place we've recommended can be viewed as hospitable (though, of course, creeps can be found in any bar).

Epernay   This stylish watering hole with a view of the ocean adds a touch of Europe to the neighborhood. You can order glasses of at least six different brands of champagne and vintage wines by the glass. Appetizers include sushi and caviar. You can also order main courses, plus tempting desserts, such as chocolate-dipped strawberries. A mature, sophisticated crowd seeks out this spot. Open Monday to Wednesday 11:30am to 11pm, Thursday to Saturday 11:30am to midnight. Rue de St. Barthélemy (next to Alexander's Restaurant), Frenchtown. ✆ 340/774-5348.

Fat Tuesday   This bar, attracting a wide age group, is located on the waterfront in downtown Charlotte Amalie. Specialties include the Tropical Itch (a frozen punch made with bourbon and 151-proof rum) and the Moko Jumbi Juice (made with vodka, bourbon, 151-proof rum, and banana and cocoa liqueurs). There's also a variety of beer, highballs, and shooters, including the "Head Butt," which contains Jagermeister, Bailey's, and amaretto. Each night the bar has a special event. Open daily 10am to midnight or 1am (perhaps later on Friday and Saturday, depending on business). 26A Royal Dane Mall. ✆ 340/777-8676.

The Greenhouse   Set directly on the waterfront, this bar and restaurant (listed in "Dining," earlier in this chapter) is one of the few night spots we recommend in the heart of Charlotte Amalie. You can park nearby and walk to the entrance. Each night a different entertainment is featured, ranging from reggae to disco. Almost all of the 30-something patrons are visitors. There's no cover, except on Wednesday and Friday nights, when you pay $5 to $7 for the live reggae music. Veterans Drive. ✆ 340/774-7998.

Iggie's Bolongo   This place functions during the day as an informal, open-air restaurant serving hamburgers, sandwiches, and salads. After dark, it presents karaoke and occasional live entertainment. This establishment attracts the broadest spectrum of age groups and professions in all of Charlotte Amalie. Call to find out what's happening. Bolongo Beach Resort, 7150 Bolongo. ✆ 340/779-1800.

Larry's Hideaway   This retreat has a laid-back, casual atmosphere, attracting, in the words of a bartender, "people from all walks of life, from boaters to condo renters." Many locals like to spend lazy Sunday afternoons here. It's also a cheap place to eat—hot dogs and hamburgers are served until 3:45pm. After 5pm, you can order affordable main courses in the restaurant, including the catch of the day and the chef's pork stew. 10 Hull Bay. ✆ 340/777-1898.

Latitude 18   This is the hot spot on the east coast, where the ferry boats depart for St. John. The ceiling is adorned with boat sails. The place is both a restaurant and bar, opening nightly at 6pm. Live entertainment is featured regularly, especially on Tuesday and Saturday nights. This casual spot is particularly popular. Red Hook Marina. ✆ 340/779-2495.

Turtle Rock Bar   This popular bar presents live music, steel bands, and karaoke to a young crowd. There's space to dance, but most patrons just sway and listen to the steel-pan bands that play from 2pm to closing or the more elaborate bands that play on Tuesday, Sunday, and some other nights. Thursday night is karaoke. Burgers, salads, steaks, and grilled fish are available at the Mangrove Restaurant a few steps away. There's no cover. Happy hour (when most drinks are half price) is 4 to 6pm every night. In the Mangrove Restaurant at the Wyndham Sugar Bay Beach Club, 6500 Estate Smith Bay (a few minutes' drive west of Red Hook). ✆ 340/777-7100.

Walter's Livingroom   This intimate, dimly lit, two-level bar attracts locals, often gay men, in season, drawing more off-island visitors in winter. It's located about 100 yards from the island's famous synagogue, in a clapboard town house built around 1935. The music here ranges from the 1950s to the 1970s. 3 Trompeter Gade. ✆ 340/774-5025.

GAY & LESBIAN NIGHTLIFE
St. Thomas might be the most cosmopolitan of the Virgin Islands, but it is no longer the "gay paradise" it was in the 1960s and 1970s—the action has shifted mainly to San Juan. The major gay scene in the U.S. Virgins is on St. Croix (see chapter 5). That doesn't mean that gay men and lesbians aren't drawn to St. Thomas. They are, but many attend predominantly straight establishments, such as **Hotel 1829** and the **Greenhouse** on Veterans Drive (see "Bars & Clubs" above).

4

St. John

A few miles east of St. Thomas, across a glistening turquoise channel known as Pillsbury Sound, lies St. John, the smallest and least densely populated of the three main U.S. Virgin Islands.

St. John is a wonder of unspoiled beauty. Along its rocky coastline are beautiful crescent-shaped bays and white-sand beaches, and the interior is no less impressive. The variety of wildlife on St. John is the envy of naturalists around the world. And there are miles of serpentine hiking trails, leading past the ruins of 18th-century Danish plantations to magnificent panoramic views. At scattered spots along the trails, you can even find mysteriously geometric petroglyphs of unknown age and origin incised into boulders and cliffs.

Today St. John (unlike the other U.S. islands) remains truly pristine, its preservation rigidly enforced by the U.S. Park Service. Thanks to the efforts of Laurance Rockefeller, who purchased many acres of land here and donated them to the United States, the island's shoreline waters, as well as more than half of its surface area, make up the Virgin Islands National Park. The hundreds of coral gardens that surround St. John are protected rigorously—any attempt to damage or remove coral from the water is punishable with large and strictly enforced fines.

Despite the unspoiled beauty of much of St. John, the island manages to provide visitors with modern amenities and travel services, including a sampling of restaurants, car-rental kiosks, yacht-supply facilities, hotels, and campgrounds. Cinnamon Bay, founded by the National Park Service in 1964, is the most famous campsite in the Caribbean. In addition, the roads are well maintained; there's even a small commercial center, Cruz Bay, on the island's western tip. Don't come here for nightlife, though: St. John is definitely sleepy, and that's why people love it.

One of the most exciting ways to see St. John is by four-wheel-drive vehicle, which you can easily rent in town (in winter it's best to reserve in advance). The steep roadside panoramas are richly tinted with tones of forest green and turquoise and liberally accented with flashes of silver and gold from the strong Caribbean sun.

St. John is the friendliest of the U.S. Virgin Islands, although it lies only a short ferry ride from the more commercialized St. Thomas. There isn't even an airport here, and life is more laid-back than in the other U.S. Virgins. The people actually have time to talk to you and perhaps provide you with directions. Whereas you'll never meet the managers of most East End properties on St. Thomas, you may end up sitting up, drinking, and talking with a St. John innkeeper until late into the night. If you show up for a visit same time next year, you might even be welcomed as one of the family; you'll certainly be considered a "regular."

1 Orientation

ARRIVING

The easiest and most common way to get to St. John is by **ferryboat** (© 340/ 776-6282), which leaves from the **Red Hook** landing pier on St. Thomas's eastern tip and goes to Cruz Bay or St. John; trip time is 20 minutes each way. Beginning at 6:30am, boats depart more or less every hour, with minor exceptions throughout the day. The last ferry back to Red Hook departs from St. John's Cruz Bay at 11pm. Departures are so frequent that even cruise-ship passengers temporarily anchored in Charlotte Amalie for a short visit can visit St. John for a quick island tour. The one-way fare is $3 for adults, $1 for children under age 11. Schedules can change without notice, so call in advance of your intended departure.

To reach the ferry at Red Hook Marina from Charlotte Amalie, grab a taxi or take the Vitran bus ($1 one-way) from the stop near Market Square.

You can also board a boat for St. John at the **Charlotte Amalie waterfront.** The ride takes 45 minutes and costs $7. The ferryboat departs from Charlotte Amalie at 9am and continues at intervals of between 1 and 2 hours until the last boat leaves at around 5:30pm. However, the last boat departing St. John's Cruz Bay to go back to Charlotte Amalie is at 3:45pm.

VISITOR INFORMATION

The **tourist office** (© 340/776-6450; www.usvi.net) is located near the Battery, a 1735 fort that's a short walk from the St. Thomas ferry dock. It's open Monday to Friday from 8am to 1pm and 2 to 5pm. A **National Park Visitors Center** (© 340/776-6201) is also found at Cruz Bay, offering two floors of information and wall-mounted wildlife displays, plus a video presentation about the culture of the Virgin Islands.

You can pick up a map of the island from the tourist office and also a copy of *St. Croix This Week,* which is distributed free. If you plan extensive touring, you can purchase *The Official Road Map of the U.S. Virgin Islands* at a bookstore, **The Bookie** (© 340/773-2592) in Christiansted.

2 Getting Around

The 20-minute ferry ride from St. Thomas will take you to **Cruz Bay,** the capital of St. John, which seems a century removed from the life you left behind. Cruz Bay is so small its streets have no names, but it does have the **Mongoose Junction** shopping center (definitely worth a visit), a scattering of restaurants, and a small park. Cruise ships are nonexistent here, so you won't find hordes of milling shoppers. After a stroll around town, seek out the natural attractions of the island.

BY BUS OR TAXI The most popular way to get around is by the local **Vitran** service, the same company that runs bus service on St. Thomas. Buses now run hourly between Cruz Bay and Coral Bay, (every two hours on Saturday and Sunday); the fare is $1 for adults and 75¢ for children (ages 4 and under free). An open-air **surrey-style taxi** (© 340/693-7530) is more fun, however. Typical fares are $5 to Trunk Bay, $8.50 to Cinnamon Bay, or $10 to Mahoe Bay. Between midnight and 6am fares are increased by 40%. Call for more information.

BY CAR OR JEEP The island's undeveloped roads offer some of the best views anywhere. Because of this, many visitors opt to rent a vehicle (sometimes

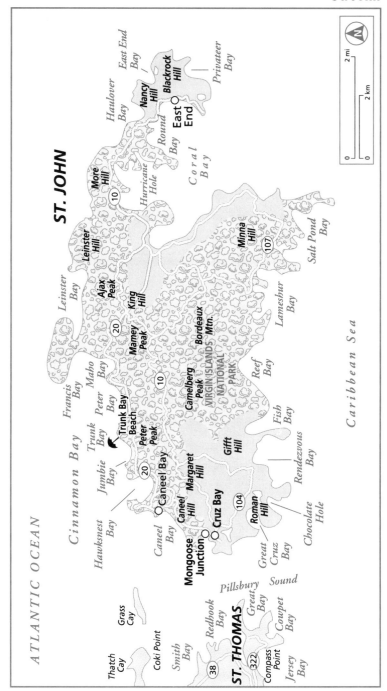

St. John

ST. JOHN

ATLANTIC OCEAN

Caribbean Sea

Cinnamon Bay

Coral Bay

East End Bay

Haulover Bay

Privateer Bay

Blackrock Hill

Nancy Hill

Round Bay

East End

More Hill

Hurricane Hole

Salt Pond Bay

Minna Hill

Leinster Hill

Leinster Bay

Ajax Peak

King Hill

Bordeaux Mtn.

Lameshur Bay

Mahoe Bay

Francis Bay

Mamey Peak

VIRGIN ISLANDS NATIONAL PARK

Camelberg Peak

Reef Bay

Peter Bay

Trunk Bay Beach

Peter Peak

Fish Bay

Trunk Bay

Jumbie Bay

Gifft Hill

Rendezvous Bay

Hawksnest Bay

Caneel Bay

Caneel Bay

Caneel Hill

Margaret Hill

Cruz Bay

Roman Hill

Chocolate Hole

Mongoose Junction

Great Cruz Bay

Pillsbury Sound

Thatch Cay

Grass Cay

Coki Point

Smith Bay

Redhook Bay

Great Bay

ST. THOMAS

Compass Point

Cowpet Bay

Jersey Bay

10 · 20 · 107 · 104 · 322 · 38

2 mi

2 km

with four-wheel drive) to tour the island. Just remember to *drive on the left,* and follow posted speed limits, which are generally very low. Because of the island's relatively limited facilities, most visitors need a car for only a day or two.

Unless you have luggage, which should probably be locked away in a trunk, you might consider one of the sturdy, open-sided, Jeep-like vehicles that offers the best view of the surroundings (most have manual transmissions). This is the most fun way to tour St. John.

Miscellaneous V.I. (© 800/331-1212 or 340/776-6374) charges $71 per day for a Suzuki Sidekick. In winter, they tend to be fully booked for many weeks in advance, so be sure to call ahead. Drivers must be age 25 or older and must present a valid credit or charge card at the time of rental. A collision-damage waiver costs $13.95 per day.

Hertz (© 800/654-3001 or 340/693-7580) rents six types of vehicles, some of which have four-wheel drive. Depending on the model, the cost ranges from $65 to $85 per day; a collision-damage waiver is around $12 extra per day. Drivers must be at least 25 years old and must present a valid credit or charge card at the time of rental.

If you want a local firm, try **St. John Car Rental,** across from the post office in Cruz Bay (© 340/776-6103). It offers daily or weekly rentals. A Jeep Wrangler rents for $60 to $70 a day, a Jeep Cherokee for $75, and a Suzuki Sidekick for $55.

FAST FACTS: St. John

American Express You'll have to visit St. Thomas for service. The representative is Caribbean Travel Agency/Tropic Tours, 9716 Estate Thomas, Havensight (© **340/774-1855**).

Area Code The area code is **340.** You can dial direct from North America.

Banks Chase Manhattan Bank is at 90C Cruz Bay (© **340/776-6881**).

Business Hours Stores are generally open Monday through Friday from 9am to 5pm, Saturday from 9am to 1pm.

Cameras & Film To purchase film or have it developed, go to Sparky's, Cruz Bay Park (© **340/776-6284**).

Currency Exchange Go to the branch of Chase Manhattan Bank in Cruz Bay (© **340/776-6881**).

Dentists The Virgin Islands Dental Association (© **340/775-9110**) is a member of the American Dental Association and is also linked with various specialists. Call for information or an appointment.

Doctor Call © **922** for a medical emergency. Otherwise, go to St. John Myrah Keating Smith Community Health Clinic, 28 Sussanaberg (© **340/693-8900**).

Drugstores Go to St. John Drugcenter, Boulon Shopping Center, Cruz Bay (© **340/776-6353**). The staff here not only fills prescriptions but also sells film, cameras, magazines, and books. Hours are Monday through Saturday from 9am to 6pm and Sunday from 10am to 2pm.

Electricity 110 to 115 V, 60 cycles, as in the mainland United States.

Emergencies For the police, call ℂ **911**; ambulance, **922**; fire, **921**.

Liquor Laws Persons must be at least 21 years of age to patronize bars or purchase liquor in St. John.

Maps See "Visitor Information," earlier in this chapter.

Newspapers & Magazines Copies of U.S. mainland newspapers, such as the *New York Times* and the *Miami Herald* arrive daily and are for sale at Mongoose Junction, Caneel Bay, and the Westin Resort. The latest copies of *Time* and *Newsweek* are also for sale. *What to Do: St. Thomas/St. John,* the official guidebook of the St. Thomas and St. John Hotel Association, is available at the tourist office (see "Visitor Information," earlier in this chapter) and at various hotels.

Post Office The Cruz Bay Post Office is at Cruz Bay (ℂ **340/779-4227**).

Safety There is some crime here, but it's relatively minor compared to St. Thomas. Most crime against tourists consists of muggings or petty theft, but rarely violent attacks. Precautions, of course, are always advised. You are most likely to be the victim of a crime if you leave valuables unguarded on Trunk Bay, as hundreds of people seem to do every year.

3 Accommodations

The number of accommodations on St. John is limited, and that's how most die-hard fans would like to keep it. There are four basic types of choices here: luxury resorts, condominiums and villas, guest houses, and campgrounds. Prices are often slashed in summer by 30% to 60%.

Chances are your location will be determined by your choice of resort. However, if you're dependent on public transportation and want to make one or two trips to St. Thomas by ferry, Cruz Bay is the most convenient place to stay. It also offers easy access to shopping, bars, and restaurants if you want to walk.

LUXURY RESORTS

Caneel Bay *⊛⊛⊛*   Conceived by megamillionaire Laurance S. Rockefeller in 1956, this is the Caribbean's first ecoresort. Though it's long been one of the premier resorts of the Caribbean, Caneel Bay is definitely not one of the most luxurious. A devoted fan once told us, "It's like living at summer camp." That means no phones or TVs in the rooms. Nevertheless, the movers and shakers of the world continue to descend on this place, though younger people tend to head elsewhere. To attract more families, young children are now allowed here. Go to Westin Resort St. John (see below) for glitz and glitter; head here for a touch of class.

The resort lies on a 170-acre portion of the national park, offering a choice of seven beaches. Surrounded by lush greenery, the main buildings are strung along the bays, with a Caribbean lounge and dining room at the core. Other buildings housing guest rooms stand along the beaches. Try to get one of the six rooms in cottage no. 7, overlooking two of the most idyllic beaches, Scott and Paradise. Most rooms, however, are set back on low cliffs or headlands. The decor within is understated, with Indonesian wicker furniture, hand-woven fabrics, sisal mats, and plantation fans.

The resort has consistently maintained a high level of cuisine, often quite formal for the laid-back Caribbean. In recent years the food has been considerably improved and modernized, with more variety and more healthy choices on the menu.

Virgin Islands National Park, St. John, U.S.V.I. 00831. © **340/776-6111.** Fax 340/693-8280. www.caneelbay. com. 166 units. Winter $550–$1,000 double. Off-season $370–$650 double. MAP (breakfast and dinner) $80 per person extra. One child under age 16 can stay free in parents' room. AE, DC, MC, V. **Amenities:** 4 restaurants; 11 tennis courts; boating; dive shop; snorkeling; windsurfing; dock; fitness center; children's play area; kayaks; deep-sea fishing; laundry; baby-sitting. *In room:* A/C, coffeemaker, minibar, hair dryer. No phone.

Westin Resort St. John ✳✳✳ Come here if you like megaresort flash and glitter as opposed to the "old school ties" of Caneel Bay. (Madonna would check in here; Walter Cronkite would prefer Caneel Bay.) This is the most architecturally dramatic and visually appealing hotel on St. John. The complex is set on 34 gently sloping, intricately landscaped acres on the southwest side of the island. It consists of 13 cedar-roofed postmodern buildings, each with ziggurat-shaped angles, soaring ceilings, and large windows. Herringbone-patterned brick walkways connect the gardens (with 400 palms imported from Puerto Rico) with the 1,200-foot white-sand beach and the largest pool in the Virgin Islands. Some of the stylish accommodations contain fan-shaped windows and curved ceilings. Most units open onto private balconies, and some have their own whirlpools. All bedrooms come with full state-of-the-art bathrooms.

Cuisine is more versatile than at Caneel, but that doesn't mean it's always as good. Expect nouvelle, buffets, even New York deli sandwiches.

Great Cruz Bay, St. John U.S.V.I. 00831. © **800/808-5020** or 340/693-8000. Fax 340/693-8888. www. westinresortstjohn.com. 285 units. Winter $359–$469 double; $859–$989 suite. Off-season $229–$410 double; $475–$860 suite. AE, DISC, DC, MC, V. Round-trip shuttle bus and private ferryboat transfers from St. Thomas airport $65 per person. **Amenities:** 3 restaurants, 3 bars; pool; 6 tennis courts; fitness center; dive shop; 24-hour room service; children's programs; sailboats; windsurfing; snorkeling gear; fishing expeditions; laundry; baby-sitting. *In room:* A/C, TV, minibar, coffeemaker, hair dryer, iron/ironing board, safe.

CONDOS & VILLAS

Villa vacations are on the rise in St. John for travelers who want a home away from home. There are actually more villa and condo beds available on St. John than there are hotel beds. These units offer spaciousness and comfort, as well as privacy and freedom, and they often come with fully equipped kitchens, dining areas, bedrooms, and such amenities as VCRs and patio grills. Rentals range from large multi-room resort homes to simply decorated one-bedroom condos.

Caribbean Villas & Resorts, P.O. Box 458, St. John, U.S.V.I. 00831 (© **800/338-0987** in the U.S., or 340/776-6152; fax 340/779-4044), the island's biggest real estate agency, is an excellent choice if you're seeking a villa, condo, or private home. Most condos go for less than $225 per night. In the off-season you can get substantial reductions, perhaps as little as $135 a night. Children age 5 and under stay free; no credit cards are accepted.

EXPENSIVE

Estate Zootenvaal ✳ This property is located within the boundaries of the U.S. National Park at the edge of a horseshoe-shaped bay. It's a good choice for escapees from urban areas who want privacy. The accommodations have been renovated, now sporting designer fabrics in muted tones. Each has its own color scheme and comes with a fully equipped kitchen and a shower-only bathroom. Rooms have ceiling fans, but no air-conditioning, telephones, or televisions.

St. John Accommodations

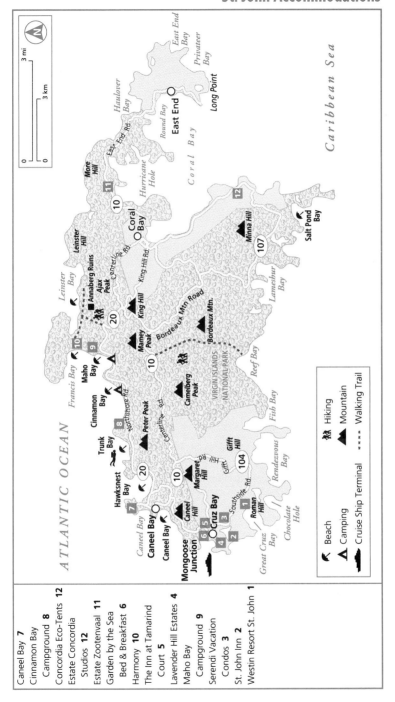

Caneel Bay **7**
Cinnamon Bay
Campground **8**
Concordia Eco-Tents **12**
Estate Concordia
Studios **12**
Estate Zootenvaal **11**
Garden by the Sea
Bed & Breakfast **6**
Harmony **10**
The Inn at Tamarind
Court **5**
Lavender Hill Estates **4**
Maho Bay
Campground **9**
Serendi Vacation
Condos **3**
St. John Inn **2**
Westin Resort St. John **1**

129

Maid service can be arranged at an extra cost. Guests can use the private beach that's known for its great snorkeling.

Hurricane Hole, St. John, U.S.V.I. 00830. © **340/776-6321** or 216/861-5337. www.usviguide.com/ zootenvaal. 4 units. $220 one-bedroom for two; $275 two-bedroom for two. Each additional person $70. No credit cards. *In room:* Coffeemaker, kitchen, refrigerator. No phone.

Lavender Hill Estate *(★ (Value)* This outfit offers some of the best condominium values on the island. It's a short walk away from the shops, markets, restaurants, and safari buses of Cruz Bay. The units overlook Cruz Bay Harbor, and each one has a spacious central living/dining area opening onto a tiled deck, along with a fully equipped kitchen and one or two bedrooms.

P.O. Box 8306, Lavender Hill, Cruz Bay, St. John, U.S.V.I. 00831-8306. © **800/562-1901** or 340/779-4647. Fax 340/776-6969. 10 condo apts. Winter $1,350 one-bedroom apt; $2,250 two-bedroom apt. Off-season $1,100 one-bedroom apt; $1,995 two-bedroom apt. Rates for 7 days (minimum stay). DISC, MC, V. **Amenities:** Pool; laundry. *In room:* Kitchen. No phone.

MODERATE

Estate Concordia Studios This environmentally sensitive 51-acre development is widely praised for its integration with the local ecosystem. Its elevated structures were designed to coexist with the stunning southern edge of St. John. The secluded property is nestled on a low cliff above a salt pond, surrounded by hundreds of acres of pristine national park. It's best for those with a rental vehicle. Each building was designed to protect mature trees, and is connected to its neighbors with boardwalks. The nine studios are contained in six postmodern cottages. Each unit comes with a kitchen, shower-only bathroom, balcony, and ceiling fan; some have an extra bedroom. On-site management assists with activity suggestions. For information on the on-site **Eco-Tents,** refer to "Campgrounds," below.

20–27 Estate Concordia, Coral Bay, St. John, U.S.V.I. 00830. © **800/392-9004** in the U.S. and Canada, or 212/472-9453. Fax 212/861-6210. www.maho.org. 9 units. Winter $135–$190 studio for 2. Off-season $95–$195 studio for 2. Extra person $25 in winter, $15 in off-season. MC, V. **Amenities:** Pool; laundry. *In room:* Ceiling fan, kitchenette. No phone.

Garden by the Sea Bed & Breakfast *(★ (Finds)* Overlooking the ocean, this little B&B lies a 10-minute walk south from the little port of Cruz Bay. It has easy access to the north shore beaches and lies between Frank and Turner Bays. From the gardens of the house, a 1-minute path along Audubon Pond leads to Frank Bay Beach. Be sure to reserve as it offers only three bedrooms. Each

---

(Kids Family-Friendly Accommodations

Lavender Hill Estates *(see p. 130)* Families often save money by staying at one of these condos. There's a swimming pool, and units have fully equipped kitchens. Children under age 12 stay free; older kids are charged $25 extra per night.

Cinnamon Bay Campground *(see p. 132)* Tents or cottages come with cooking gear at this National Park Service site.

Maho Bay Campground *(see p. 133)* The tents in this laid-back hideaway are really more like small canvas houses with kitchen areas and sundecks.

bedroom features elephant bamboo canopy beds, Japanese fountains, and hardwood floors. Artifacts from around the world have been used to furnish the units. Don't expect phones or TVs, as this is a getaway, not a communications center. The 1970s house is designed in a Caribbean gingerbread style with cathedral beamed ceilings. Breakfast is served on the veranda (try their homemade muffins and quiche).

P.O. Box 1469 Cruz Bay, St. John, U.S.V.I. © **340/779-4731**. www.gardenbythesea.com/rates/htm. 3 units. Winter $170–$190 double. Off-season $115–$130 double. No credit cards. *In room:* Ceiling fan. No phone.

Harmony ⨶ Built on a hillside above the Maho Bay Campground, this is a small-scale cluster of 12 luxury studios in six two-story houses with views sweeping down to the sea. The complex is designed to combine both ecological technology and comfort; it's one of the few resorts in the Caribbean to operate exclusively on sun and wind power. Most of the building materials are derived from recycled materials, including reconstituted plastic and glass containers, newsprint, old tires, and scrap lumber. The managers and staff are committed to offering educational experiences, as well as the services of a small-scale resort. The studios contain tiled shower-only bathrooms, kitchenettes, dining areas, and outdoor terraces. Guests can walk a short distance downhill to use the restaurant, grocery store, and water-sports facilities at the Maho Bay campground.

P.O. Box 310, Cruz Bay, St. John, U.S.V.I. 00831. © **800/392-9004** in the U.S. and Canada, 212/472-9453 in New York City, or 340/776-6226. Fax 340/776-6504, or 212/861-6210 in New York City. www.maho.org. 12 units. Winter $175–$210 studio for 2. Off-season $105–$135 studio for 2. Extra person $25. Seven-night minimum stay in winter. MC, V. **Amenities:** Restaurant; windsurfing; snorkeling. *In room:* Ceiling fan. No phone.

Serendi Vacation Condos This property is set on sloping land on a hillside above Cruz Bay. Its angular lines and concrete verandas are shielded by masses of shrubbery. The units contain slightly dated furniture, concrete latticework, a kitchenette, a ceiling fan, and a terrace or balcony. Maid service is usually not included here. A gas-heated barbecue grill on the grounds is available. Costs here are especially attractive for vacationers who include extra guests in their plans.

P.O. Box 293, Cruz Bay, St. John, U.S.V.I. 00831. © and fax **340/776-6646**. 10 apts, all with kitchenette. Winter $135 studio apt for two, $165 one-bedroom apt for two. Off-season $95 studio apt for two, $110 one-bedroom apt for two. Extra person $20; children ages 3–10 $10 each; children age 2 and under stay free in their parents' apt. AE, MC, V. **Amenities:** Nearby tennis and water sports. *In room:* No phone.

GUEST HOUSES

The following places offer just the basics, but they're fine if you're not too finicky.

The Inn at Tamarind Court Right outside Cruz Bay but still within walking distance of the ferryboat dock, this modest place consists of a small hotel and an even simpler West Indian inn. Bedrooms are small, evoking those in a little country motel. Most have twin beds. Shower-only bathrooms in the inn are shared; units in the hotel have small private bathrooms. The social life here revolves around its courtyard bar and restaurant, Pa Pa Bulls. From the hotel, you can walk to shuttles taking you to the beaches.

South Shore Rd. (P.O. Box 350), Cruz Bay, St. John, U.S.V.I. 00831. © **800/221-1637** or 340/776-6378. Fax 340/776-6722. www.tamarindcourt.com. 23 units, 13 with bathroom. Winter $89 double without bathroom, $108 double with bathroom; $145 apt; $165 suite. Off-season $59 double without bathroom, $78 double with bathroom; $98 apt; $128 suite. Rates include continental breakfast. AE, DISC, MC, V. *In room:* Ceiling fan. No phone.

St. John Inn *(Value)*   The old Cruz Inn, once the budget staple of the island, enjoys a new lease on life. Although its rates have gone up, it has also been much improved. The inn overlooks Enighed Pond, only a few blocks from the Cruz Bay Dock area. Accommodations have a light, airy, California feel. The small- to medium-size bedrooms have wrought-iron beds and new mattresses, hand-crafted pine armoires, and a touch of Ralph Lauren flair to make for an inviting nest. The junior suites contain full sofa beds, kitchenettes, and sitting areas. The shower-only bathrooms are small. The inn offers a 43-foot motor yacht, *Hollywood Waltz,* for daily excursions to private snorkeling spots along the coast and private beaches on uninhabited islands.

P.O. Box 37, Cruz Bay, St. John, U.S.V.I. 00831. © **800/666-7688** in the U.S., or 340/693-8688. www. stjohninn.com. 12 units. Winter $120–$195 double. Off-season $60–$120 double. Extra person $15. AE, DC, DISC, MC, V. **Amenities:** Pool, bar. *In room:* A/C, TV, coffeemaker, some kitchenette, hair dryer on request, refrigerator.

CAMPGROUNDS

Cinnamon Bay Campground *(finds)*   This National Park Service campground is the most complete in the Caribbean. The site is directly on the beach, surrounded by thousands of acres of tropical vegetation. Life is simple here: You have a choice of a tent, a cottage, or a bare site. At the bare campsites, nothing is provided except general facilities. The canvas tents are 10 by 14 feet with a floor, and come with a number of extras, including all cooking equipment; even your linen is changed weekly. The cottages are 15 by 15 feet, consisting of a room with two concrete walls and two screen walls. They contain cooking facilities and four twin beds with thin mattresses; two cots can be added. Lavatories and cool-water showers are in separate buildings nearby. Camping is limited to a 2-week period in any given year. Near the road is the office, with a grocery and a cafeteria.

P.O. Box 720, Cruz Bay, St. John, U.S.V.I. 00831. © **340/776-6330.** Fax 340/776-6458. www.cinnamonbay. com. 126 units, none with bathroom. Winter $105 cottage for two; $80 tent site; $25 bare site. Off-season $70 cottage for two; $62 tent site; $20 bare site (5-day minimum). Extra person $15. AE, MC, V. **Amenities:** Restaurant; snorkeling; windsurfing. No phone.

Concordia Eco-Tents   This is the newest addition to Stanley Selengut's cele-brated Concordia development project on the southern tip of St. John, over-looking Salt Pond Bay and Ram Head Point. These solar- and wind-powered tent-cottages combine sustainable technology with some of the most spectacu-lar views on the island. The light framing, fabric walls, and large screened-in windows lend a treehouse atmosphere to the guests' experience. Set on the windward side of the island, the tent-cottages enjoy natural ventilation from the cooling tradewinds. Inside, each has two twin beds with rather thin mattresses in each bedroom, one or two twin mattresses on a loft platform, and a queen-size futon in the living-room area (each unit can sleep up to six people com-fortably). Each kitchen comes equipped with a running-water sink, propane stove, and cooler. In addition, each Eco-Tent has a small private shower, rather meager towels, and a composting toilet.

The secluded hillside location, surrounded by hundreds of acres of pristine national park land, requires guests to arrange for a rental vehicle. Beaches, hikes, and the shops and restaurants of Coral Bay are only a 10-minute drive from the property. For a recommendation of regular on-site studios, see the Estate Con-cordia Studios, above.

20–27 Estate Concordia, Coral Bay, St. John, U.S.V.I. 00830. © **800/392-9004** or 212/472-9453 for reserva-tions. Fax 212/861-6210. www.maho.com. 11 tent-cottages. Winter $120 tent for two. Off-season $75–$85 tent for two. Extra person $25 in winter, $15 in off-season. AE, DISC, MC, V. **Amenities:** Pool. No phone.

Maho Bay Campground ⚓ An 8-mile drive northeast of Maho Bay, this is an interesting concept in ecology vacationing, where you camp close to nature but with considerable comfort. It's set on a hillside above the beach surrounded by the Virgin Islands National Park. To preserve the existing ground cover, all 114 tent-cottages are on platforms above a thickly wooded slope. Utility lines and pipes are hidden under wooden boardwalks and stairs. Each tent-cottage, covered with canvas and screens, has two twin beds with thin mattresses, a couch, electric lamps and outlets, a dining table, chairs, a propane stove, an ice chest (cooler), linen, thin towels, and cooking and eating utensils. Guests share communal bathhouses. Maho is more intimate and slightly more luxurious than its nearest competitor, Cinnamon Bay.

P.O. Box 310, Cruz Bay, St. John, U.S.V.I. 00831. © **800/392-9004**, 212/472-9453 in New York City, or 340/776-6226. Fax 340/776-6504, or 212/861-6210 in New York City. www.maho.org. 114 tent-cottages, none with bathroom. Winter $110–$125 tent-cottage for 2 (minimum stay of 7 nights). Off-season $75 tent-cottage for 2. Extra person $15. AE, DISC, MC, V. **Amenities:** Restaurant; snorkeling; windsurfing. No phone.

4 Dining

St. John has some posh dining, particularly at the luxury resorts like Caneel Bay, but it also has West Indian restaurants with plenty of local color and flavor. Many of the restaurants command high prices, but you can lunch almost anywhere at reasonable rates. Dinner is often quite an event on St. John, since it's about the only form of nightlife the island has.

VERY EXPENSIVE

Caneel Bay Beach Terrace Dining Room ⚓ INTERNATIONAL/ SEAFOOD Right below the Equator (see below) is an elegant, open-air dining room, overlooking the beach. The resort restaurant caters to elite palates. Start with an appetizer of papaya with prosciutto, and move on to one of the wonderful fresh salads. The best main dishes are likely to include baked fillet of red snapper or roast prime rib of blue-ribbon beef, carved to order with natural juices. For dessert, try strawberry cheesecake or Boston cream pie. Menus change nightly. The self-service buffet luncheon is one of the best in the Virgin Islands. Although the cuisine here has varied over the years, the professional standards remain high.

In the Caneel Bay Hotel. © **340/776-6111**. Reservations required for dinner. Main courses $25–$40; Mon night grand buffet $50; lunch buffet $20–25. AE, DC, MC, V. Daily 11am–2pm and Thurs–Sat 7–9pm.

EXPENSIVE

Asolare ⚓ FRENCH/ASIAN This is the most beautiful and elegant restaurant on St. John, with the hippest and best-looking staff. Asolare sits on top of a hill overlooking Cruz Bay and some of the British Virgin Islands. *Asolare* translates as "the leisurely passing of time without purpose," and that's what many diners prefer to do here. The chef roams the world for inspiration and cooks with flavor and flair, using some of the best and freshest ingredients available on island. To begin, try the prawn and coconut-milk soup or the stone-seared carpaccio. For a main course, you might be tempted by crispy Peking duckling with a chestnut glaze, or perhaps catfish wrapped in banana leaves with a plantain and lime curry sauce. Two truly excellent dishes are the lime-sautéed chicken with a yellow curry sauce and the sashimi tuna on a sizzling plate with a plum-passion fruit sake vinaigrette. For dessert, try the frozen mango guava soufflé or the chocolate pyramid cake.

Cruz Bay. © **340/779-4747**. Reservations required. Main courses $19–$40. AE, MC, V. Daily 5:30–9:30pm.

Ellington's ⚓ CONTINENTAL   This restaurant is set near the neocolonial villas of Gallows Point, to the right after you disembark from the ferry. Its exterior has the kind of double staircase, fan windows, louvers, and low-slung roof found in an 18th-century Danish manor house. Drop in at sunset for a drink on the panoramic upper deck, where an unsurpassed view of St. Thomas and its neighboring cays unfolds. The dinner menu changes often to accommodate the freshest offerings of the sea. Conch fritters or toasted ravioli might get you started, or else you could opt for one of the soups—none finer than a Caribbean seafood chowder. For a main course, we always go for the Caribbean mixed grill, with lobster, shrimp, and fresh fish grilled to perfection. Blackened swordfish and wahoo or mahi-mahi with Cajun spices are also excellent choices, as are the pastas. Vegetarian specials are featured nightly.

Gallows Point, Cruz Bay. ☎ 340/693-8490. Reservations required only for seating upstairs. Main courses $13–$45. AE, MC, V. Daily 5–10pm.

Equator ⚓ CARIBBEAN   This restaurant lies behind the tower of an 18th-century sugar mill, where ponds with waterlilies fill former crystallization pits for hot molasses. A flight of stairs leads to a monumental circular dining room, with a wraparound veranda and sweeping views of a park. In the center rises the stone column that horses and mules once circled to crush sugarcane stalks. In its center the restaurant grows a giant poinciana-like Asian tree of the *Albizia lebbeck* species. Islanders call it "woman's tongue tree."

The cuisine is the most daring on the island, and for the most part chefs pull off their transcultural dishes. A spicy and tantalizing opening is an appetizer of Caribbean jerk seasoned crab cakes with a smoked yellow pepper aïoli (get *Gourmet* magazine on the phone). A classic Caribbean callaloo soup is offered, and the salads use farm greens, such as roma tomatoes and endive. Daily Caribbean selections are offered, or else you can opt for such fine dishes as seared Caribbean mahi-mahi with a lentil or pumpkin mélange or lemon and pepper-crusted tuna loin with lemongrass. There's always a dry, aged Angus steak or a grilled veal chop for the more traditional palate.

In the Caneel Bay Hotel, Caneel Bay. ☎ 340/776-6111. Reservations required. Main courses $25–$40. Dec 15–Jan 10 daily 6:30–9pm. The rest of the year Wed–Thurs and Sun 6:30–9pm.

Le Château de Bordeaux ⚓ CONTINENTAL/CARIBBEAN   This restaurant is 5 miles east of Cruz Bay, near the geographical center of the island and close to one of its highest points. It's known for having some of the best views on St. John. A lunch grill on the patio serves burgers and drinks Monday to Saturday from 10am to 4:30pm. In the evening, amid a Victorian decor with lace tablecloths, you can begin with a house-smoked chicken spring roll or a velvety carrot soup. After that, move on to one of the saffron-flavored pastas or a savory West Indian seafood chowder. Smoked salmon and filet mignon are a bow to the international crowd, although the wild-game specials are more unusual. The well-flavored Dijon mustard and pecan-crusted roast rack of lamb with a shallot port reduction is also a good choice. For dessert, there's a changing array of cheesecakes, among other options. The specialty drink is a passion-fruit daiquiri.

Junction 10, Centerline Rd., Bordeaux Mountain. ☎ 340/776-6611. Reservations recommended. Main courses $22–$36. AE, MC, V. Cash only for lunch. Mon–Sat 11am–2:30pm. Mon–Sat two nightly seatings, 5:30–6:30pm and 7:30–8:45pm. Closed Sun–Mon in summer.

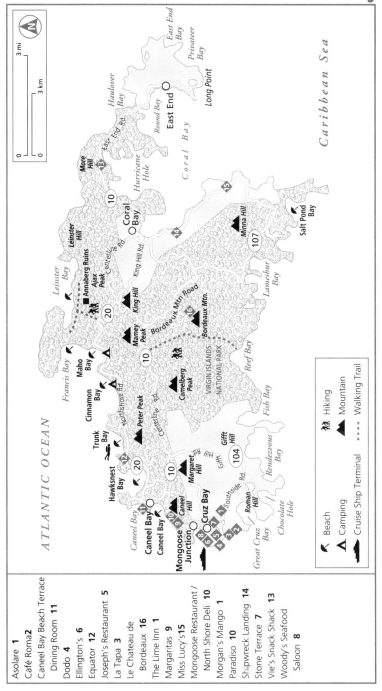

Asolare **1**
Café Roma**2**
Caneel Bay Beach Terrace
    Dining Room **11**
Dodo **4**
Ellington's **6**
Equator **12**
Joseph's Restaurant **5**
La Tapa **3**
Le Chateau de
    Bordeaux **16**
The Lime Inn **1**
Margaritas **9**
Miss Lucy's**15**
Mongoose Restaurant /
    North Shore Deli **10**
Morgan's Mango **10**
Paradiso **10**
Shipwreck Landing **14**
Stone Terrace **7**
Vie's Snack Shack **13**
Woody's Seafood
    Saloon **8**

Paradiso ✿✿ CONTEMPORARY/AMERICAN   This is the most talked-about restaurant on St. John, other than Asolare (see above), and the only one that's air-conditioned. The interior has lots of brass, glowing hardwoods, and nautical antiques, not to mention the most beautiful bar on the island, crafted from mahogany, purpleheart, and angelique.

Every dish has real flavor. Try such appetizers as shrimp and lobster dumplings with pineapple salsa and mango vinaigrette. A roasted garlic Caesar salad with sun-dried tomatoes and a Parmesan grizzini is a new twist on this classic dish. But the chefs truly shine in their main dishes, especially pan-roasted sea bass with baby beets and cannellini or grilled veal medallions with pastrami-cured duck breast and arugula. Even chicken breast is given new zest and flair, stuffed with prosciutto, Asiago cheese, and basil, and served with garlic-mashed potatoes.

Mongoose Junction. 📞 340/693-8899. Reservations recommended. Main courses $18–$35. AE, MC, V. Daily 5:30–9:30pm. Bar daily 5–10:30pm. Closed Aug–Nov.

Stone Terrace ✿ ECLECTIC   On the waterfront at Cruz Bay this charmer overlooks the sea where the ferries from St. Thomas dock. Named for the native stone-built structure it occupies, it serves some of the freshest and best dishes on island. For inspiration, the chef roams the world.

As the pelicans dive in the bay, you can pursue Chef Aaron Willis's eclectic menu. Dinner seating is on a covered archway with a terrace. The lively repertoire of dishes is crafted with a generous, personal touch. We especially like the appetizer of crab cakes with lime aïoli over jicama and mango slaw, and have equal affection for portobello and basil-wrapped shrimp with a roasted red pepper puree horseradish cream, and exotic greens in a light Parmesan dressing. Soups and salads play a large role on the menu, the shrimp bisque with a sherry crème fraîche worthy of a recipe in *Gourmet*. On our most recent rounds, the chef heightened our enjoyment with such main courses as black peppercorn–encrusted tuna with fried artichoke hearts and truffle oil served with a creamy lemon risotto.

Our party was also captivated by the macadamia and tamarind–encrusted pork tenderloin with plantain mashed potatoes and chipotle-braised fennel. But what really won our hearts was the arrival of a Dijon and dried Vidalia onion–encrusted rack of lamb with Gorgonzola sauce, carrot gnocchi, and wilted greens.

Cruz Bay. 📞 340/693-9370. Reservations required. Main courses $18–$30. AE, MC, V. Tues–Sun two seatings at 6pm and 8pm.

Café Roma ITALIAN   This restaurant in the center of Cruz Bay is not a place for great finesse in the kitchen, but it's a longtime favorite and has pleased a lot of diners who just want a casual meal. To enter, you have to climb a flight of stairs. You might arrive early and have a strawberry colada, then enjoy a standard pasta, veal, seafood, or chicken dish. There are usually 30 to 40 vegetarian items on the menu. The owner claims, with justification, that his pizzas are the best on the island; try the white pizza. Italian wines are sold by the glass or bottle, and you can end the evening with an espresso.

Cruz Bay. 📞 340/776-6524. Reservations not necessary. Main courses $8–$22. MC, V. Wed–Mon 5–10pm

Dobo ITALIAN   Located 200 yards from the public docks, this old traditional building is a great location for casual dining with good food. In this category, though, we prefer Joseph's (see review below). But if Joseph's is booked, try to get a table at this large, open dining room with white walls and an ornate central chandelier. It's a good place to spend part of the evening, dining and chatting with fellow patrons, likely to be composed almost equally of visitors and locals. The food is as traditional as can be. We call it "Frank Sinatra" cookery, and that means veal scaloppini, chicken and eggplant parmigiana, and savory spaghetti with seafood. The bar is also a good place for hanging out.

Cruz Bay. ✆ **340/693-9200.** Main courses $15–$24. AE, MC, V. Daily 5–10pm. Bar 6pm–1am.

Joseph's Restaurant ITALIAN   Set within 200 yards of the public docks, this is a pavilion that's open on two sides, with lots of comfortable chairs. We come here mainly for the chef's specialty, lobster ravioli, although there is a succulent array of fresh seafood, pastas, and meat and poultry courses, including such classics as chicken parmigiana. The food is quite traditional and rather heartwarming, reminding you of the cuisine served on those backwater streets in New York City's Greenwich Village. "We don't get too many movie stars," the waiter assured us, "but we have satisfied customers who don't go away hungry."

Cruz Bay. ✆ **340/693-9200.** Reservations recommended. Main courses $10–$17. AE, MC, V. Daily 6–10pm. Bar daily 4pm–2am.

La Tapa INTERNATIONAL   This is one of our favorite restaurants in Cruz Bay, where you can sample the tapas, Spanish-inspired bite-size morsels of fish, meat, or marinated vegetables, accompanied by pitchers of sangria. There's a tiny bar with no more than five stools, a two-tiered dining room, and lots of original paintings (the establishment doubles as an art gallery for emerging local artists). Menu items are thoughtful and well conceived, and include fast-seared tuna with a Basque-inspired relish of onions, peppers, garlic, and herbs; filet mignon with Gorgonzola, caramelized onions, and port; and linguine with shrimp, red peppers, and leeks in a peanut sauce.

Centerline Road, across from Scotia Bank, Cruz Bay. ✆ **340/693-7755.** Reservations recommended. Tapas from $4; main courses $18–$36. AE, MC, V. Fri–Wed 5:30–10pm.

Miss Lucy's 🖈 (Finds) WEST INDIAN   For the broadest array of island cookery, nobody does it better than Miss Lucy. Her food is the way it used to taste in the Caribbean long before anyone ever heard of high-rise resorts. Her paella is the most scrumptious on the island, a kettle brimming with hot Italian sausage, deep-fried chicken, shrimp, and mussels over perfectly cooked saffron rice. Traditional conch fritters appear with a picante sauce, and you can gobble them down with Miss Lucy's callaloo soup. Her fish is pulled from Caribbean waters, and does she ever know how to cook it! When a local fisherman catches a wahoo, he is often likely to bring it here for Miss Lucy to cook. Main dishes come with fungi, a cornmeal and okra side dish. At one of her "full moon parties," she'll cook a roast suckling pig. Before becoming the island's most famous woman chef, Miss Lucy was a big hit with tourists as St. John's first female taxi driver. For dessert, try her banana pancakes.

Salt Pond Road, near Estate Concordia, Coral Bay. ✆ **340/693-5244.** Reservations recommended. Main courses $15.50–$22.50. AE, MC, V. Tues–Sat 11am–3pm and 6–9pm; Sun 10am–2pm.

Mongoose Restaurant/North Shore Deli AMERICAN   There's a hint of New Age California at this popular deli and outdoor restaurant, which occupies a setting that's soothing, woodsy, and very, very tropical. The to-go service at the deli provides one of the best options on St. John for an overstuffed sandwich. There's a cluster of wooden tables near the deli if you prefer to eat here. Breads are baked fresh every day.

More substantial (and more esoteric) fare is served in the restaurant, where the vegetation of a tropical forest extends up to the deck, and where a high roof and a lack of walls give the impression of eating outdoors. You can always precede or end a meal at the centerstage bar. Perennially popular drinks include rum-and-fruit–based painkillers or a dessert-inspired "chocolate chiquita" (rum, bananas, and chocolate ice cream). Menu items at lunch include quesadillas, burgers, grilled chicken, and blackened tuna sandwiches. At dinner, they include fresh grilled or sautéed fish, often served with a salsa made from local fruits; margarita-marinated shrimp; mahi-mahi with a cashew crust; and lots of vegetarian options as well.

Mongoose Junction. Ⓒ **340/693-8677**. Reservations not necessary. Sandwiches in deli $5–$9. Main courses in restaurant $7–$12 at lunch, $14–$28 at dinner. AE, DISC, MC, V. Deli daily 7am–7pm; Mon–Sat 8:30am–10pm; Sun 10am–9pm.

Morgan's Mango CARIBBEAN   The chefs here roam the Caribbean for tantalizing flavors, which they adapt for their ever-changing menu. The restaurant is easy to spot, with its big canopy, the only protection from the elements. The bar wraps around the main dining room and offers some 30 frozen drinks. Thursday is Margarita Night, when soft music plays. Some think the kitchen tries to do too much with the nightly menu, but it does produce some zesty fare—everything from Anegada lobster cakes to a spicy Jamaican pickapepper steak. Try flying fish served as an appetizer, followed by Haitian voodoo snapper pressed in Cajun spices, then grilled and served with fresh fruit salsa. Equally delectable is mahi-mahi in a Cruzan rum and mango sauce. The knockout dessert is the mango-banana pie.

Cruz Bay (across from the National Park dock). Ⓒ **340/693-8141**. Reservations recommended. Main courses $7.95–$24.95. AE, MC, V. Daily 5:30–10pm. Bar opens at 5pm.

The Lime Inn SEAFOOD   This lively open-air restaurant is located at the Lemon Tree Mall in the heart of Cruz Bay. It's known for its fresh grilled Caribbean-style lobster. Other grilled seafood choices range from shrimp to the fresh catch of the day. If you're not in the mood for seafood, try one of the daily chicken and pasta specials or one of the grilled steaks. There's also a tender grilled filet mignon stuffed with crabmeat. The most popular night of the week here is Wednesday when the Lime Inn offers an all-you-can-eat, peel-and-eat shrimp feast for $19.95.

In the Lemon Tree Mall, Konges Gade, Cruz Bay. Ⓒ **340/776-6425**. Reservations recommended. Main courses $8–$22; lunch $5–10. AE, MC, V. Mon–Fri 11:30am–3pm and 5:30–10pm, Sat 5:30–10pm. Closed 3 weeks in July.

Margaritas MEXICAN   With a name like Margaritas, you know what to expect. On the western side of the island at Cruz Bay, next to Mongoose Junction, this eatery offers open-air dining with a view of the water. Tables are placed both outside and inside the building whose decor evokes a fantasy version of Santa Fe, with religious icons competing for wall space with decorated tiles and Mexican sombreros. It's a bit corny, but the food is tasty. The menu offers a wide choice of standard Mexican fare and a decent selection of vegetarian dishes. The cookery is no better than it should be, but is quite acceptable especially if you down one or even two of those *margaritas Gigantes.*

Cruz Bay. Ⓒ **340/693-8400**. Reservations not needed. Main courses $7–$18. Lunch $7–$12. Mon–Sat 11am–9pm.

Kids Family-Friendly Restaurants

Café Roma (see p. 136) This informal place is a family favorite with the best pizza on the island.

Mongoose Restaurant (see p. 137) The best choice for children if you're visiting Cruz Bay. The well-stuffed sandwiches and island fish cakes are perennial favorites.

Miss Lucy's (see p. 137) There is no better place in St. John to introduce your child to West Indian cookery than this restaurant. It's fun, it's local, and families enjoy it, often ordering a big paella that all members can feast on. The fish is among the best on the island.

Shipwreck Landing SEAFOOD/CONTINENTAL Eight miles east of Cruz Bay on the road to Salt Pond Beach, Shipwreck Landing offers palms and tropical plants on a veranda overlooking the sea. The intimate bar specializes in tropical frozen drinks. Lunch isn't ignored here, and there's a lot more than sandwiches, salads, and burgers—try pan-seared blackened snapper in Cajun spices, or conch fritters to get you going. The chef shines brighter at night, though, offering a pasta of the day along with such specialties as a rather tantalizing Caribbean blackened shrimp. A lot of the fare is routine, including New York strip steak and fish and chips, but the grilled mahi-mahi in lime butter is worth the trip. Entertainment, including jazz and rock, is featured Wednesday night, with no cover.

34 Freeman's Ground, Rte. 107, Coral Bay. ✆ **340/693-5640.** Reservations requested. Main courses $10–$18; lunch from $8–$14. AE, MC, V. Daily 11am–10pm. Bar daily 11am–11pm.

INEXPENSIVE

Vie's Snack Shack ★ (Finds) WEST INDIAN Vie's looks like little more than a plywood-sided hut, but its charming and gregarious owner is known as one of the best local chefs on St. John. Her garlic chicken is famous. She also serves conch fritters, johnnycakes, island-style beef pâtés, and coconut and pineapple tarts. Don't leave without a glass of homemade limeade. The place is open most days, but as Vie says, "Some days, we might not be here at all"—so you'd better call before you head out.

East End Rd. (12½ miles east of Cruz Bay). ✆ **340/693-5033.** Main courses $7–$12. No credit cards. Tues–Sat 10am–5pm (but call first!).

Woody's Seafood Saloon SEAFOOD/AMERICAN This local dive and hangout at Cruz Bay is more famous for its beers on tap than for its cuisine. A mix of local fishers, taxi drivers, tour guides, aimless island drifters, and an occasional husband and wife show up here to sample the spicy conch fritters. Shrimp appears in various styles, and you can usually order fresh fish and other dishes, including burgers, blackened shark, drunken shellfish, and mussels and clams steamed in beer. There's reggae on Wednesday, and, as a patron said, "a little bit of everything and anything" on Saturday night.

Cruz Bay (50 yards from the ferry dock). ✆ **340/779-4625.** Reservations not accepted. Main courses $8–20; lunch $6–11. AE, DC, MC, V. Mon–Thurs 11am–1am, Fri–Sun 11am–2am.

5 Beaches

The best beach, hands down, is **Trunk Bay** ✿✿, the biggest attraction on St. John and a family favorite. To miss its picture-perfect shoreline of white sand would be like touring Paris and skipping the Eiffel Tower. One of the loveliest beaches in the Caribbean, it offers ideal conditions for diving, snorkeling, swimming, and sailing. The only drawback is the crowds (watch for pickpockets). Beginning snorkelers in particular are attracted to the underwater trail near the shore (see "Sports & Outdoor Pursuits," below); you can rent snorkel gear here. Lifeguards are on duty. Admission is $4 per person for those over age 16. If you're coming from St. Thomas, both taxis and "safari buses" to Trunk Bay meet the ferry from Red Hook when it docks at Cruz Bay.

Caneel Bay, the stomping ground of the rich and famous, has seven beautiful beaches on its 170 acres, and all are open to the public. **Caneel Bay Beach** is open to everyone and easy to reach from the main entrance of the Caneel Bay resort. A staff member at the gatehouse will provide directions. **Hawksnest Beach** is one of the most beautiful near the Caneel Bay properties. It's not a wide beach, but what's there is choice. Because it lies near Cruz Bay, where the ferry docks, it is the most overpopulated especially when cruise-ship passengers come over from St. Thomas. Safari buses and taxis from Cruz Bay will take you along North Shore Road.

The campgrounds of **Cinnamon Bay** have their own beach, where forest rangers sometimes have to remind visitors to put their swim trunks back on. This is our particular favorite, a beautiful strip of white sand with hiking trails, great windsurfing, ruins, and wild donkeys (don't feed or pet them!). Couples are attracted to this beach. Changing rooms and showers are available, and you can rent water-sports equipment. Snorkeling is especially popular; you'll often see big schools of purple triggerfish. This beach is better in the morning or at midday; afternoons are likely to be windy. A marked nature trail, with signs identifying the flora, loops through a tropical forest on even turf before leading straight up to Centerline Road.

Maho Bay Beach is immediately to the east of Cinnamon Bay, and also borders campgrounds. As you lie on the sand here, you can take in a whole hillside of pitched tents. This is also a popular beach, often with the campers themselves, mainly couples.

Francis Bay Beach and **Watermelon Cay Beach** are just a few more of the beaches you'll encounter traveling eastward along St. John's gently curving coastline. The beach at **Leinster Bay** is another haven for those seeking the solace of a private sunny retreat. Singles often frequent this beach. You can swim in the bay's shallow water or snorkel over the spectacular and colorful coral reef, perhaps in the company of an occasional turtle or stingray.

The remote **Salt Pond Bay** is known to locals, couples, and singles but often missed by visitors. It's on the beautiful coast in the southeast, adjacent to Coral Bay. The bay is tranquil, but the beach is somewhat rocky. It's a short walk down the hill from a parking lot (be careful if you park here, as a few cars have recently been broken into). The snorkeling is good, and the bay has some fascinating tidal pools. The Ram Head Trail beginning here and winding for a mile leads to a belvedere overlooking the bay. Facilities are meager but include an outhouse and a scattering of tattered picnic tables.

If you want to escape the crowds, head for **Lameshur Bay Beach,** along the rugged south coast, west of Salt Pond Bay and accessible only via a bumpy dirt road. The sands are beautiful and the snorkeling is excellent. The beach is popular with singles. You can also take a 5-minute stroll down the road past the beach to explore the nearby ruins of an old plantation estate that was destroyed in a slave revolt.

Bay Beach is a contender, although park rangers of late have sometimes asked beach buffs, mainly couples and singles, to put their swimwear back on. Leave Cruz Bay on Route 20 and turn left at the park service sign, about a quarter mile past the visitor center. Park at the end of a cul-de-sac, then walk along the trail for about 15 minutes. Go early, and you'll practically have the beach to yourself.

6 Sports & Outdoor Pursuits

St. John offers some of the best snorkeling, scuba diving, swimming, fishing, hiking, sailing, and underwater photography in the Caribbean. The island is known for Virgin Islands National Park, as well as for its coral-sand beaches, winding mountain roads, hidden coves, and trails that lead past old, bush-covered sugar cane plantations. Just don't visit St. John expecting to play golf.

The most complete line of water-sports equipment available, including rentals for windsurfing, snorkeling, kayaking, and sailing, is offered at the **Cinnamon Bay Watersports Center,** on Cinnamon Bay Beach (© **340/776-6330**). One- and two-person sit-on-top kayaks rent for $12 to $20 per hour. You can also sail away in a 12- or 14-foot Hobie monohull **sailboat,** for $25 to $30 per hour.

BOAT EXCURSIONS   You can take half- and full-day boat trips, including a full-day excursion to the Baths at Virgin Gorda, for $85. A snorkel excursion on St. John costs $55 per person. Call **Vacation Vistas and Motor Yachts** (© **340/776-6462**) for details. **Cruz Bay Watersports,** P.O. Box 252, Palm Plaza, St. John (© **340/776-6234**), offers trips to the British Virgin Islands (bring your passport) for $85, including food and beverages. British Customs fees are another $15.

FISHING   Outfitters located on St. Thomas offer sport-fishing trips here—they'll come over and pick you up. Call the **St. Thomas Sportfishing Center** (© **340/775-7990**) at Red Hook. Count on spending from $370 to $550 per party (up to 6 people) for a half day of fishing.

HIKING   St. John has the most rewarding hiking in the Virgin Islands. The terrain ranges from arid and dry (in the east) to moist and semitropical (in the northwest). The island boasts more than 800 species of plants, 160 species of birds, and more than 20 trails maintained in fine form by the island's crew of park rangers. Much of the land on the island is designated as the **Virgin Island National Park.** Visitors are encouraged to stop by the Cruz Bay Visitor Center, where you can pick up the park brochure, which includes a map of the park, and the *Virgin Islands National Park News,* which has the latest information on park activities. It's important to carry a lot of water and wear sunscreen and insect repellent when you hike.

St. John is laced with a wide choice of clearly marked walking paths. At least 20 of these originate from North Shore Road (Route 20) or from the island's main east-west artery, Centerline Road (Route 10). Each is marked at its starting point with a preplanned itinerary; the walks can last anywhere from 10 minutes to 2 hours. Maps are available from the national park headquarters at Cruz Bay.

One of our favorite hikes, the **Annaberg Historic Trail** (identified by the National Park Service as trail no. 10) requires only about a half-mile stroll. It departs from a clearly marked point along the island's north coast, near the

---

⟨Moments⟩ A Water Wonderland

At Trunk Bay, you can take the **National Park Underwater Trail** (© **340/776-6201**), stretching for 650 feet, allowing you to identify what you see, everything from false coral to colonial anemones. You'll pass lavender sea fans and schools of silversides. Rangers are on hand to provide information.

---

junction of Routes 10 and 20. This self-guided tour passes the partially restored ruins of a manor house built during the 1700s. Signs along the way give historical and botanical data. Visiting the ruins costs $4 per person for those over age 16. If you want to prolong your hiking experience, take the **Leinster Bay Trail** (trail no. 11), which begins near the point where trail no. 10 ends. It leads past mangrove swamps and coral inlets rich with plant and marine life; markers identify some of the plants and animals.

Near the beach at **Cinnamon Bay,** there's a marked nature trail, with signs identifying the flora. It's a relatively flat walk through a tropical forest, eventually leading straight up to Centerline Road.

Another series of hikes traversing the more arid eastern section of St. John originates at clearly marked points along the island's **southeastern tip,** off Route 107. Many of the trails wind through the grounds of 18th-century plantations, past ruined schoolhouses, rum distilleries, molasses factories, and great houses, many of which are covered with lush, encroaching vines and trees.

The **National Park Service** (© 340/776-6201) provides a number of ranger-led activities. One of the most popular is the guided 2½-mile **Reef Bay Hike.** Included is a stop at the only known petroglyphs on the island and a tour of the sugar-mill ruins. A park ranger discusses the area's natural and cultural history along the way. The hike starts at 10am on Monday, Thursday, and Friday and costs $15 per person. Reservations are required and can be made by phone.

SCUBA DIVING & SNORKELING   Cruz Bay Watersports (© 340/776-6234), is a PADI and NAUI five-star diving center. Certifications can be arranged through a dive master for $350. Beginner scuba lessons start at $95. Two-tank reef dives with all dive gear cost $85; wreck dives, night dives, and dive packages are available. In addition, snorkel tours are offered daily.

Divers can ask about scuba packages at **Low Key Watersports,** Wharfside Village (© **800/835-7718** or 340/693-8999). All wreck dives offered are two-tank/two-location dives. One-tank dives cost $55 per person, with night dives going for $75. Snorkel tours are also available at $55 to $75 per person. Parasailing costs $55 per person. The center also rents water-sports gear, including masks, fins, snorkels, and dive skins, and arranges day sailing trips, kayaking tours, and deep-sea fishing.

Snorkeling gear can be rented from the **Cinnamon Bay Watersports Center** (© **340/776-6330**) for $5, plus a $25 deposit. Two of the best snorkeling spots around St. John are **Leinster Bay** and **Haulover Bay.** Usually uncrowded Leinster Bay offers some of the best snorkeling in the U.S. Virgins. The water is calm, clear, and filled with brilliantly hued tropical fish. Haulover Bay is a favorite among locals. It's often deserted, and the waters often clearer than in other spots around St. John. The ledges, walls, and nooks here are set very close together, making the bay a lot of fun for anyone with a little bit of experience.

SEA KAYAKING   Arawak Expeditions, based in Cruz Bay (© **800/ 238-8687** in the U.S., or 340/693-8312), provides kayaking gear, healthful meals, and experienced guides for full- and half-day outings. Trips cost $80 and $48, respectively. Multi-day excursions with camping are also available; call their toll-free number if you'd like to arrange an entire vacation with them. These trips range in price from $950 to $1,200.

WINDSURFING   The windsurfing at Cinnamon Bay is some of the best any-where, for either the beginner or the expert. The **Cinnamon Bay Watersports Center** (© **340/776-6330**) rents high-quality equipment for all levels, even for kids. Boards cost $15 an hour; a 2-hour introductory lesson costs $45.

7 Exploring St. John

Many visitors spend time at **Cruz Bay,** where the ferry docks. This village has interesting bars, restaurants, boutiques, and pastel-painted houses. It's a bit sleepy, but relaxing after the fast pace of St. Thomas.

Most cruise-ship passengers dart through Cruz Bay and head for the island's biggest attraction, **Virgin Islands National Park** ✷✷ (© **340/776-6201**). The park totals 12,624 acres, including submerged lands and water adjacent to St. John, and has more than 20 miles of hiking trails to explore. See "Sports & Out-door Pursuits," above, for information on trails and organized park activities.

Other major sights on the island include **Trunk Bay** (see "Beaches," earlier in this chapter), one of the world most beautiful beaches, and **Fort Berg** (also called Fortsberg), at Coral Bay, which served as the base for the soldiers who brutally crushed the 1733 slave revolt. Finally, try to make time for the **Annaberg Ruins** on Leinster Bay Road, where the Danes maintained a thriving plantation and sugar mill after 1718. It's located off North Shore Road east of Trunk Bay. Admission is $4 for those over age 16. On certain days of the week (dates vary), guided walks of the area are given by park rangers. For information on the **Annaberg Historic Trail,** see "Sports & Outdoor Pursuits," above.

The best way to see St. John in a nutshell, especially if you're on a cruise-ship layover, is to take a 2-hour taxi tour. The cost is $35 for one or two passengers, or $15 per person for three or more. Almost any taxi at Cruz Bay will take you on these tours, or else you can call **St. John Taxi Association** (© **340/ 693-7530**). If you have more time and you've already rented a car, try the driv-ing tour below.

DRIVING TOUR   ST. JOHN

Start & Finish: Ferry docks in Cruz Bay.

Time: 3 to 7 hours, depending on beach time, bar stops, and pedestrian detours.

Best Time: Any warm sunny day.

Worst Time: Any rainy day, when you are likely to get stuck in the mud on bad roads.

Important note: Before you begin this tour, make sure you have at least three-quarters of a tank of gas, because there are only two gas stations on St. John, one of which is often closed. The more reliable of the two stations is in the upper regions of Cruz Bay, beside Route 104. Ask for directions when you pick up your rented vehicle. And **remember to drive on the left!**

Head out of Cruz Bay, going east on Route 20. Within about a minute, you'll pass the catwalks and verandas of:

❶ Mongoose Junction

This shopping emporium, a major island attraction, contains some unusual art galleries and jewelry shops. (See "Shopping," later in this chapter.)

❷ Caneel Bay

Past the security guard, near the resort's parking lots, are a gift shop and a handful of bars and restaurants. Continuing on, you'll see within a mile the first of many stunning vistas. (Note the complete absence of billboards and electrical cables, a prohibition rigidly enforced by the National Park Service.) In less than 3 miles, you'll come to:

❸ Hawksnest Beach

Hawksnest is one of the island's best beaches. Continuing your drive, you'll pass, in this order, Trunk Bay, Peter Bay (private), and Cinnamon Bay, all of which have sand, palm trees, and clear water. A few steps from the entrance to the Cinnamon Bay Campground is a redwood sign marking the beginning of the:

● Cinnamon Bay Trail

Laid out for hikers by the National Park Service, this 1.2-mile walk takes about an hour. Its clearly marked paths lead through shaded forest trails along the rutted cobblestones of a former Danish road, past ruins of abandoned plantations.

A short drive beyond Cinnamon Bay is the sandy sweep of **Maho Bay**, site of one of the most upscale campgrounds in the Caribbean. Shortly after Maho Bay, the road splits. Take the left fork, which merges in a few moments with an extension of Centerline Road. Off this road will appear another NPS signpost marked Danish Road; this detour takes you on a 5-minute trek along a potholed road to the ruins of an 18th-century school.

At the next fork, bear right toward Annaberg. (Make sure you don't go toward Francis Bay.) You'll pass the beginning of a 0.8-mile walking trail to the Leinster Bay Estate, which leads to a beach said to be good for snorkeling. In less than a minute, you'll reach the parking lot of the:

❺ Annaberg Historic Trail

The highlight of this driving tour, the Annaberg Trail leads pedestrians within and around the ruined buildings of the best-preserved plantation on St. John. During the 18th and 19th centuries, the smell of boiling molasses permeated the air here. About a dozen NPS plaques identify and describe each building within the compound. The walk takes about 30 minutes. From a terrace near the ruined windmill, a map identifies the British Virgin Islands to the north, including Little Thatch, Tortola, Watermelon Cay, and Jost Van Dyke.

After your visit to Annaberg, retrace your route to the first major division, and take the left fork. Soon a sign will identify your road as Route 20 East. Stay on this road, forking left wherever possible, until you come, after many bends in the way, to sandy bottomlands that contain an elementary school, a baseball field, and, on a hilltop, a simple barnlike building known as the:

● Emmaus Moravian Church

This church, with its yellow clapboards and red roof, is often closed to visitors. Near its base yet another NPS walking trail begins: the 1½-mile Johnny Horn Trail, known for its scenic views and steep hills. You will now be about 12½ miles east of Cruz Bay.

The roads at this point are not very clearly marked. Avoid the road beyond the elementary school below the church; it's pretty, but leads only to the barren and rather dull expanses of the island's East End. Instead, backtrack a very short distance to a cluster

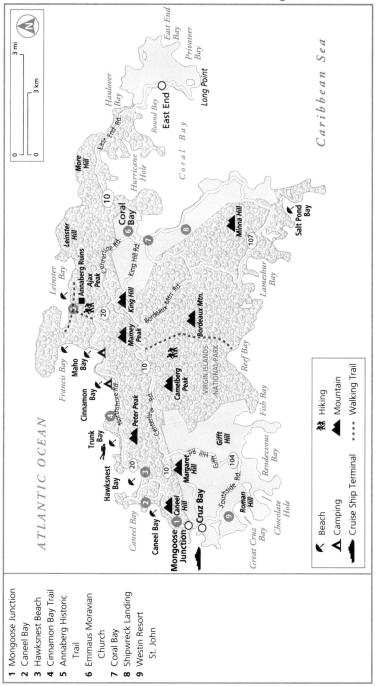

1 Mongoose Junction
2 Caneel Bay
3 Hawksnest Beach
4 Cinnamon Bay Trail
5 Annaberg Historic
   Trail
6 Emmaus Moravian
   Church
7 Coral Bay
8 Shipwreck Landing
9 Westin Resort
   St. John

of signs that point to the restaurant The Still and Shipwreck Landing. Follow these signs heading south about a mile to:

❼ Coral Bay

Claimed by the Danes in the 1600s, the bay still contains a crumbling stone pier and used to unload Danish ships. This was also the site of the first plantation on St. John, which was established in 1717 (and long ago abandoned); it predated the far better developed facilities of Cruz Bay. The bay shelters a closely knit community of yachting enthusiasts, who moor and live on their yachts here between excursions to other parts of the Caribbean. Ringing the bay's perimeter is a widely spaced handful of restaurants and bars. One of these is called:

● Shipwreck Landing

This is an ideal place to drop in for a meal or a tropical drink (see "Dining," earlier in this chapter). You can sit amid palms and tropical plants on a veranda overlooking the sea.

After your break, continue driving south along Coral Bay, perhaps stopping in at another of the two or three shops and bars beside the road.

Backtrack north along Coral Bay to a point near the Emmaus Moravian Church, which you'll see in the distance. At the cluster of restaurant signs, turn left onto Route 10 West (Centerline Road), which has high-altitude views in all directions as you follow it back toward Cruz Bay. (An alternate, but much steeper, way is King Hill Road, which merges later with Route 10 West.)

Within 7 or 8 miles, Route 10 merges with Route 104 (Gifft Hill Road) just after the island's only hospital, the St. John Myrah Keating Smith Community Health Clinic. Take Route 104 and begin one of the steepest descents of your driving tour. (Use low gear whenever possible, and honk around the many blind curves.) When the land levels off, you'll see, on your left, the entrance to the most imaginative pieces of modern architecture on the island, the postmodern:

● Westin Resort St. John

If you're a gardening or architecture enthusiast, stop in for a look at a hotel whose inspirations included ancient Mesopotamia, colonial Denmark, and the coast of California. What makes all of this even more impressive is that it was built on what was unusable swampland only a few years ago.

From here, your return to Cruz Bay entails only a short drive along Route 104, through a slightly urbanized periphery of private homes.

8 Shopping

Compared to St. Thomas, St. John's shopping isn't much, but what's here is interesting. The boutiques and shops of Cruz Bay are individualized and quite special. Most of the shops are clustered at Mongoose Junction, in a woodsy area beside the roadway, about a 5-minute walk from the ferry dock. See "Dining," earlier in this chapter, for our restaurant recommendations in this complex.

Before you leave the island, you'll want to visit the recently expanded **Wharfside Village,** just a few steps from the ferry-departure point. Here in this complex of courtyards, alleys, and shady patios is a mishmash of all sorts of boutiques, along with some restaurants, fast-food joints, and bars.

The most fun shopping on the island takes place on **St. John Saturday,** a colorful, drum beating, spice-filled feast for the senses, held on the last Saturday of every month. This daylong event begins early in the morning in the center of town and spills across the park. Vendors hawk handmade items, ranging from jewelry to handcrafts and clothing, and especially food made from local ingredients. One vendor concocts soothing salves from recipes passed on by her ancestors; another designs and makes porcelain earrings; another flavors chicken and burgers with her own wonderful secret hickory barbecue sauce; yet another hollows out and carves gourds from local calabash trees.

Bamboula, Mongoose Junction (© **340/693-8699**), has an exotic and very appealing collection of gifts from St. John, the Caribbean, India, Indonesia, and Central Africa. The store also has clothing for both men and women under its own label—hand-batiked soft cottons and rayons made for comfort in a hot climate.

The Canvas Factory, Mongoose Junction (© **340/776-6196**), produces its own handmade, rugged, colorful canvas bags, as well as sailing hats, soft-sided luggage, and cotton hats.

Clothing Studio, Mongoose Junction (© **340/776-6585**), is the Caribbean's oldest hand-painted-clothing studio. Here you can watch talented artists create original designs on fine tropical clothing, including swimwear and daytime and evening clothing, mainly for women and babies, with a few items for men.

Coconut Coast Studios, Frank Bay (© **340/776-6944**), is the studio of Lucinda Schutt, one of the best watercolor artists on the island, and Elaine Estern, who's especially known for her Caribbean landscapes. Elaine is the official artist for Westin Resorts; Lucinda is the artist for Caneel Bay. Frank Bay is 5 minutes from Cruz Bay; walk along the waterfront, bypassing Gallows Point, to reach the outlet.

Donald Schnell Studio, Mongoose Junction (© **340/776-6420**), is a working studio and gallery where Mr. Schnell and his assistants have created one of the finest collections of handmade pottery, sculpture, and blown glass in the Caribbean. The staff can be seen working daily. They're known for their rough-textured coral work. Water fountains are a specialty item, as are house signs and coral-pottery dinnerware. The studio will ship its work all over the world. Go in and discuss any particular design you may have in mind.

Fabric Mill, Mongoose Junction (© **340/776-6194**), features silk-screened and batik fabrics from around the world. Vibrant rugs and bed, bathroom, and table linens can add a Caribbean flair to your home. Whimsical soft sculpture, sarongs, scarves, and handbags are also made here.

R and I Patton Goldsmithing, Mongoose Junction (© **340/776-6548**), is one of the oldest businesses on the island. Three-quarters of the merchandise here is made on St. John. There's a large selection of island-designed jewelry in sterling silver, gold, and precious stones. Also featured are the works of goldsmiths from outstanding American studios, as well as Spanish coins.

The location of **The Shop at Caneel Bay,** Caneel Bay Resort, Caneel Bay (© **340/776-6111**), guarantees both an upscale clientele and an upscale assortment of merchandise. Scattered over two simple, elegant floors are drugstore items, books, sundries, and handcrafts, as well as some unusual artwork and pieces of expensive jewelry. There are also racks of resort wear and sportswear for men and women.

9 St. John After Dark

Bring a good book. When it comes to nightlife, St. John is no St. Thomas, and everybody here seems to want to keep it that way. Most people are content to have a leisurely dinner and then head for bed.

The **Caneel Bay Bar,** at the Caneel Bay Resort (© **340/776-6111**), presents live music nightly from 8 to 11pm. The most popular drinks here include the Cool Caneel (local rum with sugar, lime, and anisette) and the trademark of the house, the Plantation Punch (lime and orange juice with three different kinds of rum, bitters, and nutmeg).

The Caneel Bay Bar is very touristy. If you'd like to drink and gossip with the locals, try **JJ's Texas Coast Café,** Cruz Bay (© **340/776-6908**), a real dive, across the park from the ferry dock. The margaritas here are lethal.

Also at Cruz Bay, check out the action at **Fred's** (© **340/776-6363**), across from the Lime Inn. Fred's brings in bands and has dancing on Wednesday, Friday, and Sunday nights. It's just a little hole-in-the-wall and can get crowded fast.

The best sports bar on the island is **Skinny Legs,** Emmaus, Coral Bay, beyond the fire station (© **340/779-4982**). This shack made of tin and wood happens to have the best burgers in St. John. (The chili dogs aren't bad, either.) The yachting crowd likes to hang out here, though you wouldn't know it at first glance—it often seems that the richer they are, the poorer they dress. The bar has a satellite dish, dartboard, and horseshoe pits. Live music is presented on Saturday night.

Morgan's Mango (© **340/693-8141**), a restaurant, is also one of the hottest watering holes on the island. It's in Cruz Bay, across from the national park dock. Count yourself lucky if you get in on a crowded night in winter. The place became famous locally when it turned away Harrison Ford, who was vacationing at Caneel Bay. Thursday is Margarita Night.

St. Croix

At 84 square miles, St. Croix is the largest of the U.S. Virgin Islands. At the east end—which actually is the easternmost point of the United States—the terrain is rocky and arid. The west end is more lush and even includes a small "rain forest" of mango, mahogany, tree ferns, and dangling lianas. Between the two extremes are beautiful beaches, rolling hills, pastures, and, increasingly, miles of condos.

Christopher Columbus named the island *Santa Cruz* (Holy Cross) when he landed on November 14, 1493. He anchored his ship off the north shore but was quickly driven away by the spears, arrows, and axes of the Carib Indians. The French laid claim to the island in 1650; the Danes purchased it from them in 1773. Under their rule,

the slave trade and sugar cane fields flourished until the latter half of the 19th century. Danish influence still permeates the island today.

St. Croix is a lot more relaxed with friendlier people than St. Thomas, although there have been acts of violence and hostility against visitors in the past.

It is nowhere near as inviting or welcoming as St. John, and St. Croix doesn't approach the graciousness encountered in the British Virgin Islands. Additionally, the introduction of gambling has brought a more jaded Atlantic City or Las Vegas type of tourist to the island. Even with gambling, St. Croix has a long way to go to reach the sharp edge projected by the mass tourism of St. Thomas.

1 Orientation

ARRIVING

BY PLANE All flights to St. Croix land at the Alexander Hamilton Airport on the southern coast of the island.

American Airlines (© **800/433-7300**) currently offers the most frequent and most reliable service to St. Croix. Passengers flying connect through San Juan from either New York City's JFK airport or from Newark, New Jersey. From San Juan, **American Eagle** offers several daily nonstop flights to St. Croix. There's also one flight daily from Miami, with one stop (but no change of plane) in St. Thomas. The flight originates in Dallas–Fort Worth, American's biggest hub.

Delta (© **800/221-1212**) offers daily flights to St. Croix from Atlanta, with one stop in St. Thomas. Convenient connections are also available through San Juan.

Travel time to St. Croix from New York is 4 hours, from Chicago 5½ hours, from Miami 3½ hours, and from Puerto Rico 20 minutes. There are no direct flights to St. Croix from Canada or the United Kingdom; connections are made via Miami.

Tips **Package Deals**

Often, an airline can arrange discounted hotel accommodations in conjunction with airfare. Ask an airline reservations agent to explain the various package options.

There are also easy air links between St. Thomas and St. Croix. **American Eagle** (© **340/778-1140**) has three daily flights, costing $61 per person one-way. In addition, **Sea-Borne** (© **340/773-6442**) offers 10 to 11 flights daily, at $75 per person one-way. Flight time is only 30 minutes.

VISITOR INFORMATION

You can begin your exploration at the **visitors bureau,** Queen Cross Street, in Christiansted (© **340/773-0495**), a yellow-sided building with a cedar-capped roof near the harbor. It was originally built as the Old Scalehouse in 1856. In its heyday, all taxable goods leaving and entering the harbor were weighed here. The bureau is open Monday through Friday from 8am to 5pm; the staff is available to answer questions about shopping, sightseeing, beaches, and transportation on the island.

The U.S. Virgin Islands Division of Tourism has offices in Christiansted at 1AB Queen Cross St. (© **340/773-0495**) and at the Customs House Building, Strand Street (© **340/772-0357**) in Frederiksted.

Tourist offices provide free maps to the island. *St. Croix This Week,* distributed free to cruise-ship passengers and air passengers, has detailed maps of Christiansted, Frederiksted, and the entire island, pinpointing individual attractions, hotels, shops, and restaurants. If you plan to do extensive touring of the island, purchase *The Official Road Map of the U.S. Virgin Islands,* available at island bookstores.

ISLAND LAYOUT

St. Croix has only two sizable towns: Christiansted on the north central shore and Frederiksted in the southwest. The Alexander Hamilton Airport is on the south coast, directly west of the Hess Oil Refinery, the major industry on the island. No roads circle St. Croix's coast.

To continue east from Christiansted, take Route 82 (also called the East End Road). Route 75 will take you west from Christiansted through the central heartland, then south to the Hess Oil Refinery. Melvin H. Evans Highway, Route 66, runs along the southern part of the island. You can connect with this route in Christiansted and head west all the way to Frederiksted.

FREDERIKSTED It's hard to get lost in tiny Frederiksted. Most visitors head for the central historic district, where the Frederiksted Pier juts out into the sea. The two major streets, both of which run parallel to the water, are Strand Street and King Street. See the map of Frederiksted on page 183.

CHRISTIANSTED This town's historic district is in the center bordering Veterans Drive, which runs along the waterfront. The district is split by Kronprindsens Gade (Route 308 or Main Street), which is connected to Veterans Drive by a number of shop-filled little streets, including Gutters Gade, Trompeter Gade, and Raadets Gade. The Visitors Information Center lies at the end of King Street (Kongens Gade) near the water. The center of Christiansted can get very congested, and driving around is difficult because of the one-way

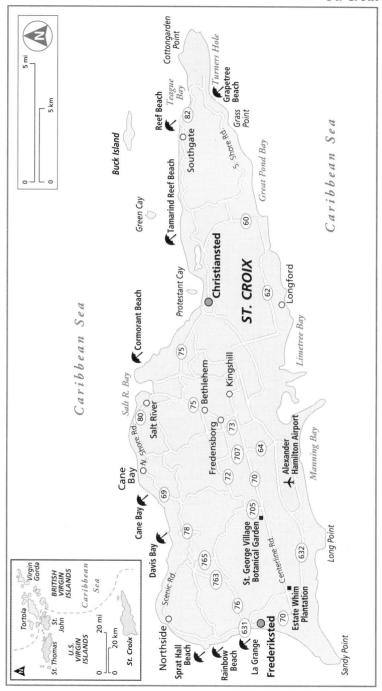

streets. It's usually more practical to park your car and cover the relatively small district on foot. You will find open-air parking on both sides of Fort Christiansvaern. See the map of Christiansted on page 181.

2 Getting Around

BY TAXI At Alexander Hamilton Airport you'll find official taxi rates posted. Expect to pay about $12 to $15 for a ride from the airport to Christiansted and about $10 from the airport to Frederiksted. As the cabs are unmetered, agree on the rate before you get in. The **St. Croix Taxicab Association** (① 340/ 778-1088) offers door-to-door service.

If you plan to do some serious sightseeing on the island, you'll need to rent a car, as getting around by public transportation is a slow, uneven process. There is bus service, but you might end up stranded somewhere and unable to reach your destination without a taxi.

BY BUS Air-conditioned **buses** run between Christiansted and Frederiksted about every 30 minutes daily between the hours of 5:30am and 9pm. They start at Tide Village, to the east of Christiansted, and go along Route 75 to the Golden Rock Shopping Center. Then they make their way to Route 70, with stopovers at the Sunny Isle Shopping Center, La Reine Shopping Center, St. George Village Botanical Garden, and Whim Plantation Museum before reaching Frederiksted. Bus service is also available from the airport to both Christiansted and Frederiksted. The fare is $1, or 55¢ for senior citizens and children. For more information, call ① **340/778-0898.**

BY CAR Remember to **drive on the left.** In most rural areas, the speed limit is 35 m.p.h.; certain parts of the major artery, Route 66, are 55 m.p.h. In towns and urban areas, the speed limit is 20 m.p.h. Keep in mind that if you're going into the "bush country," you'll find the roads very difficult. Sometimes the government smoothes the roads out before the rainy season begins (often in October or November), but they still deteriorate rapidly.

St. Croix offers moderately priced car rentals, even on cars with automatic transmissions and air-conditioning. However, because of the island's higher than normal accident rate (which is partly the result of visitors who forget about driving on the left-hand side of the road), insurance costs are a bit higher than elsewhere. **Avis** (① **800/331-2112**), **Budget** (① **888/227-3359** or 340/778-9636), and **Hertz** (① **800/654-3001** or 340/778-1402) all maintain their headquarters at the island's airport; look for their kiosks near the baggage claim areas. All three companies offer Suzuki Swifts, Suzuki Esteems, and Ford Escorts, usually with automatic transmission and air-conditioning.

Collision-damage insurance costs $13.95 per day, depending on the company, and we feel that it's a wise investment. Some credit-card companies grant you collision-damage protection if you pay for the rental with their card. Verify coverage before you go.

BY BIKE **St. Croix Bike and Tours,** 5035 Cotton Valley, Christiansted (① **340/773-5004**), offers bike rentals. Its 21-speed mountain bikes are best suited for the rugged terrain of St. Croix. The company also features a moderate 12-mile historical-eco-tour, which runs along the rolling western coast, and a 14-mile ridge line tropical mountain bike tour for more experienced bikers. Guides are knowledgeable about the social, political, and natural history of the island. Call for more information.

FAST FACTS: St. Croix

American Express The American Express travel representative is Southerland, Chandler's Wharf, Gallows Bay (📞 **800/260-2603** or 340/773-9500).

Area Code The area code is **340.** You can dial direct from North America.

Banks Several major banks are represented in St. Croix. Chase Manhattan Bank is at 1101 King St. in Christiansted (📞 **340/773-1200**). Most are open Monday through Thursday from 9am to 3pm and Friday from 9am to 4:30pm. Virgin Islands Community Bank has a branch at 12 King's St. (📞 **340/773-0440**) in Christiansted.

Bookstores Head to The Bookie, 111 Strand St. (📞 **340/773-2592**), in Christiansted. The shop is open Monday through Friday from 7:30am to 5pm.

Business Hours Typical business hours are Monday through Friday from 9am to 5pm, Saturday from 9am to 1pm.

Cameras & Film V.I. Express Photo, 2A Strand St. (📞 **340/773-2009**), in Christiansted, offers 1-hour photo finishing.

Dentist Call the Sunny Isle Medical Center, Sunny Isle (📞 **340/778-6356**) for an appointment.

Doctors A good local doctor is Dr. Frank Bishop, Sunny Isle Medical Center (📞 **340/778-0069**). Call for an appointment.

Drugstores Try the Golden Rock Pharmacy, Golden Rock Shopping Center (📞 **340/773-7666**), or People's Drugstore, Sunny Isle Shopping Center (📞 **340/778-5537**), which also has a more convenient branch at 1A King St. (📞 **340/778-7355**) in Christiansted.

Embassies & Consulates St. Croix has no embassies or consulates. Visitors with a problem can drop in at the local police station on Market Street in Christiansted for advice about what to do.

Emergencies To reach the police, call 📞 **915;** fire, **921;** ambulance, **922.**

Hospitals The main facility is Governor Juan F. Luis Hospital, Estate Ruby (📞 **340/778-6311**).

Laundry Try Tropical Cleaners and Launderers, 16–17 King Cross St. (📞 **340/773-3635**), in Christiansted. Hours are Monday to Saturday 7:30am to 6pm.

Liquor Laws You must be at least 21 years of age to purchase liquor.

Maps See "Visitor Information," earlier in this chapter.

Newspapers & Magazines Newspapers, such as the *Miami Herald,* are flown into St. Croix daily. St. Croix also has its own newspaper, *St. Croix Avis. Time* and *Newsweek* are widely sold as well. Your best source of local information is *St. Croix This Week,* which is distributed free by the tourist offices.

Police The police headquarters (📞 **915**) is on Market Street in Christiansted. In case of emergency, dial 📞 **911;** for non-emergency assistance, call 📞 **340/778-6311.**

Post Office The U.S. post office is on Company Street (© **340/ 773-3586**), in Christiansted. The hours of operation are Monday through Friday from 7:30am to 4:30pm and Saturday from 7:30am to noon.

Rest Rooms There are few public rest rooms, except at the major beaches and airport. In Christiansted, the National Park Service maintains some rest rooms within the public park beside Fort Christiansvaern.

Safety St. Croix is safer than St. Thomas. Although there have been random acts of violence against tourists in the past, even murder, most crime on the island is petty theft, usually of possessions left unguarded at the beach while vacationers go into the water for a swim, or muggings (rarely violent) of visitors wandering the dark streets and back alleys of Frederiksted and Christiansted at night. Exercise caution at night by sticking to the heart of Christiansted and not wandering around in Frederiksted. Avoid night strolls along beaches. Night driving in remote parts of the island can also be risky; you might be carjacked and robbed at knifepoint.

Taxis For an airport taxi, call © **340/778-1088**; in Christiansted call © **340/773-5020**.

Telephone, Telex & Fax A local call at a phone booth costs 25¢. You can dial direct to St. Croix from the mainland by using the 340 area code. Omit the 340 for local calls. The bigger hotels will send telexes and faxes, or you can go to the post office (see above).

3 Accommodations

St. Croix's deluxe resorts lie along the North Shore; its charming old waterfront inns are mostly in Christiansted. You may also choose to stay at a former plantation or in a condo complex, which offers privacy and the chance to save money by preparing your own meals. The choice is yours: a location in Christiansted or Frederiksted close to shops and nightlife, but away from the beach; or an isolated resort where, chances are, your accommodation will be either on the beach or a short walk away from it. From such resorts, you'll have to drive into one of the towns for a shopping binge or for restaurants and clubs.

In general, rates are steep, but in summer, hotels slash prices by about 25% to 50%. All rooms are subject to an 8% hotel room tax, which is not included in the rates given below.

Note: If you need a hair dryer, you should pack your own. Apparently, a lot of visitors have packed up hotel hair dryers upon departure, and some innkeepers are reluctant to provide them.

NORTH SHORE
VERY EXPENSIVE
The Buccaneer 𝘈𝘈𝘈 (Kids) This large, luxurious, family-owned resort boasts three of the island's best beaches, and the best sports program on St. Croix. The property was once a cattle ranch and a sugar plantation; its first estate house, which dates from the mid–17th century, stands near a freshwater pool. Although

St. Croix Hotels at a Glance	Access for disabled	A/C in bedrooms	Child-care facilities	Children are welcome	Convention facilities	Credit cards accepted	Directly beside beach	Fitness facility	Golf course nearby	Live entertainment	Marina facilities	Restaurant & bar	Spa facilities	Swimming pool	Tennis courts	TV in bedroom	Water sports
Anchor Inn		✓		✓	✓			✓				✓		✓		✓	
Breakfast Club					✓											✓	
The Buccaneer	✓	✓	✓	✓	✓	✓	✓	✓	✓	✓		✓	✓	✓	✓	✓	✓
Cane Bay Reef			✓		✓	✓		✓				✓		✓			✓
Caravelle		✓		✓	✓							✓		✓		✓	
Chenay Bay		✓		✓		✓			✓			✓		✓	✓		✓
Club Comanche					✓							✓		✓			
Club St. Croix		✓		✓		✓		✓				✓		✓	✓	✓	
Colony Cove		✓		✓	✓	✓						✓		✓	✓	✓	✓
Cormorant	✓	✓		✓		✓	✓	✓	✓			✓		✓	✓		✓
Cottages by the Sea	✓	✓				✓	✓		✓							✓	✓
Danish Manor		✓		✓	✓							✓				✓	
Divi Carina Bay Casino	✓	✓	✓	✓	✓	✓	✓	✓	✓	✓		✓	✓	✓	✓	✓	✓
The Fredricksted		✓		✓	✓							✓		✓		✓	
Hibiscus	✓	✓		✓	✓	✓	✓			✓		✓		✓		✓	✓
Hilty House												✓					
Holger Danske	✓	✓		✓	✓			✓				✓		✓		✓	
Hotel on the Cay		✓		✓	✓	✓	✓			✓	✓	✓				✓	✓
Kings Alley Hotel		✓			✓								✓			✓	
King Christian Hotel		✓		✓	✓					✓	✓	✓				✓	✓
Kronegade Inn		✓			✓											✓	
Pink Fancy		✓		✓	✓							✓				✓	
Sandcastle on the Beach			✓		✓	✓						✓		✓		✓	
Seaview Farm Inn					✓							✓					
Sprat Hall Plantation	✓	✓		✓	✓							✓				✓	✓
Sugar Beach Condos		✓		✓	✓	✓		✓						✓	✓		
Sunterra Resorts Carambola Beach		✓	✓	✓	✓	✓	✓	✓	✓	✓		✓	✓	✓	✓	✓	✓
Tamarind Reef Hotel		✓	✓	✓		✓	✓				✓	✓		✓			✓
Villa Madeleine		✓		✓	✓	✓			✓			✓		✓		✓	
Waves at Cane Bay	✓	✓		✓		✓	✓		✓			✓				✓	✓

it faces competition from Sunterra and Villa Madeleine (see reviews below), the Buccaneer remains the premier choice for St. Croix. It is far better organized and managed than the two properties below. Accommodations are either in the main building or in one of the beachside properties. The baronially arched main building has a lobby opening onto drinking or viewing terraces, with a sea vista on two sides and Christiansted to the west. The rooms are fresh and comfortable, though some of the standard units are a bit small. All have wicker furnishings and full bathrooms. The best bathrooms are in the "Beachside Doubloons," which come complete with whirlpool tubs.

2 miles east of Christiansted on Rte. 82 (P.O. Box 25200), Gallows Bay, Christiansted. St. Croix, U.S.V.I. 00824. © 800/255-3881 in the U.S., or 340/773-2100. Fax 340/778-8215. www.thebuccaneer.com. 138 units. Winter $280–$660 double; $450–$630 suite. Off-season $205–$410 double; $285–$450 suite. Rates include American breakfast. **Amenities:** 4 restaurants; 2 pools; golf course; 8 tennis courts; water sports; fitness center; kids program. *In room:* A/C, TV, fridge, coffeemaker, hair dryer, safe.

Sunterra Resorts Carambola Beach ⚓   This hotel is set on 28 acres above Davis Bay, about a 30-minute drive from Christiansted. It's one of the largest hotels on St. Croix and lies adjacent to an outstanding golf course, in a lovely, lush setting on a white-sand beach whose turquoise waters boast fine snorkeling. Try as it may, this resort never achieves the class and style of Buccaneer. Originally built as a Rock Resort, it has suffered hurricane attacks and management changes, and today it's hot on the trail of the time-share market.

Guests are housed in red-roofed, two-story buildings, each of which contains six units. The accommodations are furnished in rattan and wicker, with pastel colors; each has a balcony partially concealed from outside view, overlooking either the garden or the sea. Rooms have an upscale flair, with louvered doors, tile floors, mahogany trim, and sometimes such extras as screened-in porches with rocking chairs. Bathrooms are luxurious and roomy, with oversized showers (with seats) and tiled vanities. If you want the very finest room here, ask for the Davis Bay Suite, which was a former Rockefeller private beach home. Its veranda alone is capable of entertaining 100 people, should that many drop in on you.

P.O. Box 3031, Kingshill, St. Croix, U.S.V.I. 00851. © 800/503-8760 in the U.S., or 340/778-3800. Fax 340/778-1682. www.sunterra.com. 151 units. Winter $170–$270 double; $600 suite. Off-season $135–$195 double; $410 suite. AE, DC, DISC, MC, V. **Amenities:** 2 restaurants; pool; golf course; 4 tennis courts; fitness center; dive shop; snorkeling; fishing; library; 24-hour room service; baby-sitting; massage; car rentals. *In room:* A/C, TV, fridge, coffeemaker, hair dryer.

Villa Madeleine ⚓   This deluxe 6½-acre property has some of the island's poshest rooms. When it first opened, the Villa showed great promise of overtaking the Buccaneer. That never happened. The property remains distinguished, but service here has fallen off greatly, and the Buccaneer still sails mightly in the wind.

The Villa is very independent of everything else on St. Croix—guests check in here and often never leave the grounds. Many of the well-heeled occupants are retirees who live here full-time. The focal point is the great house, whose Chippendale balconies and proportions emulate the Danish colonial era. Inside, a splendidly conceived decor incorporates masses of English chintz and mahogany paneling. Each stylish one- or two-bedroom villa has its own kitchen, privacy wall, and plunge pool. The marble bathrooms have double dressing areas and oversized showers. The villas making up the resort are handled by different management companies; therefore, standards can vary greatly depending on which one you're assigned. Beach-lovers willingly travel the third of a mile to the nearest beaches, Reef and Grapetree.

8 miles east of Christiansted at Teague Bay (P.O. Box 26160), St. Croix, U.S.V.I. 00824. © 800/496-7379 or 340/778-8782. Fax 340/773-2150. www.villamadeleine.com. 43 units. Winter $375 one-bedroom villa; $475 two-bedroom villa. Off-season $275 one-bedroom villa; $375 two-bedroom villa. AE, MC, V. Children ages 11 and under are discouraged. **Amenities:** 2 restaurants; bar; tennis court; golf course below the property; library; laundry; baby-sitting. *In room:* A/C, TV, coffeemaker, kitchen.

St. Croix Accommodations

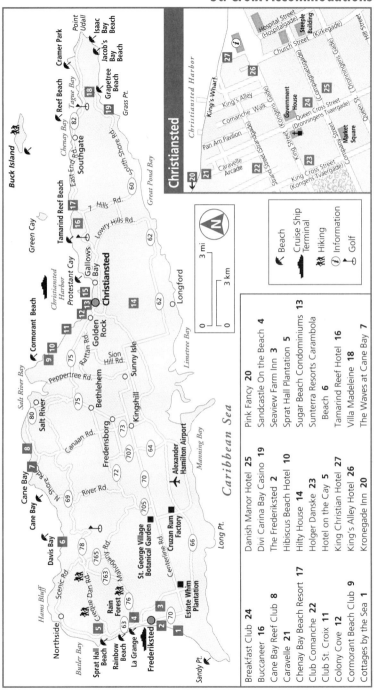

Christiansted

Legend:
- Beach
- Cruise Ship Terminal
- Hiking
- (i) Information
- Golf

Breakfast Club **24**
Buccaneer **16**
Cane Bay Reef Club **8**
Caravelle **21**
Chenay Bay Beach Resort **17**
Club Comanche **22**
Club St. Croix **11**
Colony Cove **12**
Cormorant Beach Club **9**
Cottages by the Sea **1**

Danish Manor Hotel **25**
Divi Carina Bay Casino **19**
The Frederiksted **2**
Hibiscus Beach Hotel **10**
Hilty House **14**
Holger Danske **23**
Hotel on the Cay **5**
King Christian Hotel **27**
King's Alley Hotel **26**
Kronegade Inn **20**

Pink Fancy **20**
Sandcastle On the Beach **4**
Seaview Farm Inn **3**
Sprat Hall Plantation **5**
Sugar Beach Condominiums **13**
Sunterra Resorts Carambola Beach **6**
Tamarind Reef Hotel **16**
Villa Madeleine **18**
The Waves at Cane Bay **7**

EXPENSIVE

Cormorant Beach Club ⚞ This is the poshest gay resort in the Caribbean Basin, located on a sandy beach and dwarfing all competition. About 70% of its clientele are gay males, mostly from the eastern United States or California. The 12-acre property is designed in a boxy, modern-looking series of rectangles, with strong horizontal lines and outcroppings of exposed natural stone. It strikes a well-coordinated balance between seclusion and accessibility. Long Reef lies a few hundred feet offshore from the resort's sandy beachfront.

Bedrooms contain a restrained decor of cane and wicker furniture, spacious bathrooms with tubs and showers, and sliding-glass doors that flood the interior with sunlight. The social life here revolves around an open-air clubhouse, with views of the sea. Off the central core is a bar (see "St. Croix After Dark," below) and an airy dining room. The restaurant is St. Croix's leading gay eatery (see "Dining," below).

4126 La Grande Princesse (about 3 miles northwest of Christiansted, beside route 75), St. Croix, U.S.V.I. 00820. ℂ **800/548-4460** in the U.S., or 340/778-8920. Fax 340/778-9218. www.cormorant-stcroix.com. 38 units. Winter $180–$300 double; $265 suite. Off-season $130–$210 double; $225 suite. Extra bed $20. AE, DC, DISC, MC, V. Dive, golf, scuba, and commitment ceremony packages available. **Amenities:** Restaurant, bar; 2 tennis courts, gym, pool, snorkeling. *In room:* A/C, TV, coffeemaker, hair dryer.

Divi Carina Bay Casino ⚞ Set along 1,000 feet of sugar-white beach, this resort has brought gambling to the U.S. Virgin Islands. That fact seems to obscure its success as a place of barefoot elegance and a top new resort property. The resort was built on the ruins of the former Grapetree Shores, which was wiped away by Hurricane Hugo. The Divi has both smoking and no-smoking rooms available and opens onto a good beach. Accommodations feature ocean-front guest rooms and villa suites with views of the Caribbean. Rooms are good-sized and well equipped with full bathrooms and balconies. We prefer the accommodations on the ground floor because they are closer to the water's edge. The 20 villas across the street are about a 3-minute walk from the sands. There's not only that casino but also "The Spa," where experts work you over to create a new you.

25 Estate Turner Hole, St. Croix, U.S.V.I. 00820. ℂ **800/823-9352** in the U.S., or 340/773-9700. Fax 340/773-6802. www.diviresorts.com. 146 units. Winter $225–$250 double; from $400 suite. Off-season $175–$200 double; from $275 suite. AE, DISC, DC, MC, V. **Amenities:** 2 restaurants, bar; 5 pools; 2 tennis courts; spa; fitness center; dock; snorkeling; casino; water sports center; room service; children's program. *In room:* A/C, TV/VCR, fax, minibar, coffeemaker, kitchenette, safe.

Tamarind Reef Hotel There's a sandy beach at your doorstep and good snorkeling along the reef. Each motel-style room features a garden patio or private balcony, affording guests a view of the blue Caribbean. In addition, 19 of the suites provide fully equipped kitchenettes for up to four people. Guests can relax by the pool and enjoy cocktails, light lunches, and snacks from the poolside bar and grill. For those who want to explore St. Croix underwater, the hotel offers complimentary water-sports equipment. Adjoining the hotel is the Green Cay Marina where guest can charter boats for deep-sea fishing or sailing expeditions.

5001 Tamarind Reef, St. Croix, U.S.V.I. 00820. ℂ **800/619-0014** in the U.S., or 340/773-4455. Fax 340/773-3989. www.usvi.net/hotel/tamarind. 46 units. Winter $188–$220 double. Off-season $155–$165 double. Includes daily continental breakfast. Extra person $25. Children under age 7 stay free in parents' room. Dive, golf, and honeymoon packages available. AE, MC V. **Amenities:** Restaurant; pool. *In room:* A/C, TV, fridge, coffeemaker, hair dryer, iron.

Chenay Bay Beach Resort ** (Kids)* These West Indian–style cottages are nestled on a 30-acre beach, with an open-air swimming pool. Home to one of the island's finest beaches for swimming, snorkeling, and windsurfing, Chenay Bay is just 3 miles east of Christiansted and is a terrific beach for families. With a quiet and barefoot-casual ambience, each cottage contains a fully equipped kitchenette and bathroom. The 20 original cottages are smaller and more weathered than the newer duplexes numbered 21 to 50. Accommodations are medium in size, with firm mattresses resting on comfortable beds. Most bathrooms are compact but with adequate shelf space and tubs.

Route 82, East End Road (P.O. Box 24600), St. Croix, U.S.V.I. 00824. *C* **800/548-4457** in the U.S., or 340/773-2918. Fax 340/773-6665. www.chenaybay.com. 50 cottages. Winter $157–$220 cottage for one or two. Off-season $145–$187 cottage for one or two. Additional person $25 extra. Children under age 18 stay free. $65 per person extra for all meals and drinks. AE, MC, V. **Amenities:** Restaurant, bar; picnic area; pool; 2 tennis courts; snorkeling; kayaking; children's program; baby-sitting. *In room:* A/C, TV, coffeemaker; hair dryers available at front desk.

CHRISTIANSTED
MODERATE

Hotel Caravelle ** (Value)* The biggest hotel in the historic core of Christiansted, Hotel Caravelle often caters to international business travelers who prefer to be near the center of town. Many sports activities, such as sailing, deep-sea fishing, snorkeling, scuba, golf, and tennis, can be arranged at the reception desk. A swimming pool and sun deck face the water, and all the shopping and activities in town are close at hand. Reaching the nearest beach requires a ferryboat ride from the harbor. There's an Andalusian-style fountain in the lobby, and the restaurant, Banana Bay Club, is a few steps away.

Accommodations, which are generally spacious and comfortably furnished, are priced according to their views. Bedrooms are a bit small but comfortable. We prefer the rooms on the third floor because they have high ceilings and the best views, although there are no elevators. The least expensive units open onto a parking lot. Bathrooms, also small, are neatly maintained, with adequate shelf space and shower stalls.

44A Queen Cross St., Christiansted, St. Croix, U.S.V.I. 00820. *C* **800/524-0410** or 340/773-0687. Fax 340/778-7004. www.hotelcaravelle.com. 44 units. Winter $140–$150 double; $400 suite. Off-season $110–$120 double; $280 suite. AE, DC, DISC, MC, V. **Amenities:** Restaurant, bar; pool; exercise room. *In room:* A/C, TV, fridge.

Danish Manor Hotel *** This is a good hotel in the heart of Christiansted. It features hand-painted tropical friezes around the postage-stamp swimming pool, plus art and mementos strewn about the courtyard bar. The only drawback is that there's no view of the sea from most rooms. However, some rooms on the top (third) floor overlook the sands of Protestant Cay. An L-shaped three-story addition stands in the rear, with spacious but sterile rooms with air-conditioning and ceiling fans. Bathrooms are small, with shower stalls. You can park in a public lot off King Street. The popular Italian/seafood restaurant Tutto Bene fronts the hotel (see review in "Dining," later in this chapter). Guests can swim at the beach in Christiansted Harbor, about a 5-minute ferry ride from the hotel.

2 Company St., Christiansted, St. Croix, U.S.V.I. 00820. *C* **800/524-2609** in the U.S., or 340/773-1377. Fax 340/773-1913. www.danishmanor.com. 36 units. Winter $128–$147 double; $206 suite. Off-season $89–$105 double; $175 suite. Rates include continental breakfast. AE, DC, DISC, MC, V. **Amenities:** Bar; pool. *In room:* A/C, TV, hair dryer. No phone.

Hibiscus Beach Hotel *ℱ* This hotel, located on one of the island's best beaches, attracts a lively clientele. The accommodations are in five two-story pink buildings. Each guest room is a retreat unto itself, with a private patio or balcony and a view of the Caribbean, plus tasteful Caribbean furnishings and floral prints. Even though all rooms face the water, those further back are cheaper and called "oceanfront" rather than "oceanview." We think Hotel Caravelle has more character, but this inn is still a worthy choice in spite of its somewhat antiseptic look. Shower-only bathrooms are small but well maintained.

4131 La Grande Princesse (next to the Cormorant, 10 minutes from Christiansted), St. Croix, U.S.V.I. 08820. ✆ 80/442-0121 or 340/773-4042. Fax 340/773-7668. www.st-croix.com/hibiscus. 37 units. Winter $180–$190 double; $290 efficiency. Off-season $130–$140 double; $220 efficiency. Honeymoon, dive, and golf packages available. AE, DISC, MC, V. **Amenities:** Restaurant; pool; snorkeling. *In room:* A/C, TV, minibar, hair dryer, safe.

Hotel on the Cay With its buff-colored stucco, terra-cotta tiles, and archways, this rather sterile-looking hotel evokes Puerto Rico or the Dominican Republic, but it's the most prominent building on a 3-acre island set in the middle of Christiansted's harbor. Reaching it requires a 4-minute boat ride from a well-marked quay in the town center (hotel guests ride free; nonguests pay $3 round-trip). Its position in the clear waters of the harbor is both its main plus and its main drawback: Its wide, sandy beaches provide the only pollution-free swimming in the town center, but it's the first hotel to be wiped off the map when a hurricane strikes.

In theory, this battered old place should be a lavishly landscaped, upscale retreat; unfortunately, it's not. Nonetheless, it does provide adequate, simple, and clean accommodations near the beach. Units are fairly roomy; most have two double beds, glass tables, wicker armchairs, desks and bureaus, adequate closet space, and laminate shower-only bathrooms. Rooms open onto small metal-railed balconies with a view of the garden or the Christiansted harbor.

Protestant Cay, Christiansted, St. Croix, U.S.V.I. 00820. ✆ 800/524-2035 or 340/773-2035. Fax 809/773-7046. 55 units. Winter $189 double; $225 suite. Off-season $130 double; $165 suite. Extra person $25. AE, DISC, MC, V. **Amenities:** Restaurant; bar; 2 tennis courts; pool. *In room:* A/C, TV.

King Christian Hotel This hotel is directly on the waterfront, right in the heart of everything. All of its front rooms have two double beds, refrigerator, safe, and private balcony overlooking the harbor. No-frills economy rooms have two single beds or one double and no view or balcony. Rooms are either small or medium in size. All have been redone in the past few years, with fresh mattresses on the comfortable beds, rugs and draperies, and renewed fixtures in the tiny, shower-only bathrooms. You can relax on the sun deck or on the shaded patio. There's a beach a few hundred yards across the harbor, reached by ferry. Mile Mark Charters water-sports center offers daily trips to Buck Island's famous snorkeling trail. In this category, however, we find King's Alley, a neighbor, far more appealing; see the review below.

59 King St. (P.O. Box 3619), Christiansted, St. Croix, U.S.V.I. 00824. ✆ 800/524-2012 in the U.S., or 340/773-6330. Fax 340/773-9411. www.kingchristian.com. 39 units. Winter $147–$150 double. Off-season $125–$159 double. AE, DC, DISC, MC, V. **Amenities:** Pool. *In room:* A/C, TV.

King's Alley Hotel *ℱ* This inn stands at water's edge, near Christiansted Harbor's yacht basin, a 4-minute ferry ride to the nearest beach at Hotel on the Cay. The place is furnished with a distinctly Mediterranean flair. Many of its rooms—which are small to medium-size—overlook its swimming-pool terrace

Kids Family-Friendly Hotels

The Buccaneer *(see p. 154)* Children get a big welcome at this family-owned resort, and those ages 11 and under stay free in their parents' room. During school holidays, the hotel has organized activities for kids.

Colony Cove *(see p. 165)* Families staying at Colony Cove have their own kitchens, clothes washers, and dryers. The hotel is near a beach and has a swimming pool.

Chenay Bay Beach Resort *(see p. 159)* Guests have their own cottages here overlooking the Caribbean. The resort has a swimming pool and a fine beach nearby.

surrounded by tropical plants. The galleries opening off the bedrooms are almost spacious enough for entertaining. All rooms have twin or king-size beds with good mattresses, and the deluxe units have four-poster mahogany beds. The shower-only bathrooms are very comfortable here, with good lighting and concealed vanities.

57 King St., Christiansted, St. Croix, U.S.V.I. 00820. © **800/843-3574** or 340/773-0103. Fax 340/773-4431. 35 units. Winter $119–$169 double. Off-season $108–$148 double. AE, DC, MC, V. **Amenities:** Pool. *In room:* A/C, TV, coffeemaker.

INEXPENSIVE

Breakfast Club *Value* Here you'll get the best value of any bed-and-breakfast on St. Croix. This comfortable place combines a 1950s compound of efficiency apartments with a traditional-looking stone house that was rebuilt from a ruin in the 1930s. Each of the units has a kitchenette, a cypress-sheathed ceiling, white walls, a beige tile floor, and simple, summery furniture. Shower-only bathrooms are small and adequately maintained. The centerpiece of the place is the hot tub on a raised deck, where impromptu parties are likely to develop at random hours of the day or night, and where views stretch as far off as St. John. Toby Chapin, the Ohio-born owner, cooks one of the most generous and appealing breakfasts on the island; try the banana pancakes or the chile rellenos.

18 Queen Cross St., Christiansted, St. Croix, U.S.V.I. 00820. © **340/773-7383.** Fax 340/773-8642. http://nav.to/thebreakfastclub. 9 units. Year-round $60 double. Rates include breakfast. AE, V. Free parking. **Amenities:** Hot tub. *In room:* TVs available for rent for $5 a day, kitchenette; hair dryer. No phone.

Club Comanche This famous old West Indian inn is right on the Christiansted waterfront. It's based around a 250-year-old Danish-inspired main house, once the home of Alexander Hamilton. Some of its small to medium-size bedrooms have slanted ceilings with carved four-poster beds, old chests, and mahogany mirrors. The public areas have a W. Somerset Maugham aura (or at least Sydney Greenstreet). A more modern addition, reached by a covered bridge, passes over a shopping street to the waterside. Some rooms are at poolside or harborfront buildings. Because accommodations come in such a wide range of styles and sizes, your opinion of this place is likely to be influenced almost entirely by your room assignment. Most of the units face the pool instead of the ocean. The place also has the most popular restaurant in Christiansted (see review in "Dining," below). Four minutes by ferry will take you to the beach at Hotel on the Cay.

1 Strand St., Christiansted, St. Croix, U.S.V.I. 00820. © **800/524-2066** or 340/773-0210. Fax 340/713-9145. www.usvi.nct/comanche. 45 units. Winter $75–$125 double; $175 suite. Off-season $60–$110 double; $120 suite. AE, DC, V. **Amenities:** Restaurant, bar. *In room:* A/C, TV, hair dryer.

Hilty House ✦   This tranquil B&B perches on a hilltop surrounded by mountains on the east side of St. Croix. It's a 15-minute ride from the airport, and the nearest beach is a 10-minute drive away. The place is housed in a 200-year-old building that was once a rum distillery. On arriving, guests pass through a shaded courtyard to a set of iron gates that lead to the inn's gardens. The beautifully appointed plantation-style house has a high-ceilinged living room and an enormous fireplace. The master bedroom is the most lavish room, with a four-poster bed and sunken shower over which hangs a chandelier. There are also two self-catering cottages that can be rented. Accommodations are generous in size, containing fine beds and small but beautifully kept shower-only bathrooms. The Danish Kitchen, one of the cottages, has a covered porch, TV, and phone. A three-course dinner is usually served on Monday night. The overall atmosphere here is very homey and warm.

Questa Verde Rd. (P.O. Box 26077), Gallows Bay, St. Croix, U.S.V.I. 00824. © and fax **340/773-2594.** hilty house@worldnet.att.net. 6 units. Winter $120 double; $145 cottage. Off-season $95 double; $110 cottage. Three-night minimum stay in cottages. Extra person $25. Room rates include continental breakfast. No credit cards. No children under age 12. **Amenities:** Dining room, pool. *In room:* Ceiling fan. No phone.

Holger Danske ✦ (Value)   This Best Western hotel is one of the best bets in town for the budget traveler. It's located right in the heart of Christiansted. The rooms are pleasantly furnished but small; each has a private furnished balcony. Some units also offer efficiency kitchens. The property has a pool patio and a garden path walkway, but only the superior rooms open onto the harbor and its offshore cay. Water sports and other activities are nearby. The nearest beach is a 4-minute ferry ride away.

1200 King Cross St., Christiansted, St. Croix, U.S.V.I. 00821. © **800/528-1234** or 340/773-3600. Fax 340/773-8828. golgerdan@aol.com. 44 units. Winter $104–$155 double. Off-season $90–$135 double. AE, DC, DISC, MC, V. **Amenities:** Pool. *In room:* A/C, TV, fridge.

Kronegade Inn ✦ (Finds)   This small inn offers a certain down-home charm at reasonable rates. Some guests call it the "best-kept secret in Christiansted." The inn has 12 suites or apartments, each with full kitchen. The beds are comfortable, and the shower-only bathrooms, though small, are tidily maintained. The nearest beach is at the Hotel on the Cay, a 4-minute ferry ride away. The decor is in a tropical motif, with white rattan furnishings. The inn doesn't offer food service, but a number of restaurants and cafes are nearby.

1112 Western Suburb, Christiansted, St. Croix, U.S.V.I. 00820. © **340/692-9590.** Fax 340/692-9591. www.kronegadeinn.com. 15 units. Winter $87 suite for two; $107 two-bedroom suite. Off-season $75 suite for two; $95 two-bedroom suite. AE, MC, V. *In room:* A/C, TV, kitchen, coffeemaker, fridge.

Pink Fancy ✦   This small, unique hotel is a block from the Annapolis Sailing School. You get more atmosphere here than anywhere else in town, far more than at either King's Alley or King Christian. The oldest part of the four-building complex is a historic 1780 Danish town house. In the 1950s, the hotel became a mecca for writers and artists, including, among others, Noël Coward. New owners have made major renovations, installing more antiques and fine furnishings. Guest rooms have a bright, tropical feel, with ceiling fans, floral prints, and rattan furnishings; they all have kitchenettes. The deluxe rooms are furnished with canopy or iron beds, as well as antiques and artwork. The medium-size bathrooms have combination shower/tubs. A 3-minute launch ride takes guests to the beach on the Cay, the sandy islet in Christiansted's harbor.

27 Prince St., Christiansted, St. Croix, U.S.V.I. 00820. Ⓒ 800/524-2045 in the U.S., or 340/773-8460. Fax 340/773-6448. www.pinkfancy.com. 13 units. Winter $95–$125 double. Off-season $75–$105 double. Extra person $20. Rates include continental breakfast. Ask about packages and weekly rates. AE, MC, V. **Amenities:** Pool. *In room:* A/C, TV, kitchenette, fridge.

FREDERIKSTED
MODERATE
Sandcastle On the Beach This small place is the best-known gay and lesbian hotel in Frederiksted. It lies just half a mile from the town's shopping and dining facilities. Rooms are comfortably furnished but small; all have kitchenettes, good mattresses, tiny private bathrooms, and extras such as VCR, computer hookups and coolers. There are two freshwater swimming pools, a hot tub, and a beachfront patio, where you'll often encounter middle-aged men in G-strings. The resort's restaurant is excellent.

Frederiksted Beach (P.O. Box 1908), Frederiksted, St. Croix, U.S.V.I. 00841. Ⓒ 800/524-2018 or 340/772-1205. Fax 340/772-1757. www.gaytravelling.com/onthebeach. 23 units. Winter $115–$159 double. Off-season $65–$145 double. Rates include continental breakfast. AE, DISC, MC, V. **Amenities:** Restaurant; 2 pools; hot tub; beachfront patio. *In room:* A/C, TV/VCR, coffeemaker, hair dryer, kitchenette, fridge, iron.

Seaview Farm Inn This is one of the most artfully unstructured small-scale inns in St. Croix, with views that extend out over Frederiksted's cruise-ship pier. There's no swimming pool and not many formal amenities, but the inn has a great location near the northern tip of the Great Salt Pond, with Dorsch Beach within a 5-minute walk, allowing guests to appreciate the sense of living in a backwater hideaway. Set on 3 acres of rolling land, the four-building complex has a stylized West Indian decor. Each of the unexpectedly large units contains a private porch, a living room with a kitchenette, a separate bedroom, a shower-only bathroom, a supply of paperback books for low-key reading, and beach towels and beach chairs. Most have iron four-poster beds, comfortable wicker and rattan furnishings, and the ingredients for the day's continental breakfast stocked in the refrigerators.

180 Estate Two Brothers (about a mile south of central Frederiksted), Frederiksted, St. Croix, U.S.V.I. 00840. Ⓒ 800/792-5060 in the U.S., or 340/772-5367. Fax 340/772-5060. www.seaviewfarm.net. 8 suites. Winter $100 double; off-season $65 double. DC, MC, V. **Amenities:** Restaurant, bar. *In room:* Ceiling fan, kitchenette.

Sprat Hall Plantation ⓐ (Finds) This shabbily genteel resort is the oldest plantation great house (and the only French-built plantation house) left in the Virgin Islands, dating from St. Croix's French occupation in the late 1600s. It's set on 20 acres of grounds, with private white-sand beaches. The plantation has room for about 40 people, depending on how many guests use the cottage units. The rooms in the Great House are all nonsmoking because of the value of the antiques inside. Within the annex, which was originally built in the 1940s, each unit has simple furnishings and a view of the sea. If you want an old-fashioned and homey room that gives a sense of the region's historic origins, insist on staying in the Great House. Compared to the rest of the property, the cottages aren't very romantic and are furnished in a haphazard, rundown way. Maintenance is lacking here; stay here at your own risk. It's so offbeat that it's fun for many adventurous clients. Others who want a hotel where service and comfort are more important might prefer one of the self-sufficient units recommended, including the Waves at Cane Bay.

You can be assured of good food, either at the Beach Restaurant during the lunch hour or in the Sprat Hall Restaurant. Clients are requested to dress with decorum—no jeans or T-shirts, please. Only guests of the hotel and their friends can eat here. On the grounds is a good equestrian stable. Hiking, bird-watching, snorkeling, and shore fishing are all offered. Jet-skiing and water-skiing can be arranged.

1 mile north of central Frederiksted on Route 63 (P.O. Box 695), Frederiksted, St. Croix, U.S.V.I. 00841. ✆ 800/843-3584 or 340/772-0305. Fax 340/772-2880. 17 units. $130–$150 double; $150 cottage. No credit cards. **Amenities:** Restaurants, bar; laundry, baby-sitting. *In room:* A/C, TV.

INEXPENSIVE

The Frederiksted   This contemporary four-story inn is a good choice for the heart of historic Frederiksted. It's located in the center of town, about a 10-minute ride from the airport. Much of the activity takes place in the outdoor tiled courtyard, where guests enjoy drinks and listen to live music on Friday and Saturday nights. The cheery rooms are like those of a motel on the mainland, perhaps showing a bit of wear, and with good ventilation but bad lighting. They're done in a tropical motif of pastels and are equipped with small fridges. The best (and most expensive) rooms are those with an ocean view; they're subject to street noise but have the best light. Each accommodation comes with a small, tiled shower-only bathroom. The nearest beach is Dorch Beach, a 1-mile walk or a 5-minute drive from the hotel, along the water.

20 Strand St., Frederiksted, St. Croix, U.S.V.I. 00840. ✆ 800/595-9519 in the U.S., or 340/772-0500. Fax 340/772-0500. www.frederikstedhotel.com. 40 units. Winter $100–$110 double. Off-season $90–$100 double. Extra person $10. AE, DISC, MC, V. **Amenities:** Pool. *In room:* A/C, TV, kitchenette, fridge.

Cottages by the Sea ⟨Value⟩   These isolated cottages are located on the water right outside Frederiksted, about 6 miles from the airport. Some cottages are made of cinder blocks, and others are wood. The paneled interiors are a bit worn. The look is a bit spartan, but reasonably comfortable. All cottages have private patios. Most bedrooms have king-size or twin beds, with tight, compact bathrooms with shower stalls. Maintenance is excellent. There are big patios out front where the guests can grill their dinners. Water sports have to be arranged elsewhere, but guests are welcome to go snorkeling in the waters just outside the grounds. *Note:* No children under age 8 are allowed.

127A Smithfield, Frederiksted, St. Croix, U.S.V.I. 00840. ✆ 800/323-7252 or 340/772-1753. Fax 340/772-1753. www.caribbeancottages.com. 22 units. Winter $119–$145 cottage for two; $225 villa for four. Off-season $85–$105 cottage for two; $155 villa for four. Extra person $20 in winter, $15 off-season. AE, DISC, MC, V. **Amenities:** snorkeling; water sports. *In room:* A/C, TV, coffeemaker, kitchenette, fridge. No phone.

SELF-SUFFICIENT UNITS AROUND THE ISLAND

If you're interested in a villa or condo rental, contact **Island Villas,** Property Management Rentals, 6 Company St., Christiansted, St. Croix, U.S.V.I. 00820 (✆ 800/626-4512 or 340/773-8821; fax 340/773-8823), which offers some of the best properties on St. Croix. Some are really private residences with pools; many are on the beach. The range goes from one-bedroom units to seven-bedroom villas, with prices from $1,000 to $14,000 per week year-round.

EXPENSIVE

Cane Bay Reef ⟨✿⟩   Attracting a loyal clientele, this resort offers large suites, each with a living room, a full kitchen, and a balcony overlooking the water. It's located on the north shore of St. Croix, about a 20-minute taxi ride from Christiansted, fronting the rocky Cane Bay Beach near the superior Waves at Cane

Bay. Sunsets are beautiful here, and the snorkeling's great. The decor is breezily tropical, with cathedral ceilings, overhead fans, and Chilean tiles. Bedrooms are spacious, cool, and airy, with comfortable beds and fine mattresses; living rooms also contain futons. Full bathrooms are medium in size and excellently maintained. There's a golf course nearby, and a dive shop within walking distance. You can cook in your own kitchen, barbecue, or walk to several restaurants.

P.O. Box 1407, Kingshill, St. Croix, U.S.V.I. 00851. ☎ **800/253-8534** in the U.S., or 340/778-2966. Fax 340/778-2966. www.canebay.com. 9 units. Winter $150–$250 daily; $970–$1,600 weekly. Off-season $100–$160 daily; $600–$990 weekly. Extra person $20. AE, DISC, MC, V. **Amenities:** Pool. *In room:* A/C, TV, kitchen, coffeemaker. No phone.

Club St. Croix   This is a well-managed, upscale apartment complex, located next to its own private beach. It's a slightly better choice than its nearest competitor, Sugar Beach Condominiums (see review below). Each private apartment has its own kitchenette, one or two bedrooms, and good views over Buck Island to the glittering lights of Christiansted. All units are clean, well maintained and furnished, and partially tiled. The setting is a three-story, cream-colored building. On the ground floor is a restaurant (Breezes) that's open daily for lunch and dinner.

3280 Estate Golden Rock (about ¼ mile north of the town center on Route 70), Christiansted, St. Croix, U.S.V.I. 00820. ☎ **800/524-2025** or 340/773-4800. Fax 340/773-8726. www.antillasresorts.com. 54 units. Winter efficiencies and junior suites $150 double; one-bedroom apartment for up to four occupants $205; two-bedroom apartments for up to six occupants $260. Off-season efficiencies and junior suites $125 double; one-bedroom apartment for up to four occupants $160; two-bedroom apartments for up to six occupants $185. AE, MC, V. **Amenities:** Restaurant, bar; pool; 3 tennis courts; dock. *In room:* A/C, TV, coffeemaker, kitchenette.

Colony Cove ⚑ (Kids)   Of all the condo complexes on St. Croix, Colony Cove is the most like a full-fledged hotel, with a relatively large staff on hand. Its four three-story buildings ring a swimming pool next to a palm-shaded beach. Apartments contain a washer and dryer (rare for St. Croix), an especially modern kitchen with microwave, an enclosed veranda or gallery, two air-conditioned bedrooms, and a pair of full bathrooms. All have a light, airy, tropical feel.

3221 Estate Golden Rock (about a mile west of Christiansted), St. Croix, U.S.V.I. 00820. ☎ **800/828-0746** in the U.S., or 340/773-1965. Fax 340/773-5397. www.usvi.net/hotel/colony. E-mail: colcove@islands.vi. 60 units. Winter $195 apt for 2; $255 apt for 4. Off-season $140 apt for 2; $170 apt for 4. Extra person $20 in winter, $10 in summer. Children under age 6 stay free. AE, DISC, MC, V. Go east on Rte. 75 heading toward Christiansted as far as Five Corners; turn left and pass Mill Harbor; Colony Cove is the next driveway to the left. **Amenities:** Snack bar; pool; snorkeling; 2 tennis courts. *In room:* A/C, TV, kitchen.

Sugar Beach Condominiums   This row of modernized studios and one-, two-, and three-bedroom apartments is strung along 500 feet of sandy beach on the north coast, off North Shore Road. Its location, however—near a housing development—is a turn-off for some visitors. The apartments, with enclosed balconies, are staggered to provide privacy. All open toward the sea, are tastefully decorated, and have fully equipped kitchens, tasteful furnishings, full bathrooms, and ample closet space. When you tire of the sand, you can swim in the free-form freshwater pool nestled beside a sugar mill where rum was made three centuries ago.

3245 Estate Golden Rock, St. Croix, U.S.V.I. 00820. ☎ **800/524-2049** in the U.S., or 340/773-5345. Fax 340/773-1359. www.sugarbeachstcroix.com. 46 studios and apts. Winter $165 studio; $195 one-bedroom apt; $235 two-bedroom apt; $285 three-bedroom apt. Off-season $99 studio; $130 one-bedroom apt; $155 two-bedroom apt; $195 three-bedroom apt. Maid service extra. AE, MC, V. **Amenities:** Pool; 2 tennis courts. *In room:* A/C, TV, kitchens.

The Waves at Cane Bay *(Finds)* This intimate and tasteful condo property is about 8 miles from the airport, midway between the island's two biggest towns. It's set on a well-landscaped plot of oceanfront property on Cane Bay, the heart of the best scuba and snorkeling at Cane Bay Beach, though the beach here is rocky and tends to disappear at high tide. There's a PADI dive shop on the property. It's a more comfortable and better-run choice than its nearest competitor, Cane Bay Reef (see review above). Accommodations are in two-story units with screened-in verandas, all directly on the ocean. The high-ceilinged and very large rooms come with fresh flowers, well-stocked kitchenettes, private libraries, tile floors, and shower-only bathrooms. A two-room villa next to the main building has a large oceanside deck. The beachside bar serves as the social center, and a restaurant on the premises is open Monday through Saturday in the evenings.

Cane Bay (P.O. Box 1749, Kingshill), St. Croix, U.S.V.I. 00851. © **800/545-0603** in the U.S., or 340/778-1805. Fax 340/778-4945. www.canebaystcroix.com. 12 units. Winter $140–$195 double. Off-season $75–$140 double. Extra person $20. AE, MC, V. From the airport, go left on Rte. 64; after 1 mile, turn right on Rte. 70; after another mile, go left at the junction with Rte. 75; after 2 miles, turn left at the junction with Rte. 80; follow for 5 miles. **Amenities:** Restaurant, bar; pool. *In room:* A/C, TV, kitchenette, safe.

4 Dining

Don't limit yourself to your hotel for dining. St. Croix's many independently owned restaurants serve up some of the best food in the Caribbean.

Most visitors sample diversity in their dining during lunch when, chances are, they are out indulging in beach life, shopping, or visiting attractions during the day. Christiansted is filled with excellent restaurants offering lunch, but lunch in Frederiksted is a bit dicey if cruise ships have arrived. If so, the few restaurants here may be packed with your next-door neighbors (the ones you went to St. Croix to avoid).

At night dining on island becomes more of a problem if you want to venture out. If you're not familiar with badly lit roads and driving on the left, driving to the restaurant of your choice might present some difficulties. Of course, the easiest way to go is have your hotel call a taxi and let the driver deliver you to a restaurant. Agree upon the hour you're to be picked up, and he'll even return for you, or else the restaurant will summon a cab for you if you don't want to lock yourself into a time frame. Most of the resorts are along the north shore and dining at a different resort every night (unless you're on a meal plan) is easily arranged by taxi.

If you're staying at one of the small hotels or guest houses in and around Christiansted, you can even walk to your restaurant of choice. If you're at a hotel in Frederiksted, the night is yours, as the cruise-ship crowds have departed and there is a less expensive, earthier, and more laid-back feeling in the small dining rooms here.

CHRISTIANSTED
EXPENSIVE

Indies *(Finds)* CARIBBEAN Catherine Plav-Drigger is one of the best chefs in the Caribbean, and at her restaurant you're likely to get your finest meal on St. Croix. Indies is a welcoming retreat, set in a 19th-century courtyard lined with antique cobblestones. You dine adjacent to an 1850s carriage and cookhouse in a sheltered courtyard protected from the noise of the street outside. The menu changes depending on what's fresh. The fresh fish and lobster are caught in Caribbean waters, and local seasonal fruits and vegetables are featured. Try the swordfish with fresh artichokes, shiitake mushrooms, and thyme, or perhaps the

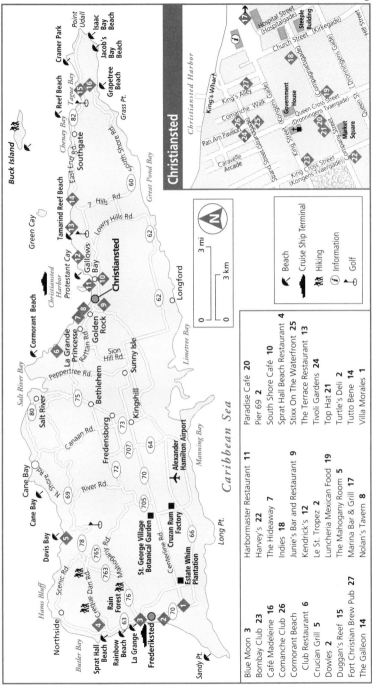

Christiansted

Buck Island

Point Udall
Isaac Bay Beach
Cramer Park
Jacob's Bay Beach

Reef Beach
Grapetree Beach
Southgate

Tamarind Reef Beach

Green Cay

Gallows Bay

Christiansted

Cormorant Beach

La Grande Princesse

Golden Rock

Protestant Cay
Christiansted Harbor

Longford

Sion Hill Rd.

Sunny Isle

Bethlehem

Kingshill

Salt River

Fredensborg

Alexander Hamilton Airport

Cane Bay

Davis Bay

St. George Village Botanical Garden

Cruzan Rum Factory

Estate Whim Plantation

Rain Forest

La Grange
Frederiksted

Sprat Hall Beach
Rainbow Beach

Northside

Hams Bluff

Caribbean Sea

Legend
- Beach
- Cruise Ship Terminal
- Hiking
- ℹ Information
- Golf

N
3 mi
3 km

Christiansted Harbor

Hospital Street (Hospitalgade)
Steeple Building
Church Street (Kirkegade)
King's Wharf
King's Alley
Comanche Walk
Government House
Pan Am Pavilion
Queen Cross Street (Dronningens Tvaergade)
Market Square
Caravelle Arcade
King Cross Street (Kongens Tvaergade)

Strand Street (Strandgade)
King Street (Kongens Gade)
Company Street (Companiegade)
Queen Street

Blue Moon **3**
Bombay Club **23**
Café Madeleine **16**
Comanche Club **26**
Cormorant Beach Club Restaurant **6**
Crucian Grill **5**
Dowles **2**
Duggan's Reef **15**
Fort Christian Brew Pub **27**
The Galleon **14**

Harbormaster Restaurant **11**
Harvey's **22**
The Hideaway **7**
Indies **18**
Junie's Bar and Restaurant **9**
Kendrick's **12**
Le St. Tropez **2**
Luncheria Mexican Food **19**
The Mahogany Room **17**
Marina Bar & Grill **17**
Nolan's Tavern **8**

Paradise Café **20**
Pier 69 **2**
South Shore Café **10**
Sprat Hall Beach Restaurant **4**
Stixx On The Waterfront **25**
The Terrace Restaurant **13**
Tivoli Gardens **24**
Top Hat **21**
Turtle's Deli **2**
Tutto Bene **14**
Villa Morales **1**

baked wahoo with lobster curry and fresh chutney and coconut. Soup choices may include an excellent island lobster and shrimp bisque or a spicy black-bean soup. A different pasta dish is offered nightly. All the desserts are freshly made.

55–56 Company St. ✆ 340/692-9440. Reservations recommended. Main courses $13–$27. AE, DISC, MC, V. Mon–Fri 11:30am–2:30pm; daily 6–10pm.

Kendricks ✒ FRENCH/CONTINENTAL   This restaurant, the island's toniest, lies in the historic Quin House complex at King Cross and Company Streets. It has both upstairs and downstairs dining rooms, the downstairs being more informal. Some of its recipes have been featured in *Bon Appétit,* and deservedly so. You'll immediately warm to such specialties as homemade eggplant ravioli with a tomato-basil butter or grilled filet mignon with black truffle in a bordelaise sauce. The signature appetizer is seared scallops and artichoke hearts in a lemon-cream sauce. Another great choice is the pecan-crusted roast pork loin with a ginger mayonnaise.

2132 Company St. ✆ 340/773-9199. Reservations required for dinner upstairs. Main courses $19–$28. AE, MC, V. Tues–Sat 6–9:30pm.

Top Hat ✒ CONTINENTAL/SCANDINAVIAN   This staid restaurant, set on the second floor of an 18th-century merchant's house, is a long-enduring favorite, despite its rather standard cuisine. It's the only Danish restaurant in the Virgin Islands. Choices include well-prepared dishes such as crisp roast duck prepared Danish-style with apples, prunes, red cabbage, sugar-brown Irish potatoes, and demi-glace sauce; chilled cucumber soup; local mahi-mahi sautéed with butter and lime; and an interesting version of Wiener Schnitzel. This may be the only place around where you can order smoked eel and scrambled eggs, as well as Scandinavian meatballs. The Top Hat platter comes with herring, roast beef, pâté, frikadeller, cheese, and fried fish.

52 Company St. (opposite Market Square, 2 blocks inland from Christiansted's wharves). ✆ 340/773-2346. Reservations recommended. Main courses $20–$32, including salad bar. AE, DC, DISC, MC, V. Mon–Sat 6–10pm. Closed July.

MODERATE

The Bombay Club INTERNATIONAL   This is one of the most enduring restaurants in Christiansted. It's concealed from the street by the brick foundations of an 18th-century planter's town house. You enter through a low stone tunnel and eventually end up near the bar and the courtyard that contains many of its tables. The food, though not overly fancy, is plentiful, full of flavor, and reasonably priced. The best items include the catch of the day, regional dishes such as conch, veal dishes, beef fillet, and pasta. The island's best fresh lobster pasta is served here.

5A King St. ✆ 340/773-1838. Reservations recommended. Main courses $10–$18. MC, V. Mon–Fri 11am–4pm and 5–10pm, Sat–Sun 6–10pm.

Comanche Club CARIBBEAN/CONTINENTAL   Relaxed yet elegant, Comanche is one of the island's most popular restaurants. It's not the best, but the specialties are eclectic—everything from fish and conch chowder to shark cakes. Each night, a different special and a different local dish are featured. Other choices include salads, a cold buffet, curries, fish sautéed with lemon butter and capers, and typical West Indian dishes, such as conch Creole with fungi. There are also standard international dishes such as filet mignon in a béarnaise sauce.

1 Strand St. ✆ 340/773-2665. Reservations recommended. Main courses $13–$25; lunch from $12. AE, MC, V. Mon–Sat 11:30am–2:30pm and 5:30–9:30pm.

South Shore Café AMERICAN   Set in a simple, breezy building on an isolated inland region ("in the middle of nowhere"), this is a charming and intensely
personalized family-style restaurant. Decorating quirks (including a collection of
umbrellas hanging from the ceiling of the lattice-trimmed dining room) add a
funky, offbeat note to what are usually well-turned-out meals with a rural North
American twist. Excellent choices include ravioli stuffed with sweet potatoes and
spring onions; a tomato-based Sicilian clam chowder; baked Brie with a rum
sauce; local grilled fish with herb-flavored butter sauce; and homemade grilled
chicken lasagna with sun-dried tomatoes and a sherry-flavored cream sauce.

2 miles southeast of Christiansted at the junction of Routes 62 and 624. Ⓒ **340/773-9311.** Reservations
required. Main courses $12–$25. MC, V. Mid-Dec–Apr Wed–Sun 6–9pm. May–mid-Dec Thurs–Sun 6–9pm.

Stixx on the Waterfront INTERNATIONAL/AMERICAN   This rustic
two-story establishment is located at the Pan Am Pavilion on the waterfront in
downtown Christiansted. Its deck extends out over the harbor. Lobster is the
house specialty. Stixx is also known for its stuffed mushrooms, swordfish served
with a mango salsa, and grilled vegetables over angel-hair pasta. Most dishes are
democratically priced at the lower end of the scale.

39 Strand St. Ⓒ **340/773-5157.** Reservations recommended. Main courses $10–$30; lunches from $5.50;
all-you-can-eat Sun brunch $12.50 adults, $6.50 children. AE, MC, V. Daily 7am–10pm.

Tivoli Gardens INTERNATIONAL   The large second-floor porch festooned
with lights affords the same view of Christiansted Harbor that a sea captain
might have. This well-known local gathering spot has white beams, trellises, and
hanging plants that evoke its namesake, the pleasure gardens of Copenhagen.
Ingredients are fresh and deftly handled. Begin with the house special soup,
Tivolienne, made with onions and cabbage in a hearty beef broth, with added
flavor from Swiss cheese. There's also a West Indian pea soup made with ham
and island spices. Main courses come with garlic bread and include succulent
pastas, such as linguine with Italian sausage or penne with chicken and broccoli.
Other choices are the Thai seafood curry and the fresh grilled fish of the day—
perhaps wahoo, tuna, or dolphin. If there's still room left, opt for the peanut
butter pie with chocolate frosting or the local favorite, guava cream pie. The
kitchen is also known for its homemade ice creams, especially the lemon cheesecake ice cream.

39 Strand St., upstairs in the Pan Am Pavilion. Ⓒ **340/773-6782.** Reservations recommended after 7pm.
Main courses $14–$25. AE, MC, V. Mon–Fri 11am–2:30pm; daily 5:30–9:30pm.

Tutto Bene ITALIAN   In the heart of town, this place seems more like a
bistro-cantina than a full-fledged restaurant. The owners, Smokey Odom and
Kelly Williams, believe in simple, hearty, and uncomplicated *paysano* dishes, the
kind that mamas fed their sons in the old country. You'll dine on wooden tables
covered with painted tablecloths, amid warm colors and often lots of hubbub.
Menu items are written on a pair of oversize mirrors against one wall. At lunch,
you can enjoy bistro-style veggie frittatas, a chicken pesto sandwich, or spinach
lasagna. A full range of delectable pastas and well-prepared seafood is offered
nightly. Fish might be served parmigiana, or you can order seafood Genovese
with mussels, clams, and shrimp in a white wine/pesto sauce over linguine. The
large mahogany bar in back does a brisk business of its own.

2 Company St. Ⓒ **340/773-5229.** Reservations accepted only for parties of five or more. Main courses
$12.95–$24.95. AE, MC, V. Daily 6–10pm.

INEXPENSIVE

Fort Christian Brew Pub CAJUN   This fish house and brewery boasts one of the best harbor views in Christiansted. It's the only licensed microbrewery in the U.S. Virgin Islands. Beer choices include a pale ale (Frigate), a red beer (Blackbeard's), and a dark stout (Jump-Up), all of which have already earned a formidable reputation on the island. Many patrons here come just to drink, staying until the pub's closing at around 1am. But if you're hungry, a roster of burgers and sandwiches is served on street level at lunch and dinner. In the evening, the upstairs dining room offers a two-fisted menu that includes 16-ounce rib-eye with caramelized onions. A favorite of ours is Bourbon Street Jambalaya. Maybe it's better in New Orleans, but this version tastes very much of Louisiana, as does the shrimp étouffée, slow cooked in a blend of Creole spices and stock. The blackened or pan-seared catfish takes you way down south. For something West Indian, order the red snapper with fungi (okra and cornmeal).

King's Alley Walk. (C) **340/713-9820.** Reservations recommended for upstairs dining room, not for meals in the brew pub. Platters in brew pub $8–$12; main courses in upstairs restaurant $12–$24. MC, V. Mon–Sat 11am–11pm.

Harbormaster Restaurant AMERICAN   This is where guests at the local town inns head for a day at the beach. It's a 4-minute ferry ride across the harbor from Christiansted. While here, you don't want to go back into town for lunch, so the hotel has wisely decided to accommodate its many day visitors by offering this quite acceptable restaurant. It offers the usual array of salad platters, sandwiches, omelets, and burgers, but many main dishes are more elaborate and appealing, especially the grilled fillet of mahi-mahi (or swordfish); the conch in a lemon, garlic, and butter sauce; and the barbecued ribs. The excellent Tuesday evening West Indian barbecue costs $23 for all you can eat; steel band music accompanies the feast.

At the Hotel on the Cay, Protestant Cay. (C) **340/773-2035.** Main courses $6.50–$17.50; breakfast from $3.50. AE, DISC, MC, V. Mon–Fri 8am–5pm, Tues 7–9:30pm.

Harvey's CARIBBEAN/CONTINENTAL   Forget the plastic and the flowery tablecloths that give this place a 1950s ambience and enjoy the thoroughly zesty cooking of island matriarch Sarah Harvey, who takes joy in her work and definitely aims to fill your stomach with her basic but hearty fare. Try one of her homemade soups, especially the callaloo or chicken. She'll even serve you conch in butter sauce as an appetizer. For a main dish you might choose from barbecue chicken, barbecue spareribs, boiled fillet of snapper, and sometimes even lobster. Fungi comes with just about everything. For dessert, try one of the delectable tarts made from guava, pineapple, or coconut.

11B Company St. (C) **340/773-3433.** Main courses $7–$10. No credit cards. Mon–Sat 11:30am–5pm.

The Hideaway ⭐ (Value) AMERICAN   This open-air restaurant fronts one of the island's best beaches. It's a true hideaway, known for serving one of the island's best breakfasts, including eggs Benedict or salmon with sour cream. The chef also makes one of the island's best omelets. At lunch, you get the usual burgers and sandwiches, as well as main-dish specialties. At night, the menu is considerably upgraded, based on the market that day. You can usually get fresh fish prepared as you like it and sometimes lobster. The baby back ribs are a winner. The Wednesday night beach barbecue is all you can eat for $18.

Three miles west of Christiansted at the Hibiscus Beach Hotel, La Grande Princesse. (C) **340/773-4042.** Reservations recommended. Main courses $11–$25; lunch $7–$12. Breakfast $4.50–$9. AE, DISC, MC, V. Daily 7am–10pm.

Junie's Bar and Restaurant ⭐ (Finds) WEST INDIAN/SEAFOOD   A favorite of local residents, and particularly the island's corps of taxi drivers, this restaurant occupies a white-painted cement building about a half-mile south of Christiansted's main core, adjacent to a church and a discount store. Inside, wooden tables, metal chairs, bowls of cut flowers, and a well-scrubbed kind of simplicity add to the appeal. Your hosts, Junie Allen and her daughter Denise, prepare a flavor-filled but basic medley of West Indian staples, including a roster of drinks that you might not have tasted before, such as sea moss (a kind of eggnog flavored with pulverized seaweed), mauby (fermented from rain water and tree bark), and ginger beer. Good menu choices include boiled fish, conch, lobster in butter sauce, stewed goat, stewed Creole-style lobster, and pork chops with greens and yams. Desserts include carrot cake, cheesecake, and key lime pie. Because the place has been here for about 30 years, it's known by virtually everybody on the island.

132 Peter's Rest. © **340/773-2801.** Reservations not necessary. Lunch main courses $8–$12; dinner main courses $8–$22. AE, DC, DISC, MC, V. Mon–Sat 10am–11pm; Sun 11am–8pm.

Luncheria Mexican Food (Value) MEXICAN/CUBAN/PUERTO RICAN This Mexican restaurant offers great value. You get the usual tacos, tostadas, burritos, nachos, and enchiladas, as well as chicken fajitas, enchiladas verde, and arroz con pollo (spiced chicken with brown rice). Daily specials feature both low-calorie and vegetarian choices (the chef's refried beans are lard-free), and whole-wheat tortillas are offered. The complimentary salsa bar has mild to hot sauces, plus jalapeños. More recently, some Cuban and Puerto Rican dishes have appeared on the menu, including a zesty chicken curry, black-bean soup, and roast pork. The bartender makes the island's best margaritas.

In the historic Apothecary Hall Courtyard, 2111 Company St. © **340/773-4247.** Main courses $7–$12. No credit cards. Mon–Sat 11am–9pm.

Marina Bar & Grill CARIBBEAN/CONTINENTAL   Locals are fond of dining on the waterfront here, watching the seaplane land. Some in-the-know boaters head here for their morning pick-me-up, a great, spicy Bloody Mary. You can join them for breakfast, which is rather standard fare of bagels, muffins, and eggs. Lunch is also standard; many opt for one of the burgers, even a veggie burger. The best bet is one of the daily specials. In the evening the menu perks up, and fresh fish is the best item to order. Your dinner is often accompanied by steel drum music. If you show up Monday night you can get in on the crab races.

At the Kings Landing Yacht Club. © **340/773-0103.** Main courses $5.50–$12. AE, MC, V. Daily 24 hours.

Nolan's Tavern (Value) INTERNATIONAL/WEST INDIAN   This is the best place to go for a warm, cozy tavern with no pretensions. It's across from the capital's most prominent elementary school, the Pearl B. Larsen School. Your host is Nolan Joseph, a Trinidad-born chef who makes a special point of welcoming guests and offering "tasty food and good service." No one will mind if you stop in just for a drink. Mr. Joseph, referred to by some diners as "King Conch," prepares that mollusk in at least half a dozen ways, including versions with curry, Creole sauce, and garlic-pineapple sauce. He reportedly experimented for 3 months to perfect a means of tenderizing the conch without artificial chemicals. His ribs are also excellent.

5A Estate St. Peter (2 miles east of Christiansted's harbor), Christiansted East. © **340/773-6660.** Reservations recommended only for groups of six or more. Burgers $7–$9; main courses $12.75–$20. AE, DISC, MC, V. Kitchen daily 5–9pm; bar from 3pm.

Paradise Café *(Value)* DELI/AMERICAN   This neighborhood favorite draws locals seeking good food and great value. Its brick walls and beamed ceiling were originally part of an 18th-century great house. New York–style deli fare is served during the day. Enjoy the savory homemade soups or freshly made salads, to which you can add grilled chicken or fish. At breakfast, you can select from an assortment of omelets, or try the steak and eggs. Dinners are more elaborate. The 12-ounce New York strip steak and the freshly made pasta specialties are good choices. Appetizers include stuffed mushrooms and crab cakes.

53B Company St. (at Queen Cross St., across from Government House). ✆ **340/773-2985.** Breakfast $3.50–$8.50; lunch $5–$12; dinner $13–$20. No credit cards. Mon–Sat 7:30–10pm.

NORTH SHORE
EXPENSIVE
The Mahogany Room *✶* INTERNATIONAL   This elegant, exclusive enclave is located in the previously recommended hotel. The restaurant seats 100 under a vaulted cathedral ceiling. Tables lit by softly glowing lamps have a 180° view that includes the ocean. Ambience is important here, but the cuisine continues to lure upscale patrons. The menu changes, but count on dishes such as perfectly grilled wahoo from the deep ocean, made even more delightful by a roasted pepper couscous, charcoal-grilled scallions, and a hoisin sesame glaze. For a touch of island flavor, opt for tuna, which is quickly seared and served with a papaya and mango chutney. Steaks are handled with care and grilled to your preference; lamb and veal, although flown in frozen, still turn out tasty. Tangy appetizers include jumbo prawn cocktail with black bean salsa instead of the traditional cocktail sauce.

In Sunterra Resorts Carambola Beach. ✆ **340/778-3800.** Reservations required. Main courses $26–$40. AE, DC, DISC, MC, V. Winter Tues–Sat 6–9pm. Off-season Fri–Sat only 6–9pm.

The Terrace Restaurant *✶* INTERNATIONAL   This is the island's finest dining room in a hotel. Menu items vary but are likely to include grilled local lobster cakes, served with lemon caper beurre blanc (white butter) and accented with fresh tarragon. You might also opt for the poached shrimp with a fresh lime cocktail sauce or a hand-cut New York strip steak in a tamarind dark rum sauce. The delectable pecan-crusted roast pork tenderloin is served sliced over pesto mashed potatoes and red-eye gravy. The chef prepares a fresh soup nightly, but many patrons begin with a Caesar salad.

At the Buccaneer, Gallows Bay. ✆ **340/773-2100.** Reservations recommended. Main courses $18–$28. AE, DC, DISC, MC, V. Daily 6–9pm.

MODERATE
Crucian Grill INTERNATIONAL   Many guests at this luxury resort come to this informal restaurant because of its authentic island dishes, zesty flavors, and reasonable prices. It offers a wide array of lunch fare, ranging from sandwiches to coconut shrimp and conch fritters (both tasty specialties). Freshly made salads run the gamut from chicken Caesar to hearts of palm. You can also order hamburgers; try the Jamaican jerk burger. A full selection of main courses for dinner is offered as well, including a Caribbean spiced seafood brochette. You might also try the excellent Mangrove Mama's mahi-mahi, which is grilled and served on a bed of sesame seaweed with green mango salsa, or the jerk spiced pork tenderloin in a gingered guava glaze.

In Sunterra Resorts Carambola Beach. ✆ **340/778-3800.** Reservations not needed. Main courses $10–$18, sandwiches $7.50–$9.50. AE, DC, DISC, MC, V. Daily 7am–6pm.

Cormorant Beach Club Restaurant ✿ INTERNATIONAL   This is the premier gay restaurant on St. Croix. Both the restaurant and its bar are a mecca for gay and gay-friendly people who appreciate its relaxed atmosphere, well-prepared food, and gracefully arched premises overlooking the sea. The menu isn't particularly ambitious, but food items are full of flavor and generous. Lunch specialties include meal-size salads, club sandwiches, burgers, and fresh fish. Dinner might begin with carrot-ginger soup or Caribbean spring rolls with chutney; main courses include steak au poivre, chicken breast stuffed with spinach and feta, grilled New Zealand lamb chops, and grilled fillets of salmon with roasted poblano orange sauce. Desserts feature tropical fruits baked into tempting pastries.

4126 La Grande Princesse. ⓒ **340/778-8920.** Reservations recommended. Main courses $7–$12 lunch, $12–$25 dinner. AE, DC, DISC, MC, V. Daily 11:30am–3pm and 6–9pm.

Duggan's Reef ✿ CONTINENTAL/CARIBBEAN   This is one of the most popular restaurants on St. Croix. It's set only 10 feet from the still waters of Reef Beach and makes an ideal perch for watching the windsurfers and Hobie Cats careening through the nearby waters. At lunch, a simple array of salads, crêpes, and sandwiches is offered. The more elaborate night menu features the popular house specialties: Duggan's Caribbean lobster pasta and Irish whiskey lobster. Begin with fried calamari or conch chowder. Main dishes include New York strip steak, veal piccata, and pastas. The local catch of the day can be baked, grilled, blackened Cajun style, or served island style (with tomato, pepper, and onion sauce).

East End Rd., Teague Bay. ⓒ **340/773-9800.** Reservations required for dinner in winter. Main courses $17–$37; pastas $12–$18. AE, MC, V. Daily noon–3pm and 6–9:30pm. Bar daily 11am–11:30pm. Closed for lunch in summer.

The Galleon FRENCH/NORTHERN ITALIAN   This restaurant, which overlooks the ocean, is a local favorite, and deservedly so. It offers the cuisine of northern Italy and France, including osso buco, just as good as that served in Milan. Freshly baked bread, two fresh vegetables, and rice or potatoes accompany main dishes. The menu always includes at least one local fish, such as wahoo, tuna, swordfish, mahi-mahi, or even fresh Caribbean lobster. Or you might order a perfectly done rack of lamb, which will be carved right at your table. There's an extensive wine list, including many sold by the glass. Music from a baby grand piano accompanies your dinner.

East End Rd., Green Cay Marina, 5000 Estate Southgate. ⓒ **340/773-9949.** Reservations recommended. Main courses $17–$40. AE, MC, V. Daily 6–10pm. Go east on Rte. 82 from Christiansted for 5 minutes; after going a mile past the Buccaneer, turn left into Green Cay Marina.

IN & AROUND FREDERIKSTED
MODERATE

Blue Moon INTERNATIONAL/CAJUN   The best little bistro in Frederiksted becomes a hot, hip spot during Sunday brunch and on Friday nights when it offers entertainment. The 200-year-old stone house on the waterfront is a favorite of visiting jazz musicians, and tourists have discovered (but not ruined) it. It's decorated with funky, homemade art from the States, including a trash can–lid restaurant sign. The atmosphere is casual and cafelike. Begin with the "lunar pie," with feta cheese, cream cheese, onions, mushrooms, and celery in phyllo pastry, or else the artichoke-and-spinach dip. Main courses include the catch of the day and, on occasion, Maine lobster. The clams served in garlic sauce are also from Maine. Vegetarians opt for the spinach fettuccine. There's also the usual array of steak and chicken dishes. Save room for the yummy guava pie.

17 Strand St. ✆ 340/772-2222. Reservations recommended. Main courses $16.50–$21.50. AE, DISC, MC, V. Tues–Fri 11:30am–2pm, Sun 11am–2pm; Tues–Sat 6–9:30pm, Sun 6–9pm. Closed Aug.

Le St. Tropez FRENCH/MEDITERRANEAN   This is the most popular bistro in Frederiksted. It's small, so call ahead for a table. If you're visiting for the day, make this bright little cafe your lunch stop, and enjoy crêpes, quiches, soups, or salads in the sunlit courtyard. At night, the atmosphere glows with candlelight, and becomes more festive. Try the Mediterranean cuisine, beginning with mushrooms aïoli and escargots Provençale, or one of the freshly made soups. Main dishes are likely to include medallions of beef with two mushrooms, the fish of the day, or a magret of duck. Ingredients are always fresh and well prepared.

Limetree Court, 67 King St. ✆ 340/772-3000. Reservations recommended. Main courses $12–$27. AE, DISC, MC, V. Mon–Fri 11:30am–2:30pm and 6–10pm, Sat 6–10pm.

Villa Morales PUERTO RICAN   This inland spot is the premier Puerto Rican restaurant on St. Croix. You can choose between indoor and outdoor seating areas. No one will mind if you come here just to drink; a cozy bar is lined with the memorabilia collected by several generations of the family who maintain the place. Look for a broad cross-section of Hispanic tastes here, including many that Puerto Ricans remember from their childhood. Savory examples include fried snapper with white rice and beans, stewed conch, roasted or stewed goat, and stewed beef. Meal platters are garnished with beans and rice. Most of the dishes are at the lower end of the price scale. About once a month, the owners transform the place into a dance hall, bringing in live salsa and merengue bands (the cover ranges from $5 to $12).

Plot 82C, off Route 70 (about 2 miles from Frederiksted), Estate Whim. ✆ 340/772-0556. Reservations recommended. Breakfast $4–$8; lunch main courses $7–$14; dinner main courses $10–$25. MC, V. Thurs–Sat 8am–10pm.

INEXPENSIVE

Dowies CARIBBEAN/AMERICAN   This local diner occupies a prominent position in the heart of Frederiksted. Regulars appreciate this place for its complete lack of pretense, its hearty portions, and its West Indian format. Tables are set on a bed of gravel under a corrugated tin roof, but it's a bit more elegant then you'd expect. Madras-patterned tablecloths cover most surfaces. Diners can choose from a cosmopolitan choice of American and West Indian food. Breakfast choices includes omelets (meat, vegetarian, and seafood) and French toast. On Friday and Saturday, you can get a Cruzan breakfast, featuring saltfish, johnnycakes, and banana fritters. Lunch choices include platters of grilled fish, served with beans, rice, and stewed greens; a prize-winning version of fish pudding; bullfoot soup; stewed conch in butter sauce; grilled or jerk chicken; and sandwiches.

111 Market St. ✆ 340/772-0845. Reservations not necessary. Breakfasts $4–$6. Lunch platters $4–$10. MC, V. Tues–Sat 7:30am–2:30pm.

Pier 69 AMERICAN/CARIBBEAN   You can get a decent platter of food here, but this place is far more interesting for its funky, Greenwich Village–style atmosphere than for its cuisine. New York–born Unise Tranberg is the earth mother/matriarch of the place, which looks like a warm and somewhat battered combination of a 1950s living room and a nautical bar. Counterculture fans from Christiansted make this their preferred drinking hangout, sometimes opting for a mango colada or a lime lambada. Menu items include a predictable array of salads, sandwiches, and platters.

69 King St. ℂ 340/772-0069. Reservations not accepted. Sandwiches and platters $5.50–$10.50; main courses $12–$20. AE, DC, DISC, MC, V. Mon–Thurs 10am–midnight, Fri–Sun 10am–3am.

Sprat Hall Beach Restaurant ⭐ *(Finds)* CARIBBEAN   This informal spot is on the west coast, near Sprat Hall Plantation. It's the best place on the island to combine lunch and a swim. The restaurant has been in business since 1948, feeding both locals and visitors. Try such local dishes as conch chowder, pumpkin fritters, tannia soup, and the fried fish of the day. These dishes have authentic island flavor, perhaps more so than any other place on St. Croix. You can also get salads and burgers. The bread is baked fresh daily. The owners charge $2 for use of the showers and changing rooms.

A mile north of Frederiksted on Rte. 63. ℂ 340/772-5855. Lunch $8–$15. Daily 11:30am–3pm and 5:30–10pm. MC, V.

Turtle's Deli DELI   This is the only seafront deli on St. Croix. Lots of folks take their overstuffed sandwiches to the handful of outdoor tables that sit atop the wharf at its back side. The selection includes salads, baked-on-site bread, bagels, lox, and cold cuts, as well as pastries and munchies. The place is especially good at packing boxed picnics, great for a sailing or snorkeling expedition.

625 Strand St. ℂ 340/772-3676. Sandwiches $5.50–$7.50. No credit cards. Mon–Sat 10am–4:30pm.

EAST END
MODERATE
Café Madeleine CONTINENTAL   Located in the great house built by the Roncari family in 1990 in colonial style, Café Madeleine offers a mountaintop panorama of both the north and the south sides of the island. The lavish decor was created by a battalion of hardworking decorators. Don't overlook a before-dinner drink at the mahogany-trimmed bar, where a scale model of a Maine schooner, bolted against mahogany paneling, creates a private club aura. The eclectic menu might feature baked artichoke hearts, oysters Mario, fillet of red snapper Milanese, veal scaloppine alla Madeleine, and some of the most unusual pastas on island. There's a terrace for outdoor dining.

Teague Bay (8 miles east of Christiansted). ℂ 340/778-7377. Reservations recommended. Main courses $18–$36. AE, DC, MC, V. Mon–Sat 6–10pm.

5 Beaches, Water Sports & Other Outdoor Pursuits
BEACHES
Beaches are St. Croix's big attraction. The problem is that getting to them from Christiansted, which is home to most of the hotels, isn't always easy. It can also be expensive, especially if you want to go back and forth each day of your stay. Of course, you can always rent a condo right on the water.

The most celebrated beach is offshore **Buck Island,** part of the National Park network. Buck Island is actually a volcanic islet surrounded by some of the most stunning underwater coral gardens in the Caribbean. The white-sand beaches on the southwest and west coasts are beautiful, but the snorkeling is even better. The islet's interior is filled with such plants as cactus, wild frangipani, and pigeonwood. There are picnic areas for those who want to make a day of it. The whole world seems to show up here—all sexes, all ages, whatever. Boat departures are from Kings Wharf in Christiansted; the ride takes half an hour. For more information, see "A Side Trip to Buck Island," later in this chapter.

Your best choice for a beach in Christiansted is the one at the **Hotel on the Cay.** This white-sand strip is on a palm-shaded island. The beach draws guests of the hotel, mainly a middle-age crowd, but also a lot of people in their 20s and 30s, both single or couples, who are staying at one of the inns in Christiansted. To get here, take the ferry from the fort at Christiansted; it runs daily from 7am to midnight. The 4-minute trip costs $3, free for guests of the Hotel on the Cay.

Five miles west of Christiansted is the **Cormorant Beach Club,** where some 1,200 feet of white sand shaded by palm trees attracts a gay crowd. Because a reef lies just off the shore, snorkeling conditions are ideal.

We highly recommend both **Davis Bay** and **Cane Bay,** with swaying palms, white sand, and good swimming and snorkeling. Because they're on the north shore, these beaches are often windy, and their waters are not always tranquil. Nonetheless, a lot of families staying in nearby condos frequent these sands. The snorkeling at Cane Bay is truly spectacular; you'll see elkhorn and brain corals, all lying some 250 yards off the "Cane Bay Wall." Cane Bay adjoins Route 80 on the north shore. Davis Beach doesn't have a reef; it's more popular among bodysurfers than snorkelers. There are no changing facilities. It's near Carambola Beach Resort.

On Route 63, a short ride north of Frederiksted, lies **Rainbow Beach,** which offers white sand and ideal snorkeling conditions. Nearby, also on Route 63, about 5 minutes north of Frederiksted, is another good beach, called **La Grange.** Lounge chairs can be rented here, and there's a bar nearby. A lot of single travelers are attracted to this beach area.

Sandy Point, directly south of Frederiksted, is the largest beach in all the U.S. Virgin Islands, attracting mainly families and couples. Its waters are shallow and calm, perfect for swimming. Try to concentrate on the sands and not the unattractive zigzagging fences that line the beach. Take the Melvin Evans Highway (Route 66) west from the Alexander Hamilton Airport.

There's an array of beaches at the **East End** of the island; they're somewhat difficult to get to but much less crowded, attracting the adventurous traveler, both lone beach buffs and often groups of friends. The best choice here is **Isaac Bay Beach,** ideal for snorkeling, swimming, or sunbathing. Windsurfers like **Reef Beach,** which opens onto Teague Bay along Route 82, East End Road, a half-hour ride from Christiansted. You can get food at Duggan's Reef. **Cramer Park** is a special public park operated by the Department of Agriculture. It's lined with seagrape trees and has a picnic area, a restaurant, and a bar. **Grapetree Beach** is off Route 60 (the South Shore Road); water sports are popular here.

WATER SPORTS & OTHER OUTDOOR ACTIVITIES

FISHING   The fishing grounds at **Lang Bank** are about 10 miles from St. Croix. Here you'll find kingfish, dolphin fish, and wahoo. Using light-tackle boats to glide along the reef, you'll probably turn up jack or bonefish. At **Clover Crest,** in Frederiksted, local anglers fish right from the rocks.

Serious sportfishers can board the *Fantasy,* a 38-foot Bertram special available for 4-, 6-, or 8-hour charters, with bait and tackle included. It's anchored at St. Croix Marina, Gallows Bay. Reservations can be made by calling © **340/773-7165** during the day, or 340/773-0917 at night. The cost for six

Finds **Into the Deep Without Getting Wet**

St. Croix Water Sports Center (© **340/773-7060**), located at the Hotel on the Cay, features the *Oceanique,* a semi-submersible vessel acting as part submarine and part cruiser. It takes visitors on 1-hour excursions through Christiansted Harbor and along Protestant Cay. The inch-thick windows lining the vessel's underwater observation room provide views of St. Croix's colorful marine life in a cool, dry environment. This trip is especially popular with children and nonswimmers. Day and night excursions are available for $35 for adults and $25 for children. Call for reservations.

passengers is $350–$400 for 4 hours, $550–$590 for 6 hours, and $600 for 8 hours.

GOLF   St. Croix has the best golf in the U.S. Virgins. Guests staying on St. John and St. Thomas often fly over for a day's round on one of the island's three courses.

The **Carambola Golf Course,** on the northeast side of St. Croix (© **340/ 778-5638**), was created by Robert Trent Jones Sr., who called it "the loveliest course I ever designed." It's been likened to a botanical garden. The par-3 holes here are known to golfing authorities as the best in the tropics. The greens fee of $95 in winter, or $48 in summer, allows you to play as many holes as you like. Carts are included.

Buccaneer, Gallows Bay (© **340/773-2100**, ext. 738), 2 miles east of Christiansted, has a challenging 5,810-yard, 18-hole course with panoramic vistas. Nonguests of this deluxe resort pay $65 in winter or $55 off-season, plus $15 for use of a cart.

The **Reef,** on the east end of the island at Teague Bay (© **340/773-8844**), is a 3,100-yard, nine-hole course, charging greens fees of $20 including carts. The longest hole here is a 579-yard par 5.

HIKING   Scrub-covered hills make up much of St. Croix's landscape. The island's western district, however, includes a dense, 15-acre forest known as the **"Rain Forest"** (though it's not a real one). The network of footpaths here offers some of the best nature walks in the Caribbean. For more details on hiking in this area, see "Exploring the 'Rain Forest'" in "Seeing the Sights," below. **Buck Island** (see section 9 in this chapter), just off St. Croix, also offers some wonderful nature trails.

The **St. Croix Environmental Association,** 6 Company St., Christiansted (© **340/773-1989**), has regularly scheduled hikes from December to March. A minimum of four people are required, costing $25 per person.

HORSEBACK RIDING   Paul and Jill's Equestrian Stables, Sprat Hall Plantation, Route 58 (© **340/772-2880**), the largest equestrian stable in the Virgin Islands, is known throughout the Caribbean for the quality of its horses. It's set on the sprawling grounds of the island's oldest plantation great house. The operators lead scenic trail rides through the forests, past ruins of abandoned 18th-century plantations and sugar mills, to the tops of the hills of St. Croix's western end. Beginners and experienced riders alike are welcome. A 2-hour trail ride costs $50. Tours usually depart daily in winter at 10am and 4pm, and in the off-season at 5pm, with slight variations according to demand. Reserve at least a day in advance.

KAYAKING   The beauty of St. Croix is best seen on a kayak tour offered by **Caribbean Adventure Tours** (© 340/773-4599). You'll use stable sit-on-top sea kayaks—they are a blast. You traverse the tranquil waters of Salt River and enjoy the park's ecology and wildlife, including secluded estuaries and mangrove groves. This is not necessarily an adventure for the rugged Olympic athlete but is ideal for beginners, as the helpful staff is exceedingly patient and solicitous of your well-being. The highlights of the trip are snorkeling on a pristine beach and paddling to where Columbus and his crew came ashore some 500 years ago. The tour, lasting 3 hours, costs $45 per person.

SAFARI TOURS   The best are offered by **St. Croix Safari Tours** (© 340/773-6700) in a 25-passenger open-air bus tour run by a hip tour guide who knows all about the history of the island. Tours crisscross the island with stops at former plantation houses, historic Frederiksted, the Salt River landfall of Columbus, and a drive through the "Rain Forest," with a stop for lunch. There are plenty of photo ops. The cost of the tour is $38 per person (with an absolute minimum of four people). There is no central pick-up point to start the tour; arrangements about where to meet are usually worked out when you call for a reservation. If you're staying at hotels in and around Christiansted, they will agree to pick up, but they may not if you're at a remote B&B mid-island.

SNORKELING & SCUBA DIVING   Sponge life, black coral (the finest in the West Indies), and steep drop-offs into water near the shoreline make St. Croix a snorkeling and diving paradise. The island is home to the largest living reef in the Caribbean, including the fabled north-shore wall that begins in 25 to 30 feet of water and drops to 13,200 feet, sometimes straight down. See "Beaches," above, for information on good snorkeling beaches. The St. Croix Water Sports Center (see "Windsurfing," below) rents snorkeling equipment for $20 per day if your hotel doesn't supply it.

   Buck Island is a major scuba-diving site, with a visibility of some 100 feet. It also has an underwater snorkeling trail. All the outfitters offer scuba and snorkeling tours to Buck Island. See section 9, "A Side Trip to Buck Island."

   Other favorite dive sites include the historic **Salt River Canyon** (northwest of Christiansted at Salt River Bay), which is for advanced divers. Submerged canyons walls are covered with purple tube sponges, deep-water gorgonians, and black coral saplings. You'll see schools of yellowtail snapper, turtles, and spotted eagle rays. We also like the gorgeous coral gardens of **Scotch Banks** (north of Christiansted), and **Eagle Ray** (also north of Christiansted), the latter so named because of the rays that cruise along the wall there. **Cane Bay** is known for its coral canyons.

   Davis Bay is the site of the 12,000-foot-deep Puerto Rico Trench. **Northstar Reef,** at the east end of Davis Bay, is a spectacular wall dive, recommended for intermediate or experienced divers only. The wall here is covered with stunning brain corals and staghorn thickets. At some 50 feet down, a sandy shelf leads to a cave where giant green moray eels hang out.

   The ultimate night dive is at the **Frederiksted Pier.** The old pier was damaged by Hurricane Hugo and torn down to make way for a new one. The heavily encrusted rubble from the old pier remains beneath the new one, carpeted with rainbow-hued sponges and both hard and soft coral, preserving a fantastic night dive where you're virtually guaranteed to see seahorses and moray eels.

At **Butler Bay,** to the north of the pier on the west shore, three ships were wrecked: the *Suffolk Maid,* the *Northwind,* and the *Rosaomaira,* the latter sitting in 100 feet of water. These wrecks form the major part of an artificial reef system made up mostly of abandoned trucks and cars. This site is recommended for intermediate or experienced divers.

Dive St. Croix, 59 King's Wharf (📞 **800/523-DIVE** in the U.S., or 340/778-1522; fax 340/773-7400), operates the 38-foot dive boat *Reliance.* The staff offers complete instruction, from resort courses through full certification, as well as night dives. A resort course is $80, with a two-tank dive going for $80. Scuba trips to Buck Island cost $70, and dive packages begin at $350 for five dives.

V.I. Divers Ltd., in the Pan Am Pavilion on Christiansted's waterfront (📞 **340/773-6045**), is the oldest and one of the best dive operations on the island. *Rodale's Scuba Diving* magazine rated its staff as among the top 10 worldwide. This full-service PADI five-star facility offers two-tank boat dives, guided snorkeling trips to Green Cay, night dives, and a full range of scuba-training programs. Introductory two-tank dives, which require no experience, cost $95, including all instruction and equipment. A six-dive package goes for $210, and a 10-dive package for $330. A two-tank boat or beach dive is $75. Night dives go for $60. A 2-hour guided snorkel tour costs $35, the boat snorkeling trip to Green Cay, $35.

Other recommended outfitters include **Anchor Dive** (📞 800/532-DIVE), **The Buccaneer** (📞 800/255-3881), the **Cane Bay Dive Shop** (📞 340/773-9913), **St. Croix Ocean Recreational Experience (S.C.O.R.E.)** (📞 340/778-8907), and **St. Croix Ultimate Bluewater Adventure** (📞 877/789-7282).

TENNIS   Some authorities rate the tennis at the **Buccaneer,** Gallows Bay (📞 **340/773-3136,** ext. 736), as the best in the Caribbean. This resort offers a choice of eight courts, two lit for night play, all open to the public. Nonguests pay $10 per person per hour; you must call to reserve a court. A tennis pro is available for lessons, and there's also a pro shop.

WINDSURFING   Head for the **St. Croix Water Sports Center** (📞 **340/773-7060**), located on a small offshore island in Christiansted Harbor and part of the Hotel on the Cay. It's open daily from 10am to 5pm. Windsurfing rentals are $30 per hour; lessons are available. Sea Doos, which seat two, can be rented for $45 to $55 per half hour. The center also offers parasailing for $65 per person, and rents snorkeling equipment for $25 per day.

6 Seeing the Sights

CHRISTIANSTED

This town is best seen on a walking tour, such as the one below. An additional point of interest in Christiansted is the **St. Croix Aquarium,** Caravelle Arcade (📞 **340/773-8995**), which has expanded with many new exhibits, including one of "night creatures." In all, it houses some 40 species of marine animals and more than 100 species of invertebrates. A touch pond contains starfish, sea cucumbers, brittle stars, and pencil urchins. The aquarium allows you to become familiar with the marine life you'll see while scuba diving or snorkeling. It's open Tuesday through Saturday from 11am to 4pm. Admission is $5 for adults and $2 for children.

WALKING TOUR   CHRISTIANSTED

Start: Visitors Bureau.

Finish: Christiansted harbor front.

Time: 1½ hours.

Best Times: Any day from 10am to 4pm.

Worst Times: Monday through Friday from 4 to 6pm.

Begin at:

❶ The Visitors Bureau

This yellow-sided building with a cedar-capped roof is located near the harborfront. It was originally built as the Old Scalehouse in 1856, to replace a similar structure that had burned down. In its heyday, all taxable goods leaving and entering Christiansted's harbor were weighed here. In front of the building lies one of the most charming squares in the Caribbean. Its old-fashioned asymmetrical allure is still evident despite the masses of cars.

With your back to the scalehouse, turn left and walk through the parking lot to the foot of the white-sided gazebo-like band shell that sits in the center of a park named after Alexander Hamilton. The yellow-brick building with the ornately carved brick staircase is the:

❷ Old Customs House

This is currently the headquarters of the National Park Service. The gracefully proportioned 16-step staircase was added in 1829 as an embellishment to an older building. (There are public toilets on the ground floor.)

Continue climbing the hill to the base of the yellow-painted structure, which is:

❸ Fort Christiansvaern

This is the best-preserved colonial fortification in the Virgin Islands. It's maintained as a historic monument by the National Park Service. Its original four-sided, star-shaped design was in accordance with the most advanced military planning of its era. The fort is the site of the St. Croix Police Museum, which documents police work on the island from the late 1800s to the present. Photos, weapons, and artifacts help bring alive the police force's past here. The admission price of $2 also includes admission to the Steeple Building (see below). The fort is open Monday through Thursday from 8am to 5pm and Friday and Saturday from 9am to 5pm.

Exit from the fort, and head straight down the tree-lined path toward the most visible steeple in Christiansted. It caps the appropriately named:

● Steeple Building

Also known as the Church of Lord God of Sabaoth, this building was completed in 1753 as St. Croix's first Lutheran church, and embellished with a steeple in 1794–96. The building was deconsecrated in 1831 and has served at various times as a bakery, a hospital, and a school. Inside is a museum devoted to local history. Hours are daily from 8am to 5pm; admission is included in the $2 ticket for Fort Christiansvaern (see above).

Across Company Street from the Steeple Building is a U.S. post office. The building that contains it was built in 1749 as:

❺ The West Indies and Guinea Warehouse

The structure was once three times larger than it is today and included storerooms and lodging for staff. Go to the building's side entrance, on Church Street, and enter the rear courtyard if the iron gate is open. For many years, this was the site of some of the largest slave auctions in the Caribbean.

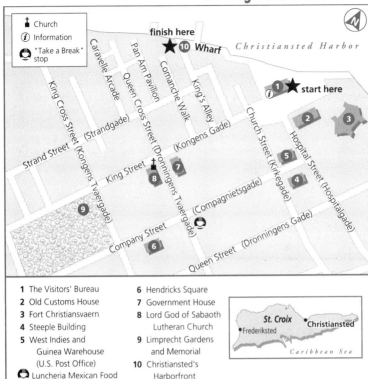

Legend:
- ✝ Church
- ⓘ Information
- ☕ "Take a Break" stop

finish here ★ ⑩ Wharf

Christiansted Harbor

ⓘ ★ start here

Caravelle Arcade
Pan Am Pavilion
Queen Cross Street (Dronningsgade)
Comanche Walk
King's Alley
King Cross Street (Strandgade)
Strand Street (Kongens Taergade)
Church Street (Kirkegade)
Hospital Street (Hospitalgade)
King Street
(Kongens Gade)
Dronningens Tvaergade
(Compagnietsgade)
Company Street
Queen Street (Dronningens Gade)

1 The Visitors' Bureau
2 Old Customs House
3 Fort Christiansvaern
4 Steeple Building
5 West Indies and Guinea Warehouse (U.S. Post Office)
☕ Luncheria Mexican Food

6 Hendricks Square
7 Government House
8 Lord God of Sabaoth Lutheran Church
9 Limprecht Gardens and Memorial
10 Christiansted's Harborfront

St. Croix
Frederiksted • • *Christiansted*
Caribbean Sea

From the post office, retrace your steps to Company Street and head west for one block. On your left, you'll pass the entrance to **Apothecary Hall,** 2111 Company St., which contains a charming collection of shops and restaurants.

TAKE A BREAK
If you need refreshment, try **Luncheria Mexican Food,** Apothecary Hall Courtyard, 2111 Company St. (☎ 340/773-4247). The bar's tables are grouped in a courtyard shaded by trees. The owners are margarita specialists, stocking more types of tequila (15-plus) than any other bar in the neighborhood. Luncheria serves burritos, tostadas, enchiladas, and tacos, as well as daily specials and vegetarian meals. See separate recommendation under "Dining."

Exit Apothecary Hall and turn left onto Company Street. Cross Queen Cross Street (Dronningens Tvergade). Half a block later, you'll arrive at the island's largest outdoor market:

● **Hendricks Square**
The square was rebuilt in a timbered, 9th-century style after the 1989 hurricane. Fruits and vegetables are sold here Monday through Saturday from 7am to 6pm.

Retrace your steps half a block along Company Street, then turn left onto Queen Cross Street. Head downhill toward the harbor, walking on the right-hand side of the street. Within half a block, you'll reach an unmarked arched iron gateway, set beneath an arcade. If it's open, enter the charming gardens of:

❼ Government House
The European-style garden here contains a scattering of very old trees, flowerbeds, and walkways. The

antique building that surrounds the gardens was formed from the union of two much older town houses in the 1830s.

Exit the same way you entered, turn right, and continue your descent of Queen Cross Street. At the first street corner (King Street), turn left, and admire the neoclassical facade of the:

● **Lord God of Sabaoth Lutheran Church**
This church was established in 1734. Continue walking southwest along King Street.

Within two blocks is the:

● **Limprecht Gardens and Memorial**
For 20 years (1888–1908) Peter Carl Limprecht served as governor of the Danish West Indies. Today, an occasional chicken pecks at seedlings planted near a Danish-language memorial to him.

At the end of the park, retrace your steps to Queen Cross Street, and go left. One very short block later, turn right onto Strand Street, which contains some interesting stores, including at least two different shopping arcades. The streets will narrow, and the pedestrian traffic will be more congested. Pass beneath the overpass belonging to a popular bar and restaurant, the Comanche Club (see "Dining," above).

Continue down the meandering curves of King's Alley. Within one block you'll be standing beside:

❶ **Christiansted's harborfront**
You can end your tour here by strolling on the boardwalk of the waterside piers.

FREDERIKSTED

This former Danish settlement at the western end of the island, about 17 miles from Christiansted, is a sleepy port town that comes to life only when a cruise ship docks at its pier. Frederiksted was destroyed by a fire in 1879, and the citizens rebuilt it by putting wood frames and clapboards on top of the old Danish stone and yellow-brick foundations.

Most visitors begin their tour at russet-colored **Fort Frederik,** at the northern end of Frederiksted next to the cruise-ship pier (✆ **340/772-2021**) This fort, completed in 1760, is said to have been the first to salute the flag of the new United States. When an American brigantine anchored at port in Frederiksted hoisted a homemade Old Glory, the fort returned the salute with cannon fire, violating the rules of neutrality. Also, on July 3, 1848, Governor-General Peter von Scholten emancipated the slaves in the Danish West Indies, in response to a slave uprising led by a young man named Moses "Buddhoe" Gottlieb. In 1998, a bust of Buddhoe was unveiled here. The fort has been restored to its 1840 appearance and today is a national historic landmark. You can explore the courtyard and stables. A local history museum has been installed in what was once the Garrison Room. Admission is free. Open Monday through Saturday from 8:30am to 4:30pm.

The Customs House, just east of the fort, is an 18th-century building with a 19th-century two-story gallery. To the south of the fort is **visitor's bureau** at Strand Street (✆ **340/772-0357**), where you can pick up a free map of the town.

EXPLORING THE "RAIN FOREST"

The island's western district contains a dense, 15-acre forest called the "Rain Forest" (though it's not a real one). The area is thick with mahogany trees, kapok (silk-cotton) trees, turpentine (red-birch) trees, samaan (rain) trees, and all kinds

Frederiksted

Customs House **3**
Fort Frederik **1**
Market Square **4**
Police Station **6**
Post Office **5**
Visitors Bureau **2**

Lagoon St.

Customs House St.

Pier

King St.

Market St.

Queen St.

Strand St.

Hill St.

Prince St.

Hospital St.

King Cross St.

New St.

Queen Cross St.

Caribbean Sea

Fisher St.

St. Croix ○ Christiansted
● Frederiksted

C a r i b b e a n   S e a

of ferns and vines. Sweet limes, mangoes, hog plums, and breadfruit trees, all of which have grown in the wild since the days of the plantations, are also interspersed among the larger trees. Crested hummingbirds, pearly eyed thrashers, green-throated caribs, yellow warblers, and perky but drably camouflaged bananaquits nest in the trees. The 150-foot-high Creque Dam is the major manmade sight in the area.

The Rain Forest is private property, but the owner lets visitors go inside to explore. To experience its charm, some visitors opt to drive along Route 76 (which is also known as Mahogany Road), stopping beside the footpaths that meander off on either side of the highway into dry riverbeds and glens. It's advisable to stick to the best-worn of the footpaths. You can also hike along some of the little-traveled four-wheel-drive roads in the area. Three of the best for hiking are the Creque Dam Road (Routes 58/78), the Scenic Road (Route 78), and the Western Scenic Road (Routes 63/78).

Our favorite trail in this area takes about 2½ hours one-way. From Frederiksted, drive north on Route 63 until you reach Creque Dam Road, where you should turn right, park the car, and start walking. About 1 mile past the 150-foot Creque Dam, you'll be deep within the forest's magnificent flora and fauna. Continue along the trail until you come to the Western Scenic Road. Eventually, you reach Mahogany Road (Route 76) near St. Croix Leap (see "Around the Island" in section 7, "Shopping"). Hikers rate this trail moderate in difficulty.

The St. Croix Heritage Trail

One of the 50 nationwide Millennium Legacy Trails launched in 2000, the St. Croix Heritage Trail helps visitors relive the Danish colonial past of the island. All you need is a brochure and map available at the tourist office in Christiansted (see p. 150), and you can set out on this 72-mile road, which is teeming with historical and cultural sights (some of which are reviewed individually in "Around the Island," below).

The route connects the two major towns of Christiansted and Frederiksted and traverses the entires 28-mile length of St. Croix, passing former sugar plantations, cattle farms, suburban communities, industrial complexes, and resorts. Although it's not all manicured and pretty, much of it is scenic and worth the drive. The route consists mainly of existing roadways, and the pamphlet you picked up will identify everything you see. Allow at least a day to follow the entire trail, with stops along the way.

Nearly everyone gets out of the car at Point Udall, the easternmost point under the American flag. Two other highlights of the trail are the Estate Mount Washington (see p. 185), a strikingly well-preserved sugar plantation, and Estate Whim Plantation (see p. 186), one of the best of the restored great houses, with a museum and gift shop. Another worthwhile stop along the way is along Salt River Bay, which cuts into the northern shoreline. This was the site of Columbus's landfall in 1493.

Of course, you'll also want get to know the locals along the way. We recommend a refreshing stop at Smithens Market along the trail. Lying off Queen Mary Highway, vendors here offer freshly squeezed sugar cane juice and sell locally grown fruits and homemade chutneys.

You could also begin near the junction of Creque Dam Road and Scenic Road. From here, your trek will cover a broad triangular swath, heading north and then west along Scenic Road. First, the road will rise, then it will descend toward the coastal lighthouse of the island's extreme northwestern tip, Hamm's Bluff. Most trekkers decide to retrace their steps after about 45 minutes of northwesterly hiking. Real diehards, however, will continue trekking all the way to the coastline, then head south along the coastal road (Butler Bay Road), and finally head east along Creque Dam Road to their starting point at the junction of Creque Dam Road and Scenic Road. Embark on this longer expedition only if you're really prepared for a hike lasting about 5 hours.

SANDY POINT WILDLIFE REFUGE ⋒

St. Croix's rarely visited southwestern tip is composed of salt marshes, tidal pools, and low vegetation inhabited by birds, turtles, and other forms of wildlife. More than 3 miles of ecologically protected coastline lie between Sandy Point (the island's westernmost tip) and the shallow waters of the Westend Saltpond. The area is home to colonies of green, leatherback, and hawksbill turtles. It's one of only two such places in U.S. waters. It's also home to thousands of birds, including herons, brown pelicans, Caribbean martins, black-necked stilts, and white-crowned pigeons. As for flora, Sandy Point gave its name to a rare form of orchids, a brown and/or purple variety.

This wildlife refuge is only open on Saturday and Sunday from 6am to 6pm. To get here, drive to the end of Route 66 (Melvin Evans highway) and continue down a gravel road. For guided weekend visits, call the **St. Croix Environmental Association** (② **340/773-1989**).

AROUND THE ISLAND

North of Frederiksted you can drop in at **Sprat Hall,** the island's oldest plantation, or continue along to the Rain Forest (see above). Most visitors come to the area to see the jagged estuary of the northern coastline's **Salt River.** The Salt River was where Columbus landed on November 14, 1493. Marking the 500th anniversary of Columbus's arrival, President George H. Bush signed a bill creating the 912-acre **Salt River Bay National Historical Park and Ecological Preserve.** The park contains the site of the original Carib village explored by Columbus and his men, including the only ceremonial ball court ever discovered in the Lesser Antilles. Also within the park is the largest mangrove forest in the Virgin Islands, sheltering many endangered animals and plants, plus an underwater canyon attracting scuba divers from around the world. The **St. Croix Environmental Association,** 3 Arawak Building, Gallows Bay (② **340/ 773-1989**), conducts tours of the area. Call for information. Tours cost $20 for adults, $12 for children under age 10.

Estate Mount Washington Plantation   This is the island's best-preserved sugar plantation and a highlight along the St. Croix Heritage Trail. It flourished from 1780 to 1820 when St. Croix was the second largest producer of sugar in the West Indies. The on-site private residence is closed to the public, but you can go on a self-guided tour of the 13 acres at any time of the day you wish (there is no admission charge, although donations are appreciated). You'll see what is the best antiques store on St. Croix, but it can only be visited by those who call ② **340/772-1026** and ask for an appointment (see "Shopping," later in this chapter).

At the very southwestern tip of the island, off Route 63, a mile inland from the highway that runs along the Frederiksted coast.

St. George Village Botanical Garden of St. Croix   This is a 16-acre Eden of tropical trees, shrubs, vines, and flowers. The garden is a feast for the eye and the camera, from the entrance drive bordered by royal palms and bougainvillea to the towering kapok and tamarind trees. It was built around the ruins of a 19th-century sugarcane workers' village. There are restrooms and a gift shop.

⌜*Moments* **Where the Sun First Shines**
        on the United States

The rocky promontory of Point Udall, jutting into the Caribbean Sea, is the easternmost point of the United States. Diehards go out to see the sun rise, but considering the climb via a rutted dirt road, you may want to wait until there's more light before heading here. Once at the top, you'll be rewarded with one of the best scenic views in the U.S. Virgin Islands. On the way to the lookout point, you'll see "The Castle," a local architectural oddity, owned by the island's most prominent socialite, the Contessa Nadia Farbo Navarro. Point Udall is reached along Route 82 (it's signposted).

Kids **Especially for Kids**

Fort Christiansvaern *(see p. 180)* Children can explore dungeons and battlements and even see how soldiers of yesteryear fired a cannon.

Buck Island *(see p. 193)* The boat ride to Buck Island is great fun for kids. Equally appealing are the island's white sandy beaches and its profuse wildlife. Bring along a picnic.

Self-guided walking-tour maps are available at the entrance to the garden's great hall.

127 Estate St. (just north of Centerline Road, 4 miles east of Frederiksted), Kingshill. ✆ **340/692-2874.** Admission $6 adults, $1 children age 12 and under; donations welcome. Nov–May daily 9am–5pm; June–Oct Tues–Sat 9am–4pm.

Cruzan Rum Factory This factory distills the famous Virgin Islands rum, which some consider the finest in the world. Guided tours (including a mixed drink) depart from the visitor's pavilion; call for reservations and information. There's also a gift shop.

W. Airport Road, Route 64. ✆ **340/692-2280.** Admission $4. Tours given Mon–Fri 9–11:30am and 1–4:15pm.

Estate Whim Plantation Museum This restored Great House is unique among those of the many sugar plantations whose ruins dot the island of St. Croix. It's composed of only three rooms. With 3-foot-thick walls made of stone, coral, and molasses, the house resembles a luxurious European château. A division of Baker Furniture Company used the Whim Plantation's collection of models for one of its most successful reproductions, the "Whim Museum— West Indies Collection." A showroom in the museum sells these reproductions, plus others from the Caribbean, including pineapple-motif four-poster beds, cane-bottomed planters' chairs with built-in leg rests, and Caribbean adaptations of Empire-era chairs with cane-bottomed seats.

Also on the museum's premises is a woodworking shop (which features tools and exhibits on techniques from the 18th century), the estate's original kitchen (where you can get a fresh-made johnnycake for $1), a museum store, and a servant's quarters. The ruins of the plantation's sugar-processing plant, complete with a restored windmill, also remain.

Centerline Road (2 miles east of Frederiksted). ✆ **340/772-0598.** Admission $6 adults, $1 children. June–Oct Tues–Sat 10am–3pm; Nov–May Mon–Sat 10am–4pm.

ORGANIZED TOURS

BUS TOURS Organized tours operate according to demand. Many are conducted at least three times a week during the winter, with fewer departures in summer. A typical 4-hour tour costs $25 per person. Tours usually go through Christiansted and include visits to the botanical gardens, Whim Estate House, the rum distillery, the Rain Forest, the St. Croix Leap mahogany workshop (see "Shopping," below), and the site of Columbus's landing at Salt River. Check with your hotel desk, or call **Travellers' Tours,** Alexander Hamilton Airport (✆ **340/778-1636**), for more information.

TAXI TOURS   Many visitors explore St. Croix on a taxi tour (𝓒 **340/ 778-1088**), which for a party of two costs $40 for 2 hours or $60 for 3 hours. The fare should be negotiated in advance. Extra fees are charged for the following sights: $10 for the botanical gardens, $10 for the Whim Estate House, and $8 for the rum distillery. Taxi tours are far more personalized than bus tours' you can get on and off where you want and stay as long or as little as you wish at a destination.

WALKING TOURS   For a guided walking tour of either Christiansted or Frederiksted, contact **St. Croix Heritage Tours** (𝓒 **340/778-6997**). The tour of Christiansted departs Tuesday at 9:30am, and costs $12 per person or $6 for children 12 and under. The Frederiksted tour leaves on Wednesday at 10:15am, and costs $8 per person or $4 for children 12 and under. Call for details and to arrange meeting places.

DRIVING TOUR   EAST ST. CROIX

Start: The Buccaneer.

Finish: Fort Christiansvaern.

Time: 1½ hours.

Best Times: Early morning or late afternoon.

Worst Times: Any evening after 5pm.

Head east from Christiansted on Route 75 (sometimes referred to as East End Road). Within a few miles, it will become Route 82. If you get confused at any time during this tour, remember the ocean should always be on your left.

Landmarks you'll pass on your way out of town will include Gallows Point and:

❶ The Buccaneer Hotel

You might want to return to this hotel for one of the nightly musical performances, which are among the island's best (see section 8, "St. Croix After Dark").

As you leave town, the landscape will open onto verdant countryside. Cows graze peacefully on a rolling landscape. Accompanying the cows are tickbirds, which feed on ticks buried in the cows' skin. An occasional small traffic jam might form as herds of goats cross the road.

Continue driving, and you'll pass:

❷ Green Cay Marina

You might want to visit this marina to admire the yachts bobbing at anchor or perhaps to have a swim at Chenay Bay. Nearby monuments include the Southgate Baptist Church and a hand-ful of stone towers that once housed the gear mechanisms of windmills that crushed the juice from sugarcane.

As you drive on, you'll pass by scatterings of bougainvillea-covered private villas.

About 7 miles along the route from Christiansted, you'll see the:

❸ Mountaintop Eyrie

Mountaintop Eyrie is owned by the island's most prominent socialite, the Contessa Nadia Farbo Navarro, the Romanian-born heiress to a great fortune. This opulent castle is the most outrageously unusual, most prominent, and most talked-about villa on St. Croix. Understandably, its privacy is rigidly maintained.

A couple of miles farther along East End Road, you'll reach one of the most popular windsurfing beaches in St. Croix, Teague Bay. This is a good spot to take a break.

TAKE A BREAK
Duggan's Reef, East End Road, Teague Bay (© **340/ 773-9800**), offers good lunches, more formal dinners, fruit daiquiris, and a bar only 10 feet from the waves. Many guests claim this is the best way to experience windsurfing without getting on a sailboard. See "Dining" for details.

After your stop, continue driving east along Route 82 to the area that most residents consider the most peaceful and dramatic on the island. It's especially memorable at sunset, when the vistas are highlighted and the sun is against your back.

At Knight Bay, near the eastern tip of the island, turn right onto Route 60 (South Shore Road), and head west. One of the several lakes you'll pass is:

● **Hartmann's Great Pond**
Also known just as Great Pond, this is a favorite of nesting seabirds. The views of the sea and the rolling grasslands are excellent.

Route 60 merges with Route 624 a short distance north of Great Pond. Fork left onto Route 624, and, a short distance later, right onto Route 62 (Lowry Hill Road). You will travel the mountainous spine of the island through districts named after former farms, such as Sally's Fancy, Marienhøøj, and Boetzberg.

Within 2 miles, Lowry Hill Road merges with Route 82 again. Fork left, and follow it as it turns into Hospital Gade and leads to the center of Christiansted. To your right will appear:

❺ **Fort Christiansvaern**
You'll see it as you pull into the parking lot in front of Christiansted's tourist office (Old Scalehouse).

7 Shopping

Christiansted is the shopping hub of St. Croix. The emphasis here is on hole-in-the-wall boutiques selling handmade goods. Most of the shops are compressed into a half-mile or so. There's also the **King's Alley Complex** (© **340/ 778-8135**), a pink-sided compound filled with the densest concentration of shops on St. Croix.

In recent years, **Frederiksted** has also become a popular shopping destination. An urban mall appeals to cruise-ship passengers arriving at Frederiksted Pier. The mall lies on a 50-foot strip of land from Strand Street to King Street, the town's bustling main thoroughfare.

CHRISTIANSTED
ANTIQUES
Estate Mount Washington Antiques   The owners may only be on site on Sunday, but when they are, you'll be able to browse through the best treasure trove of colonial West Indian furniture and "flotsam" in the Virgin Islands. Afterward, you can walk around the grounds of an 18th-century sugar plantation. Call for an appointment. 2 Estate Mount Washington. © **340/772-1026.**

ARTS & CRAFTS
Folk Art Traders   The operators of this store travel throughout the Caribbean ("in the bush") to add to their unique collection of local art and folk-art treasures—carnival masks, pottery, ceramics, original paintings, and hand-wrought jewelry. The assortment also includes batiks from Barbados and high-quality iron sculpture from Haiti. There's nothing else like it in the Virgin Islands. Strand Street. © **340/773-1900.**

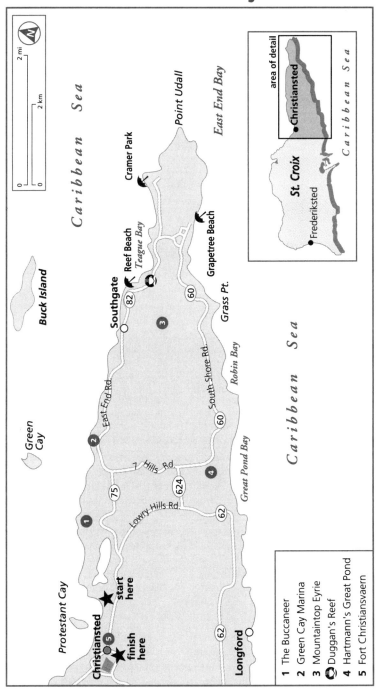

Caribbean Sea

2 mi

2 km

Caribbean Sea

area of detail

Christiansted

St. Croix

Caribbean Sea

Frederiksted

Point Udall

East End Bay

Cramer Park

Grapetree Beach

Reef Beach

Teague Bay

Southgate

82

60

Grass Pt.

3

Buck Island

Green Cay

East End Rd.

South Shore Rd.

Robin Bay

2

7 Hills Rd.

60

624

4

Great Pond Bay

75

Lowry Hills Rd.

62

1

Caribbean Sea

Protestant Cay

start here

Christiansted

5

finish here

Longford

62

1 The Buccaneer
2 Green Cay Marina
3 Mountaintop Eyrie
4 Duggan's Reef
5 Hartmann's Great Pond
5 Fort Christiansvaern

FASHIONS

The Coconut Vine   This is one of the most colorful and popular little boutiques on the island. Hand-painted batiks for both men and women are the specialty. Pan Am Pavilion. ✆ 340/773-1991.

From the Gecko   At this hip and eclectic outlet, you can find anything from
hand-painted local cottons and silks to the old West Indian staple, batiks. We
found the Indonesian collection here among the most imaginative in the U.S.
Virgin Islands—everything from ornate candle holders to banana leaf knap-
sacks. 1233 Queen Cross St. ✆ 340/778-9433.

Gone Tropical   About 60% of the merchandise in this unique shop is made
in Indonesia (usually Bali). Prices of new, semi-antique, or antique sofas, beds,
chests, tables, mirrors, and decorative carvings are the same as (and sometimes
less than) those of new furniture in conventional stores. Gone Tropical also sells
art objects, jewelry, batiks, candles, and baskets. 55 Company St. ✆ 340/773-4696.

Urban Threadz/Tribal Threadz   This is the most comprehensive clothing
store in Christiansted's historic core, with a two-story, big-city scale and appeal.
It's the store where island residents prefer to shop because of the hip, urban
styles. Men's items are on the street level, women's upstairs. The inventory
includes everything from Bermuda shorts to lightweight summer blazers and
men's suits. The store carries Calvin Klein, Nautica, and Oakley, among others.
52C Company St. ✆ 340/773-2883.

The White House   This White House is not about politics, but fashion.
Everything is white or off-white—nothing darker than beige is allowed on the
premises here. The women's clothing here ranges from dressy to casual and
breezy. King's Alley Walk. ✆ 340/773-9222.

GIFTS

Many Hands   The merchandise here includes West Indian spices and teas,
and locally made shellwork, stained glass, hand-painted china, pottery, and
handmade jewelry. The collection of local paintings is also intriguing, as is the
year-round "Christmas tree." In the Pan Am Pavilion, Strand Street. ✆ 340/773-1990.

Purple Papaya   This is the best place to go for inexpensive island gifts. It has
the biggest array of embroidered T-shirts and sweatshirts on island. Although
you're in the Caribbean and not Hawaii, there is a large selection of Hawaiian
shirts and dresses, along with beachwear for the whole family, plus island souvenirs. 39 Strand St., Pan Am Pavilion. ✆ 340/713-9412.

The Royal Poinciana   This is the most interesting gift shop on St. Croix,
looking like an antique apothecary. You'll find such items as hot sauces, seasoning blends for gumbos, island herbal teas, Antillean coffees, and a scented array
of soaps, toiletries, lotions, and shampoos. There's also a selection of museum-
reproduction greeting cards and calendars. Also featured are educational but fun
gifts for children. 1111 Strand St. ✆ 340/773-9892.

JEWELRY

Colombian Emeralds   Stunning emeralds, as well as rubies and diamonds,
will dazzle you here. The staff will also show you the wide range of 14-karat gold
jewelry, along with the best buys in watches, including Seiko quartz. Fake jewelry is peddled throughout the Caribbean, but Colombian Emeralds sells the
genuine thing. 43 Queen Cross St. ✆ 340/773-1928.

Crucian Gold   This small West Indian cottage holds the gold and silver creations of island-born Brian Bishop. His most popular item is the Crucian bracelet, which contains a "True Lovers' Knot" in its design. The outlet also sells hand-tied knots (bound in gold wire), rings, pendants, and earrings. 59 Kings Wharf. © 340/773-5241.

Elegant Illusions Copy Jewelry   This branch of a hugely successful chain based in California sells convincing fake jewelry. The look-alikes range in price from $9 to $1,000 and include credible copies of the baroque and antique jewelry your great-grandmother might have worn. If you want the real thing, you can go next door to **King Alley Jewelry** (© **340/773-4746**), which is owned by the same company and specializes in fine designer jewelry, including Tiffany and Cartier. 55 King St. © **340/773-2727.**

Sonya Ltd.   Sonya Hough is the matriarch of a cult of local residents who wouldn't leave home without wearing one of her bracelets. She's most famous for her sterling silver or gold (from 14- to 24-karat) versions of her original design, the C-clasp bracelet. Locals say that if the cup of the "C" is turned toward your heart, it means you're emotionally committed; if the cup is turned outward, it means you're available. Prices range from $20 to $2,500. She also sells rings, earrings, and necklaces. 1 Company St. © 340/778-8605.

Waterfront Larimar Mines   Everything sold in this shop is produced by the largest manufacturer of gold settings for larimar in the world. Discovered in the 1970s, larimar is a pale-blue pectolyte prized for its color. It comes from mines located in only one mountain in the world, on the southwestern edge of the Dominican Republic, near the Haitian border. Objects range from $25 to $1,000. Although other shops sell the stone as well, this emporium has the widest selection. The Boardwalk/King's Walk. © 340/692-9000.

PERFUME

Violette Boutique   This is a small department store, with many boutique areas carrying famous lines. Here you can get many famous and exclusive fragrances and hard-to-find toiletry items, as well as the latest in Cartier, Fendi, Pequignet, and Gucci. There's also a selection of gifts for children. Many famous brand names sold here are found nowhere else on the island, but are certainly found elsewhere in the Caribbean. In the Caravelle Arcade, 38 Strand St. © 340/773-2148.

AROUND THE ISLAND

If you're touring western St. Croix in the vicinity of Frederiksted, you might want to stop off at the following offbeat shops.

St. Croix Leap   If you're on western St. Croix, near Frederiksted, visit St. Croix Leap for an offbeat adventure. In this open-air shop, you can see stacks of rare and beautiful wood being fashioned into tasteful objects. This is a St. Croix Life and Environmental Arts Project, dedicated to manual work, environmental conservation, and self-development. The end result is a fine collection of local mahogany serving boards, tables, wall hangings, and clocks. Sections of unusual pieces are crafted into functional, artistic objects.

St. Croix Leap is 15 miles from Christiansted, 2 miles up Mahogany Road from the beach north of Frederiksted. Large mahogany signs and sculptures flank the driveway. Visitors should bear to the right to reach the woodworking area and gift shop. The site is open daily from 9am to 5:30pm. Mahogany Road, Route 76. © 340/772-0421.

Whim Museum Store   This unique store offers a wide selection of gifts, both imported and local. And if you buy something, your money goes to a worthy cause: the upkeep of the museum and the grounds (see "Seeing the Sights"). In the Estate Whim Plantation Museum, east of Frederiksted on Centerline Road. ✆ 340/772-0598.

8 St. Croix After Dark

St. Croix doesn't have the nightlife of St. Thomas. To find the action, you might consult the publication *St. Croix This Week,* which is distributed free to cruise-ship and air passengers and is available at the tourist office.

Try to catch a performance of the **Quadrille Dancers,** a real cultural treat. Their dances have changed little since plantation days. The women wear long dresses, white gloves, and turbans, and the men wear flamboyant shirts, sashes, and tight black trousers. When you've learned their steps, you're invited to join the dancers on the floor. Ask at your hotel if and where they're performing.

Regrettably, women entering bars alone at night in Christiansted or Frederik-sted can expect some advances from men. It is generally assumed here that a women enters a bar alone seeking companionship and not necessarily just to have a drink and survey the scene. Nonetheless, women are fairly safe in bars providing they know how to deal with some leering. It is not wise to leave the bar alone and walk the lonely streets. Take a taxi back to your hotel—it's worth the investment.

THE PERFORMING ARTS

Island Center   This 1,100-seat amphitheater, half a mile north of Sunny Isle, continues to attract big-name entertainers to St. Croix. Its program is widely varied, ranging from jazz, nostalgia, and musical revues to Broadway plays. Consult *St. Croix This Week* or call the center to see what's being presented. The Caribbean Community Theatre and Courtyard Players perform here regularly. Call for performance times. Sunny Isle. ✆ 340/778-5272. Tickets $8–$30.

THE CLUB & MUSIC SCENE

Blue Moon   This hip little dive, which is also a good bistro, is the hottest spot in Frederiksted on Friday, when a five-piece ensemble entertains. There's no cover. 17 Strand St. ✆ 340/772-2222.

The Terrace Lounge   This lounge off the main dining room of one of St. Croix's most upscale hotels welcomes some of the Caribbean's finest entertainers every night, often including a full band. In the Buccaneer, Route 82, Estate Shoys. ✆ 340/773-2100.

2 Plus 2 Disco   This is a real Caribbean disco. It features the regional sounds of the islands, not only calypso and reggae but also salsa and soca (a hybrid of calypso and reggae). Usually there's a DJ, except on weekends when local bands are brought in. The place isn't fancy or large; it has a black-tile dance floor with a simple lighting system. Come here for Saturday Night Fever. Hours are Tuesday through Sunday from 8:30pm to 2am and Friday and Saturday from 8pm to either 5 or 6am. Admission is $5 to $10 when there's a live band. At the La Grande Princess. ✆ 340/773-3710.

THE BAR SCENE

Cormorant Beach Club Bar   This romantic bar lies within a predominantly gay resort about 3 miles northwest of Christiansted (see "Accommodations"). It caters both to clients of the resort and to gay men and women from other parts of the island. You can sit at tables overlooking the ocean or around an open-centered mahogany bar, adjacent to a gazebo. The chairs are comfortable and the lighting is soft. Excellent tropical drinks are mixed here, including the house specialty, a Cormorant Cooler, made with champagne, pineapple juice, and Triple Sec. 4126 La Grande Princesse. ✆ **340/778-8920.**

The Marina Bar   This bar occupies a great position on the waterfront, on a shaded terrace overlooking the deep-blue sea and Protestant Cay. It's open throughout the day, but the most appealing activities begin here right after the last seaplane departs for St. Thomas, around 5:30pm, and continue until 8:30pm. Sunset-colored cocktails made with rum, mangos, bananas, papaya, and grenadine are the drinks of choice. You can also stave off hunger pangs with burgers, sandwiches, and West Indian–style platters. There's live entertainment most nights, usually street bands. On Monday you can bet on crab races. In The King's Alley Hotel, King's Alley/The Waterfront. ✆ **340/773-0103.**

A CASINO

Divi Casino   After much protest and controversy, this casino introduced gambling to St. Croix for the first time in spring 2000. Many visitors who heretofore went to such islands as Aruba for gambling now stay within the realm of U.S. possessions. The 10,000-square-foot casino boasts 12 gaming tables and 275 slot machines. No passport is needed to enter, but you do need some form of ID. There is no cover charge. In lieu of a nightclub, the casino offers nightly live music on an open stage on the casino floor. There are two bars, a main bar plus a smaller cafe-style bar where you can order light meals. Open Monday through Thursday from noon to 4am and Friday through Sunday from noon to 6am. In the Divi Carina Bay Resort, 25 Estate Turner Hole. ✆ **340/773-9700.**

9 A Side Trip to Buck Island 🖈🖈🖈

The crystal-clear water and white coral-sand of **Buck Island,** a satellite of St. Croix, are legendary. Some call it the single most important attraction of the Caribbean. Only ⅓ mile wide and a mile long, Buck Island lies 1½ miles off the northeastern coast of St. Croix. A barrier reef here shelters many reef fish, including queen angelfish and smooth trunkfish. In years past the island was frequented by the swashbuckling likes of Morgan, LaFitte, Blackbeard, and even Captain Kidd.

Buck Island's greatest attraction is its underwater snorkeling trails, which ring part of the island. Equipped with a face mask, swim fins, and a snorkel, you'll be treated to some of the most beautiful underwater views in the Caribbean. Plan on spending at least two-thirds of a day at this extremely famous ecological site, which is maintained by the National Park Service. There are also many labyrinths and grottoes for scuba divers. The sandy beach has picnic tables and barbecue pits, as well as rest rooms and a small changing room.

You can also take hiking trails through the tropical vegetation that covers the island. Circumnavigating the island on foot will take about 2 hours. Buck Island's trails meander from several points along its coastline to its sun-flooded summit, affording views over nearby St. Croix. *A couple of warnings, though:* Bring protection from the sun's merciless rays; even more important, don't rush to touch every plant you see. The island's western edge has groves of poisonous machineel trees, whose leaves, bark, and fruit cause extreme irritation when they come into contact with human skin.

Small boats run between St. Croix and Buck Island. Nearly all charters provide snorkeling equipment and allow for 1½ hours of snorkeling and swimming.

Mile Mark Watersports, in the King Christian Hotel, 59 King's Wharf, Christiansted (© **800/523-DIVE** or 340/773-2628), conducts three different types of tours. The first option is a half-day tour aboard a glass-bottom boat departing from the King Christian Hotel, daily from 9:30am to 1pm and from 1:30 to 5pm; it costs $35 per person. The second is a full-day tour, offered daily from 10am to 4pm on a 40-foot catamaran, for $75. Included in this excursion is a West Indian barbecue picnic on Buck Island's beach.

Captain Heinz (© **340/773-3161** or 340/773-4041) is an Austrian-born skipper with more than 25 years of sailing experience. His trimaran, *Teroro II,* leaves Green Cay Marina "H" Dock at 9am and 2pm, never filled with more than 24 passengers. This snorkeling trip costs $50 for adults, $30 for children age 10 and under. The captain is not only a skilled sailor but also a considerate host. He will even take you around the outer reef, which the other guides do not, for an unforgettable underwater experience.

The British Vir

The British Virgin Islands embrace 40-odd islands, some no more than just rocks or spits of land in the sea. Only a trio of them are of any significant size: Virgin Gorda ("Fat Virgin"), Tortola ("Dove of Peace"), and Jost Van Dyke. These craggy volcanic islands are just 15 minutes by air from St. Thomas; there is also regularly scheduled ferry service between St. Thomas and Tortola.

With its small bays and hidden coves, once havens for pirates, the British Virgin Islands are among the world's loveliest cruising areas. Despite predictions that mass tourism will invade, the islands are still an escapist's paradise. The smaller islands have colorful names, such as Fallen Jerusalem and Ginger. Norman Island is said to have been the prototype for Robert Louis Stevenson's novel *Treasure Island.* On Deadman Bay, Blackbeard reputedly marooned 15 pirates and a bottle of rum, giving rise to the well-known ditty.

Even though they lie right near each other and are part of the same archipelago, the British Virgin Islands and the U.S. Virgin Islands are as different a Dench. Islands ....
deep into mega-resort tourism, but it's still a bit sleepy in the B.V.I., where the pace is much slower and laid-back, the people more welcoming and friendlier. Tortola, the capital, is more bustling than more tranquil Virgin Gorda, but even Tortola seems to exist in a bit of a time capsule of long ago.

The islands attract mainly those who like to sail, although landlubbers can delight in the beaches. Most of the resorts on Virgin Gorda are so isolated from each other that you'll feel your hotel has the island to itself.

For those who want to be truly remote, there is a scattering of other minor hotels on a handful of the smaller islands. Peter Island is the poshest. There are modest inns on Jost Van Dyke and Anegada. Some places are so small that you virtually get to know all the locals after about a week. With no casinos, no nightlife, no splashy entertainment, and often no TV, what does one do at night? Jost Van Dyke has only 150 souls but six bars. Question answered.

1 Essentials

VISITOR INFORMATION

Before you go, you can obtain information from the **British Virgin Islands Tourist Board,** 370 Lexington Ave., Suite 313, New York, NY 10017 (© **212/ 696-0400**). You can also contact the **British Virgin Islands Information Office** at 1804 Union St., San Francisco, CA 94123 (© **415/775-0344**); at 3450 Wilshire Blvd, Suite 1202, Culver City, CA 90010 (© **213/736-8931**); and at 3390 Peachtree Rd., NE, Suite 1000, Lenox Towers, Atlanta, GA 30326 (© **404/240-8018**). In the United Kingdom, contact the **BVI Information Office,** 54 Baker St., London WIM 1DJ (© **020/7240-4259**).

ncy Tip

Virgin Islands use the U.S. dollar as their form of currency.
unds are not accepted.

e **BVI Tourist Board** on the islands is in the center of Road Town, Tor-
la, close to the ferry dock, south of Wickhams Cay (© **284/494-3134**). The
tourist board has a website at www.bviwelcome.com.

GETTING THERE

Your gateway to the B.V.I. will most likely be either Tortola or Virgin Gorda.
Supplies and services on the other islands are extremely limited.

BY PLANE   There are no direct flights from North America to Tortola or any
of the other British Virgin Islands, but you can make easy connections Miami,
through St. Thomas, St. Croix, or San Juan in Puerto Rico. Beef Island, the site
of the major airport serving the British Virgin Islands, is connected to Tortola
by the one-lane Queen Elizabeth Bridge.

American Eagle (© **800/433-7300** in the U.S.; www.aa.com) has four daily
flights from San Juan, Puerto Rico, to the airport at Beef Island. San Juan is serv-
iced by dozens of daily nonstop flights from cities in North America, including
Boston, Toronto, New York, Chicago, Miami, and Raleigh-Durham. You can
also fly **American Airlines** (© **800/433-7300**) to St. Thomas, then hop on an
American Eagle flight to Tortola.

Another choice, if you're on one of Tortola's neighboring islands, is the much
less reliable **LIAT** (© **800/468-0482** in the U.S. and Canada, 284/495-2577 or
284/495-1187). This Caribbean carrier makes short hops to Tortola from St.
Kitts, Antigua, St. Martin, St. Thomas, and San Juan in small planes not known
for their careful scheduling. Reservations are made through travel agents or
through the larger U.S.-based airlines that connect with LIAT hubs. **Air Sunshine** (© **284/495-1122**) flies from San Juan or St. Thomas to Beef Island (Tortola) and on to Virgin Gorda.

Flying time to Tortola from San Juan is 30 minutes; from St. Thomas, 15
minutes; and from the most distant of the LIAT hubs (Antigua), 60 minutes.
There's also a small airport on Virgin Gorda; see "Essentials" in section 3, "Virgin Gorda," for details.

BY FERRY   You can travel from Charlotte Amalie (St. Thomas) by public
ferry to West End and Road Town on Tortola, a 45-minute voyage. Boats making this run include **Native Son** (© 284/495-4617), **Smith's Ferry Service**
(© 284/495-4495), and **Inter-Island Boat Services** (© 284/495-4166). The
latter specializes in a somewhat obscure routing—that is, from St. John to the
West End on Tortola. One-way and round-trip fares range from $20 to $40.

GETTING AROUND

BY BOAT   On Tortola, **Smith's Ferry** (© **284/495-4495**) and **Speedy's Fantasy** (© **284/495-5240**) operate ferry links to the Virgin Gorda Yacht Club (the
trip lasts 30 minutes). The **North Sound Express** (© **284/495-2138**), near the
airport on Beef Island, has daily connections to the Bitter End Yacht Club on
Virgin Gorda. **Peter Island Boat** (© **284/495-2000**) also shuttles passengers
between Road Town on Tortola and Peter Island at least seven times a day. Ferry
fares range from $7 to $15.

The British Virgin Islands

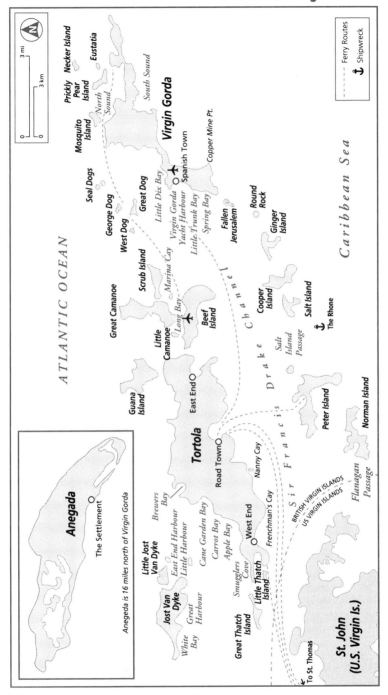

ATLANTIC OCEAN

Caribbean Sea

3 mi
3 km

Ferry Routes
⚓ Shipwreck

Necker Island
Eustatia
Prickly Pear Island
Mosquito Island
North Sound
South Sound
Virgin Gorda
Copper Mine Pt.
Spanish Town
Little Dix Bay
Virgin Gorda Yacht Harbour
Little Trunk Bay
Spring Bay
Seal Dogs
George Dog
West Dog
Great Dog
Round Rock
Fallen Jerusalem
Ginger Island
Scrub Island
Marina Cay
D r a k e   C h a n n e l
Great Camanoe
Long Bay
Little Camanoe
Beef Island
Cooper Island
Salt Island
The Rhone
Salt Island Passage
Guana Island
East End
Tortola
Road Town
Nanny Cay
S i r   F r a n c i s
Peter Island
Norman Island
Flanagan Passage
BRITISH VIRGIN ISLANDS
US VIRGIN ISLANDS

Anegada
The Settlement
Anegeda is 16 miles north of Virgin Gorda

Brewers Bay
Little Jost Van Dyke
East End Harbour
Little Harbour
Cane Garden Bay
Carrot Bay
Apple Bay
West End
Frenchman's Cay
Jost Van Dyke
Great Harbour
Smugglers Cove
Little Thatch Island
Great Thatch Island
White Bay
St. John (U.S. Virgin Is.)
To St. Thomas

197

Special Moments in the British Virgin Islands

Here are some of the best things to do in the B.V.I.:

- **Visit a Tropical Park:** If you like to explore mountainous landscape that still looks like it did when Christopher Columbus first landed, head to **Sage Mountain National Park** on Tortola (see p.217). Although it gets only 100 inches of rain a year, the park nevertheless has the appearance of a primeval rain forest.

- **Explore Remote Anegada:** Anegada Island (see p.235) is easy to miss—it covers only 15 square miles and stands only 27 feet above sea level at its highest point. Because of the treacherous coral shelf nearby, more than 300 ships have sunk just offshore. Here's the good news: The entire island is surrounded by white sandy beaches, and the population is only about 250 people, so you can often walk for miles without seeing anyone. You'll feel like a modern Robinson Crusoe.

- **Ponder the Mystery of the Baths:** The most celebrated site on the island of Virgin Gorda is the Baths (see p.231), on the island's southwest shore, where huge granite rocks are strewn along the beach. Granite is rarely found this far south, so it's been suggested that the rocks were placed here by a race of giants or moved south by some ancient glacier. Most scientists think they were spewed up by volcanic activity. The important thing is not to solve the mystery but to explore the cavelike passages between the rocks and to seek out the hidden pools, which are just right for a quick dip.

- **Exploring Deserted "Treasure Island":** Legend has it that tiny Norman Isle (see p.220), south of Tortola and east of St. John, was the inspiration for Robert Louis Stevenson's *Treasure Island*. The sea caves on this island are some of best snorkeling spots in the British Virgin Islands. Intrepid hikers climb through scrubland to the island's central ridge, Spy Glass Hill. To cut costs, ask three or four other people to rent a sailboat with you to go over for a day's adventure.

BY CAR, BUS, OR TAXI   There are car-rental agencies on Virgin Gorda and Tortola; taxis also operate on these islands, as well as on some of the smaller ones. Bus service is available on Tortola and Virgin Gorda only. See the "Essentials" section for each island for further details.

2 Tortola ⋆⋆

Road Town, on Tortola's southern shore, is the capital of the British Virgin Islands and the site of Government House and other administrative buildings. Its new development at Wickhams Cay, a 70-acre town center project, has brought in a large yacht-chartering business and has transformed the sleepy village capital into more of a bustling center.

The entire southern coast of this 24-square-mile island, including Road Town, is characterized by rugged mountain peaks. On the northern coast are white-sand beaches, banana trees, mangos, and clusters of palms.

Fast Facts

For "Fast Facts" about the British Virgin Islands, see page 58 in chapter 2, "Planning Your Trip to the Virgin Islands."

ESSENTIALS

GETTING THERE   Close to Tortola's eastern end is **Beef Island,** the site of the main airport for all of the British Virgins. The tiny island is connected to Tortola by the one-lane Queen Elizabeth Bridge. For more information on getting to Tortola by plane or by ferry, see "Getting There" in section 1.

VISITOR INFORMATION   There is a **B.V.I. Tourist Board Office** (© 284/ 494-3134) at the center of Road Town near the ferry dock, south of Wickhams Cay. Here you'll find information about hotels, restaurants, tours, and more. Pick up a copy of *The Welcome Tourist Guide,* which has a useful map of the island.

GETTING AROUND   Taxis meet every arriving flight. Government regulations prohibit anyone from renting a car at the airport—visitors must take a taxi to their hotels. The fare from the Beef Island airport to Road Town is $15 for one to three passengers. Your hotel can call a taxi for you. A **taxi tour** lasting 2½ hours costs $45 for one to three people. To call a taxi in Road Town, dial © **284/494-2322;** on Beef Island, © **284/495-2378.**

Scato's Bus Service (© **284/494-2365**) operates from the north end of the island to the west end, picking up passengers who hail it down. Fares are $1 to $3.

If you want to rent a car, you'll need to reserve it in advance, especially in winter. Rental companies include **Itgo** (© **284/494-2639**) at 1 Wickhams Cay, Road Town; **Avis** (© **800/331-1212** or 284/494-3322), opposite the police headquarters in Road Town; and **Hertz** (© **800/654-3001** or 284/495-4405) on the island's West End, near the ferryboat landing dock. Rental companies will usually deliver your car to your hotel. All three companies require a valid driver's license and a temporary B.V.I. driver's license, which they can sell you for $10; it's valid for 3 months.

Remember to **drive on the left.** Because island roads are narrow, poorly lit, and have few, if any, lines, driving at night can be quite tricky. It's a good idea to rent a taxi to take you to that difficult-to-find beach, restaurant, or bar.

WHERE TO STAY

Many of the island's hotels are small, informal, family-run guesthouses offering only the most basic amenities. Others are more elaborate, boasting a full range of resort-related facilities. None of them, however, is as big, splashy, and all-encompassing as the resorts in the U.S. Virgin Islands. Many of the island's repeat visitors seem to like that just fine. Remember that all Tortola's beaches are on the northern shore, so guests staying elsewhere (at Road Town, for example) will have to drive or take a taxi to reach them.

Note: All rates given within this chapter are subject to a 10% service charge and a 7% government tax. Rates are usually discounted significantly in summer. The term "MAP" stands for "Modified American Plan"; this means that the hotel provides breakfast and dinner (or lunch if you prefer) for an extra charge.

VERY EXPENSIVE

Long Bay Beach Resort ✦✦   A favorite of sophisticated travelers since the 1960s, this resort is the finest on Tortola lying on a mile-long sandy beach. In a lovely setting on the north shore, about 10 minutes from the West End, it's the only full-service resort on the island, a low-rise complex set in a 52-acre estate. The accommodations include hillside rooms and studios, the smallest and most basic with the simplest furnishings; poolside overview studios; and deluxe beach-front rooms and cabanas with either balconies or patios that overlook the ocean. The resort also offers two- and three-bedroom villas complete with a kitchen, living area, and large deck with a gas grill. If you're not staying right on the beach, you'll still enjoy an ocean view from any of the other accommodations. All units have one four-poster king or two queen beds, each with a first-rate mattress, plus large bathrooms with tiled showers.

The Beach Café is set in the ruins of an old sugar mill. The Garden Restaurant offers dinner by reservation only and a tantalizing variety of local and international dishes in a more elegant, alfresco setting of tropical gardens. The cuisine is among the finest of any hotel on the island, especially its fresh fish, and the wine list is extensive.

Tortola, B.V.I. ✆ **800/729-9599** in the U.S. and Canada, or 284/495-4252. Fax 914/833-3318. www. longbay.com. 117 units. Winter $275–$395 double; $595–$650 two-bedroom villa; $855–$895 three-bedroom villa. Off-season $155–$210 double; $320–$350 two-bedroom villa; $450–$485 three-bedroom villa. MAP (breakfast and dinner) $45 per person extra. AE, MC, V. **Amenities:** 2 restaurants, 2 bars; pool; snorkeling; 3 tennis courts; children's activity program (ages 3 to 8); laundry; baby-sitting; car rental. *In room:* A/C, TV, mini-bar, hair dryer, coffeemaker, kitchen.

The Sugar Mill ✦   Set in a lush tropical garden on the site of a 300-year-old sugar mill on the north side of Tortola, this secluded cottage colony sweeps down the hillside to its own little beach, with vibrant flowers and fruits brightening the grounds. Plain but comfortable apartments climb up the hillside. The accommodations are contemporary and well designed, ranging from suites and cottages to studio apartments, all self-contained with kitchenettes and private terraces with views. Rooms have twin or king-size beds, each with a good mattress, plus well-maintained private bathrooms with showers. Four of the units are suitable for families of four.

Lunch or dinner is served down by the beach at the Islands, which features Caribbean specialties along with burgers and salads. Dinner is also offered at the Sugar Mill Restaurant (see "Where to Dine," below).

Apple Bay (P.O. Box 425), Tortola, B.V.I. ✆ **800/462-8834** in the U.S., or 284/495-4355. Fax 284/495-4696. www.sugarmillhotel.com. sugmill@surfbvi.com. 24 units. Winter $310 double; $325 triple; $340 quad; $620 two-bedroom villa. Off-season $225–$245 double; $240–$260 triple; $255–$275 quad; $475–$515 two-bedroom villa. AE, MC, V. Closed Aug–Sept. Children age 11 and under not accepted in winter. **Amenities:** 2 restaurants, 2 bars; pool; snorkeling; laundry; baby-sitting. *In room:* A/C, hair dryer, coffeemaker, kitchenette, iron/ironing board.

EXPENSIVE

Frenchman's Cay Resort Hotel ✦   This intimate resort is tucked away at the windward side of Frenchman's Cay, a little island connected by bridge to Tortola. The 12-acre estate enjoys delightful year-round breezes and views of Sir Francis Drake Channel and the outer Virgins. It does not have a cuisine to match that of Sugar Mill, nor does it have the full resort services of Long Bay. The individual one- and two-bedroom villas (actually a cluster of condos) are well furnished, each with a shady terrace, full kitchen, dining room, and sitting

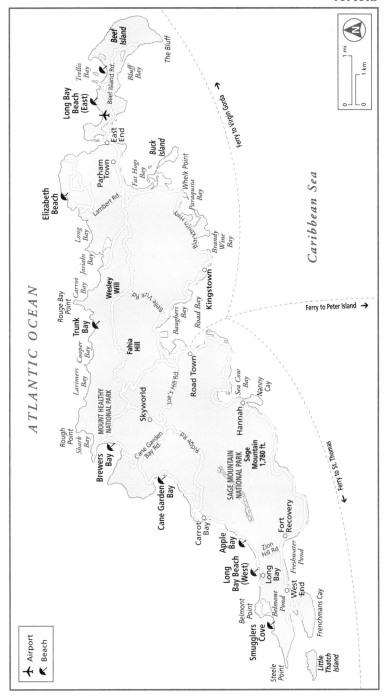

Fun Fact **The Notorious Pirate: Sir Francis Drake**

Sir Francis Drake (1543–96) was an English navigator and explorer, famous for leading his country's defense against the Spanish Armada in 1588. He was also one of the most notorious pirates in the Caribbean. Arriving in the West Indies as the young captain of *The Judith* and a favorite of Queen Elizabeth I, Drake brought the swashbuckling adventures of the Elizabethan age to the Virgin Islands. A channel through the Virgin Islands now bears his name. In 1580, Drake became the first Englishman to circumnavigate the globe. He died aboard ship off Panama on January 27, 1596, and was buried at sea.

---

room. The two-bedroom villas have two full bathrooms, a vacation in and of itself for families looking to escape the morning bathroom line. Pastel colors and tropical styling make for inviting accommodations, and each unit has quality mattresses, good linen, and shower stalls. There's a small beach with rocks offshore; it's best for snorkeling. The Clubhouse Restaurant and lounge bar is located in the main pavilion, with a good-tasting menu continental and Caribbean menu.

West End (P.O. Box 1054), Tortola, B.V.I. ✆ **800/235-4077** in the U.S., 800/463-0199 in Canada, or 284/495-4844. Fax 284/495-4056. www.frenchmans.com. 9 units. Winter $255 one-bedroom villa; $380 two-bedroom villa. Off-season $150–$165 one-bedroom villa; $210–$245 two-bedroom villa. MAP (breakfast and dinner) $45 per person extra. AE, DISC, MC, V. From Tortola, cross the bridge to Frenchman's Cay, turn left, and follow the road to the eastern tip of the cay. **Amenities:** Restaurant, bar; pool; tennis court; Sunfish sailboats; kayaks; windsurfing; snorkeling; sailing trips; horseback riding; island tours; car rentals. *In room:* Ceiling fan, coffeemaker, kitchen.

The Moorings/Mariner Inn ✦ Located right in Road Town, the Caribbean's most complete yachting resort is outfitted with at least 180 sailing yachts, some worth $2 million or more. On an 8-acre resort, the inn was obviously designed with the yachting crowd in mind, offering not only support facilities and services but also shoreside accommodations. You experience more of town life here, as opposed to the seclusion of the resorts reviewed above; it's a lively spot that's close to restaurants, shops, and bars. The rooms are spacious; all suites have kitchenettes and bathrooms with shower stalls, and most of them open onto the water. Obviously the boaties get more attention here than the landlubbers do. The nearest beach is Cane Garden Bay, about 15 minutes away by car; you'll either have to drive there in a rental car or take a taxi.

Wickhams Cay (P.O. Box 139, Road Town), Tortola, B.V.I. ✆ **800/535-7289** in the U.S., or 284/494-2332. Fax 284/494-2226. www.moorings.com. 40 units. Winter $170 double; $230 suite. Off-season $95 double; $125 suite. Extra person $15. AE, MC, V. **Amenities:** Dockside restaurant and bar; swimming pool; tennis court; gift shop; dive shop that rents underwater video cameras. *In room:* A/C, TV, minibar, hair dryer, coffeemaker, kitchenette, fridge, safe.

Treasure Isle Hotel ✦ The most central resort on Tortola is built at the edge of the capital on 15 acres of hillside overlooking a marina (not on the beach). The core of this attractive hotel is a rather splashy and colorful open-air bar done in vibrant colors and boasting lovely views. The motel-like, midsize rooms are on two levels along the hillside terraces; a third level is occupied by more elegantly decorated suites at the crest of a hill. Tropical touches, such as local art, tile floors, white stucco walls, floral upholstery, and white rattan, make for an inviting atmosphere. Each comes with a small bathroom containing a shower stall. All in all, however, Village Cay Hotel provides better value (see review below).

Adjoining the lounge and pool area is a covered open-air dining room overlooking the harbor. The cuisine is respected here, with barbecue and full a la carte menus offered at dinner. On Wednesday, the hotel puts on a West Indian "grill out," complete with live entertainment and dancing.

Pasea Estate, east end of Road Town (P.O. Box 68, Road Town), Tortola, B.V.I. © **800/334-2435** in the U.S., or 284/494-2501. Fax 284/494-2507. www.treasureislehotel.com. 43 units. Winter $187 double; $253 suite. Off-season $104–$143 double; $137–$209 suite. Extra person $15. AE, DISC, MC, V. **Amenities:** Restaurant, 2 bars; pool; dive shop. In room: A/C, TV, minibar, hair dryer, coffeemaker.

Nanny Cay Resort & Marina * * Few other resorts cater as aggressively to yacht owners as Nanny Cay, a sprawling, somewhat disorganized resort where great wealth (in the form of hyper-expensive yachts) lies cheek by jowl with more modest fishing craft. It competes with Village Cay for the boat owner or sailor, but is not as good as its competition. Accommodations are within a two-story motel-style building, where windows overlook open-air hallways. Each unit contains a kitchen and comfortable albeit bland furniture. The heart and soul of the resort, however, is the 180-slip marina, headquarters to at least three yacht chartering companies and permanent home to many fishing and pleasure boats. The resort sprawls over 25 acres of steamy flatlands, adjacent to a saltwater inlet that's favored because of the protection it offers to boats during storms and hurricanes. Don't expect the spit-and-polish of a resort catering to the conventional resort trade. This place is artfully and deliberately raffish, which seems to be the way folks here want to keep it.

P.O. Box 281, Road Town, Tortola, B.V.I. © **800/74-CHARMS** in the U.S., or 284/494-4895. Fax 284/494-0555. www.nannycay.com. 42 studios. Winter $160–$195 double; $185–$220 triple. Off-season $100–$145 double; $125–$170 triple. AE, MC, V. **Amenities:** Restaurant, bar; tennis court; pool; bike rentals; dive shop. In room: A/C, TV, hair dryer, coffeemaker, kitchen.

Prospect Reef Resort * * This is the largest resort in the British Virgin Islands, and it offers a lot of facilities to make up for the lack of a beach. It rises above a small, private harbor in a sprawling series of two-story concrete buildings scattered over 44 acres of steeply sloping, landscaped terrain. The panoramic view of Sir Francis Drake Channel from the bedrooms is one of the best anywhere.

Each of the resort's buildings contains up to 10 individual accommodations and is painted in hibiscus-inspired shades of pink, peach, purple, or aquamarine. Initially designed as condominiums, there are unique studios, town houses, and villas in addition to guest rooms. All include private balconies or patios; larger units, which are perfect for families, have kitchenettes, living and dining areas, and separate bedrooms or sleeping lofts with firm mattresses. About a third of the rooms are air-conditioned; others are cooled by ceiling fans and the trade winds. Bathrooms are tiled and well maintained and come with shower stalls.

Impressions

Question: Where are the British Virgin Islands?
Answer: I have no idea, but I should think that they are as far as possible from the Isle of Man.

—Sir Winston Churchill

The food at the hotel's Callaloo Restaurant (see "Where to Dine," below), offering a combination of continental specialties and island favorites, has been praised by *Gourmet* magazine.

Drake's Hwy. (P.O. Box 104, Road Town), Tortola, B.V.I. ℂ **800/356-8937** in the U.S., 800/463-3608 in Canada, or 284/494-3311. Fax 284/494-5595. www.prospectreef.com. 131 units. Winter $150–$280 double; $450 two-bedroom villa for 4. Off-season $99–$242 double; $319 two-bedroom villa for 4. Ask about packages. AE, MC, V. **Amenities:** 2 restaurants, 2 bars; 4 pools; snorkeling; 6 tennis courts; fitness center; sailing; snorkeling; scuba diving; sport fishing; shuttle to beaches; spa; children's programs; baby-sitting. *In room:* A/C, TV, minibar, coffeemaker, hair dryer, kitchenette in villas.

MODERATE

Coconut Point 🎯 *Finds*   Opening onto Carrot Bay, these vacation apartments are light and breezy with real Caribbean flair and style. You get comfort and taste in one- or two-bedroom units, each with a king- or queen-size bed, with ceiling fans whirling overhead. A few units also offer air-conditioning. The nicest feature is the oversize porches with dining tables set out. Some units also feature a gas-fed barbecue grill. The Orchid unit is perfect for honeymooners, and the Hibiscus, Bougainvillea, and Frangipani come with two bedrooms each, suitable for families. Bathrooms are neatly tiled, each with a shower unit.

P.O. Box 441, Carrot Bay, Road Town, B.V.I. ℂ **284/495-4892**. Fax 284/495-4466. www.go.bvi.com/coconut_point/rates.htm. 5 units. Winter $1,400–$1,750 per week. Off-season $900–$1,000 per week. MC, V. **Amenities:** pool, baby-sitting. *In room:* A/C, TV, coffeemaker.

Fort Burt Hotel   This inn, which is covered with flowering vines, rents rooms, but devotes much of its energy to its popular pub and restaurant (reviewed in "Where to Dine," below). Built in 1960 on the ruins of a 17th-century Dutch fort, the rooms are set at a higher elevation than any others in Road Town, offering views from their private terraces to the waterfront below. Simple, sun-flooded, and cozy, they have a colonial charm and freewheeling conviviality. The suite rentals are a bit expensive, but the regular doubles are spacious enough and have recently been refurbished. There's a pool on the grounds, or guests can walk to Garden Bay Beach or Smuggler's Cove Beach in just 3 minutes. Its major competitor is Fort Recovery Estate, which is also built around the ruins of a sugar mill, but Fort Recovery has a beach.

P.O. Box 3380, Fort Burt, Road Town, Tortola, B.V.I. ℂ **284/494-2587**. Fax 284/494-2002. 18 Units. Year-round $99–$135 double; $155–$205 suite with kitchen, $225–$295 suite with private pool, but no kitchen. AE, MC, V. **Amenities:** Restaurant; pub; pool. *In room:* A/C, TV, hair dryer, coffeemaker. No phone.

Fort Recovery Estate 🎯   Nestled in a small palm grove about 8 miles from Road Town, this property faces the Sir Francis Drake Channel and offers villas and two houses. The property fronts one of the best small beaches on this side of the island. It also contains the remnants of an old Dutch fort with the stone lookout tower still standing. The large house has an art gallery hallway and a large wraparound porch. The villas have living/dining areas, air-conditioned bedrooms, private bathrooms, and sliding glass doors that open onto patios facing the ocean. Although there's no restaurant on the premises, guests can enjoy dinner selected from a well-chosen menu, with each course brought to the room by courteous waiters. The accommodations come with complimentary continental breakfasts; for guests staying 7 or more nights, dinner is also complimentary, along with a boat trip.

P.O. Box 239, Road Town, Tortola, B.V.I. ℂ **800/367-8455** or 284/495-4354. Fax 284/495-4036. www.fortrecovery.com. 17 units. Winter $235–$265 villa for two; $345–$475 villa for four; $650–$725 villa for six to eight. Off-season $150–$170 villa for two; $285–$355 villa for four; $575–$590 villa for six to eight. Extra person $25. Rates include continental breakfast. AE, MC, V. **Amenities:** Dinner room service; laundry; baby-sitting; pool; car-rental desk; bike rentals. *In room:* A/C, TV, hair dryer, coffeemaker, kitchenette, fridge.

Josiah Bay Cottages   This well-designed cottage compound is located at the base of the steep and heavily forested hillsides of Tortola's northern coast. It's only a 5-minute walk from the beach. Its focal point is a swimming pool ringed with terra-cotta tiles and parasols. Red-roofed bungalows are scattered throughout the garden. Each unit contains a kitchenette. There's no restaurant or bar on-site. Costs here are especially reasonable for families.

P.O. Box 306, Road Town, Tortola, B.V.I. ✆ **284/494-6186.** Fax 284/494-2000. www.bviwelcome.com/ads/josiahbay. 7 units. Winter $195 daily; off-season $120 daily. Extra person $30; children age 12 and under $15 each. MC, V. **Amenities:** Pool; laundry; baby-sitting. *In room:* A/C, TV, kitchenette, mini-bar, coffeemaker.

Sebastians on the Beach   The hotel is located at Little Apple Bay, about a 15-minute drive from Road Town, on a long beach that offers some of the best surfing in the British Virgin Islands. The rooms are housed in three buildings, with only one on the beach. All come with rattan furniture and have small refrigerators and private shower-only bathrooms; six have air-conditioning, balconies, and porches. You should be careful here about room selection, as accommodations vary considerably. Most sought after are the beachfront rooms, only steps from the surf; they have an airy tropical feeling, with tile floors, balconies, patios, and screened jalousies. The rear accommodations on the beach side are less desirable—not only do they lack views but they're also subject to traffic noise. Also, avoid the two noisy bedrooms above the commissary. The dozen less expensive, rather spartan rooms in the back of the main building lack views, but they're only a short walk from the beach. The restaurant overlooks the bay. On Saturday and Sunday guests can enjoy live entertainment in the bar. The hotel features dive packages along with other deals that include a MAP plan, a welcome cocktail, a dozen assorted postcards, a pictorial guide to the B.V.I., and a bottle of rum.

Little Apple Bay (P.O. Box 441), West End, Tortola, B.V.I. ✆ **800/336-4870** in the U.S., or 284/495-4212. Fax 284/495-4466. www.sebastiansbvi.com. 26 units. Winter $135–$230 double. Off-season $85–$140 double. Extra person $15; MAP $40 per person extra. AE, DISC, MC, V. **Amenities:** Restaurant, bar. *In room:* A/C (only half), TV, coffeemaker, ceiling fan, fridge. Phone (only half).

Village Cay Hotel 🐾   Set in the heart of Road Town, this is the most centrally located full-service lodging facility in the British Virgin Islands. Yachties are drawn to this resort, but if you're seeking a beachfront location you'll have to look elsewhere. All rooms are medium-size to spacious and have been recently refurbished; many directly overlook a marina filled with yachts from around the world. Some of the rooms have balconies and patios; the most expensive are the waterfront rooms. These are called "A" rooms, and they are better furnished than the "B" units, which are smaller but good value if you're on a budget. Anything you need is within a 5-minute walk of the premises, including ferry service to other islands, secretarial services for traveling business clients, or taxi service to anywhere on Tortola.

Wickhams Cay, Road Town, Tortola, B.V.I. ✆ **284/494-2771.** Fax 284/494-2773. 20 units. Winter $150–$190 double, $225 one-bedroom suite, $350 two-bedroom suite. Off-season $115–$150 double, $185 1-bedroom suite, $285 2-bedroom suite. AE, MC, V. **Amenities:** Restaurant, bar; pool; marina. *In room:* A/C, TV, hair dryer, coffeemaker.

INEXPENSIVE

Castle Maria   This inn sits on a hill overlooking Road Town Harbour, just a few minutes' walk from the center of Road Town. The lush, tropical garden out front is one of the best in the British Virgin Islands. An orchard produces avocados, mangoes, and bananas, which guests can enjoy. Rooms are basic, but offer reasonable comfort, with balconies, patios, shower-only bathrooms, and kitchenettes.

P.O. Box 206, Road Town, Tortola, B.V.I. (📞) 284/494-2553. Fax 284/494-2111. www.islandsonline.com/hotelcastlemaria. 31 units. Winter $90–$95 double; $105–$110 triple; $130–$140 quad. Off-season $80–$85 double; $99–$105 triple; $120–$130 quad. MC, V. **Amenities:** Restaurant, bar; pool; room service; baby-sitting. *In room:* A/C, TV, fridge, coffeemaker; kitchenette in some units.

Icis Vacation Villas   These apartment units, though rather basic, are spotlessly maintained, and they're just yards from Brewers Bay, with its good swimming. Doors open onto a patio or porch in three white-and-pink concrete buildings. The rooms have both air-conditioning and ceiling fans, plus small, shower-only bathrooms. There are no room phones, but an on-site pay phone is available. This place is in a tranquil part of the island.

P.O. Box 383, Road Town, Tortola, B.V.I. (📞) 284/494-6979. Fax 284/494-6980. www.icisvillas.com. 5 efficiencies, 5 one-bedroom apts, 1 three-bedroom apt. Winter $99–$115 efficiency; $159 one-bedroom apt; $260 three-bedroom apt. Off-season $69–$79 efficiency; $89–$99 one-bedroom apt; $179 three-bedroom apt. Children age 11 and under stay free in parents' unit. DC, DISC, MC, V. **Amenities:** Secretarial services; laundry; baby-sitting; pool; car-rental desk. *In room:* A/C, TV, kitchenette, coffeemaker. No phone.

The Jolly Roger Inn   This small harborfront hotel is located at Soper's Hole, only 100 yards from the dock for the ferry to St. Thomas and St. John. The accommodations are clean and very simple. The small rooms have recently been refurbished with new draperies, bedspreads, and fresh paint, though only two have a private bathroom. There's no air-conditioning, but the rooms are breezy. The atmosphere is fun, casual, and definitely laid-back. The beach at Smuggler's Cove is a 20- to 30-minute walk over the hill.

West End, Tortola, B.V.I. (📞) 284/495-4559. Fax 284/495-4184. 5 units, 2 with bathroom. Winter $66 double without bathroom, $76 double with bathroom; $88 triple without bathroom, $99 triple with bathroom. Off-season $59 double without bathroom, $70 double with bathroom; $65 triple without bathroom, $83 triple with bathroom. AE, MC, V. Closed Aug 10–Oct 1. **Amenities:** Dinghy dock; fax service; sports fishing; sailing; diving trips. *In room:* Ceiling fan. No phone.

Maria's by the Sea   Right in the heart of Road Town, the hotel has a certain Caribbean charm from its little balconies that open right on the lapping waves of the harbor. The staff is friendly and helpful, catering to your needs. Bedrooms, though fairly minimalist, depend for their allure on the sea breezes that seem to blow here constantly. All units include a kitchenette, balcony, and a small shower-only bathroom. At night you can enjoy the harbor lights from your balcony perch. It's a 10- to 15-minute drive to the nearest beach. Maria, the owner and manager, serves an excellent local Caribbean cuisine. From her famous conch chowder to her home-baked rolls fresh from the oven, dining here in the evening is a delight.

P.O. Box 206, Road Town, Tortola, B.V.I. (📞) 284/494-2595. Fax 284/494-2420. www.islandsonline.com/mariasbythesea. 41 units. Winter $110–$125 double. Off-season $95–$125 double. AE, DC, MC, V. **Amenities:** Restaurant, bar; pool; water sports. *In room:* A/C, TV, kitchenette.

Mongoose Apartments   Just minutes from the beach, in the Cane Garden Bay area, lies one of the most reasonably priced apartment units on the island. All the apartments, although simply furnished, have a living room, kitchen and balcony, a shower-only bathroom, a twin sleeper couch in the living room, and ceiling fans. Two units have TV, but you'll have to rely on the office phone. The apartments are in a U-shaped two-story building. Some have an ocean view. A number of restaurants are close at hand. The owner, Sandra Henley, grows medicinal teas, which guests are invited to try.

P.O. Box 581, Cane Garden Bay, Tortola, B.V.I. © 284/495-4421. Fax 284/495-9721. www.mongoose apartments.com. 6 one-bedroom apts. Winter $135 apt for two. Off-season $95 apt for two. Extra person $20; children age 12 and under $10. AE, MC, V. **Amenities:** Baby-sitting. *In room:* Ceiling fan, hair dryer, fridge, coffeemaker. No phone.

Ole Works Inn ⭐ *Finds*   This hotel occupies the historic premises of a 300-year-old sugar refinery. It is also a far less expensive alternative to the island's other Sugar Mill, although it doesn't have the cuisine or the facilities of the more famed property. Still, it puts you right on the beach. It's set inland from Cane Bay, across the road from a beautiful white-sand beach, and has the best musical venue on Tortola—the rustic indoor/outdoor bar, Quito's Gazebo. The rooms are cramped but cozy, outfitted with angular furniture and pastel colors; many have water views. Each contains a small refrigerator and ceiling fan. Some are built as hillside units with ceiling fans (plus air-conditioning), refrigerators, and clock radios. Others are older and smaller. Regardless, the shower-only bathrooms are all a bit too small. The most romantic unit is the honeymoon suite in the venerable tower; it's larger than you'd expect. On the premises is a boutique-style art gallery showing watercolors by local artists and souvenirs. There are seven different restaurants on the beach.

The in-house bar is a magnet for fans of modern calypso music, largely because it's supervised by the hotel owner Quito (Enriquito) Rhymer, who's the most famous recording star ever produced on Tortola. Quito himself performs several times a week.

P.O. Box 560, Cane Garden Bay, Tortola, B.V.I. © 284/495-4837. Fax 284/495-9618. 18 units. Winter $80–$200 double, from $165 suite. Off-season, $60–$175 double, from $140 suite. Rates include continental breakfast. Extra person $25; children age 11 and under stay free in parents' room. Rates include breakfast. MC, V. Closed Sept. **Amenities:** Bar. *In room:* TV, hair dryer, ceiling fan, coffeemaker, fridge.

Rhymer's Beach Hotel   This comfortable, unpretentious mini-resort is housed in a low-slung pink building that sits next to a white-sand beach on the island's north shore. The hotel's social center is a wide ground-floor veranda where beach life and bar orders merge. The simple accommodations have ceiling fans, basic kitchenettes, and small, shower-only bathrooms. Music lovers can head for the bar of the nearby Ole Works Inn, where live music by island star Quito Rhymer is presented.

P.O. Box 570, Cane Garden Bay, Tortola, B.V.I. © 284/495-4639. Fax 284/495-4820. 21 units. Winter $90 double. Off-season $55 double. Extra person $10. AE, MC, V. **Amenities:** Restaurant; beauty salon; commissary. *In room:* A/C, ceiling fans, TV, coffeemaker, kitchenette.

Ronneville Cottages   If you'd like an inexpensive, week-long vacation in the Brewers Bay area, this is a good choice. The cottages may not be romantic, but they're well designed for basic beach living. They're set in concrete structures on ground level, and feature lots of tropical foliage and flowers. The units are clean and basic, with ceiling fans in the living rooms and standing fans in the bedrooms. Each has a porch or patio and TV, plus a small, shower-only bathroom. There's no pool, however, and no restaurant. But if you'd like some local cookery, the owner will prepare a dinner (give sufficient notice), and a beach bar serving burgers and the like is only a 5-minute walk away.

P.O. Box 2652, Brewers Bay, Tortola, B.V.I. ⓒ **284/494-3337.** 2 two-bedroom cottages, 1 three-bedroom/two-bathroom house. Winter $675 cottage per week. Off-season $475 cottage per week. Extra person $25 year-round; children age 2 and under stay free with parents. No credit cards. **Amenities:** Meals prepared with notice. *In room:* Ceiling fan, TV. No phone.

CAMPING

Brewers Bay Campground   Most camping buffs appreciate this place, located 3 miles from Road Town, for its low costs and for its easy access to some of the best snorkeling off the coast of Tortola. Both tent and bare-site options are available, and both include access to cookout areas, showers, and flush toilets. There's also a simple beachfront bar selling sandwiches, hot dogs, and beer. Dinner can be provided with advance notice. On Friday night there's a communal fish fry and on Sunday night a barbecue—both meals cost $10 per person. There's no on-site commissary, but shops in Road Town sell groceries and camping paraphernalia.

Brewers Bay (P.O. Box 185), Road Town, Tortola, B.V.I. ⓒ **284/494-3463.** 20 tents, 20 bare sites. $35 tent for two; $10 bare site for two. No credit cards. A camp shuttle is sometimes available. **Amenities:** Beachfront bar. No phone.

WHERE TO DINE

Most guests dine at their hotels, but if you want to venture out, try one these suggestions below. *Note:* Many of the less expensive restaurants here serve rotis, Indian-style turnovers stuffed with such good things as potato and peas or curried chicken.

EXPENSIVE

Brandywine Bay Restaurant ⋳⋳ ITALIAN/INTERNATIONAL   This restaurant is set on a cobblestone garden terrace along the south shore, overlooking Sir Francis Drake Channel. It's the most elegant choice for romantic dining. Davide Pugliese, the chef, and his wife, Cele, the hostess, have earned a reputation for their outstanding Florentine fare. Davide changes his menu daily, based on the availability of fresh produce. The best dishes include beef carpaccio, homemade pasta, his own special calf liver dish (the recipe is a secret), and homemade mozzarella with fresh basil and tomatoes. The skillful cookery ranges from the classic to the inspired.

Brandywine Estate, Sir Francis Drake Hwy. ⓒ **284/495-2301.** Reservations required. Main courses $22–$40. AE, MC, V. Mon–Sat 6–9:30pm. Closed Aug–Oct. Drive 3 miles east of Road Town (toward the airport) on South Shore Rd.

Callaloo ⋳ INTERNATIONAL   One of the better hotel restaurants on Tortola, this place is rather romantic at night, especially if it's a balmy evening and the tropical breezes are blowing. It's the kind of clichéd Caribbean setting that is forever a turn-on, and the food is quite good, too. The menu is hardly imaginative, but the chefs do well with their limited repertoire. Begin with the conch fritters or shrimp cocktail, and don't pass on the house salad, which has a zesty papaya dressing. The best dishes are fresh lobster when available (not as good as the Maine variety, though), as well as fresh fish like tuna, swordfish, or mahi-mahi. For dessert, make it the orange bread pudding or the key lime pie. Downstairs is the less expensive Scuttlebutt Pub. Most dishes are at the lower end of the price scale.

In Prospect Reef Resort, Drake's Hwy. ⓒ **284/494-3311.** Reservations recommended. Main courses $17–$45; fixed-price lunch $13. AE, MC, V. Daily 7am–11pm.

Mrs. Scatliffe's Restaurant ✿ (Finds) WEST INDIAN   This Tortola mama offers home-cooked meals on the deck of her island home, and some of the vegetables come right from her garden. You'll be served excellent authentic West Indian dishes, perhaps spicy conch soup, followed by curried goat, "ole wife" fish, or possibly chicken in a coconut shell. After dinner, your hostess and her family will entertain you with a fungi-band performance (except on Sunday) or gospel singing. *Be duly warned:* This entertainment isn't for everyone, including one reader who compared the hymns to a "screeching caterwaul." Service, usually from an inexperienced teenager, is not exactly efficient.

You may also be exposed to Mrs. Scatliffe's gentle and often humorous form of Christian fundamentalism. A Bible reading and a heartfelt rendition of a gospel song might be served up with a soft custard dessert. She often serves lunch in winter, but call ahead just to be sure.

Carrot Bay. ✆ **284/495-4556.** Reservations required by 5:30pm. Fixed-price meal $25–$30. No credit cards. One seating daily begins 7–8pm.

Pegleg Landing ✿ INTERNATIONAL   This restaurant lies 1½ miles southwest of Road Town and overlooks the yachts of the Nanny Cay Marina. You'll find accents of stained glass, mastheads from old clipper ships, lots of rustic paneling, and a nautical theme enhanced by the views and breezes from the sea. Specialties include sautéed breast of chicken in a champagne and orange sauce, charbroiled New York strip steak with mushrooms, and fresh fillets of fish, such as dolphin, swordfish, tuna, and wahoo. This is the type of food that appeals to yachties in many parts of the Western world—it's competent, but hardly exciting.

Nanny Cay Hotel and Marina, Road Town. ✆ **284/494-4895.** Reservations required. Main courses $18–$25. AE, MC, V. Daily 11am–11pm.

Skyworld ✿✿ INTERNATIONAL   Skyworld continues to be all the rage, one of the best restaurants on the island and the equal of Brandywine (see review above). On one of Tortola's loftiest peaks, at a breezy 1,337 feet, it offers views of both the U.S. Virgin Islands and the British Virgin Islands. The restaurant is divided into two sections—a more upscale area, with a dress code for men (collared shirts and long trousers), and an enclosed garden area, where you can dine in shorts. Both sections offer the same menu.

The fresh pumpkin soup is an island favorite, but you can also begin with seafood chowder or, our favorite, mushrooms stuffed with conch. The fresh fish of the day is your best bet (we prefer to skip the steak with port and peaches). The best key lime pie on the island awaits you at the end of the meal, unless you succumb to chocolate-fudge ice-cream pie.

Ridge Rd., Road Town. ✆ **284/494-3567.** Reservations required. Main courses $18–$24. AE, MC, V. Daily 11am–3pm and 5:30–8:30pm.

Sugar Mill Restaurant ✿ CALIFORNIA/CARIBBEAN   Transformed from a 3-centuries-old sugar mill (see "Where to Stay," above), this is a romantic spot for dining with many dishes that evoke recipes in *Gourmet* magazine. Colorful works by Haitian painters hang on the old stone walls, and big copper basins have been planted with tropical flowers. Before going to the dining room, once part of the old boiling house, visit the open-air bar on a deck that overlooks the sea.

Your hosts, the Morgans, know a lot about food and wine. One of their most popular creations, published in *Bon Appétit,* is a curried-banana soup. You might also begin with smoked conch pâté. A good choice for dinner is Jamaican jerk pork roast with a green-peppercorn salsa, or perhaps ginger-lime scallops with pasta and toasted walnut sauce.

Lunch by the beach can be ordered at the second restaurant, **Islands,** where dinner is also served Tuesday through Saturday from 6:30 to 9pm, from January to May. Try jerk ribs or stuffed crabs here.

Apple Bay. ✆ **284/495-4355.** Reservations required. Main courses $20–$30. AE, MC, V. Daily noon–2pm and 7–8:30pm. Closed Aug–Sept. From Road Town, drive west for about 7 miles, take a right turn over Zion Hill going north, and turn right at the T-junction opposite Sebastians; Sugar Mill is about half a mile down the road.

MODERATE

Gourmet picnic, anyone? **Fort Wines Gourmet,** Main Street, Road Town (✆ **284/494-2211**), offers fabulous fixings, including Hediard pâté terrines and fine chocolates.

Captain's Table CONTINENTAL   Set amid a cluster of palm trees on the marina, the Captain's Table offers outdoor dining in an inviting atmosphere. For appetizers you can enjoy selections from gazpacho to escargots. Also included is honey-dipped chicken, which is lightly coated with flour and deep-fried to a golden brown, then served with french fries on the side. For a lighter meal, you may want to try the Cajun chicken over a Caesar salad. For even more substantial appetites, the menu offers dolphin, served sautéed or grilled, along with grilled salmon and lobster. For something unusual, try filet of Jamaican jerk duck or one of the Asian specialties.

Wickhams Cay II. ✆ **284/494-3885.** Reservations recommended in winter. Main courses $12.50–$28. DC, MC, V. Mon–Fri 11am–3pm and 5–11pm, Sat–Sun 5–9pm.

Fort Burt Restaurant & Pub INTERNATIONAL   The food here is quite passable, but hardly the best on the island. Chalk it up as a "local favorite." This restaurant was built on rocks mortared together with lime and molasses in the 17th century by the Dutch and French. Lunches consist of soups, salads, grilled fish, and sandwiches. Dinners are by candlelight and are more elaborate, with such choices as fresh asparagus with aïoli sauce, conch fritters, shepherd's pie, baby back ribs, and roast duck with orange-and-tarragon sauce.

Fort Burt, Road Town. ✆ **284/494-2587.** Reservations recommended for dinner. English breakfast $8.75; dinner platters $15–$25; lunch sandwiches and platters $5–$8.50. AE, MC, V. Daily 8–10am, noon–3pm, and 6–11pm (bar, daily 10am–midnight).

North Shore Shell Museum Bar & Restaurant WEST INDIAN   When Egberth and Mona Donovan, both chefs, got married, they naturally decided to open a restaurant to showcase their culinary talents. They have succeeded admirably. Mona learned from her mother, Mrs. Scatliffe, who is the most celebrated local chef in the British Virgin Islands. The cuisine here is local and authentic. If you're in the area for breakfast, by all means drop in to sample the pancakes, made with coconut, guava, and mango—they're delectable. At lunch you can sample typical island fare along with some spicy conch fritters. For dinner you can try what was good at the market that day. The best soursop daiquiri on the island will get you in the mood. Tuesday and Saturday are barbecue nights, with chicken, lobster, and ribs. After dining, patrons hang out for a hoedown, a music fest featuring such instruments as a ukulele, a washtub, or a gourd maraca.

Main Road, Carrot Bay. ✆ **284/495-4714.** Dinner $28; breakfast from $5; lunch $5–$10. No credit cards. Daily 7am–10pm.

Pusser's Landing CARIBBEAN/ENGLISH PUB/MEXICAN   This second Pusser's (see Pusser's Road Town Pub, below, for the first) is even more desirably located in the West End, opening onto the water. Within this nautical setting you can enjoy fresh grilled fish, or perhaps an English-inspired dish like shepherd's pie. Begin with a hearty bowl of homemade soup and follow it with filet mignon, West Indian roast chicken, or a filet of mahi-mahi. "Mud pie" is the classic dessert here, or else you can try key lime pie, or, even better, the mango soufflé. Some dishes occasionally miss the mark, but on the whole this is a good choice. Happy hour is daily from 4 to 6pm.

Frenchman's Cay, West End. ✆ 284/495-4554. Reservations recommended. Main courses $13–$22. AE, DISC, MC, V. Daily 11am–10pm.

Spaghetti Junction ITALIAN/SEAFOOD   Boaters like this funky place. It's located near several marinas, and the bar remains open long after the food service has stopped. There's occasional impromptu dancing late at night. The Italian dishes, although standard, are quite good. Chicken or veal parmigiana, beef Marsala, and several seafood items are featured. Look for the blackboard specials. The *frutta di mare* (medley of seafood) is always a winner—it's served in a light cream sauce over angel-hair pasta. The Cajun jambalaya is another crowd-pleaser.

Administration Drive, Wickham's Cay, Road Town. ✆ 284/494-4880. Main courses $9.75–$24. AE, MC, V. Daily 6–10pm. Closed mid-Aug–mid-Oct.

INEXPENSIVE

Capriccio di Mare ✿ ITALIAN   Created in a moment of whimsy by the more upscale Brandywine (see above), this place is small, casual, laid-back, and a local favorite. It's the most authentic-looking Italian *caffè* in the Virgin Islands. At breakfast time, many locals stop in for a refreshing Italian pastry along with a cup of cappuccino, or else a full breakfast. You can come back for lunch or dinner. If it's evening, you might also order the mango Bellini, a variation of the famous cocktail (which is made with fresh peaches) served at Harry's Bar in Venice. Begin with such appetizers as *piedini* (flour tortillas with various toppings), then move on to fresh pastas with succulent sauces, the best pizza on the island, or even well-stuffed sandwiches. We prefer the pizza topped with grilled eggplant. If you arrive on the right night, you might even be treated to lobster ravioli in a rosé sauce. Also try one of the freshly made salads: We like the *insalata mista* with large, leafy greens and slices of fresh Parmesan.

Waterfront Dr., Road Town. ✆ 284/494-5369. Reservations not accepted. Main courses $6–$13. MC, V. Mon–Sat 8am–9pm.

Flying Iguana CARIBBEAN/CONTINENTAL   Don't make a special trip here, but if you're in the vicinity this is a good lunch spot. It serves tasty dinners as well. Don't be scared off by the $45 price for surf-and-turf. Most dishes are under $7, and the portions are so big they are a meal unto themselves. This open-air restaurant is painted in vivid Caribbean colors. At lunch order one of the iguana burgers (actually made with beef), the conch chowder, or one of the spicy conch fritters, along with a selection of sandwiches and pasta. The kitchen shines brighter at dinner, with an array of steak and seafood dishes, filet mignon, and roast duck. Puck, the chef and co-owner, will also prepare pretty much what you want to eat that night—within reason, of course. Just tell him your culinary desires, and he'll try to whip something up for you.

At the airport. ✆ 284/495-5277. Reservations not needed. Main courses $3–$45, lunch $3–$16. MC, V. Daily 7am–10pm.

The Jolly Roger ℞ SEAFOOD/INTERNATIONAL   This open-air bar and restaurant is a local favorite. People come for the stewed and cracked conch, unique pizzas, and great burgers—but the best thing about the Jolly Roger is the people. Just stick your head into the kitchen and ask Wanda for one of her great omelets for breakfast (she's here for lunch, too). The house specialty is home-made key lime pie—don't miss it. The bar is very popular with locals and sailors. Check the schedule or call to ask about the weekend Caribbean barbecue and live entertainment several nights a week.

West End (just past the ferry dock). ✆ 284/495-4559. Main courses $10.95–$19.75; pizzas from $10.25. AE, MC, V. Daily 8–10pm. Closed mid-Aug–Oct 1.

Marlene's WEST INDIAN   This centrally located restaurant provides take-out as well as casual dining indoors. Try the Caribbean pâtés—conch, swordfish, chicken, or beef wrapped in pastry dough, then baked or fried. Other examples of local fare include rotis and curries. You can also order baked chicken, steak, or seafood like lobster and other shellfish. The desserts are made from scratch.

Wickhams Cay. ✆ 284/494-4634. Pâtés $1.50–$2.50; main courses $6.50–$12; breakfast $2.50–$5. No credit cards. Mon–Sat 7:30am–6pm.

Midtown Restaurant CARIBBEAN   Set in the heart of Road Town, this hangout offers typical local fare, such as curried chicken and mutton. The menu also includes soups, such as conch, pea, and even boiled cow-foot soup. Other choices are stewed beef ribs, baked chicken, and a wide selection of fresh seafood, depending on the day's catch. Most dishes come with your choice of fungi, plantains, or Caribbean carrots. There's also a good breakfast here.

Main Street, Road Town. ✆ 284/494-2764. Main courses $6–$15. No credit cards. Mon–Sat 7am–10pm, Sun 7am–5pm.

Paradise Pub INTERNATIONAL   This establishment is housed in a low-slung timbered building on a narrow strip of land between the coastal road and the southern edge of Road Town's harbor. It has a grangelike interior and a rambling veranda built on piers over the water. The pub attracts many of the island's yachties, as well as the local sports teams, who celebrate here after their games. More than 25 different kinds of beer are available. If you're here for a meal, you can order Bahamian fritters, Caesar or Greek salad, pasta, four kinds of steaks, and burgers. The chef also prepares a catch of the day. Different nights of the week are devoted to all-you-can-eat theme dinners, including pasta on Tuesday, prime rib on Thursday, mussels on Wednesday, and barbecue on Saturday. Happy hour brings discounted drinks from 5 to 7pm Monday through Thursday and from 11am to 7pm on Friday, when hot wings and raw vegetable platters are offered.

Fort Burt Marina, Harbour Rd. ✆ 284/494-2608. Reservations recommended. Main courses $8.50–$22. AE, MC, V. Mon–Sat 6am–10pm.

Pusser's Road Town Pub CARIBBEAN/ENGLISH PUB/MEXICAN   Standing on the waterfront across from the ferry dock, the original Pusser's serves Caribbean fare, English pub grub, and good pizzas. This is not as fancy or as good as the Pusser's in the West End, but it's a lot more convenient and has faster service. The complete lunch and dinner menu includes English shepherd's pies and deli-style sandwiches. *Gourmet* magazine asked for the recipe for its chicken-and-asparagus pie. John Courage ale is on draft, but the drink to order here is the famous Pusser's Rum, the same blend of five West Indian rums that the Royal Navy has served to its men for more than 300 years. Thursday is nickel beer night.

Waterfront Dr. and Main St., Road Town. ℂ **284/494-3897**. Reservations recommended. Main courses $7–$19. AE, DISC, MC, V. Daily 10am–midnight.

Rita's Restaurant CARIBBEAN/AMERICAN   If you're looking for an inexpensive eatery with a touch of the island, then stop at Rita's for some local fare. The surroundings are simple, but the atmosphere is lively. Breakfast ranges from the standard American fare to local favorites such as fried fish or saltfish, which is chopped up with a variety of spices and sautéed in butter. Both are served with johnnycakes. The lunch menu includes pea soup, curried chicken, and stewed mutton. For those who want a taste of the mainland, try the barbecued chicken and ribs, sandwiches, or that old standby, spaghetti and meatballs.

Round-A-Bout, Road Town. ℂ **284/494-6165**. Reservations not required. Breakfast $3–$8; lunch or dinner $10–$16. No credit cards. Daily 8am–10pm.

Rôti Palace INDIAN   The best rotis in the British Virgin Islands are served here, right on the old main street of the island's capital—they're just as good as those in Port-of-Spain, Trinidad. This is primarily a lunch stop, although it's also a good choice for an affordable dinner or a standard breakfast. Choices include a wide selection of vegetables and local conch, along with lobster, beef, and chicken dishes, often spicy and tasty. Sea snails are a specialty; they're mixed with onions, garlic, and celery and spiced with curries, then served in a butter sauce. Ginger beer, along with the usual juices and wines, might accompany your meal.

Abbot Hill, Road Town. ℂ **284/494-4196**. Main courses $6–$18. No credit cards. Mon–Sat 7am–9:30pm.

Virgin Queen WEST INDIAN/ENGLISH   This restaurant offers casual dining in a modest cinder-block building with nautical pictures scattered throughout. The menu includes a wide spectrum of dishes ranging from local fare, such as curried chicken, to a more international offering of pastas, such as the fettuccine served with a tomato-basil sauce, and barbecued chicken and baby back ribs. Included among the British specialties are shepherd's pie, bangers and mash, and a steak-and-ale pie. The portions are substantial.

Fleming St., Road Town. ℂ **284/494-2310**. Reservations recommended. Main courses $8.50–$16.50; lunch $9. MC, V. Mon–Fri 11am–10pm, Sat 6:30–10pm.

Quito's Gazebo ★ Ⓕⁱⁿᵈˢ WEST INDIAN   This restaurant, owned by Quito Rhymer, the island's most acclaimed musician, is the most popular of those located along the shore of Cane Bay. Quito himself performs after dinner several nights a week. The place, which is designed like an enlarged gazebo, is set directly on the sands of the beach. It serves frothy rum-based drinks (ask for the piña colada or a Bushwacker, made with four different kinds of rum). Lunch includes sandwiches, salads, and platters. Evening meals are more elaborate, and might feature conch or pumpkin fritters, mahi-mahi with a wine-butter sauce, a conch dinner with (Callwood) rum sauce, chicken roti, and steamed local mutton served with a sauce of island tomatoes and pepper. On Friday night for only $16 you can enjoy an all-you-can-eat buffet of barbecue ribs, chicken, roti, corn on the cob, and johnnycakes. The food has a true island flavor and a lot of zest.

Cane Garden Bay. ℂ **284/495-4837**. Main courses $12–$18; lunch platters, sandwiches, and salads $5–$10. AE, MC, V. Mon–Fri 7am–6pm, Fri–Sat 7am–4pm. (Bar, Tues–Sun 11am–midnight.)

Tips Down Among the Sheltering Palms

If you decide to navigate the roller-coaster hills of the British Virgin Islands, then head to **Cane Garden Bay,** one of the choicest pieces of real estate on the island, long ago discovered by the sailing crowd. Its white sandy beach with sheltering palms is the epitome of Caribbean charm.

Rhymer's, Cane Garden Bay (© **284/495-4639**), is the place to go for food and entertainment. Skippers of any kind of craft like to stock up on supplies here, and you can also order cold beer and refreshing rum drinks. If you're hungry, try the conch, lobster, black bean gazpacho, or barbecued spareribs. The beach bar and restaurant are open daily from 8am to 9pm. Main courses cost $12 to $25. On some nights a steel-drum band plays. Ice and freshwater showers are available (and you can rent towels). Ask about renting Sunfish next door. Major credit and charge cards are accepted.

Scuttlebutt Bar & Grill INTERNATIONAL/CARIBBEAN   This cafe's greatest asset is its location—it's 1 mile west of the center of Road Town, beside a small, charming marina. You can order your meal at the counter, then carry it to one of the picnic tables, which are sheltered from the sun, but not from the breezes off the water. The simple setting here keeps prices down, and the food—especially breakfast—is plentiful and good. Specialties include beef crêpes, crab-meat salads, sandwiches, burgers, and a house drink that combines several kinds of rum into a lethal combination known as a Painkiller. The place is especially popular at breakfast, when eight different kinds of "rooster omelets" draw the yachters. Upstairs is a more expensive restaurant, Callaloo (see review earlier in this section).

In the Prospect Reef Resort, Slaney Hill, Drake's Highway. © **284/494-3311.** Sandwiches, platters, and salads $5.50–$14. AE, MC, V. Daily 7am–1am.

Sebastians on the Beach INTERNATIONAL   Sebastians is a good choice if you're in the area for lunch. The wooden tables and rush-bottomed chairs here are scattered, Polynesian-style, beneath a rustic yet comfortable pavilion a few feet from the waves of the island's West End. Sun lovers sit within the open courtyard nearby. Choices include hot sandwiches, West Indian fritters, a home-made soup of the day, and burgers—nothing special, but it's all satisfying. At night, dishes have more flair and flavor. Your best bet is the fresh fish of the day, which can be pan-fried, grilled, or blackened, with a choice of sauces, including a local blend of seasonings and spices. You might also try their Jamaican jerk chicken, or vegetable casserole. Surf-and-turf items are also available.

West End. © **284/495-4212.** Reservations required for dinner only. Main courses $15–$35; lunch from $5.50. AE, DISC, MC, V. Daily 8–11am, noon–3pm, and 6:30–9:30pm (bar daily 7am–10:30pm).

BEACHES

Beaches are rarely crowded on Tortola unless a cruise ship is in port. You can rent a car or a Jeep to reach them, or take a taxi (but arrange for a time to be picked up).

Tortola's finest beach is **Cane Garden Bay,** on Cane Garden Bay Road directly west of Road Town. You'll have to navigate some roller-coaster hills to get there, but these fine white sands, with sheltering palm trees, are among the most popular in the B.V.I., and the lovely bay is beloved by yachties. There are outfitters that rent Hobie Cats, kayaks, and sailboards. Windsurfing is possible as well. Beware of crowds in high season. There are some seven places here to eat, along with a handful of bars.

Surfers like **Apple Bay,** west of Cane Garden Bay, along North Shore Road. The beach isn't very big, but that doesn't diminish activity when the surf's up. Conditions are best in January and February. After enjoying the white sands here, you can have a drink at the Bomba Shack, a classic dive of a beach bar at the water's edge (see "Tortola After Dark," below).

Smugglers Cove, known for its tranquility and for the beauty of its sands, lies at the extreme western end of Tortola, opposite the offshore island of Great Thatch and just north of St. John. It's a lovely crescent of white sand, with calm turquoise waters. A favorite local beach, it's at the end of bumpy Belmont Road. Once you get here, a little worse for wear, you'll think the crystal clear water and the beautiful palm trees are worth the effort. Snorkelers like this beach, which is sometimes called "Lower Belmont Bay." It's especially good for beginning snorkelers, because the reef is close to shore and easily reached. You'll see sea fans, sponges, parrot fish, and elkhorn and brain corals.

East of Cane Garden Bay and site of a campground, **Brewers Bay,** reached along the long, steep Brewers Bay Road, is ideal for snorkelers and surfers. This clean, white-sand beach is a great place to enjoy walks in the early morning or at sunset. Sip a rum punch from the beach bar, and watch the world go by.

The mile-long, white-sand beach at **Long Bay West,** reached along Long Bay Road, is one of the most beautiful in the B.V.I. Joggers run along the water's edge; it's also a lovers' walk at dusk, with spectacular sunsets. The Long Bay Beach Resort stands on the northeast side of the beach; many visitors like to book a table at the resort's restaurant overlooking the water.

At the very east end of the island, **Long Bay East,** reached along Beef Island Road, is a great spot for swimming. Cross Queen Elizabeth Bridge to reach this mile-long beach with great views and white sands.

EXPLORING THE ISLAND

Travel Plan Tours, Romasco Place, Wickhams Cay 1, Road Town (© **284/ 494-2347**), offers a 3½-hour tour that touches on the panoramic highlights of Tortola (a minimum of four participants is required). The cost is $28 per person, with a supplement of $5 per person if you want to extend the tour with hill-climbing in the rain forest. The company also offers 2½-hour snorkeling tours for $35 per person, or full-day snorkeling tours for $42 per person (with lunch included). A full-day sailing tour aboard a catamaran that goes from Tortola to either Peter Island or Norman Island costs $80 to $85 per person; a full-day

---

Finds The B.V.I.'s Tropical Showcase

It's free and it's a gem. The **J. R. O'Neal Botanic Gardens,** Botanic Station (© **284/494-4997**), is a 3-acre park in Road Town. It was created by the B.V.I. National Parks Trust and is run by local volunteers eager to show you around. The orchid house and a small rain forest are reached by crossing a charming lily pond, and other paths lead to a cactus garden and a palm grove. The aptly named flamboyant tree, with its brilliant scarlet flowers, is just one of the highlights here.

The Wreck of the *Rhone* & Other Top Dive Sites

The wreck of the HMS *Rhone*, which sank in 1867 near the western point of Salt Island, is perhaps the premier dive spot in the Caribbean. *Skin Diver* magazine called this "the world's most fantastic shipwreck dive." It teems with marine life and coral formations.

Although it's no *Rhone*, **Chikuzen** is another intriguing dive site off Tortola. This 270-foot steel-hulled refrigerator ship sank off the island's east end in 1981. The hull, still intact under about 80 feet of water, is now home to a vast array of tropical fish, including yellowtail, barracuda, black-tip sharks, octopus, and drum fish.

Another top dive site is a brilliant coral wall with the evocative name of **Alice in Wonderland.** It lies off Ginger Island. The wall slopes from 40 feet to a sandy bottom at 100 feet. This dreamlike site earned its name because of its monstrous overhangs, large mushroom-shaped corals, rainbow-hued colors, and wide variety of sea animals, including everything from the longnose butterfly fish to garden eels.

The best way for novice and expert divers to see these and other great dive sites is with one of the following outfitters:

Baskin in the Sun (② **800/233-7938** in the U.S., or **284/494-2858**), a PADI five-star facility on Tortola, is a good outfitter, with locations at the Prospect Reef Resort, near Road Town, and at Soper's Hole, on Tortola's West End. Baskin's most popular trip is the supervised "Half-Day Scuba Diving" experience for $95, catered to beginners, but there are trips for all levels of experience. Daily excursions are scheduled to the HMS *Rhone*, as well as "Painted Walls" (an underwater canyon, the walls of which are formed of brightly colored coral and sponges) and the "Indians" (four pinnacle rocks sticking out of the water, which divers follow 40 feet below the surface).

Underwater Safaris (② **284/494-3235**) takes you to all the best sites, including the HMS *Rhone*, "Spyglass Wall," and Alice in Wonderland. It has two offices: "Safari Base" in Road Town and "Safari Cay" on Cooper Island. Get complete directions and information when you call. The center, connected with the Moorings (see below), offers a complete PADI and NAUI training facility. An introductory resort course and three dives costs $168, while an open-water certification, with 4 days of instruction and four open-water dives, goes for $385, plus $40 for the instruction manual.

tour, which goes as far afield as the Baths at Virgin Gorda and includes lunch, costs $80 per person. If deep-sea fishing appeals to you, a half-day excursion, with equipment, for four fishers and up to two "nonfishing observers" will cost $600 to $700.

A **taxi tour** costs $45 for two passengers for 2 hours or $55 for 3 hours. To call a taxi in Road Town, dial ② **284/494-2322;** on Beef Island, ② **284/495-2378.**

No visit to Tortola is complete without a trip to **Sage Mountain National Park** (*, rising to an elevation of 1,780 feet. Here you'll find traces of a primeval rain forest, and you can enjoy a picnic while overlooking neighboring islets and cays. Go west from Road Town to reach the mountain. Before you head out, stop by the tourist office and pick up the brochure called *Sage Mountain National Park.* It has a location map, directions to the forest (where there's a parking lot), and an outline of the main trails through the park. Covering 92 acres, the park protects the remnants of Tortola's original forests not burned or cleared during the island's plantation era. From the parking lot, a trail leads to the main entrance to the park. The two main trails are the Rain Forest Trail and the Mahogany Forest Trail.

Shadow's Ranch, Todman's Estate (© 284/494-2262), offers horseback rides through the national park or down to the shores of Cane Garden Bay. Call for details, Monday through Saturday from 9am to 4pm. The cost is from $30 per hour.

OUTDOOR ACTIVITIES

SNORKELING   A good beach for snorkeling is **Brewer's Bay** (see "Beaches," above). Snorkelers should also consider heading to the islet of **Marina Cay** (see "A Nearby Island: Marina Cay," below), or taking an excursion to **Cooper Island,** across the Sir Francis Drake Channel. **Underwater Safaris** (see "The Wreck of the *Rhone* & Other Top Dive Sites" box) leads expeditions to both sites.

But the best choice for a snorkeling trip is **High Sea Adventures** (© 284/495-1300; fax 284/495-1301; www.highseabvi.com), led by one of Tortola's best charter captains, Capt. Roy. The company expanded this year to include Anegada day trips (see Loblolly Bay elsewhere in this chapter). The excursions are designed to make any level of swimmer feel comfortable. Capt. Roy patiently spends all his time in the water pointing out the fascinating underwater plants, coral, and countless species of colorful marine life. Make sure to ask him about the parrotfish "poop" (it's how coral is "made"). Equipment rental is included, or you can bring your own. Capt. Roy even throws in his special tropical punch on the way home.

YACHT CHARTERS   Tortola boasts the largest fleet of bareboat sailing charters in the world. The best place to get outfitted is **The Moorings,** Wickhams Cay (© 800/535-7289 in the U.S., or 284/494-2332), whose waterside resort is also recommended in "Where to Stay," above. This outfit, along with a handful of others, make the British Virgins the cruising capital of the world. You can choose from a fleet of sailing yachts, which can accommodate up to four couples in comfort and style. Depending on your nautical knowledge and skills, you can arrange a bareboat rental (with no crew) or a fully crewed rental with a skipper, a staff, and a cook. Boats come equipped with a portable barbecue, snorkeling gear, dinghy, linens, and galley equipment. The Moorings has an experienced staff of mechanics, electricians, riggers, and cleaners. If you're going out on your own, you'll get a thorough briefing session on Virgin Island waters and anchorages.

If you'd like sailing lessons, consider **Steve Colgate's Offshore Sailing School** (© 284/494-5119) or Tortola's **Treasure Isle Hotel** (© 284/494-2501), which offers courses in seamanship year-round.

Start & Finish: Harbour Drive, in the center of Road Town.

Time: 2 hours, not counting stops.

Best Time: Any day before 5:30pm.

Worst Time: Sunday, when many places close.

This tour concentrates on Tortola's West End, site of some of the lovelier beaches and vistas. See map on page 201.

Begin your tour at:

❶ Wickhams Cay

Here you'll find the densest concentration of shops and restaurants in Road Town. At first glance, Road Town seems to be a scattered sprawl of modern buildings that form a crescent along the harbor front and up the hillsides. At Wickhams Cay, however, some of the town's charm is more apparent.

From Road Town, head southwest along the coastal road, passing the capital's many bars and restaurants, including Pusser's, a popular watering hole. You'll also pass St. Paul's Episcopal Church (established 1937) and the Faith Tabernacle Church.

Less than 2 miles away on your left is the sandy peninsula containing:

❷ Nanny Cay Hotel and Marina

There's an attractive restaurant here called Pegleg Landing (see "Where to Dine," earlier in this section) and the opportunity to view some fine yachts bobbing at anchor.

Along the same road, 2½ miles southwest of Road Town, you'll get panoramic views to the left of 5-mile-wide Sir Francis Drake Channel, loved by yachters throughout the world, and of many rocks, cays, inlets, and uninhabited offshore islands. This curvy expanse of uncluttered road is one of the loveliest on Tortola.

The crumbling antique masonry on the right side of the road (look through the creeping vegetation) is the ruins of a stone prison built by the English for pirates and unruly slaves. Lush St. John will appear across the distant channel.

Continuing on, you'll come to the unpretentious hamlet of:

❸ West End

You'll also see the pier at Soper's Hole. Yachters and boaters report to the immigration and Customs officer stationed here.

Turn left on the hamlet's only bridge to:

● Frenchman's Cay

Here you can enjoy the scenic view and, to the west, Little Thatch Island.

Retrace your route toward Road Town. At the first major intersection, turn left up Zion's Hill. Tucked into a hollow in the hillside, is the:

❺ Zion Hill Methodist Church

This church boasts a devoted local following despite its rural isolation.

Continue on the road that runs along the island's northern coast, site of many of its least-developed beaches, with imaginative names like Apple Bay, Little and Great Carrot Bays, and Ballast Bay. Stop at any of them to swim or snorkel wherever it looks safe; if in doubt, ask a local. Continuing along the coast, you'll pass the Methodist Church of Carrot Bay and the Seventh-Day Adventist Church of Tortola.

TAKE A BREAK
Quito's Gazebo ((℗ 284 495-4837) is located at Cane Garden Bay, on the island's north coast. The owner is Quito Rymer, one of the island's best musicians. The place serves piña coladas (either virgin or laced with liberal quantities of Callwood's local rum) in an enlarged gazebo built almost directly above the waves.

After Quito's, the road will cut inland, climbing dramatically through forests and fields; a sweeping view will unfold continuously behind you. Soon, you'll be forced to make a turn. Fork left, and continue for a short distance along the rocky spine that runs down the length of the island. A sign will point to a platform offering one of the finest views on Tortola:

● **SkyWorld**
This eagle's-nest aerie has survived the most violent hurricanes. It offers unparalleled views of the entire island,

as well as food and drink. Many daytime visitors return to SkyWorld for a candlelit dinner.

After passing SkyWorld, continue east for about 1 mile. Take a right whenever the road forks. After the second right fork, the road will descend, passing houses, churches, suburbs, and schools, and eventually joining the main road running beside the waterfront at Road Town.

SHOPPING
Most of the Tortola's shops are on Main Street, Road Town. Unlike the U.S. Virgin Islands, the British Virgin Islands have no duty-free-port shopping. A wise shopper may, however, be able to find some good deals among items imported from the Great Britain. In general, store hours are from 9am to 4pm Monday through Friday and from 9am to 1pm on Saturday.

Caribbean Corner Spice House Co., Soper's Hole (© **284/495-9567**), offers the island's finest selection of spices and herbs, along with local handcrafts and botanical skin-care products, many of which you may find useful in the fierce sun. There's also a selection of Cuban cigars, but you'll have to smoke them on the island, as U.S. Customs does not allow their importation.

Caribbean Fine Arts Ltd., Main Street, Road Town (© **284/494-4240**), has one of the most unusual collections of art from the West Indies. It sells original watercolors and oils, limited-edition serigraphs and sepia photographs, and pottery and primitives.

Caribbean Handprints, Main Street, Road Town (© **284/494-3717**), features island handprints, all hand-made by local craftspeople. It also sells colorful (and expensive) fabric by the yard.

Flamboyance, Soper's Hole (© **284/495-4099**), is the best place to shop for perfume. There's also an upscale assortment of quality cosmetics.

Fort Wines Gourmet, Main Street, Road Town (© **284/494-2211**), is a store-cum-cafe. This is the best place on the island for stocking up for a picnic. Sample the full line of Hediard pâtés terrines along with a wide selection of chocolates, including some of the best from Paris. There's also an elegant showcase of glassware, lacquered boxes, and handmade Russian filigree items plated in 24-karat gold.

J. R. O'Neal, Upper Main Street, Road Town (© **284/494-2292**), stands across from the Methodist church. This home accessories store has an extensive collection of terra-cotta pottery, wicker and rattan furnishings, Mexican glassware, Dhurrie rugs, baskets, ceramics, and more, all at good prices.

Bargain hunters should also head to **Sea Urchin,** Columbus Centre, Road Town (© **284/494-3129**), where you'll find print shirts and shorts, along with stuff for the beach, including T-shirts, cover-ups, bathing suits, and sandals.

Good prices in swimwear are also available at **Turtle Dove Boutique,** Fleming Street, Road Town (© **284/494-3611**), which has a wide international selection. Linen and silk dresses here are sold here, too.

Pusser's Company Store, Main Street and Waterfront Road, Road Town (© **284/494-2467**), sells nautical memorabilia. A long, mahogany-trimmed bar

Moments Exploring Deserted "Treasure Island"

Across Drake Channel from Tortola lies **Norman Isle.** Although it used to be a pirate den with treasure ships at anchor, it is now deserted by all except some seabirds and small wild animals. Legend has it that Norman Isle was the inspiration for Robert Louis Stevenson's *Treasure Island,* first published in 1883. You can row a dinghy into the southernmost cave of the island—with bats overhead and phosphorescent patches—where Stevenson's Mr. Fleming supposedly stowed his precious treasure. Norman Isle has a series of other caves whose waters are teeming with marine life. The caves are one of the most well-known snorkeling spots in the B.V.I., with spectacular fish, and maybe even a small octopus, squid, garden eel, and colorful coral. Intrepid hikers climb through scrubland to the island's central ridge, Spy Glass Hill. To cut costs ask three or four other people to go in with you and rent a sailboat to go over for a cheap thrill adventure.

is accented with many fine nautical artifacts. There's also a line of Pusser's sports and travel clothing and gift items. Pusser's Rum is one of the best-selling items here. A Pusser's ceramic flask makes a good memento.

Sunny Caribbee Herb and Spice Company, Main Street, Road Town (© **284/494-2178**), was the first hotel on Tortola. Today it's a shop specializing in Caribbean spices, seasonings, teas, condiments, and handcrafts. You can buy two world-famous specialties here: the West Indian hangover cure and the Arawak love potion. A Caribbean cosmetics collection, Sunsations, is also sold here; it includes herbal bath gels, island perfume, and sunshine lotions. With its sweet aroma of spices, this factory is an attraction in itself. Every day, there's a different sampling of island products—perhaps tea, coffee, sauces, or dips. Right next-door is the **Sunny Caribbee Gallery,** which features original paintings, prints, wood carvings, and hand-painted furniture, plus crafts from throughout the Caribbean.

TORTOLA AFTER DARK

Ask around to find out which hotel might have entertainment on any given evening. Steel bands and fungi or scratch bands (made up of African-Caribbean musicians who improvise on locally available instruments) appear regularly, and nonresidents are usually welcome. Pick up a copy of *Limin' Times,* an entertainment magazine listing what's happening locally; it's available at most hotels.

Bomba's Surfside Shack, Cappoon's Bay (© **284/495-4148**), is the oldest, most memorable, and most uninhibited hangout on the island, sitting on the beach near the West End. It's covered with luminescent graffiti and odds and ends of plywood, driftwood, and abandoned rubber tires. Despite its makeshift appearance, the shack has the sound system to create a really great party. Every month (dates vary), Bomba's stages a full-moon party, with free house tea spiked with hallucinogenic mushrooms. (The tea is free because it's illegal to sell it.) The place is also wild on Wednesday and Sunday nights, when there's live music and an $8 all-you-can-eat barbecue. It's open daily from 10am to midnight (or later, depending on business).

The bar at **The Moorings/Mariner Inn,** Wickhams Cay (© **284/ 494-2332**), is the preferred watering hole for some upscale yacht owners, but drink prices are low. Open to a view of its own marina, and bathed in a dim and flattering light, the place is relaxed. Another popular choice is the **Spyglass Bar,** in the Treasure Isle Hotel, Road Town (☎ **284/494-2501**), where a sunken bar on a terrace overlooks the pool and faraway marina facilities of this popular hotel.

The **Bat Cave,** Waterfront Drive, Road Town (☎ **284/494-4880**), is one of the newest hot spots, on the ground floor of Spaghetti Junction. The latest recorded hits are played nightly. On the last Friday of each month, the staff throws a big themed costume party.

Other little hot spots, worth at least a stop on a bar-hopping jaunt, include the **Jolly Roger,** West End (☎ **284/495-4559**), where you can hear local or sometimes American bands, playing everything from reggae to blues. In the same area, visit **Stanley's Welcome Bar,** Cane Garden Bay (☎ **284/495-9424**), where a rowdy frat-boy crowd gathers to drink, talk, and drink some more. Finally, check out **Sebastians,** Apple Bay (☎ **284/495-4212**), especially on Saturday and Sunday, when you can dance to live music under the stars, at least in winter.

Rhymer's, on the popular stretch of beach at Cane Garden Bay (☎ **284/495-4639**), serves up cold beer or tropical rum concoctions, along with a casual menu of ribs, conch chowder, and more. The beach bar and restaurant is open daily from 8am to 9pm, with occasional steel-drum bands entertaining in the evening.

The joint is jumping at the **Tower Night Club,** West End (☎ **284/494-1776**), on Friday through Sunday nights. The place is packed with locals and a scattering of visitors who come to listen to a DJ but often live salsa and reggae.

A NEARBY ISLAND: MARINA CAY

Marina Cay is a private 6-acre islet near Beef Island. It was the setting of the 1953 Robb White book *Our Virgin Isle,* which was later filmed with Sidney Poitier and John Cassavetes. For 20 years after White's departure, the island lay uninhabited, until its hotel (see below) opened. That hotel was recently taken over by Pusser's, the famous Virgin Islands establishment.

The island is only 5 minutes by launch from Tortola's Trellis Bay, adjacent to Beef Island International Airport. The ferry running between Beef Island and Marina Cay is free of charge. There are no cars here. We only mention this tiny island at all because of the Marina Cay Resort, which non-guest can visit for the day.

WHERE TO STAY & DINE

Pusser's Marina Cay Resort 🐾   This small cottage hotel attracts the sailing crowd. It houses guests in simply furnished double rooms, all overlooking a reef and the islands of the Sir Francis Drake Channel. Each room has a private balcony. Furnishings are in a light, airy, tropical motif. For privacy, accommodations are set on a bluff, which also makes them well ventilated. Ceiling fans also help keep the rooms cool (there's no air-conditioning). The tiled bathrooms contain large showers.

There's casual dining in the beachside restaurant, with a cuisine that features Continental and West Indian dishes. Activities include snorkeling, Hobie Cat sailing, scuba diving (with certification courses taught by a resident dive master), castaway picnics on secluded beaches, and kayaking.

Marina Cay (mailing address: P.O. Box 626, Road Town, Tortola), B.V.I. ☎ **284/494-2174.** Fax 284/494-4775. www.pussers.com. 4 units, 2 villas. Winter $175 double; $450 villa. Off-season $120 double; $295 villa. Rates include continental breakfast. AE, MC, V. **Amenities:** Room service; Laundromat. *In room:* Ceiling fan, coffeemaker, fridge.

3 Virgin Gorda ⟨★⟨★⟨★

The second-largest island in the British cluster, Virgin Gorda is 10 miles long and 2 miles wide with a population of some 1,400 people. It's located 12 miles east of Tortola and 26 miles east of St. Thomas.

In 1493, on his second voyage to the New World, Christopher Columbus named the island Virgin Gorda or "Fat Virgin," because the mountain on the island looked (in his opinion) like a protruding stomach.

Virgin Gorda was a fairly desolate agricultural community until Laurance Rockefeller established the resort of Little Dix here in the early 1960s, following his success with Caneel Bay on St. John in the 1950s. He envisioned a "wilderness beach," where privacy and solitude reigned. Other major hotels followed in the wake of Little Dix, but privacy and solitude still reign supreme.

ESSENTIALS

GETTING THERE   You can get to Virgin Gorda by air via St. Thomas in the U.S. Virgin Islands. **Air St. Thomas** (𝓒 **800/522-3084**) flies to Virgin Gorda daily from St. Thomas. A one-way trip (40 minutes) costs $71, round-trip, $140.

Or you can arrive by boat from either St. Thomas or Tortola. **Speedy's Fantasy** (𝓒 **284/495-5240**) operates a ferry service between Road Town, Tortola, and the Valley, Virgin Gorda (at the end of Main Street). Five ferries a day leave from Road Town Monday to Saturday (there's two on Sunday). The cost is $10 one-way or $19 round-trip. From St. Thomas to Virgin Gorda, there is service three times a week (Tuesday, Thursday, and Saturday), costing $31 one-way or $50 round-trip.

You'll also find that the more luxurious hotels have their own boats to take you from the airport on Beef Island, Tortola, to Virgin Gorda.

VISITOR INFORMATION   The island's **tourist office** is in Virgin Gorda Yacht Harbor, Spanish Town (𝓒 **284/495-5182**).

GETTING AROUND   Independently operated, open-sided **safari buses** run along the main road. These buses, which hold up to 14 passengers, charge upward from $3 per person.

If you'd like to rent a car, try one of the local firms, including **Mahogany Rentals,** The Valley, Spanish Town (𝓒 **284/495-5469**), across from the yacht harbor. A representative will meet you at the airport or ferry dock and do the paperwork there. This company is the least expensive on the island, charging around $50 daily for a Suzuki Samurai. An alternative choice is **Andy's Taxi and Jeep Rental** (𝓒 **284/495-5511**), 7 minutes from the marina in Spanish Town. A representative here will also meet you at the airport or ferry dock for the paperwork. Rates begin at $50 daily year-round.

An aerial view of the island shows what looks like three bulky masses connected by two very narrow isthmuses. The most northeasterly of these three masses (which contains two of the most interesting hotels) is not even accessible by road at all, requiring ferryboat transit from the more accessible parts of the island.

One possibility for exploring Virgin Gorda by car is to drive from the southwest to the northeast along the island's rocky and meandering spine. This route will take you to the **Baths** (in the extreme southeast), **Spanish Harbour** (near the middle), and eventually, after skirting the mountainous edges of **Gorda Peak,** to the most northwesterly tip of the island's road system, near **North**

Virgin Gorda

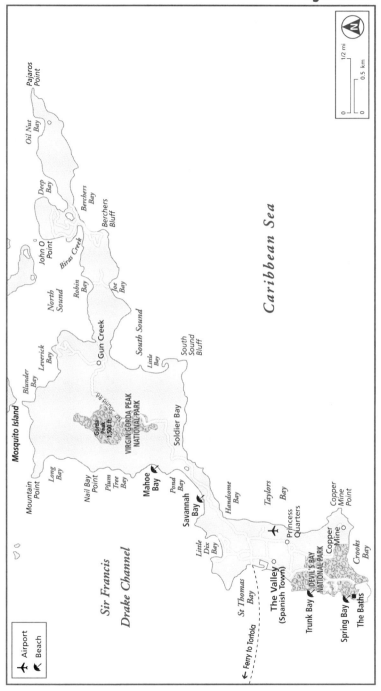

Airport
Beach

Sir Francis
Drake Channel

Caribbean Sea

Pajaros
Point

Oil Nut
Bay

Deep
Bay

Berchers
Bay

Berchers
Bluff

John O
Point

Biras Creek

Robin
Bay

Joe
Bay

North
Sound

South Sound

Little
Bay

South
Sound
Bluff

Gun Creek

Leverick
Bay

Blunder
Bay

Mosquito Island

Mountain
Point

Long
Bay

Nail Bay
Point

Plum
Tree
Bay

Gorda
Peak
1,500 ft.

North Sound Rd.

VIRGIN GORDA PEAK
NATIONAL PARK

Soldier Bay

Mahoe
Bay

Savannah
Bay

Pond
Bay

Handsome
Bay

Taylors
Bay

Copper
Mine
Point

Princess
Quarters

Copper
Mine

Crooks
Bay

Little
Dix
Bay

St Thomas
Bay

The Valley
(Spanish Town)

Trunk Bay

DEVIL'S BAY
NATIONAL PARK

Spring Bay

The Baths

Ferry to Tortola

1/2 mi
0.5 km

223

Sound. Here, a mini-armada of infrequently scheduled ferryboats departs and arrives from Biras Creek and the Bitter End Yacht Club.

FAST FACTS   The local American Express representative is **Travel Plan,** Virgin Gorda Yacht Harbour (© **284/494-2347**).

There are **police stations** on Virgin Gorda (© **284/495-5222**) and on Jost Van Dyke (© **284/495-9828**).

Barclay Bank (© **284/495-5217**) is located in Spanish Town at the Virgin Gorda Shopping Centre. It has an ATM machine.

For cameras and film, try **Kysk Tropix,** Virgin Gorda Yacht Harbour (© **284/495-5636**), open Monday through Saturday from 9am to 5:45pm. **Stevens Laundry and Dry Cleaning,** near the Virgin Gorda Yacht Harbour (© **284/495-5525**), is open daily from 8am to noon and 1 to 9pm.

WHERE TO STAY

The best agency for a villa rental is **Virgin Gorda Villa Rentals Ltd.,** P.O. Box 63, The Valley, Virgin Gorda, B.V.I. (© **284/495-7421;** fax 284/495-7367). This company manages villas throughout the island, most of which are quite expensive. A 5-night minimum stay is required in the off-season, a 7-night minimum in winter. The cheapest weekly rentals in winter are around $1,150 per week, dropping to $800 per week off-season.

Remember that all accommodation rates given within this chapter are subject to a 10% service charge and a 7% government tax.

VERY EXPENSIVE

Biras Creek Estate ✿✿✿   This private and romantic resort stands at the northern end of Virgin Gorda like a hilltop fortress, opening onto a decent beach, much of which is man-made. This sophisticated and relaxing hideaway has vastly improved after a major face-lift. This is the class joint of the island— stay here if you want a retreat from the world. (Bitter End is more family oriented, and Little Dix Bay more of a conventional resort.) On a 150-acre estate with its own marina, it occupies a narrow neck of land flanked by the sea on three sides. All the attractive, tropically decorated units have well-furnished bedrooms and private patios. Most have king beds, with deluxe mattresses, plus spacious bathrooms with inviting garden showers. There are no phones, radios, or TVs, but you do get such amenities as ocean-view verandas. Even the latest editions of the *Wall Street Journal* and the *New York Times* are delivered daily. Guests get their own bikes for their stay, and there are lots of hiking trails near the property.

The food has won high praise; the wine list is also excellent. The hotel restaurant and open-air bar are quietly elegant, and there's always a table with a view. A barbecued lunch is often served on the beach.

North Sound (P.O. Box 54), Virgin Gorda, B.V.I. © **800/608-9661** in the U.S., or 284/494-3555. Fax 284/494-3557. www.biras.com. 33 units. Winter $650 double; $1,150 two-bedroom suite for 2; $1,350 suite for 4. Off-season $425 double; $1,085 suite for 2; $1,285 suite for 4. Rates include all meals. Ask about packages. AE, MC, V. Take the private motor launch from the Beef Island airport. No children under age 6. **Amenities:** 3 restaurants; bar; pool; snorkeling; Sunfish; 2 tennis courts; kayaks; free bikes; laundry; baby-sitting; taxi service to launch; free trips to beaches. *In room:* A/C, coffeemaker, fridge, hair dryer. No phone.

The Bitter End Yacht Club ✿✿✿   This is the liveliest of B.V.I. resorts and even better equipped than the more exclusive Biras Creek. It's the best sailing and diving complex in the British chain. It opens onto one of the most unspoiled and secluded deep-water harbors in the Caribbean. Guests have unlimited use of the resort's million-dollar fleet, the Nick Trotter Sailing and

Windsurfing School. The Bitter End offers an informal yet elegant experience, as guests settle into one of the hillside chalets or well-appointed beachfront and hillside villas overlooking the sound. Most units have varnished hardwood floors, sliding-glass doors, and wicker furnishings. All villas have either twin or king-size beds, each with a deluxe mattress, plus a large dressing area and a shower with sea views.

For something novel, you can stay aboard one of the 30-foot yachts, yours to sail, with dockage and daily maid service, meals in the Yacht Club dining room, and overnight provisions. Yachts contain a shower with pressure water. Each yacht can accommodate four comfortably.

Dining on a first-rate cuisine is in the Clubhouse Steak and Seafood Grille, the English Carvery, or the Pub, with entertainment by a steel-drum or reggae band.

John O'Point, North Sound (P.O. Box 46), Virgin Gorda, B.V.I. © 800/872-2392 in the U.S. for reservations, or 284/494-2746. Fax 312/944-2860 or 284/494-4756. www.beyc.com. 86 units, 3 yachts. Winter (double occupancy) $555–$770 beachfront villa, suite, or yacht; $600 hillside villa. Off-season (double occupancy) $400–$550 all units. Rates include all meals. AE, MC, V. Take the private ferry from the Beef Island airport. **Amenities:** 2 restaurants, bar; Sunfish; windsurfing; Boston whalers; reef snorkeling; scuba diving; sports fishing; fitness center; boat trips to nearby cays; pool; laundry. *In room:* Ceiling fan, fridge, hair dryer. No phone.

Little Dix Bay Hotel 🐾🐾   Full of low-key luxury, along a curving white sand beach, the Little Dix Bay Hotel is a resort discreetly scattered along a half-mile, crescent-shaped, private bay on a 500-acre preserve. Many guests find this resort too pricey and stuffy; we prefer the more casual elegance of Biras Creek Estate and the Bitter End Yacht Club, though Little Dix Bay does have an undeniably lovely setting, fine service, and a quiet elegance (but, surprisingly, no pool).

All rooms, built in the woods, have private terraces with views of the sea or gardens. Tradewinds come through louvers and screens, and the units are further cooled by ceiling fans or air-conditioning (in 80% of the rooms). Some units are two-story *rondavels* (like tiki huts) raised on stilts to form their own breezeways. Accommodations are roomy, airy, and decorated with tropical flair each with a smart private bathroom with shower stall. All guest rooms have been renovated with new furnishings and fabrics, evoking a Southeast Asian style with beautiful wicker or reed furniture, bamboo beds, Balinese boxes and baskets, and ceramic objets d'art.

On the northwest corner of the island (P.O. Box 70), Virgin Gorda, B.V.I. © 800/928-3000 in the U.S., or 284/495-5555. Fax 284/495-5661. www.rosewood-hotels.com. 98 units. Winter $550–$775 double; $1,500 suite. Off-season $275–$525 double; $800–$950 suite. MAP (breakfast and dinner) $80 per person extra. Extra person $90. AE, DC, MC, V. Take the private ferry service from the Beef Island airport to the resort; $65 per person round-trip. **Amenities:** 3 restaurants, 2 bars; 7 tennis courts; Sunfish; kayaks; snorkeling; scuba diving; water-skiing; boat rentals; deep-sea fishing; fitness center; children's programs; massage; jeep rental; island tours. *In room:* A/C (in some rooms), ceiling fan.

EXPENSIVE

Nail Bay Resort 🐾   Below Gorda Peak National Park, and a short walk from a trio of usually deserted beaches, this resort enjoys an idyllic position. From its 147-acre site, some of the best sunset views of Sir Francis Drake Channel and the Dogs Island can be enjoyed. All the well-furnished units, each with a bathroom containing a shower stall, are comfortable and tasteful. Accommodations are wide ranging, including deluxe bedrooms, suites, apartments and villas. The best accommodations are the four "estate villas"—Diamond Beach, Flame Trees, Sunset Watch, and Turtle Bay. The most modest units are hotel-style bedrooms in the main building. At night it evokes a luxury property in Asia, its landscaping highlighted by circuitous stone walkways. One devotee told us that when she found the resort, it had the "terra-ultima exclusitivity of Mustique without that island's elitism."

Nail Bay, (P.O. Box 69) Virgin Gorda, B.V.I. ✆ **800/871-3551** in the U.S., or 284/494-8000. Fax 284/495-5875. www.nailbay.com Winter $200–$425 double. Off-season $120–$286 double. AE, DC, MC, V. **Amenities:** Swim-up bar and grill; tennis court; kayaking; snorkeling. In room: A/C, TV, coffeemaker, hair dryer, iron.

The Olde Yard Inn *𝒻* For those who shun the super-expensive and chic resorts recommended above, there is this little charmer outside Spanish Town. It's not on a beach, but a free shuttle hauls guests to nearby Savannah Bay where there is an excellent white sandy beach. The inn lies a mile from the airport, surrounded by tropical gardens and a wall for privacy. Near the main house are two long bungalows with large renovated bedrooms, each with its own bathroom (shower only) and patio, done in a charming style. Half of the rooms have airconditioning (for an extra $10), and all have ceiling fans. Three of the rooms also contain minifridges. You can go for a sail on a yacht or embark on a snorkeling adventure at one of 16 beaches nearby.

The French-accented dinners are one of the reasons for coming here. Lunch is served poolside at the Sip and Dip Grill. There's live entertainment three times a week in the dining room.

The Valley (P.O. Box 26), Virgin Gorda, B.V.I. ✆ **800/653-9273** in the U.S., or 284/495-5544. Fax 284/495-5986. http://oldeyardinn.com. 14 units. Winter $195 double; $220 triple; $245 quad. Off-season $110 double; $130 triple; $150–$190 quad. MAP (breakfast and dinner) $50 per person extra. Honeymoon packages available. AE, MC, V. **Amenities:** 2 restaurants, bar; health club; Jacuzzi; library; pool. In room: A/C, ceiling fan, fridge, coffeemaker, hair dryer.

MODERATE

Fischers Cove Beach Hotel There's swimming at your doorstep in this group of units nestled near the sandy beach of St. Thomas Bay. Erected of native stone, each of the eight cottages is self-contained, with one or two bedrooms and a combination living/dining room with a kitchenette, plus a small bathroom with shower stall. You can stock up on provisions at a food store near the grounds. There are also 12 pleasant but simple rooms with views of Drake Channel. Each has its own private bathroom (with hot and cold showers) and private balcony.

The Valley (P.O. Box 60), Virgin Gorda, B.V.I. ✆ **284/495-5252.** Fax 284/495-5820. 20 units. Winter $145–$150 double; $170–$285 studio cottage. Off-season $100 double; $125–$205 studio cottage. MAP (breakfast and dinner) $40 per person extra. AE, MC, V. **Amenities:** Jeeps available; children's playground; occasional live entertainment. In room: A/C. No phone.

Guavaberry Spring Bay Vacation Homes *𝒻* Staying in one of these hexagonal, white-roofed redwood houses built on stilts is like living in a tree house, with screened and louvered walls to let in sea breezes. The Baths with their excellent sandy beach are nearby. Each home, available for daily or weekly rental, has one or two bedrooms; all have private bathrooms, with showers, small kitchenettes, and dining areas. Each unique vacation house also has its own elevated sundeck overlooking Sir Francis Drake Passage. Within a few minutes of the cottage colony is the beach at Spring Bay, and the Yacht Harbour Shopping Centre is a mile away.

Spring Bay (P.O. Box 20), Virgin Gorda, B.V.I. ✆ **284/495-5227.** Fax 284/495-5283. www.guavaberryspring bay.com. 18 houses. Winter $175 one-bedroom house; $265 two-bedroom house. Off-season $120 one-bedroom house; $175 two-bedroom house. Extra person $17–$22. No credit cards. **Amenities:** Commissary; scuba diving; fishing; jeep tours; sailing. In room: Ceiling fan, kitchenette. No phone.

Leverick Bay Resort & Marina   Set at the southern edge of the sheltered waters of Virgin Gorda's North Sound, this establishment offers a well-designed row of town house–style hotel rooms on a white-sand beach. The facade of each unit is painted a different pastel color, and the building is capped with an orange-red roof and fronted by three tiers of ocean-facing balconies. The units are stylish, comfortable, and graced with fine architectural touches. The bedrooms are pastel-colored, breezy, and filled with original art and have seafront balconies or verandas. The site contains a food market, an art gallery and two small beaches (a larger beach at Savannah Bay is within a 10-minute drive). A quartet of condo units is set in modern, red-roofed hexagons flanked on four sides by wraparound porches.

North Sound (P.O. Box 63), Virgin Gorda, B.V.I. © **800/848-7081** in the U.S., 800/463-9396 in Canada, or 284/495-7421. Fax 284/495-7367. 16 units, 4 condos. Winter $149 double. Off-season $119 double. Extra person $36 in winter, $24 off-season. Condos (by the week only): $1,470 for two, $1,800 for six. Off-season $1,200 for two, $1,350 for six. AE, MC, V. **Amenities:** Restaurant, bar; pool; dive shop. *In room:* A/C, TV.

Mango Bay Resort ⋆ *Value*   This well-designed compound of eight white-sided villas is set on lushly landscaped grounds overlooking the scattered islets of Drake's Channel on the island's western shore. You get good value for your money here. The accommodations are the most adaptable on the island—doors can be locked or unlocked to divide each villa into as many as four independent units. Costs vary with the proximity of your unit to the nearby beach. Interiors are stylish yet simple, often dominated by the same turquoise as that of the seascape in front of you. Daily maid service is included. You can cook in, or dine on-site at Giorgio's Table, which is quite good and serves three meals a day. There's also a bar.

Mahoe Bay (P.O. 1062), Virgin Gorda, B.V.I. © **800/223-6510** in the U.S., 800/424-5500 in Canada, or 284/495-5672. Fax 284/495-5674. www.mangobayresort.com. 12 units (all with kitchen). Winter $220 efficiency studio for two; $450 two-bedroom villa for four; $645–$900 three-bedroom villa for six. Off-season $99–$130 efficiency studio for two; $235–$465 two-bedroom villa for four; $365–$515 three-bedroom villa for six. Extra person on foldaway couch $25–$45. AE, MC, V. **Amenities:** Restaurant, bar. *In room:* A/C, ceiling fan. No phone.

Paradise Beach Resort   This resort was designed "for the plucky" who prefer vacations as unstructured as possible and who want to spend most of their holiday in their swimsuits. Don't even consider this place if you're looking for gregarious contact with lots of other travelers. This beachfront complex was created by Italian designers, who made ample use of marble, terra-cotta tile, and a breezy indoor-outdoor exposure to the sea. Bougainvillea and oleander climb up pergolas that shelter some of the amenities from too much direct exposure to the sun. If you stay here you're rather isolated, but the management will rent you a jeep. The design of each unit permits the combination of any two into a three-bedroom "villa." Units have indoor-outdoor kitchens, high ceilings, and sofa beds. Bathrooms, though small, are well organized, with marble vanities and showers.

P.O. Box 1105, Virgin Gorda, B.V.I. © **800/225-4255** in the U.S. or Canada, or 284/495-5871. Fax 284/495-5872. 7 units. Winter $185 studio for two; $265–$375 one-bedroom suite for two; $360–$440 two-bedroom suite for four; $500–$595 three-bedroom villa for six. Off-season $135 studio for two; $180–$245 one-bedroom suite for two; $210–$290 two-bedroom suite for four; $300–$405 three-bedroom villa for six. Extra person $30; children age 3 and under stay free in parents' room. MC, V. Closed the first 2 weeks of Sept. *In room:* Ceiling fan, kitchen.

INEXPENSIVE

The Wheelhouse/Ocean View Hotel This cinder-block building is definitely no-frills, although it is conveniently located, near a shopping center and the Virgin Gorda Marina and a 15-minute walk from the beach. The rooms are clean and simply furnished, often done in pastels with two single beds or a double bed. All are equipped with a small bathroom with a shower stall. Children are welcome, and baby-sitting can be arranged. The rooms are on the second floor with a long porch front and back, and downstairs is an inexpensive restaurant. There's also a garden in back.

P.O. Box 66, Virgin Gorda, B.V.I. ✆ 284/495-5230. 12 units. $85 double. AE, MC, V. **Amenities:** Restaurant, bar. *In room:* A/C, TV, ceiling fan.

WHERE TO DINE

EXPENSIVE

Biras Creek Estate *𝒞𝒞* INTERNATIONAL Even better than the cuisine at Little Dix (see The Pavillion, below), this hilltop restaurant is our longtime island favorite. And for good reason: The resort hires the island's finest chefs, who turn out a superb cuisine based on quality ingredients. The menu changes every night, but not that panoramic view of North Sound. It's as super as the key lime pie with raspberry sauce served here. On our latest visit, the chef launched us into an appetizer of lobster medallions dressed in a bed of tomatoe confit enhanced with a fresh black truffle vinaigrette. Our tastebuds were enthralled by the open ravioli made with octopus, scallops, vegetables, prawns, and olives. Our dining partner preferred an equally good (and more Caribbean) pan-roasted chicken leg served with avocado, served with sweet mashed potatoes and a red pepper mango salsa. Those warm berries in a champagne sauce made us not regret having passed on the iced white chocolate parfait with cherry griottes.

In Biras Creek, North Sound. ✆ 284/494-3555. Reservations required. Fixed price lunches from $36. Fixed price dinner $59. Daily 12:30–2pm and 7–10:30pm. AE, MC, V.

The Pavillion *𝒞* INTERNATIONAL The most romantic of the dining spots on Virgin Gorda, this pavilion is our preferred choice at this deluxe resort, which also operates The Beach Grill and The Sugar Mill. At the Pavilion guests sit under a large thatched roof, with the doors open to the trade winds. A middle-aged crowd frequents the place, and there are few objections to the high prices as this resort caters to the well-heeled traveler. The chefs change the menu daily, so you could dine here every night and have nothing repeated. Although many of the ingredients are shipped in frozen, especially meats and some seafood, there is much that is fresh and good. The most expensive item on the menu is a perfectly roasted lamb, but we prefer the pan-seared red snapper with a ratatouille made not with eggplant but with christophene, "the squash of the islands." Many vegetables evoke the Pacific Rim, and the seafood keeps us returning again and again.

In the Little Dix Bay Hotel, northeast corner of the island. ✆ 284/495-5555. Reservations recommended. Main courses $26–$40. AE, DC, MC, V. Daily noon–3pm and 7–9pm.

MODERATE

Chez Bamboo *𝒞* INTERNATIONAL The closest approximation to New Orleans supper club you're likely to find in Virgin Gorda lies here, in a building with a big veranda and a location that's within a 5-minute walk north of the yacht club. Inside, there's a wraparound mural showing a jazz band playing within a forest of bamboo, as well as bamboo artifacts that highlight the restaurant's choice of names. Owner Rose Giacinto and chef Monica Guglielmina concoct superb versions of dishes that their tastiest creations—conch gumbo, red snapper *en papillotte* (cooked in parchment) and New Orleans–style strip steak that's covered with a creamy Worcestershire sauce. Desserts such as apple crostini and crème brûlée are among the very best of their ilk on the island. Live music, usually blues or jazz, is presented every Friday night on the terrace.

In the Virgin Gorda Yacht Harbour. ✆ **284/495-5752.** Reservations recommended. Main courses $18–$32. AE, MC, V. Tues–Sun 6–10pm.

The Flying Iguana MEDITERRANEAN/FRENCH/WEST INDIAN   The owner of this place, Puck (a.k.a. Orlington Baptiste), studied his craft in Kansas City, with the Hilton Group, before setting up this amiable restaurant overlooking the airport's landing strip and the sea. Potted hibiscus and lots of effigies of iguanas, stuffed and carved, ornament a room that's a celebration of West Indian mystique. The house drink is a "happy" concoction whose secret ingredients change according to the whim of the bartender; it usually produces a lightheaded effect that goes well with the carefully conceived cuisine. The finest examples include fresh fish and all kinds of shellfish, including calamari, shrimp, scallops, and conch, often served in combinations with each other. There are also "the usual suspects"—steak, chicken, and lamb, seasoned in a way that emulates both the Caribbean and the faraway Mediterranean.

The Valley, at the airport. ✆ **284/495-5277.** Reservations not necessary. Lunch main courses $8–$16; dinner main courses $18.50–$45. MC, V. Daily 7am–10:30pm (last order).

Giorgio's Table ✷ ITALIAN   This is the only authentic Italian restaurant on the island. Located a 15-minute drive north of Spanish Town, it opens onto a big covered terrace, although its varnished interior evokes a yacht. We like to sit out here at night starstruck, gazing up at the heavens with the sounds of the surf nearby. The chef says he cooks Italian instead of "American Italian," and the food is good in spite of its reliance on a lot of imported ingredients. Fresh locally caught fish is generally your best bet, although you can order an array of succulent pastas and such standard fare Italian staples as veal scallopine. Pizzas and sandwiches will fill you at lunch. Looking at this place, we decided its owner, Giorgio, had an appropriate last name—"Paradisio."

Mahoe Bay ✆ **284/495-5684.** Reservations recommended. Lunch main courses $13.50–$18; dinner main courses $25–$34. AE, DISC, MC, V. Daily noon–2:30pm and 6:30–9pm.

INEXPENSIVE

Bath & Turtle Pub INTERNATIONAL   At the end of the waterfront shopping plaza in Spanish Town sits the most popular pub on Virgin Gorda, packed with locals during happy hour from 4 to 6pm. Even if you don't care about food, you might join the regulars over midmorning guava coladas or peach daiquiris. There's live music every Wednesday and Sunday night, in summer only (no cover). From its handful of indoor and courtyard tables, you can order fried fish fingers, nachos, very spicy chili, pizzas, fresh pasta, barbecue chicken, steak, lobster, and daily seafood specials, such as conch fritters, from the simple menu here.

Virgin Gorda Yacht Harbour, Spanish Town. ✆ **284/495-5239.** Reservations recommended. Breakfast $4.50–$8.95; main courses $6.75–$9 lunch, $9–$20 dinner. AE, MC, V. Daily 7am–11pm.

The Crab Hole WEST INDIAN   This is a clean and decent West Indian restaurant, far removed from the expense and glitter of such resorts as Little Dix Bay and Biras Creek Estate in the private home of Kenroy and Janet Millington (look for a concrete house surrounded by fields and other simple private dwellings). Order your food from the chalkboard posted above the bar. They have their good days and their bad days here, depending on what the market turned up. You might get stewed whelk with a Creole sauce made from local spices or tomatoes, perhaps stewed chicken, and most definitely fried fish. Stewed oxtail is sometimes on the menu, and guests, often hotel workers in the area, drop in for a noon hamburger.

South Valley. ✆ 284/495-5307. Main courses $10–$15. No credit cards. Mon–Sat 9am–9pm. Head south along the road to the Baths, and turn left at the sign to the Crab Hole.

The Lighthouse Restaurant CONTINENTAL   A combined restaurant and beach bar, this recently renovated place is today's version of the old Pusser's, which now operates only a store here. During the day, you can enjoy all sorts of light meals, including croissant sandwiches, burgers, fried snapper, and pizza. There's also a special menu for children. At night, the menu is more ambitious, with appetizers like conch chowder and hearty main courses such as rack of barbecued ribs or penne pesto. The best food here is the fish, including mahi-mahi, wahoo, snapper, grouper, or swordfish, all prepared any way you want it (charcoal-grilled, blackened, pesto crusted, sautéed in butter, or Caribbean-style with white wine and butter with pepper and onions).

Leverick Bay, North Sound. ✆ 284/495-7154. Reservations recommended. Main courses $14.95–$21.95; lunch $3.25–$18.95; pizzas from $6.95. AE, MC, V. Daily 7:30am–midnight. Closed Sept–Oct.

Mad Dog PIÑA COLADAS/SANDWICHES   This is the most skillful and charming reconstruction of a West Indian cottage on Virgin Gorda. The wide veranda and the brightly painted 19th-century wooden timbers and clapboards create a cozy and convivial drink and sandwich bar. The piña coladas are absolutely divine. The owner and supervisor of this laid-back place is London-born Colin McCullough, a self-described "mad dog" who sailed the British Virgin Islands for almost 30 years before establishing his domain here.

The Baths, The Country. ✆ 284/495-5830. Sandwiches $5; piña coladas $4. No credit cards. Daily 9am–7pm.

Thelma's Hideout ✔ *Finds* WEST INDIAN   Mrs. Thelma King, one of the most outspoken grandes dames of Virgin Gorda (who worked in Manhattan for many years before returning to her native B.V.I.), runs this convivial gathering place for the island's local community. It's located in a concrete house with angles softened by ascending tiers of verandas. Food choices include grilled steaks, fish fillets, and West Indian stews containing pork, mutton, or chicken. Limeade or mauby are available, but many stick to rum or beer. Live music is presented on Saturday night in winter, and every other Saturday off-season.

The Valley. ✆ 284/495-5646. Reservations required for dinner. Dinner $15–$18; lunch $9–$10. No credit cards. Daily 7–10am, 11:30am–2:30pm, and (only on notification before 3pm) 6–10pm (bar, daily 11am–midnight).

Top of the Baths CARIBBEAN   This aptly named green-and-white restaurant offers a patio with a swimming pool. Locals gather here to enjoy the food they grew up on. At lunch, you can order an array of appetizers, sandwiches, and salad plates. You're invited to swim in the pool either before or after dining. At night, the kitchen turns out good home-style cookery, including fresh fish,

lobster, chicken, and steaks. Look for one of the daily specials. Save room for a piece of that rum cake! On Wednesdays and Thursdays live steel bands perform.
The Valley. ✆ **284/495-5497.** Reservations not necessary. Dinner $16–$26; sandwiches and salad plates $6.50–$10. AE, MC, V. Daily 8am–10pm.

EXPLORING THE ISLAND

The northern side of Virgin Gorda is mountainous, with Gorda Peak reaching 1,370 feet, the highest spot on the island. However, the southern half is flat, with large boulders appearing at every turn.

The best way to see the island if you're over for a day trip is to call **Andy Flax** at the Fischers Cove Beach Hotel. He runs the **Virgin Gorda Tours Association** (✆ **284/495-5252**), which will give you a tour of the island for $20 per person. The tour leaves twice daily, or more often based on demand. You can be picked up at the ferry dock if you give 24-hour notice.

HITTING THE BEACH   The best beaches are at **the Baths** ✱✱, where giant boulders form a series of tranquil pools and grottoes flooded with sea water (nearby snorkeling is excellent, and you can rent gear on the beach). Scientists think the boulders were brought to the surface eons ago by volcanic activity.

Devil's Bay National Park can be reached by a trail from the Baths. The walk to the secluded coral-sand beach takes about 15 minutes through boulders and dry coastal vegetation.

The Baths and surrounding areas are part of a proposed system of parks and protected areas in the B.V.I. The protected area encompasses 682 acres of land, including sites at Little Fort, Spring Bay, the Baths, and Devil's Bay on the east coast.

Neighboring the Baths is **Spring Bay,** one of the best of the island's beaches, with white sand, clear water, and good snorkeling. **Trunk Bay** is a wide, sandy beach reachable by boat or along a rough path from Spring Bay.

Savannah Bay is a sandy beach north of the yacht harbor, and **Mahoe Bay,** at the Mango Bay Resort, has a gently curving beach with neon-blue water.

DIVING   **Kilbrides Sunchaser Scuba** is located at the Bitter End Resort at North Sound (✆ **800/932-4286** in the U.S., or 284/495-9638). Kilbrides offers the best diving in the British Virgin Islands at 15 to 20 dive sites, including the wreck of the ill-fated HMS *Rhone.* Prices range from $80 to $90 for a two-tank dive on one of the coral reefs. A one-tank dive in the afternoon costs $60. Equipment, except wet suits, is supplied at no charge, and videos of your dives are available.

HIKING IN VIRGIN GORDA PEAK NATIONAL PARK

Consider a trek up the stairs and hiking paths that crisscross Virgin Gorda's largest stretch of undeveloped land, the **Virgin Gorda Peak National Park.** To reach the best departure point for your uphill trek, drive north of the Valley on the only road leading to North Sound for about 15 minutes of very hilly drives (using a four-wheel-drive vehicle is a very good idea). Stop at the base of the stairway leading steeply uphill. There's a sign pointing to the Gorda Peak National Park.

It will take between 25 and 40 minutes to reach the summit of Gorda Peak, the highest point on the island, where views out over many scattered islets of the Virgin Islands archipelago await you. There's a tower at the summit, which you can climb for enhanced views. Admire the flora and the fauna (birds, lizards, nonvenomous snakes) en route. Because the vegetation you'll encounter is not particularly lush, wear protection against the sun. Consider bringing a picnic—tables are scattered along the hiking trails.

SHOPPING

There isn't much here. Your best bet is the **Virgin Gorda Craft Shop** at Yacht Harbour (© **284/495-5137**), which has some good arts and crafts, especially straw items. Some of the more upscale hotels have boutiques, notably the Bitter End Yacht Club's **Reeftique** (© **284/494-2745**), with its selection of sports clothing, including sundresses and logo wear. You can also purchase a hat here for protection from the sun. You might also check **Island Silhouette in Flax Plaza,** near Fischer's Cove Beach Hotel (no phone), which has a good selection of resort wear hand-painted by local artists. **Pusser's Company Store,** Leverick Bay (© **284/495-7369**), sells rum products, sportswear, and gift and souvenir items. **Tropical Gift Collections,** the Baths (© **284/495-5380**), is a good place to shop for local crafts. Here you'll find island spices, bags, and pottery on sale at good prices.

VIRGIN GORDA AFTER DARK

There isn't a lot of action at night, unless you want to make some of your own. The **Bath & Turtle Pub,** at Yacht Harbour (© **284/495-5239**), brings in local bands for dancing on Wednesdays and Sundays at 8pm. Most evenings in winter, the **Bitter End Yacht Club** (© **284/494-2746**) has live music. Reached only by boat, this is the best bar on the island. With its dark wood, it evokes an English pub and even serves British brews. Call to see what's happening at the time of your visit.

Andy's **Chateau de Pirate,** at the Fischers Cove Beach Hotel, The Valley (© **284/495-5252**), is a sprawling, sparsely furnished local hangout. It has a simple stage, a very long bar, and huge oceanfront windows that almost never close. The complex also houses the Lobster Pot Restaurant, the Buccaneer Bar, and the nightclub EFX. The **Lobster Pot,** open from 7am to 10pm, is a famous showcase for the island's musical groups, which perform Wednesday through Sunday from 8pm to midnight. There's a $5 cover Friday through Sunday nights. You might also check out the **Lighthouse Restaurant** (© **284/ 495-7154**), which has live bands on Saturday night and Sunday afternoon. Call the **Olde Yard Inn** (© **284/495-5544**) to see if its Sip and Dip Grill is staging live local bands at its Sunday night barbecues.

4 Jost Van Dyke

This 4-square-mile rugged island (population 150) on the seaward (west) side of Tortola was named after a Dutch settler. In the 1700s, a Quaker colony settled here to develop sugarcane plantations. (One of the colonists, William Thornton, won a worldwide competition to design the Capitol in Washington, D.C.) Smaller islands surround this one, including Little Jost Van Dyke, the birthplace of Dr. John Lettsom, founder of the London Medical Society.

On the south shore are some good beaches, especially at **White Bay** and **Great Harbour.** The island only has a handful of places to stay, but offers several dining choices, as it's a popular stopover point, not only for the yachting set but also for many cruise ships. Jost Van Dyke is very tranquil, but only when cruise ships aren't in port.

GETTING THERE

Take the ferry from either St. Thomas or Tortola. (Be warned that departure times can vary widely throughout the year and sometimes don't adhere very closely to the printed timetables.) Ferries from Red Hook, St. Thomas, depart 3 days a week (Friday, Saturday, and Sunday) about twice a day. More convenient (and more frequent) are the daily ferryboat shuttles from Tortola's isolated West End; they depart three times a day on the 25-minute trip, and charge $8 each way, $15 round-trip. Call the **Jost Van Dyke Ferryboat service** (☎ **284/ 494-2997**) for information about either of the above services. If all else fails, try one of the handful of privately operated water taxis—but negotiate the fee carefully.

WHERE TO STAY

The **White Bay Campground** (☎ **284/495-9312**) rents bare sites costing $15 for three people or equipped tent sites going for $35 for two. Facilities include showers and toilets.

Don't try to write to these accommodations (or anywhere else) on Jost Van Dyke, as it can take months for mail to arrive.

Rudy's Mariner Inn   This simple place is modesty itself, but it's got a lot of yachties who like the hospitality of Rudy George, the owner. It's also one of the best places to eat on the island (see "Where to Dine," below), with simply prepared food. This place is the social gathering point for much of the island. It's also a bar and nightclub of sorts, and a ship's commissary. Expect bare-bone rooms with a bed and shower, and that's about it.

Great Harbour (next to the boat dock at the west end of the harbor), Jost Van Dyke, B.V.I. ☎ **284/495-9282,** or 284/775-3558 in the U.S.V.I. 5 units. Winter $125–$240 double. Off-season $90–$160 double. DISC, MC, V. **Amenities:** Restaurant, bar; snorkeling; fishing; windsurfing. *In room:* Ceiling fan. No phone.

Sandcastle Hotel ⚑   A retreat for escapists who want few neighbors and absolutely nothing to do, these six cottages are surrounded by flowering shrubbery and bougainvillea and have panoramic views, opening onto a white sandy beach. Bedrooms are spacious, light, and airy, furnished in a tropical motif, with tile floors, local art, rattan furnishings, day beds, and king-size beds with excellent mattresses. Two units are air-conditioned. There are large, tiled bathrooms, plus solar-heated showers outside. You mix your own drinks at the beachside bar, the Soggy Dollar, and keep your own tab. Visiting boaters often drop in to enjoy the beachside informality and order a drink called the "Painkiller." A line in the guest book proclaims, "I thought places like this only existed in the movies."

White Bay, Jost Van Dyke, B.V.I. ☎ **284/495-9888.** Fax 284/495-9999. www.sandcastle-bvi.com. (For reservations and information, call or write the Sandcastle, Suite 201, Red Hook Plaza, St. Thomas, U.S.V.I. 00802-1306; ☎ **340/495-9888**). 6 units. Winter $170–$220 double. Off-season $110–$150 double. Extra person $35–$45. 3-night minimum. MC, V. Take the private motor launch from Tortola; it's a 20-minute ride. **Amenities:** Restaurant, bar; diving; sailing; fishing trips. *In room:* Ceiling fan. No phone.

Sandy Ground   These self-sufficient apartments are along the edge of a beach on a 17-acre hill site on the eastern part of Jost Van Dyke. The complex rents two- and three-bedroom villas. One of our favorites was constructed on a cliff that seems to hang about 80 feet over the beach. If you've come all this way, you might as well stay a week, which is the way the rates are quoted. The airy villas, each privately owned, are fully equipped with kitchenettes. The interiors vary widely, from rather fashionable to bare bones. The living space is most generous, and extra amenities include private balconies or terraces. Most rooms have showers only.

The managers help guests with boat rentals and water sports. Diving, day sails, and other activities can also be arranged, and there are dinghies available. Snorkeling and hiking are among the more popular pastimes.

East End (P.O. Box 594, West End), Tortola, B.V.I. ✆ **284/494-3391.** Fax 284/495-9379. www.sandy ground.com. 8 units. Weekly rates: winter $1,650 villa for 2. Off-season $1,200 villa for 2. Extra person $300 per week in winter, $200 off-season. MC, V. Take a private water taxi from Tortola or St. Thomas. **Amenities:** Diving; day sails; dinghies; snorkeling. *In room:* Ceiling fan, coffeemaker, fridge.

WHERE TO DINE

Abe's by the Sea WEST INDIAN   In this local bar and restaurant, sailors are satisfied with a menu of fish, lobster, conch, and chicken. Prices are low, too, and it's money well spent, especially when a fungi band plays for dancing. For the price of the main course, you get peas and rice, coleslaw, and dessert. On some nights, Abe's will host a festive pig roast.

Little Harbour. ✆ **284/495-9329.** Reservations recommended for groups of five or more. Dinner $12–$35; nightly barbecue $20. MC, V. Daily 8–11am, noon–3pm, and 7–10pm. Take the private motor launch or boat from Tortola; as you approach the east side of the harbor, you'll see Abe's on your right.

Foxy's Tamarind Bar ⚓ WEST INDIAN   Arguably the most famous bar in the B.V.I., this mecca of yachties and other boat people spins entirely around a sixth-generation Jost Van Dyke native, Philicianno ("Foxy") Callwood. He opened the place some 3 decades ago, and sailors and the world have been coming back ever since. A songwriter and entertainer, Foxy is part of the draw. He creates impromptu calypso—almost in the Jamaican tradition—around his guests. If you're singled out, he'll embarrass you, but it's all in good fun. He also plays the guitar and takes a profound interest in preserving the environment of his native island.

Thursday through Saturday nights, a live band entertains. On other evenings, it's rock-and-roll, perhaps reggae or soca. The food and drink aren't neglected, either—try Foxy's Painkiller Punch. During the day, flying-fish sandwiches, rotis, and the usual burgers are served, but evenings might bring freshly caught lobster, spicy steamed shrimp, or even grilled fish, depending on the catch of the day. No lunch is served on Saturday and Sunday.

Great Harbour (✆ **284/495-9258.** Reservations recommended. Dinner $12–$26; lunch $7–$12. Daily 9am "until."

Rudy's Mariner's Rendezvous WEST INDIAN   Rudy's, at the western end of Great Harbour, serves good but basic West Indian food—and plenty of it. The place looks and feels like a private home with a waterfront terrace for visiting diners. A welcoming drink awaits sailors and landlubbers alike, and the food that follows is simply prepared and inexpensive. Conch always seems to be available, and a catch of the day is featured.

Great Harbour. ✆ **284/495-9282.** Reservations required by 6:30pm. Dinner $18–$35. MC, V. Daily 7pm–midnight.

The Sandcastle INTERNATIONAL/CARIBBEAN   This hotel restaurant serves food that has often been frozen, but, even so, the flavors remain consistently good. Lunch is served in the open-air dining room, while lighter fare and snacks are available at the Soggy Dollar Bar. Dinner is by candlelight and features four courses, including such dishes as mahi-mahi Martinique (marinated in orange-lemon-lime juice and cooked with fennel, onions, and dill). Sandcastle hen is another specialty likely to appear on the menu: It's a grilled Cornish hen that's been marinated in rum, honey, lime, and garlic. But we'd skip all that for the sesame snapper, if available. Meals are served with seasonal vegetables and fresh pasta, along with a variety of salads and homemade desserts. Those desserts are luscious, including a piña-colada cheesecake and a mango mousse.

On White Bay. ⓒ 284/495-9888. Reservations required for dinner by 5pm. Lunch main courses $6–$8; fixed-price dinner $32. MC, V. Daily 9:30am–3pm and one seating at 7:30pm.

5 Anegada ⓐ

Anegada (population 250) is the most northerly and isolated of the British Virgin Islands, lying 30 miles east of Tortola. The island has more than 500 ship-wrecks lying off its notorious Horseshoe Reef. Many of Anegada's inhabitants have looked unsuccessfully for the legendary hidden treasures on these sunken vessels, including the *Paramatta,* which has rested on the sea bottom for more than a century.

Anegada is different from the other British Virgin Islands in that it's a flat coral-and-limestone atoll. At its highest point, it reaches only 28 feet. The island hardly appears on the horizon, which explains why it has always been so dan-gerous for sailors. It's 11 miles long and 3 miles wide, and has a 2,500-foot airstrip.

At the northern and western ends of the island, there are some good beaches, which might be your only reason for coming here. This is a remote little corner of the Caribbean. Don't expect any frills, and be prepared to put up with some nuisances, such as mosquitoes.

Most of the island is off-limits to development and is reserved for birds and other wildlife. The **B.V.I. National Parks Trust** has established a bird sanctuary, which is the protected home of a flamingo colony, a variety of herons, and plenty of ospreys and terns. Thanks to the trust, the island's interior is also a pre-served habitat for some 2,000 wild goats, donkeys, and cattle. The preservation effort is giving a new lease on life to the rock iguana, an endangered, fierce-looking but actually harmless reptile that can grow to a length of 5 feet and weigh up to 20 pounds. Though rarely seen, these creatures have called Anegada home for thousands of years, and their surroundings have hardly changed.

ESSENTIALS

GETTING THERE   Most people get here by private boat; there's no ferry service. As an alternative, **Clair Aero Service** (ⓒ 284/495-2271), offers flights from Tortola to Anegada on six- to eight-passenger prop planes. It flies four times a week, on Monday, Wednesday, Friday, and Sunday, charging $59 per person round-trip. In addition, **Fly BVI** (ⓒ 284/495-1747) operates a charter/sightseeing service between Anegada and Beef Island off Tortola. The one-way cost is $125 for two to three passengers.

You can also take a day excursion to Anegada by charter boat from Tortola, with either **Speedy's** (ⓒ 284/495-5240) or **High Sea Adventures** (ⓒ 284/495-1300), which charges $110 per person for a day trip that includes a taxi tour, snorkeling, and a stop at Pam's Kitchen and Bakery (ⓒ 284/495-8031) for homemade pastries (lunch isn't included).

GETTING AROUND   Limited taxi service is available on the island—not that you'll have many places to go. **Tony's Taxis** (ⓒ 284/495-8027), which you'll easily spot when you arrive, will take you around the island. It's also pos-sible to rent bicycles—ask around.

Finds **Loblolly Bay**

Any trip to Anegada has to include a visit to the fantastic beach and reef at Loblolly Bay. If you're taking a day trip from Tortola, make sure you call Tony's Taxi (© **284/495-8027**) ahead of time; he'll take you across the island to the bay, with one quick stop to see the legendary pink flamingos on the way. Once you pull up at Loblolly Bay, stake out a place on the beach and enjoy some of the most spectacular snorkeling in the B.V.I. Break for lunch at Big Bamboo, and have a drink at the small thatched-roof bar where scrawled signatures on the bar and roof supports are from Cindy Crawford, Brooke Shields, and Andre Agassi (the bartender swears they're real).

WHERE TO STAY & DINE

Guests who stay on this remote island are basically hiding out. The accommodations below are bare bones, but great for those seeking tranquility.

Anegada Reef Hotel *☆*   The only major hotel on the island is 3 miles west of the airport, right on the beachfront. It's one of the most remote places covered in this guide—guests who stay here are, in effect, hiding out. It's a favorite of the yachting set, who enjoy the hospitality provided by Lowell Wheatley. He offers motel-like and very basic rooms with private porches, with either a garden or ocean view. Mattresses are just adequate and bathrooms are cramped, with shower stalls. Come here for tranquility, not for pampering.

You can arrange to go inshore fishing, deep-sea fishing, or bonefishing (there's also a tackle shop); they'll also set up snorkeling excursions and secure taxi service and jeep rentals. There's a beach barbecue nightly, the house specialty is lobster, and many attendees arrive by boat. Reservations for the 7:30pm dinner must be made by 4pm. If you're visiting just for the day, you can use the hotel as a base. Call, and they'll have a van meet you at the airport.

Setting Point, Anegada, B.V.I. © **284/495-8002**. Fax 284/495-9362. www.anegada.com. 19 units. Winter $250–$275 double. Off-season $215–$250 double. Rates include all meals. MC, V. **Amenities:** Restaurant, bar. *In room:* A/C. No phone.

Anegada Beach Campground   Despite its isolated setting on one of the least developed islands in the British Virgin Islands, this campground boasts excellent amenities. It lies near waters that are great for snorkeling, at the edge of about a dozen miles of secluded beachfront. There's also a woodsy but relatively elaborate restaurant, access to cookout areas for budgeteers who want to barbecue, flush toilets in the restaurant, and outdoor showers whose privacy is ensured by artfully woven palm fronds. For tent sites, the management provides a sponge-foam mattress, but campers usually bring their own pillows. The campsite also contains two breezy beach cottages for rent, equipped with private kitchenettes.

Anegada, B.V.I. © **284/495-9466**. 10 tent sites, 10 bare sites, 2 cottages. Year-round, $36 tent for two; $7 per person bare site; $100 cottage. No credit cards. **Amenities:** Restaurant. No phone.

Neptune's Treasure *Finds* INTERNATIONAL   Set near its own 24-slip marina, near the southern tip of the island in the same cluster of buildings that includes the more high-priced Anegada Reef Hotel, this funky bar and restaurant usually hosts a mix of yacht owners and local residents. Dining is in a spacious indoor area whose focal point is a bar and lots of nautical memorabilia. The drink of choice is a Pink Whopee, composed of fruit juices and rum. The Soares family and their staff serve platters of swordfish, lobster, fish fingers, chicken, steaks, and ribs; dispense information about local snorkeling sites; and generally maintain order and something approaching a (low-key) party atmosphere.

They also offer four simple bedrooms and about four tents for anyone looking for super-low-cost lodgings. Depending on the season, rooms with private bathroom rent for $70 to $95 double. Tents share the plumbing facilities of the restaurant and go for $25 a night for two. Continental breakfast is included in the rates, and discounts are offered for stays of a week or more.

Between Pomato and Saltheap Points, Anegada, B.V.I. (©) **284/495-9439**, or VHF Channel 16 or 68. www.islandsonline.com. Reservations not necessary. Breakfast $9; fixed-price meals $16–$40. AE, MC, V. Daily 8am–10pm.

6 Peter Island *

Half of this island, boasting a good marina and docking facilities, is devoted to the yacht club. The other part is deserted. Beach facilities are found at palm-fringed Deadman's Bay, which faces the Atlantic but is protected by a reef. All goods and services are at the one resort (see below). The island is so private that except for an occasional mason at work, about the only company you'll encounter will be an iguana or a feral cat whose ancestors were abandoned generations ago by shippers (the cats are said to have virtually eliminated the island's rodent population).

A hotel-operated ferry, **Peter Island Boat** (© **284/495-2000**), picks up any overnight guest who arrives at the Beef Island airport. It departs from the pier at Trellis Bay, near the airport. The round-trip fare is $35. Other boats depart eight or nine times a day from Baughers Bay in Road Town. Passengers must notify the hotel 2 weeks before their arrival so transportation can be arranged.

WHERE TO STAY & DINE

Peter Island Resort *** This 1,800-acre tropical island is solely dedicated to Peter Island Resort guests and yacht owners who moor their crafts here. The island's tropical gardens and hillside are bordered by five gorgeous private beaches, including Deadman's Beach (in spite of its name, it's often voted one of the world's most romantic beaches in travel-magazine reader polls).

The resort contains 30 rooms facing Sprat Bay and Sir Francis Drake Channel (oceanview or garden rooms) and 20 larger rooms on Deadman's Bay Beach (beachfront). Designed with a casual elegance, each has a balcony or terrace. The least desirable rooms are also the smallest and housed in two-story, A-frame structures next to the harbor. Baths range from standard motel-unit types to spectacular luxurious ones, depending on your room assignment. The Crow's Nest, a luxurious four-bedroom villa, overlooks the harbor and Deadman Bay and features a private swimming pool. The two Hawk's Nest villas are two-bedroom villas situated on a tropical hillside.

Peter Island (P.O. Box 211, Road Town, Tortola), B.V.I. (©) **800/346-4451** in the U.S., or 284/495-2000. Fax 284/495-2500. www.peterisland.com. 53 units. Winter $595–$930 double; $1,320 two-bedroom villa; $5,950 four-bedroom villa. Off-season $595 double; $895 two-bedroom villa; $3,150 four-bedroom villa. Hawk's and Crow's Nest rates include all meals. MAP $75 per person extra. AE, MC, V. **Amenities:** 2 restaurants, 2 bars; fitness center; pool; 4 tennis courts; scuba diving; library; spa; marina with complimentary use of Sunfish; snorkeling gear; sea kayaks; Windsurfers; Hobie Cats; water-skiing; deep-sea fishing; room service (breakfast only); laundry; massage; baby-sitting. *In room:* A/C, minibar, hair dryer, fridge, safe.

7 Guana Island 🖈

This 850-acre island, a nature preserve and wildlife sanctuary, is one of the most private hideaways in the Caribbean. Don't come here looking for action; rather, consider vacationing here if you want to retreat from the world. This small island right off the coast of Tortola offers seven virgin beaches and nature trails ideal for hiking; it abounds in unusual species of plant and animal life. Arawak relics have been found here. Head up to the 806-foot peak of Sugarloaf Mountain for a panoramic view. It's said that the name of the island came from a jutting rock that resembled the head of an iguana.

The Guana Island Club will send a boat to meet arriving guests at the Beef Island airport (trip time is 10 minutes).

WHERE TO STAY & DINE

Guana Island Club 🖈🖈   The sixth or seventh largest of the British Virgin Islands, was bought in 1974 by Henry and Gloria Jarecki, dedicated conservationists who run this resort as a nature preserve and wildlife sanctuary. On your arrival on the island, a Land Rover will meet you and transport you up one of the most scenic hills in the region, in the northeast of Guana.

The cluster of white cottages was built as a private club in the 1930s on the foundations of a Quaker homestead. The stone cottages never hold more than 30 guests (and only two phones), and because the dwellings are staggered along a flower-dotted ridge overlooking the Caribbean and the Atlantic, the sense of privacy is almost absolute. The entire island can be rented by groups of up to 30. Although water is scarce on the island, each airy accommodation has a shower. The decor is rattan and wicker, and each unit has a ceiling fan. North Beach cottage, the most luxurious, is like renting a private home. The panoramic sweep from the terraces is spectacular, particularly at sunset. There are seven beaches, some of which require a boat to reach.

Guests will find a convivial atmosphere at the rattan-furnished clubhouse. Casually elegant dinners by candlelight are served on the veranda, with menus that include homegrown vegetables and continental and stateside specialties.

P.O. Box 32, Road Town, Tortola, B.V.I. © 800/544-8262 in the U.S., or 284/494-2354. For reservations, write or call the Guana Island Club Reservations Office, 10 Timber Trail, Rye, NY 10580 (© 800/544-8262 in the U.S., or 914/967-6050; fax 914/967-8048). www.guana.com. 16 units. Winter $850 double; $1,500 cottage. Off-season $475–$640 double; $1,200 cottage. Rent the island, $9,200–$11,800. Rates include all meals and drinks served with meals. No credit cards. Closed Sept–Oct. **Amenities:** Restaurant; 2 tennis courts; fishing; snorkeling; windsurfing; kayaks; sailboats; water-skiing; laundry; baby-sitting. *In room:* Ceiling fan, kitchen, fridge, coffeemaker. No phone except in cottage.

Appendix:
The Virgin Islands in Depth

Golden beaches shaded by palm trees and crystalline waters teeming with rainbow-hued sea creatures—it's all just a few hours' flight from the east coast of the United States. Both the U.S. Virgin Islands and the British Virgin Islands are noted for their diversity. From sleepy islands that appear to be time capsules from the 1950s to the shopping bazaars and cruise-port terminals of St. Thomas, there is much here to attract the widest range of visitors. Food from most continents of the world, spicier music, and a leisurely lifestyle draw a never-ending stream of visitors seeking their own place in the sun.

1 The Virgin Islands Past & Present

A BRIEF HISTORY
Christopher Columbus is credited with "discovering" the Virgin Islands in 1493, but, in fact, they had already been inhabited for 3,000 years. It is believed that the original settlers were the nomadic Ciboney Indians who migrated from the mainland of South America and lived off the islands' fish and vegetation. The first real homesteaders were the peaceful Arawak Indians, who arrived from Venezuela, presumably in dugout canoes with sails.

For about 500 years, the Arawaks occupied the Virgin Islands until the arrival of the cannibalistic Carib Indians in the 15th century. The Caribs destroyed the Arawaks, either by working them to death as slaves or by eating them. With the advent of European explorers and their diseases, these tribes were completely wiped out.

THE AGE OF COLONIZATION In November 1493, on his second voyage to the New World, Columbus spotted the Virgin Islands, naming them *Las Once Mil Virgenes,* after the Christian St. Ursula and her martyred maidens. Short of drinking water, he decided to anchor at what is now Salt River on St. Croix's north shore. His men were greeted by a rainfall of arrows. Embittered, Columbus called that part of the island *Cabo de Flechas,* or "Cape of the Arrows," and sailed toward Puerto Rico.

As the sponsor of Columbus's voyage, Spain claimed the Virgin Islands; however, with more interest in the Greater Antilles, Spain chose not to colonize the Virgins, leaving the door open to other European powers. In 1625, both the English and the Dutch established opposing frontier outposts on St. Croix. Struggles between the two nations for control of the island continued for about 20 years, until the English finally prevailed.

The islands soon became a battleground, as the struggle among European powers widened. In 1650, Spanish forces from Puerto Rico overran the British garrison on St. Croix. Soon after, the Dutch invaded; in 1653 the island fell into the hands of the Knights of Malta, who gave St. Croix its name. However, these aristocratic French cavaliers weren't exactly prepared for West Indian plantation life, and their debts quickly mounted. By 1674 King Louis XIV of France took control of St. Croix and made it part of his kingdom.

The English continued to fight Dutch settlers in Tortola, which was considered the most important of the British Virgin Islands. It wasn't until 1672 that England added the entire archipelago to its growing empire.

A year before, in March 1671, the Danish West India Company made an attempt to settle St. Thomas. The company sent two ships, but only one, the *Pharaoh,* completed the voyage, with about a third of its crew. Eventually, reinforcements arrived, and by 1679, at least 156 Europeans were reported living on St. Thomas, along with their slaves.

Captain Kidd, Sir Francis Drake, Blackbeard, and other legendary pirates of the West Indies continued to use St. Thomas as their base for maritime raids in the area. Its harbor also became notorious for its bustling slave market.

In 1717 Danish planters sailed to St. John from St. Thomas to begin cultivating plantations. By 1733 an estimated 100 sugar, tobacco, and cotton plantations were operating on the island. That same year the slaves rebelled against their colonial masters, taking control of the island for about 6 months and killing many Europeans. It took hundreds of French troops to quell the rebellion.

In that same year France sold St. Croix to the Danish West India Company, which divided the island into plantations, boosting the already flourishing slave trade. Some historians say that nearly 250,000 slaves were sold on the auction blocks at Charlotte Amalie before being sent elsewhere, often to America's South. By 1792 Denmark changed its tune and announced that it officially planned to end the slave trade. It was not until 1848, however, that it did so. The British had freed their 5,133 slaves in 1834.

Dateline

- **1493** Columbus sails by the Virgin Islands and is attacked by Carib Indians on St. Croix.
- **1625** Dutch and English establish frontier outposts on St. Croix.
- **1650** Spanish forces from Puerto Rico overrun English garrison on St. Croix.
- **1671** Danes take over St. Thomas.
- **1672** England adds British Virgin Islands to its empire.
- **1674** King Louis XIV of France makes St. Croix part of his empire.
- **1717** Danish planters from St. Thomas cultivate plantations on St. John.
- **1724** St. Thomas is declared a free port.
- **1733** Danish West India Company purchases St. Croix from France; slaves revolt on St. John.
- **1792** Denmark announces plans to abandon the slave trade.
- **1807–15** England occupies Danish Virgin Islands.
- **1834** England frees 5,133 slaves living in British Virgin Islands.
- **1848** Under pressure, the governor of St. Croix grants slaves emancipation.
- **1916** Denmark signs treaty with the United States and sells islands for $25 million.
- **1917** Virgin Islands fall under the control of the U.S. Navy for 14 years.
- **1927** United States grants citizenship to island residents.
- **1936** Under Franklin Roosevelt, the first Organic Act is passed, granting voting rights to U.S. Virgin Islanders.
- **1940** Population of U.S. Virgin Islands increases for the first time since 1860.
- **1946** First black governor of the islands is appointed.
- **1954** Revised Organic Act passed; islands fall under jurisdiction of Department of the Interior.
- **1966** Queen Elizabeth II visits the British Virgin Islands.
- **1989** Hurricane Hugo rips through the islands, hitting St. Croix especially hard.

continues

The great economic boom that resulted from the Virgin Islands plantations began to wilt by the 1820s. The introduction of sugar beet virtually bankrupted plantation owners as the demand for cane sugar drastically declined.

- 1995 Hurricane Marilyn causes millions of dollars of damage and leaves thousands homeless.
- 1996 Water Island, off the coast of St. Thomas, is officially declared the fourth U.S. Virgin Island.
- 2000 St. Croix becomes the first "casino island" in the Virgin Islands.

Cuba eventually took over the sugar market in the Caribbean. By 1872 the British had so little interest in the British Virgins that they placed them in the loosely conceived and administered Federation of the Leeward Islands.

ENTER THE UNITED STATES   In 1867 the United States attempted to purchase the islands from Denmark, but the treaty was rejected by the U.S. Senate in 1870. The asking price was $7.5 million.

Following its acquisition of Puerto Rico in 1902, the United States expressed renewed interest in acquiring the Danish islands. This time, the United States offered to pay only $5 million, and the Danish parliament spurned the offer.

On the eve of its entry into World War I, the U.S. Navy began to fear a possible German takeover of the islands. The United States was concerned that the kaiser's navy, using the islands as a base, might prey on shipping through the Panama Canal. After renewed attempts by the United States to purchase the islands, Denmark agreed to sell them for $25 million, a staggering sum to pay for island real estate in those days.

By 1917, the United States was in full control of the islands, and Denmark retreated from the Caribbean after a legacy of nearly 2½ centuries. The U.S. Navy looked after the islands for 14 years, and in 1954 they came under the sovereignty of the U.S. Department of the Interior.

Some money was diverted to the area during the Prohibition era, as some islanders made rum and shipped it illegally to the United States, often through Freeport, Bahamas. In 1927, the United States granted citizenship to the island residents. In 1936, under Franklin Roosevelt, the first Organic Act was passed, giving the islanders voting rights in local elections. This act was revised in 1954, granting them a greater degree of self-government.

Jobs generated by World War II finally woke the islands from their long economic slumber. Visitors started to appear on the islands, and in the postwar economic boom that swept across America, the Virgin Islands at long last found a replacement for sugar cane.

The British Virgin Islands were finally freed from the Leeward Islands Federation in 1956, and in 1966 Queen Elizabeth II visited this remote colonial outpost. By 1967 the British Virgin Islands received a new constitution. Tourism was slower to come to the British Virgins than to the U.S. Virgin Islands, but it is now the mainstay of the economy.

THE ISLANDS TODAY   The American way of life prevails today in the U.S. Virgin Islands, and it has even swept across to the British Virgin Islands as well. The region's traditional recipes and remedies, as well as the self-reliant arts of fishing, boat building, farming, and even hunting, are all but gone. When islanders need something, they have it shipped from Miami. In clothes, cars, food, and entertainment, America, not Great Britain, rules the seas around both archipelagos. The British Virgins even use American dollars as their official currency, instead of British pounds.

A 51st State?

U.S. Virgin Islanders are not allowed to vote in national elections, a sore spot among some of the local residents. Many hope to see another star added to the American flag in the near future, but others prefer not to rock the boat.

When the 1936 Organic Act of the Virgin Islands was passed under the Roosevelt administration, residents age 21 and over were granted suffrage and could elect two municipal councils and a legislative assembly for the islands. In 1946, the first black governor of the islands, William Hastie, was appointed; by 1970 the U.S. Virgin Islanders had the right to elect their own governor and lieutenant governor.

Today, the U.S. Virgin Islands remain an unincorporated territory administered by the U.S. Department of the Interior. Politically speaking, the Virgin Islands, like Puerto Rico, remain outside the family of the United States. They are only permitted to send a nonvoting delegate to the U.S. House of Representatives.

Today, islanders are beginning to demand more representation. Many feel that only full statehood will provide the respect, power, and influence needed to turn the islands into more than just a "colony." But as of yet, it seems unlikely. The question of statehood is raised at each new election of Congress or of a president, but progress in this direction moves sluggishly along, if at all.

In late 1996, Water Island, off the coast of St. Thomas, became the fourth U.S. Virgin Island when Washington officials agreed to transfer it to the U.S.V.I. government. About 430 acres of the island, currently owned by the U.S. Department of the Interior, remain to be transferred. The U.S. government also agreed to allocate $3 million for an island-wide cleanup.

Also in 1996, U.S. senators agreed to allow the opening of gambling casinos in the U.S. Virgin Islands, granting permission for the building of two hotel casino hotels on St. Croix. In a bow to the islanders, senators agreed that majority ownership of the casino hotels will be reserved for locals. The arrival of gambling, conflicts with the interest of many islanders who want to save the scenic beauty of their land. Nonetheless, the gambling wheels are spinning at St. Croix's newest resort, the Divi Bay Casino Resort. Local governments are struggling to balance the preservation of the islands' number-one resource—scenic beauty—with modern economic realities.

These days the news coming out of the Virgin Islands is most often about the weather, as it was in 1995 when Hurricane Marilyn ripped through. The islands have now bounced back and are welcoming more tourists than ever before, especially cruise-ship passengers. But each year at hurricane season they live in dread, having been hit hard so many times in the past.

2 The Cuisine: A Taste of the Virgin Islands

Just as food critics were composing eulogies for traditional cooking in the Virgin Islands, there was a last-minute resurgence. Many of the old island dishes have made a comeback, and little taverns, often shanties, offering regional specialties are popping up everywhere. You can now escape hamburger hell and taste some real Caribbean flavors. In the individual island chapters, we recommend specific restaurants offering the best in local cuisine. The islands are also home to many fine restaurants with some of the Caribbean's best chefs—many hailing from the United States and Europe—who prepare a variety of sumptuous cuisines, from French and Italian to Mexican and Asian.

When dining in the Virgins, try **fresh fish,** especially mahi-mahi, wahoo, yellowtail, grouper, and red snapper. These fish, accompanied by a hot lime sauce, are among the tastiest island specialties. Watch out for the sweet Caribbean lobster. It's likely to be overpriced and overcooked, and many diners, especially those from Maine, feel that it's not worth the price.

The major resort hotels often feature elaborate **buffets,** which inevitably include some West Indian dishes along with more standard continental fare. They're almost always reasonable in price, and you'll most likely enjoy the sounds of a West Indian fungi band while you eat (fungi music is a melodious, usually improvised blend of African and Spanish sounds). You don't have to be a hotel guest to indulge, but you often need to make a reservation.

THE CUISINE

APPETIZERS   The most famous soup of the islands is *kallaloo,* or **callaloo,** made in an infinite number of ways with a leafy green vegetable similar to spinach. It's often flavored with salt beef, pig mouth, pig tail, hot peppers, ham bone, fresh fish, crab, or perhaps corned conch, along with okra, onions, and spices.

Many **soups** are sweetened with sugar and often contain fruit; for example, the classic red bean soup—made with pork or ham, various spices, and tomatoes—is sugared to taste. *Tannia* soup is made with its namesake, a starchy root known

Fun Fact   Don't Let the Jumbies Get Ya!

"Don't let the jumbies get ya!" is an often-heard phrase in the Virgin Islands, particularly when people are leaving their hosts and heading home in the dark. Jumbies, capable of good or evil, are supernatural beings that are believed to live around households. It is said that new settlers from the mainland of the United States never see these jumbies and, therefore, need not fear them. But many islanders believe in their existence and, if queried, may enthrall you with tales of sightings.

No one seems to agree on exactly what a jumbie is. Some claim it's the spirit of a dead person that didn't go where it belonged. Others disagree. "They're the souls of live people," one islander told us, "but they live in the body of the dead." The most prominent jumbies are "mocko jumbies," carnival stilt-walkers seen at all parades.

as the "purple elephant ear" because of its color and shape; it's combined with salt-fat meat and ham, tomatoes, onions, and spices. *Souse* is an old-time favorite made with the feet, head, and tongue of a pig and flavored with a lime-based sauce.

Salt-fish salad is traditionally served on Maundy Thursday or Good Friday in the Virgin Islands. It consists of boneless salt fish, potatoes, onions, boiled eggs, and an oil and vinegar dressing.

Herring gundy is another old-time island favorite; it's a salad made with salt herring, potatoes, onions, green sweet and hot peppers, olives, diced beets, raw carrots, herbs, and boiled eggs.

SIDE DISHES   Rice—seasoned, not plain—is popular with Virgin Islanders, who are fond of serving several starches at one meal. Most often rice is flavored with ham or salt pork, tomatoes, garlic, onion, and shortening.

Fungi is a simple cornmeal dumpling, made more interesting with the addition of okra and other ingredients. Sweet fungi is served as a dessert, with sugar, milk, cinnamon, and raisins.

Okra (often spelled *ochroe* in the islands) is a mainstay vegetable, usually accompanying beef, fish, or chicken. It's fried in an iron skillet and flavored with hot pepper, tomatoes, onions, garlic, and bacon fat or butter. *Accra,* another popular dish, is made with okra, black-eyed peas, salt, and pepper, and fried until golden brown.

The classic vegetable dish, which some families eat every night, is **peas and rice.** It usually consists of pigeon peas flavored with ham or salt meat, onion, tomatoes, herbs, and sometimes slices of pumpkin. Pigeon peas, one of the most common vegetables in the islands, are sometimes called congo peas or *gunga.*

FISH & MEAT   Way back when, locals gave colorful names to the various fish brought home for dinner, everything from "ole wife" to "doctors," both of which are whitefish. "Porgies and grunts," along with yellowtail, kingfish, and bonito, also show up on many Caribbean dinner tables. Fish is usually boiled in a lime-flavored brew seasoned with hot peppers and herbs and is commonly served with a Creole sauce of peppers, tomatoes, and onions, among other ingredients. **Salt fish and rice** is an excellent low-cost dish, the fish flavored with onion, tomatoes, shortening, garlic, and green pepper.

Conch Creole is a savory brew, seasoned with onions, garlic, spices, hot peppers, and salt pork. Another local favorite is chicken and rice, usually made with Spanish peppers. More adventurous diners might try **curried goat,** the longtime classic West Indian dinner prepared with herbs, cardamom pods, and onions.

The famous **johnnycakes** that accompany many of these fish and meat dishes are made with flour, baking powder, shortening, and salt, then fried or baked.

DESSERTS   **Sweet potato pie** is a Virgin Island classic, made with sugar, eggs, butter, milk, salt, cinnamon, raisins, and chopped raw almonds (it's been perfected at Eunice's Terrace on St. Thomas). The exotic fruits of the islands lend themselves to various **homemade ice creams,** including mango. Long ago, islanders invented many new dishes using local ingredients, like orange-rose sherbet made with fragrant rose petals that are mortar-pounded into a paste and flavored with sugar and orange juice. Guava ice cream is our favorite concoction, but we also like *soursop,* banana, and papaya. Sometimes **dumplings,** made with guava, peach, plum, gooseberry, cherry, and apple, are served for dessert.

DRINKS

The islands' true poison is **Cruzan rum.** To help stimulate the local economy, U.S. Customs allows you to bring home an extra bottle of Cruzan rum, in addition to your usual 5-liter liquor allowance.

Long before the arrival of Coca-Cola and Pepsi, many islanders concocted their own drinks with whatever was available, mostly from locally grown fruits. From the guavaberry comes an unusual liqueur rum, which is a mixture of sorrel, fruit, ginger, prunes, raisins, cinnamon, and rum.

Water is generally safe to drink on the islands. Much of the water is stored in cisterns and filtered before it's served. Delicate stomachs, however, should stick to mineral water or club soda. American sodas and beer are sold in both the U.S. Virgin Islands and the British Virgin Islands. Wine is sold, too, but it's usually quite expensive.

Index

See also Accommodations and Restaurant indexes, below.

FROMMER'S® COMPLETE TRAVEL GUIDES

Alaska
Amsterdam
Argentina & Chile
Arizona
Atlanta
Australia
Austria
Bahamas
Barcelona, Madrid & Seville
Beijing
Belgium, Holland &
  Luxembourg
Bermuda
Boston
British Columbia & the
  Canadian Rockies
Budapest & the Best of Hungary
California
Canada
Cancún, Cozumel & the
  Yucatán
Cape Cod, Nantucket &
  Martha's Vineyard
Caribbean
Caribbean Cruises & Ports
  of Call
Caribbean Ports of Call
Carolinas & Georgia
Chicago
China
Colorado
Costa Rica
Denmark
Denver, Boulder & Colorado
  Springs
England
Europe

European Cruises & Ports of Call
Florida
France
Germany
Greece
Greek Islands
Hawaii
Hong Kong
Honolulu, Waikiki & Oahu
Ireland
Israel
Italy
Jamaica
Japan
Las Vegas
London
Los Angeles
Maryland & Delaware
Maui
Mexico
Montana & Wyoming
Montréal & Québec City
Munich & the Bavarian Alps
Nashville & Memphis
Nepal
New England
New Mexico
New Orleans
New York City
New Zealand
Nova Scotia, New Brunswick &
  Prince Edward Island
Oregon
Paris
Philadelphia & the Amish
  Country
Portugal

Prague & the Best of the Czech
  Republic
Provence & the Riviera
Puerto Rico
Rome
San Antonio & Austin
San Diego
San Francisco
Santa Fe, Taos & Albuquerque
Scandinavia
Scotland
Seattle & Portland
Shanghai
Singapore & Malaysia
South Africa
Southeast Asia
South Florida
South Pacific
Spain
Sweden
Switzerland
Texas
Thailand
Tokyo
Toronto
Tuscany & Umbria
USA
Utah
Vancouver & Victoria
Vermont, New Hampshire
  & Maine
Vienna & the Danube Valley
Virgin Islands
Virginia
Walt Disney World & Orlando
Washington, D.C.
Washington State

FROMMER'S® DOLLAR-A-DAY GUIDES

Australia from $50 a Day
California from $70 a Day
Caribbean from $70 a Day
England from $70 a Day
Europe from $70 a Day

Florida from $70 a Day
Hawaii from $70 a Day
Ireland from $60 a Day
Italy from $70 a Day
London from $85 a Day

New York from $80 a Day
Paris from $80 a Day
San Francisco from $60 a Day
Washington, D.C.,
  from $70 a Day

FROMMER'S® PORTABLE GUIDES

Acapulco, Ixtapa &
  Zihuatanejo
Alaska Cruises & Ports
  of Call
Amsterdam
Australia's Great Barrier Reef
Bahamas
Baja & Los Cabos
Berlin
Boston
California Wine Country
Charleston & Savannah
Chicago

Dublin
Hawaii: The Big Island
Hong Kong
Houston
Las Vegas
London
Los Angeles
Maine Coast
Maui
Miami
New Orleans
New York City
Paris

Phoenix & Scottsdale
Portland
Puerto Rico
Puerto Vallarta, Manzanillo &
  Guadalajara
San Diego
San Francisco
Seattle
Sydney
Tampa & St. Petersburg
Vancouver
Venice
Washington, D.C.

FROMMER'S® NATIONAL PARK GUIDES

Family Vacations in the
  National Parks
Grand Canyon

National Parks of the American
  West
Rocky Mountain
Yellowstone & Grand Teton

Yosemite & Sequoia/
  Kings Canyon
Zion & Bryce Canyon

FROMMER'S® MEMORABLE WALKS

Chicago	New York	San Francisco
London	Paris	Washington, D.C.

FROMMER'S® GREAT OUTDOOR GUIDES

Arizona & New Mexico	Northern California	Southern New England
New England	Southern California & Baja	Vermont & New Hampshire

FROMMER'S® BORN TO SHOP GUIDES

Born to Shop: France	Born to Shop: Italy	Born to Shop: New York
Born to Shop: Hong Kong, Shanghai & Beijing	Born to Shop: London	Born to Shop: Paris

FROMMER'S® IRREVERENT GUIDES

Amsterdam	Los Angeles	Seattle & Portland
Boston	Manhattan	Vancouver
Chicago	New Orleans	Walt Disney World
Las Vegas	Paris	Washington, D.C.
London	San Francisco	

FROMMER'S® BEST-LOVED DRIVING TOURS

America	France	New England
Britain	Germany	Scotland
California	Ireland	Spain
Florida	Italy	Western Europe

THE UNOFFICIAL GUIDES®

Bed & Breakfasts in California	Golf Vacations in the Eastern U.S.	New Orleans
Bed & Breakfasts in New England	The Great Smoky & Blue Ridge Mountains	New York City
Bed & Breakfasts in the Northwest	Inside Disney	Paris
Bed & Breakfasts in Southeast	Hawaii	San Francisco
Beyond Disney	Las Vegas	Skiing in the West
Branson, Missouri	London	Southeast with Kids
California with Kids	Mid-Atlantic with Kids	Walt Disney World
Chicago	Mini Las Vegas	Walt Disney World for Grown-ups
Cruises	Mini-Mickey	Walt Disney World for Kids
Disneyland	New England with Kids	Washington, D.C.
Florida with Kids		World's Best Diving Vacations

SPECIAL-INTEREST TITLES

Frommer's Britain's Best Bed & Breakfasts and Country Inns	Hanging Out in Europe
Frommer's France's Best Bed & Breakfasts and Country Inns	Hanging Out in France
	Hanging Out in Ireland
Frommer's Italy's Best Bed & Breakfasts and Country Inns	Hanging Out in Italy
	Hanging Out in Spain
Frommer's Caribbean Hideaways	Israel Past & Present
Frommer's Adventure Guide to Australia & New Zealand	Frommer's The Moon
	Frommer's New York City with Kids
Frommer's Adventure Guide to Central America	The New York Times' Guide to Unforgettable Weekends
Frommer's Adventure Guide to India & Pakistan	Places Rated Almanac
Frommer's Adventure Guide to South America	Retirement Places Rated
Frommer's Adventure Guide to Southeast Asia	Frommer's Road Atlas Britain
Frommer's Adventure Guide to Southern Africa	Frommer's Road Atlas Europe
Frommer's Gay & Lesbian Europe	Frommer's Washington, D.C., with Kids
Frommer's Exploring America by RV	Frommer's What the Airlines Never Tell You
Hanging Out in England	

Frommers.com

Travel with the Name You Trust the Most

With over 2,000 destinations, a daily newsletter highlighting the best deals, monthly vacation sweepstakes and photo contests, Frommers.com helps you plan a fabulous vacation at an affordable cost.

Visit us today at www.frommers.com

powered by

Map, Dine, and Drive on your PALM!

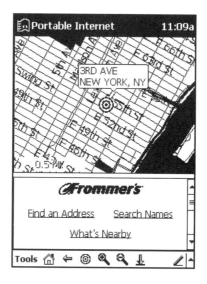

"Just plain fun" —*Business 2.0*

"Far superior to printed maps or information downloaded from the Internet" —*Pen Computing*

✓ Frommer's reviews for 29 popular travel destinations in U.S., Canada
✓ Find restaurants, attractions, shopping, entertainment, hotels near you
✓ FREE updates, new standard features, new cities*
✓ Available for Palm OS 3.1+, Pocket PC, Windows CE (PPC)

Plus:
• Instant, trusted driving directions (soon on Palm OS)
• Exact addresses with every street—intersections not required
• Up to 1 million business listings near you, including airports, ATMs, subways, mass transit, parking garages, and more
* Metro area maps for 5,000 towns and cities in Traveler's Edition

Get it now at www.portableinternet.com/frommers

See website for special offers for book purchasers.

Let Us Hear From You!

Dear Frommer's Reader,

You are our greatest resource in keeping our guides relevant, timely, and lively. We'd love to hear from you about your travel experiences—good or bad. Want to recommend a great restaurant or a hotel off the beaten path—or register a complaint? Any thoughts on how to improve the guide itself?

Please use this page to share your thoughts with me and mail it to the address below. Or if you like, send a FAX or e-mail me at frommersfeedback@hungryminds.com. And so that we can thank you—and keep you up on the latest developments in travel—we invite you to sign up for a free daily Frommer's e-mail travel update. Just write your e-mail address on the back of this page. Also, if you'd like to take a moment to answer a few questions about yourself to help us improve our guides, please complete the following quick survey. (We'll keep that information confidential.)

Thanks for your insights.

Yours sincerely,

Michael Spring

Michael Spring, *Publisher*

Name (Optional) ————————————————————————

Address ——————————————————————————————

City ————————————————— **State** ——— **ZIP** ————

Name of Frommer's Travel Guide ————————————————

Comments ——————————————————————————————

4; ( )25-39; ( )40-49; ( )50-55; ( )Over 55

.ne: ( )Under $25,000; ( )$25,000-$50,000; ( )$50,000-$100,000; ( )Over $100,000

I am: ( )Single, never married; ( )Married, with children; ( )Married, without children;
( )Divorced; ( )Widowed

Number of people in my household: ( )1; ( )2; ( )3; ( )4; ( )5 or more

Number of people in my household under 18: ( )1; ( )2; ( )3; ( )4; ( )5 or more

I am ( )a student; ( )employed full-time; ( )employed part-time; ( )not employed at this time;
( )retired; ( )other

I took ( )0; ( )1; ( )2; ( )3; ( )4 or more leisure trips in the past 12 months

My last vacation was ( )a weekend; ( )1 week; ( )2 weeks; ( )3 or more weeks

My last vacation was to ( )the U.S.; ( )Canada; ( )Mexico; ( )Europe; ( )Asia;
( )South America; ( )Central America; ( )The Caribbean; ( )Africa; ( )Middle East;
( )Australia/New Zealand

( )I would; ( )would not buy a Frommer's Travel Guide for business travel

I access the Internet ( )at home; ( )at work; ( )both; ( )I do not use the Internet

I used the Internet to do research for my last trip. ( )Yes; ( )No

I used the Internet to book accommodations or air travel on my last trip. ( )Yes; ( )No

My favorite travel site is ( )frommers.com; ( )travelocity.com; ( )expedia.com;

other _____

I use Frommer's Travel Guides ( )always; ( )sometimes; ( )seldom

I usually buy ( )1; ( )2; ( )more than 2 guides when I travel

Other guides I use include _____

What's the most important thing we could do to improve Frommer's Travel Guides?

_____

_____

_____

_____

Yes, please send me a daily e-mail travel update. My e-mail address is

_____

Mail to: Michael Spring, Publisher and Vice President, Frommer's Travel Guides
909 Third Ave., New York, NY 10022   FAX: 212.884.5432